Labour Law in Norway

Labour Law in Norway

Fourth Edition

Henning Jakhelln
Kristine Fremstad Moen
Maarten Brandsnes Faret

This book was originally published as a monograph in the International Encyclopaedia of Laws/Labour Law and Industrial Relations.

Founding Editor: Roger Blanpain
General Editor: Frank Hendrickx

Wolters Kluwer

Published by:
Kluwer Law International B.V.
PO Box 316
2400 AH Alphen aan den Rijn
The Netherlands
Website: www.wklawbusiness.com

Sold and distributed in North, Central and South America by:
Wolters Kluwer Legal & Regulatory U.S.
7201 McKinney Circle
Frederick, MD 21704
United States of America
Email: customer.service@wolterskluwer.com

Sold and distributed in all other countries by:
Turpin Distribution Services Ltd.
Stratton Business Park
Pegasus Drive, Biggleswade
Bedfordshire SG18 8TQ
United Kingdom
Email: kluwerlaw@turpin-distribution.com

ISBN 97890-411-8752-9

e-Book: ISBN 97890-411-8775-8
web-PDF: ISBN 97890-411-8805-2

This title is available on www.kluwerlawonline.com

The Author

Henning Jakhelln was born in Bodø, Norway in 1939, graduated 1957 from Oslo High School of Commerce (Oslo Handelsgymnasium), law degree (cand.jur.) in 1963, lic. jur. 1967, University of Oslo. He was Research assistant at the Scandinavian Institute of Maritime Law, Faculty of Law, University of Oslo, Norway, 1963–1964. He worked as a lawyer at a law firm in Oslo 1964–1965, and as lecturer and research fellow at the Department of Private Law, Faculty of Law, University of Oslo 1965–1971. From 1971, he worked at the Department of Public Law as associate professor, and from 1990 as professor of law with a particular obligation to give lectures in Labour Law, until 30 June 2009. Since 1 July 2009, he has worked as professor emeritus at the Department of Public and International Law, Faculty of Law, University of Oslo.

Co-writers

Kristine Fremstad Moen was born in Oslo in 1979, and gained her law degree (cand. jur.) in 2006 from the University of Oslo. She was research assistant at the Institute

The Author

of Public and International law, University of Oslo in 2005–2006. From 2006 to 2013, she was employed as a lawyer at the law firm DLA Piper Norway DA. From October 2010 until November 2011, she worked as a junior judge at Nedre Romerike district court. Fremstad Moen currently works as a lawyer at Haavind law firm, working primarily with labour law, including mergers and acquisitions, reorganizations, workforce reduction and transfer of enterprises.

Maarten Brandsnes Faret was born in Kristiansand in 1984. He obtained his Masters degree in law at the University of Oslo, in 2010. He worked as a trainee at a law firm which specializes in labour law in Oslo for most of 2008, and as an intern at a law firm in Stockholm in 2009. From 1 May 2010, he was employed as research assistant at the Institute of Public and International Law, Faculty of Law, University of Oslo, Norway. From 1 August 2010 until November 2011, he worked as a legal adviser at the Agency for Business Development Services, Licensing Division, in Oslo. From November 2011 until August 2014, he worked as an associate/lawyer at the law firm FØYEN Advokatfirma DA. Faret currently works as a lawyer at the Norwegian Association of Local and Regional Authorities (KS).

Assisted By

Richard Hindle (born 1986 in Surrey (UK)), has a Masters Degree, 2009, in publishing from University of Kingston upon Thames, London, and is currently working in England as a web consultant and freelance editor.

Stella Anne Colling (born 1940 (UK)), came to Norway in 1965, leaving behind a career in aviation, including air traffic control, Air Traffic Control Officer authorization (1962); worked for a number of years in the Legal Office, United States Air Force (NATO Support Squadron), Norway, as translator, interpreter and paralegal, dealing with a number of different fields of law, including international law. Institute of Linguists (now Chartered Institute of Linguists), Final Diploma, Special Subject Law (1978), the Norwegian Government Authorized Translator authorization for the language combination Norwegian-English (2000), working since 1994 as freelance translator in a number of fields, including labour law.

The Author

Else Leona McClimans (born 1968 in Oslo), is a lawyer and partner in the Law Firm Økland & Co, previously research network facilitator at UNDP Oslo Governance Centre (2002–2006), coordinating the human rights network HURITALK, and research assistant at the Institute of Public Law at the University of Oslo. She has, *inter alia*, been legal adviser to the Gender Equality Ombudsman and deputy leader of the Norwegian Gender and Anti-Discrimination Tribunal 2006–2008. She has published the report 'Women's political rights under the UN Womens Convention', 7/1997 Institutt for offentlig retts skriftserie and has been co-author of www.arbeidsrett.no since 2005.

Gina-Agnetha Andersen (born 1985 in Kristiansand (Norway)) has a Master of Law degree from the University of Oslo (2009), currently working as a lawyer at the labour union organization Delta.

Magnhild Eggen (born 1980 in Moss (Norway)) Master of Law degree University of Oslo (2008), currently working with labour issues in The Norwegian Correctional Services, article 'Arbeidsgivers tilrettelegging for varsling' ('The employer's duty to organize the workplace for whistleblowing') (*Arbeidsrett* 2009 pp. 1–45).

Table of Contents

Table of Contents

List of Abbreviations

AA	Agency Act (of 19 June No. 56)
ACP	Act on Civil Protection (of 25 June 2010 No. 45)
ADA	Anti-Discrimination Act (of 3 July 2005 No. 33)
ADOA	Access to Documents in the Public Administration Act (of 19 May 2006 No. 19)
ARD	Decisions of the Labour Court
BA	The Basic Agreement between LO and NHO
BoyA	Boycotting Act (of 5 December 1947 No. 1)
ConstA	Constitution Act (of 17 May 1814)
CA	Court of Appeal (*lagmannsrett*)
CCA	Contract Conclusion Act (of 31 May 1918 No. 4)
CCPR	Covenant on Civil and Political Rights (1996)
CDA	Civil Defence Act (of 17 July 1953 No. 9)
CDBANA	Closing Down Business Activities Notification Act (of 6 June 2008 No. 38)
CEDAW	Convention on the Elimination of All Forms of Discrimination against Women (1979)
CERD	Convention on the Elimination of All Forms of Racial Discrimination (1966)
CESR	Covenant on Economic, Social and Cultural Rights (1966)
COA	Claims Obsolescence Act (of 18 May 1979 No. 18)
CP	Contractual Pension
CPA	Court Proceeding Act (of 13 August 1915 No. 5)
CPDA	Court Proceeding Dispute Act (of 17 June 2005 No. 90)
CPSSCA	Contractual Pension Schemes State Contributions Act (of 23 March 1983 No. 110)
CSA	Civil Servants Act (of 4 March 1983 No. 3)
EA	Education Act (of 17 July 1998 No. 61)
ECA	Enforcement of Claims Act (of 26 June 1998 No. 86)

ECHR	Convention for the Protection of Human Rights and Fundamental Freedoms (1950)
EctHR	European Court of Human Rights
EEA	The European Economic Area
EEAAA	EEA Agreement Act (of 27 November 1992 No. 109)
EEC	The European Economic Community
EFTA	The European Free Trade Association
EinA	Employee Invention Act (of 17 April 1970 No. 21)
EPA	Employment Promotion Act (of 27 June 1947)
ETDPA	Equal Treatment of Disabled Persons Act of 20 June 2008 No. 42
EU	European Union
G	Basic Amount as per the Social Security Act
GA	Guardianship Act (of 22 April 1927 No. 3)
GACAA	General Application of Collective Agreement Act (of 4 June 1993 No. 58)
GEA	General Equality Act (of 9 June 1978 No. 45)
GDP	Gross domestic product
HPA	Holidays with Pay Act (of 29 April 1988 No. 21)
HRA	Human Rights Act (of 21 May 1999 No. 30)
IA	Industry Agreement, collective agreement between the Federation of Norwegian Industries and the Norwegian United Federation of Trade Unions (*Industrioverenskomsten*)
ICA	Insurance Contracts Act (of 16 June 1989 No. 69)
ICPLA	Integrated Circuit Protection of Layout Designs (of 15 June 1990 No. 27)
IDA	Infectious Deceases Act (of 5 August 1994 No. 55)
IIIA	Industrial Injuries Insurance Act (of 16 June 1989 No. 65)
IPA	Intellectual Property Act (of 12 May 1961 No. 2)
LCIA	Lugano Convention Implementation Act (of 8 January 1993 No. 21)
LDA	Labour Disputes Act (of 27 January 2012 No. 9)
LDPS	Labour Disputes Act for the Public Sector (of 18 July 1958 No. 2)
LFA	Lencing of Frames Act (of 25 June 1965 No. 1)
LLCA	Limited Liability Companies Act (of 13 June 1997 No. 44)

List of Abbreviations

LMAA	Labour Market Activities Act (of 13 December 2004, No. 76)
LO	Norwegian Confederation of Trade Unions
LPEFA	Legal Proceedings Entry Into Force Act (of 14 August 1918 No. 4)
MCA	Marketing Control Act (of 9 June 2009)
NAD	Court Decisions on Norwegian Labour Law (*Norsk Arbeidsrettslig Domssamling*)
NATO	North Atlantic Treaty Organization
NAV	The Norwegian Labour and Welfare Service (*Arbeids-og velferdsetaten*)
NDS	Nordic Maritime Law Reports (*Nordiske Domme i Sjøfartsanliggende*)
NHO	Confederation of Norwegian Enterprises
NIS	Norwegian International Ship Register (*Norsk Internasjonalt Skipsregister*)
NISRA	Norwegian International Ship Register Act (of 26 March 1999 No. 15)
NOU	Official Norwegian Reports (*Norges Offentlige Utredninger*)
NL	Norwegian Law Book (of 15 April 1687)
OCAA	Ombudsman for Civil Administration Act (of 22 June 1962)
OIIA	Occupational Injuries Insurance Act (of 12 December 1958 No. 10)
ONHA	Official National Holidays Act, as regards 1 and 17 May (of 26 April 1947)
OCA	Ombudsman for Children Act (of 3 March 1981 No. 5)
PA	Petroleum Act (of 22 March 1985 No. 11)
PAA	Public Administration Act (of 10 February 1967)
PC	Penal Code (of 22 May 1902 No. 10)
PDA	Personal Data Act (of 14 April 2000 No. 31)
PHPA	Public Holidays Peace Act (of 24 February 1995 No. 22)
PLLCA	Public Limited Liability Companies Act (of 13 June 1997 No. 45)
PRA	Patients' Rights Act (of 2 July 1999 No. 63)
RCA	Religious Communities Act (of 13 June 1969 No. 25)
RG	Decisions by Courts of Appeal and District Courts (*Rettens Gang*)

Rt.	Decisions by the Norwegian Supreme Court (*Norsk Rettstidende*)
SA	Seamen's Act (of 30 May 1975 No. 18)
SC	The Supreme Court of Norway *(Høyesterett)*
SCA	Settlement of Claims Act (of 8 June 1984 No. 19)
Somb	Annual reports of the Ombudsman for the Civil Administration to the Parliament
SSA	Social Security Act (of 28 February 1997 No. 19)
SSSA	Ship Safety and Security Act (of 19 December 2007 No. 9)
TCA	Torts Compensation Act (of 13 June 1969 No. 26)
TfR	Journal for Nordic jurisprudence (*Tidsskrift for Rettsvitenskap*)
TRWA	Temporary Redundancies Wage Act (of 6 May 1988 No. 22)
UDHR	Universal Declaration of Human Rights (1948)
UFITA	Archiv für Urheber- und Medienrecht (Switzerland)
UN	United Nations
UNCRC	International Convention on the Rights of the Child (1989)
WBA	Wage Board Act (of 27 January 2012 No. 10)
WEA	Working Environmental Acts (of 17 June 2005 No. 62)
WCSGA	Wage Claims State Guarantee Act (of 14 December 1973 No. 61)

Register of Acts, Regulations, International Conventions and Bilateral Agreements, EU Directives and Regulations

Norwegian Legislation

Constitution of the Kingdom of Norway (of 17 May 1814)

King Christian V's Norwegian Act (of 15 April 1687)

General Civil Penal Code (of 22 May 1902 No. 10) with subsequent amendments, the latest made by Act of 21 December 2005 No. 131

Courts of Justice Act (of 13 August 1915 No. 5)

Contract Act (of 31 May 1918 No. 4)

Act relating to the entry into force of the system(s) of legal procedure (of 14 August 1918 No. 4)

Guardianship Act (of 22 April 1927 No. 3)

Act related to 1 and 17 May as official national holidays (of 26 April 1947)

Act related to respecting measures to promote employment (of 27 June 1947)

Act relating to boycott (of 5 December 1947 No. 1)

Norwegian Civil Defence Act (of 17 July 1953 No. 9)

Labour Disputes Act for the Public Sector (of 18 July 1958 No. 2)

Occupational Injuries Insurance Act (of 12 December 1958 No. 10)

Act regarding intellectual property rights, etc. (of 12 May 1961 No. 2)

Act related to the Ombudsman for Civil Administration (of 22 June 1962)

Act related to leasing of farms (of 25 June 1965 No. 1)

Public Administration Act (of 10 February 1967)

Religious Communities Act (of 13 June 1969 No. 25)

Act relating to compensation in certain circumstances (of 13 June 1969 No. 26)

Employee Inventions Act (of 17 April 1970 No. 21)

Marketing Control Act (of 16 June 1972 – repealed by the Marketing Control Act of 9 January 2009 No. 2)

Act relating to state guarantees for wage claims in the event of bankruptcy, liquidation, etc. (of 14 December 1973 No. 61)

Seamen's Act (of 30 May 1975 No. 18 – repealed by the Ship Labour Act of 21 June 2013 No. 102)

Gender Equality Act (of 9 June 1978 No. 45 – repealed by the Gender Equality Act of 21 June 2013 No. 59)

Limitation Period for Claims Act (of 18 May 1979 No. 18)

Act relating to the children's ombudsman (of 3 March 1981 No. 5)

Civil Service Act (of 4 March 1983 No. 3)

Satisfaction of Claims Act (of 8 June 1984 No. 59)

Petroleum Act (of 22 March 1985 No. 11)

Holidays Act (of 29 April 1988 No. 21)

Act regarding salaries in connection to temporary redundancies (of 6 May 1988 No. 22)

Act relating to state contributions to contractual pension schemes (of 23 December 1988 No. 110)

Industrial Injuries Insurance Act (of 16 June 1989 No. 65)

Insurance Contract Act (of 16 June 1989 No. 69)

Act relating to the protection of layout-designs for integrated circuits (of 15 June 1990 No. 27)

Agency Act (Act relating to Commercial Agents and Commercial Travellers) (of 19 June 1992 No. 56)

Enforcement of Claims Act (of 26 June 1992 No. 86)

Act related to the implementation of the main part of the EEA Agreement (of 27 November 1992 No. 109)

General Application of Collective Agreements Act (of 4 June 1993 No. 58)

Act regarding infectious diseases (of 5 August 1994 No. 55)

Act related to public holidays (of 24 February 1995 No. 12)

Social Security Act (of 28 February 1997 No. 19)

Limited Liability Companies Act (of 13 June 1997 No. 44)

Public Limited Liability Companies Act (of 13 June 1997 No. 45)

Education Act (of 17 July 1998 No. 61)

Act related to the Norwegian International Ship Register (NIS) (of 26 March 1999 No. 15)

Human Rights Act (of 21 May 1999 No. 30)

Patients' Rights Act (of 2 July 1999 No. 63)

Personal Data Act (of 14 April 2000 No. 31)

Register of Acts, Regulations, International

Anti-Discrimination Act (of 3 July 2005 No. 33 – repealed by the Ethnicity Anti-Discrimination Act of 21 June 2013 No. 60)

Anti-Discrimination Ombudsman Act (of 10 June 2005 No. 40)

Working Environment Act (of 17 June 2005 No. 62)

Disputes Act (of 17 of June 2005 No. 90)

Access to Documents in the Public Administration Act (of 19 May 2006 No. 16)

Ship Safety and Security Act (of 19 December 2007 No. 9)

Act on notification of closure of business activities (of 6 June 2008 No. 38)

Act on amendments in the Disputes Act and on consent to ratification of the 2007 Lugano Convention on jurisdiction and the recognition and enforcement of judgments in civil and commercial matters (of 19 June 2009 No. 79)

Labour Disputes Act (of 27 January 2012 No. 9)

Wage Board Act (of 27 January 2012 No. 10)

Act on amendments in the Working Environment Act and the Civil Servants Act, etc. (equal treatment for hired employees, etc.) (of 22 June 2012 No. 33)

Sexual Orientation Anti-Discrimination Act) (of 21 June 2013 No. 58)

Gender Equality Act (of 21 June 2013 No. 59)

Ethnicity Anti-Discrimination Act (of 21 June 2013 No. 60)

Anti-Discrimination and Accessibility Act (of 21 June 2013 No. 61)

Ship Labour Act) (of 21 June 2013 No. 102)

Act on occupational pension scheme (of 13 December 2013 No. 106)

Regulations

Regulation regarding protective measures concerning industrial enterprises etc. of 29 November 1996 No. 1092

Regulation on internal control of 6 December 1996 No. 1127

Regulation on diseases to be regarded as industrial injuries of 28 July 1997 No. 902

Regulation on state guarantee for wage claims of 28 October 1998 No. 999

Regulation on employees' representatives of 18 December 1998 No. 1205

Regulation on work to be carried out in the employee's home of 5 July 2002 No. 715

Regulation on domestic work etc. to be carried out in the home of a private employer of 5 July 2002 No. 716

Regulation on employees who are sent abroad of 16 December 2005 No. 1566

Regulation regarding appointments in the public service of 15 December 2006 No. 1456, Chapter 5

Regulation of safety, health and working environment in workplaces in the building and construction area of 3 August 2009 No. 1028

Regulation regarding immigration of 15 October 2009 No. 1286

Regulation regarding organization, adaptation and management of work and employee participation of 6 December 2011 No. 1355

Regulation relating to design and installation of workplaces and work premises of 6 December 2011 No. 1356

Regulation for the execution of work, the use of work equipment and associated technical requirements of 6 December 2011 No. 1357

Regulation on action values and limit values for physical and chemical factors in the working environment and infection risk groups for biological factors of 6 December 2011 No. 1358

Regulation on construction, design and manufacture of work equipment and chemicals (producer Regulations) of 6 December 2011 No. 1359

Regulation on administrative arrangements with relevance for the scope of the Working Environment Act of 6 December 2011 No. 1360.

Regulations regarding amendments in the regulation on unemployment benefits due to layoff, of 30 January 2014 No. 82

Regulation regarding general application of collective agreements concerning the agricultural and market garden industry of 27 November 2014 No. 1481

Regulation regarding general application of collective agreements concerning construction sites generally in Norway of 27 November 2014 No. 1482

Regulation regarding general application of collective agreements concerning cleaning companies of 27 November 2014 No. 1483

Regulation regarding general application of collective agreements concerning fishing industry companies of 27 November 2014 No. 1805

Regulation regarding partly general application of collective agreements concerning the Engineering Industry Agreement within the shipping and shipyard industry of 27 November 2014 No. 1829

Regulation regarding partly general application of the National Agreement for electricians of 3 February 2015 No. 815.

Regulation regarding general application of collective agreements concerning freight transport by road of 11 May 2015 No. 554.

Regulation regarding general application of collective agreements concerning carriage of passengers by road of 27 May 2015 No. 815.

International Conventions and Bilateral Agreements

ILO Convention No. 14 (Weekly Time of Rest in the Industry, 1921)

Register of Acts, Regulations, International

ILO Convention No. 22 (Seamen's Articles of Agreement Convention, 1926)

ILO Convention No. 30 (Regulation of Working Hours in Trade and Office Activities, 1930)

ILO Convention No. 47 (Forty-Hour week etc., 1935)

ILO Convention No. 87 (Freedom of Association and Protection of the Right to Organize Convention, 1948)

ILO Convention No. 98 (Right to Organize and Collective Bargaining Convention, 1949)

ILO Convention No. 111 (Discrimination (Employment and Occupation) Convention, 1958)

ILO Convention No. 151 (Labour Relations (Public Service) Convention, 1978)

ILO Convention No. 154 (Collective Bargaining Convention, 1981)

ILO Convention MLC (Maritime Labour Convention, 2006 – in force 20 August 2013)

UDHR Universal Declaration of Human Rights (1948)

ECHR Convention for the Protection of Human Rights and Fundamental Freedoms (1950)

Brussels Convention (1968)

The European Social Charter (1961, revised in 1996)

International Covenant on Economic, Social and Cultural Rights (1966)

International Convention on the Elimination of All Forms of Racial Discrimination (1966)

Convention on the Elimination of All Forms of Discrimination against Women (1979)

EC Convention on Choice of Law in Respect of Contractual Obligations (1980)

International Convention on the Rights of the Child (1989)

The European Economic Area – Agreement (1992)

International Covenant on Civil and Political Rights (1996)

Lugano Convention on Jurisdiction and the Enforcement of Judgments in Civil and Commercial Matters (2007)

EU Directives and Regulations

Directive 94/95 EEC regarding European works councils

Council Directive 2001/23/EC on the approximation of the laws of the Member States relating to the safeguarding of employees' rights in the event of transfers of undertakings, businesses or parts of undertakings or businesses, of 12 March 2001

Directive 2002/14/EC of the European Parliament and of the Council establishing a general framework for informing and consulting employees in the European Communities (11 March 2002)

Directive 2003/88/EC (Working Hours of 4 November 2003)

Directive 2004/38/EC on the right of citizens of the Union and their family members to move and reside freely within the territory of the Member States amending Regulation (EEC) No. 1612/68 (29 April 2004)

Regulation of the Council (EC) No. 44/2001 of 22 December 2000 on jurisdiction and the recognition and enforcement of judgments in civil and commercial matters

Directive 2008/104 EC of the European Parliament and the Council of 19 November 2008 on temporary agency work

Preface

This monograph on labour law in Norway is based on Henning Jakhelln, *Oversikt over arbeidsretten (A Survey of Norwegian Labour Law)*, 4th edn (2007), but the text is updated as per 31 December 2015, rewritten and adapted for an international audience, and to the concept of the *Encyclopaedia of Laws*.

The aim of this book is to give an overall, concise and not over detailed presentation and introduction to Norwegian labour law. Certain central questions are, however, dealt with in more detail, e.g., as regards jurisdiction and choice of laws, etc.

Thus, the book deals with the individual employment relationships as well as collective labour law, trade unions and collective agreements, and certain parts of the social security legislation.

The various considerations behind the different rules and legislation are emphasized, and seen in the broader context of the legal system, as well as the general conditions of the Norwegian society. Consequently, Norwegian society is described to a certain extent, e.g., as regards population, political system, central and local administration, ombudsmen, the court system, etc.

The description and discussion of the different legal questions is exemplified by basic and illustrative cases from the practice of courts and other bodies.

It may be mentioned that the regulation regarding working hours and job security is dealt with at some length, while – of course – such questions as regards remuneration, anti-discrimination and equality are also dealt with. The similar applies to themes as trade union freedom, the legal character of collective agreements, collective bargaining, strikes and lockouts, etc.

We thank Gina-Agnetha Andersen and Magnhild Eggen for their assistance and contribution to the rewriting and translation process of parts of the manuscript.

We also thank Else Leonora McClimans, who kindly has read through large parts of the manuscript, and Anne S. Colling for her patient assistance with this translation as regards the English language, and – not least – Richard Hindle, who has gone through the manuscript in order to ensure that the whole result of the rewriting and translation process was satisfactory as far as the English language is concerned.

The 2015 updating is carried out by Maarten Brandsnes Faret and Henning Jakhelln.

Henning Jakhelln
Kristine Fremstad Moen
Maarten Brandsnes Faret

General Introduction

Chapter 1. General Background

§1. General Description of Norway

1. Norway is the fifth largest country in Europe, but the population density is the third lowest, about 15 inhabitants per square kilometre (sq. km). In 2012, Norway had a population of about 5 million inhabitants.

2. Today, Norway is one of the modern welfare countries of Western Europe. It is a country with an advanced industry. Its policy is greatly influenced by the ideas of social democracy, and also by the ideas of the market. The population is, as a whole, quite well educated – ten years' primary schooling is compulsory. The social security system is developed to an advanced degree. Public authorities are, to some extent, able to control, influence and direct the activities of different enterprises, as well as labour relations in general.

3. The great majority of Norwegian people and politicians have agreed on the basic and major lines of Norwegian post-war foreign and domestic policy. In this period, there has been little social unrest. It is typical that severe labour conflicts have mostly been avoided.

4. To a large degree, the Norwegian economy is outward oriented, and focuses on external trade and shipping. Today oil and gas activities are of great importance.

§2. Geography

5. Norway is a country of 323,882 sq. km, of which about 96,363 sq. km are north of the Arctic Circle, situated at the north-western corner of the Eurasian continent on the Scandinavian Peninsula.

6. To the north, west and south, Norway faces oceans and seas. To the north the Arctic Ocean, to the west the Atlantic Ocean and the North Sea, and to the south the Skager Rack. Thus, Norway has a very long coastline with deep fjords and high mountains. The total coast length of the main land is about 21,112 km, if the coast length of the fjords, etc. is excluded, 2,650 km. The coast line of the islands is 67,112 km.

7. The distance from the most southern point of the country (Lindesnes) to the point furthest north (Norkinn and the North Cape) is 1,752 km in a direct line. The longest distance across the country from west to east is 430 km, while the shortest is only 6 km.

8. In connection to this it may be mentioned that the name of the country – Norway – means the sailing way – the sailing lane – to the north; originally the sailing lane as such, later on also the coastal areas, and finally the inland areas as well. Even in the oldest Nordic manuscripts, the name is written *Norveg(h)r* and, somewhat later, *Noreg(h)r*. In Norwegian, the name of the country is written Norge.

9. Land frontiers to the east are about 2,531 km, a 196 km border Russia, a 716 km border Finland and a 1,619 km border Sweden.

10. To the very far north are also the Svalbard islands (61,020 sq. km, coast line 8,829 km) and Jan Mayen Island (377 sq. km, coast line 150 km). These islands are constitutionally regarded as a part of Norway.

11. In the Antarctic, Peter I-island (249 sq. km) and Bouvet Island (59 sq. km) as well as Queen Maud's Land on the Antarctic continent are Norwegian possessions.

§3. Cultural Composition: Language

12. In general, it seems fair to say that the cultural composition of the Norwegian population is quite homogeneous. It should, however, also be observed that there are certain differentiations between and within the different parts of the country – which are *inter alia* reflected in the language.

13. The Norwegian language is closely related to the other Scandinavian languages and is spoken, in different dialects, throughout the whole country. A small minority in the northern part of Norway, the Sami people, have kept their own language, which is of Finno-Ungrian origin. The Sami language is spoken by about 20,000 people, and North Sami is by law equivalent to Norwegian in some of the municipalities in the most northern parts of Norway.

14. Immigration has mainly been from Denmark and Sweden, but over the centuries immigrants have also arrived from Germany and England. Immigrants have come from Finland to Norway since the 1600s, and Finnish is spoken by some people, mainly in the most northern parts of Norway. It may also be mentioned that Russian-Norwegian was used by fishermen and tradesmen from the 1800s until 1917 along the coasts of the most northern parts of Norway. In addition, since the 1500s a few hundred gypsies have spoken the Romanés language in addition to Norwegian.

15. In more recent years, immigrants have come to Norway from more distant places (*see* paragraph 94), and the language problem has become more obvious.

16. It may also be mentioned that in spite of the fact that Norwegian is understood and spoken by the great majority of the population, there has during the last one-and-a-half centuries been a great disagreement on the language question. Until the end of the nineteenth century, there was only one official language (*riksmål*), strongly influenced by the long union with Denmark. In about 1850, inspired by the national romantic trends, a neo-Norwegian language (*nynorsk*) was construed, based on the very old Norwegian language and different dialects. Since 1980, these two languages (*riksmål* and *nynorsk*) have had equal status in official use and – to some degree – in schools. The great disagreement was the question of whether the two languages should be amalgamated – at a relatively early date, or as a result of natural development over a longer time – and possibly end up as one united language (*samnorsk*).

§4. International Relations

17. Traditionally, one of the main features of the Norwegian foreign policy is to support international cooperation and peaceful settlement of international conflicts. Norway is one of the founder members of the United Nations (UN), and loyalty to the UN and the fulfilment of the obligations under the charter is essential.

18. Since 1949, Norway has been a member of North Atlantic Treaty Organization (NATO) and has supported the idea of collective self-defence.

19. Norway is not a member of the European union (EU). Application for membership of the European Economic Community (EEC) was filed in 1962 and 1967 and renewed in 1970, but in 1972, as well as in 1994, an advisory referendum gave a majority against membership. In 1973, a trade agreement (European Economic Area (EEA)) with the EEC was concluded.

20. Since the Council of Europe was established in 1949, Norway has been a member and played an active role in establishing European Free Trade Association (EFTA) in 1959.

21. Between the Scandinavian countries, cooperation and trade is very close. In 1952, the Nordic Council was set up, consisting of parliamentarians from each of the Member States – Denmark, Finland, Iceland, Norway and Sweden. At different times, formalizing further the economic cooperation between these countries has been suggested, e.g., by establishing a Nordic Economic Community (Nordek), but such ideas have, so far, not been realized. An exception is SAS – the Scandinavian Airlines System – founded in 1946 by Denmark, Norway and Sweden; since 2004 SAS has, however, been divided into three national subsidiaries.

22. Norway has given aid to developing countries since the 1950s, with emphasis on technical assistance. Development aid amounts to 1% of the GDP. Also, development aid is financed by a special ‘development tax’, amounting to 1.3% of assessed taxable income, which is paid in addition to general income tax. The development aid is channelled through NORAD, a directorate under the Ministry of Foreign Affairs.

§5. Political System

23. It seems fair to say – generally – that the political situation in Norway is stable. In general, the relative strength of the political parties does not change much, although – over a longer span of time – certain tendencies may appear.

24. The political system of Norway is based on the principle of democracy through elections and political parties of representatives of the people controlling the highest institutions of the country, the counties and the local communities. It is further based on the principle of local political independence under central supervision.

25. The Norwegian Constitution was proclaimed – in the wake of the Napoleonic wars – on 17 May 1814 by the National Assembly. It is (still) influenced by the great ideas of the French Revolution, British political tradition and the Constitution of the United States of America (USA). Since 1814. amendments to the Constitution have been passed by the Parliament several times. The Constitution can, however, be altered every fourth year only.

26. It should be mentioned that the proclamation in 1814 of Norway as an independent state lasted for just a few months, and Norway was united with Sweden from 1814 until 1905 when the union was dissolved. Until 1814, Norway was united with Denmark and had been since 1397 (the Kalmar union).

I. Parliament (Stortinget)

27. The most important institution in the Norwegian Constitution is the Parliament (*Stortinget*) with 169 representatives elected by the people. It is a single house system. From 1814 to 2009, Norway had a reformed system consisting of two chambers, e.g., for legislative processes. When dealing with bills on legislation, Parliament was divided into two parts: the *Odelstinget* (127 members) and the *Lagtinget* (42 members), while other cases (the majority, including the budget) were dealt with by the Parliament in plenary sessions. Since 2009, bills on legislation have been dealt with in plenary sessions, like budgetary and other matters. Bills on legislation must, however, be dealt with by Parliament twice, with an interval of at least three days. Finally, the King-in-Council has to approve the bill.

28. It should be noted that every member of the Parliament is also a member of a committee of the Parliament. No bill will be presented to the *Stortinget* unless it has been dealt with by the committee. Constitutional and budgetary control is the responsibility of the *Stortinget*. The leader of the Auditor General's Office (*Riksrevisjonen*) is appointed by *Stortinget* (cf. section 75K of the Constitution Act (ConstA)).

29. Election to Parliament takes place by secret ballot, and these elections take place on the same day in every electoral district. Eligible for election are all men and women who in the year of election, have reached the age of 20 and fulfil certain other requirements. In general, representatives are elected by direct election in the individual county which is entitled to a certain number of representatives, on the basis of proportional representation. It should be noted that the members of the Parliament are elected for a period of four years, and Parliament cannot be dissolved in that period.

30. All Norwegian subjects have the right to vote, provided that they live in Norway on the day of voting and have not had their right of voting annulled. Norwegian subjects abroad may vote on certain conditions. Universal suffrage for men was introduced in 1898, while women received the right to vote in municipal elections from 1910 and in elections to Parliament from 1913. The first woman was elected to Parliament in 1911.

31. According to the Constitution, the executive power is exercised by the King-in-Council. The Council consists of the King and the ministers. These ministers must have the confidence of the majority of the Parliament, and no act of the King is effective unless it is countersigned by the prime minister (section 31 of the Constitution).

32. When Parliament is not in session, the King-in-Council has the power to pass temporary legislation (*provisoriske anordninger*), but such regulations must not be contrary to the Constitution, or to the laws passed by Parliament (section 17 of the Constitution).

II. Political Parties

33. A political system built on political parties has a long tradition in Norway. The oldest party still existing – Venstre (the Liberal Party) – was founded in 1884 as a reform party. In that same year, parliamentarianism was introduced to Norwegian constitutional law as a consequence of a decision of the Court of Impeachment.

34. Shortly after, in 1885, Høyre (the Conservative Party) was founded and in 1887 Det Norske Arbeiderparti (the Labour Party). In addition it should be noted, that Senterpartiet (the Centre Party) was founded in 1920 to promote the interests of the farming community, and Kristelig Folkeparti (the Christian Democratic Party) was founded in 1938 to promote Christianity as a basis of political life. To the left of the Labour Party are found the Communist Party, the Socialist People's Party and Democratic Socialists. These formed in 1973 the Sosialistisk Valgforbund (Socialist Electoral League), and since 1977, it has been the Sosialistisk Venstreparti (Socialist Leftwing Party). In 1973, the Communist Party (AKPm-l) left the league and Rød Valgallianse (the Red Electoral League) was founded. It obtained one seat in the Parliament in 1973, 1989, 1993, 1997 and in 2001. In 2007, it formed the party Rødt (Red), together with AKP and Rød Ungdom (Red Youth). To the right of the Conservative Party is found Fremskrittspartiet (the Progress Party), founded in 1973 as a protest party against growing state activity and the increasing burden of taxes and duties. The General election in 2013 was a national breakthrough for the Green Party. The party received 2.8% of the votes, which granted them one member in the Parliament. In addition are found smaller groups on both the left and right sides of the political line.

35. Following the 2013 election, the parties have the following representation in the *Stortinget*:

(a) Arbeiderpartiet (the Labour Party), 55
(b) Fremskrittspartiet (the Progress Party), 29
(c) Høyre (the Conservative Party), 48
(d) Kristelig Folkeparti (the Christian Democratic Party), 10
(e) Senterpartiet (the Centre Party), 10
(f) Sosialistisk Venstreparti (Socialist Leftwing Party), 7
(g) Venstre (the Liberal Party), 9
(h) Miljøpartiet De Grønne (the Green Party), 1.

36. Since the 2005 election, the central government (*Regjeringen*) consisted of a coalition of three parties (the red/green parties): Arbeiderpartiet (the Labour Party), Sosialistisk Venstreparti (Socialist Leftwing Party) and Senterpartiet (the Centre Party). Following the 2013 election, the new government is based on a coalition between the

Conservative Party and the Progress Party, based on a collaboration with the Liberal Party and the Christian Democratic Party.

§6. ADMINISTRATION

I. The Central Administration

37. The central administration consists of the ministries and directorates. To a large degree, the different ministries have been given authority to enact general regulations and to decide different cases.

38. At present there are sixteen ministries: of labour and social affairs, of children, equality and social inclusion, of finance, of trade, industry and fisheries, of defence, of health and care services, of justice and public security, of local government and modernization, of culture, of education and research, of agriculture and food, of climate and environment, of petroleum and energy, of transport and communications, of foreign affairs and of the office of the prime minister.

39. As far as labour law is concerned, special attention should be given to the Ministry of Labour and Social Affairs, which *inter alia* has administrative responsibility for the Working Environment Act (WEA) and the Labour Disputes Act (LDA). Other ministries do also deal with labour questions, e.g., the Ministry of Trade, Industry and Fisheries is responsible for the Ship Labour Act. As far as civil servants are concerned, the Ministry of Local Government and Modernization is responsible.

40. Administrative authority is to a considerable extent also delegated to subordinate bodies, such as the Norwegian Competition Authority (*Konkurransetilsynet*), the Directorate for Customs and Special Tariffs (*Tolldirektoratet*), the Directorate for Public Health (*Helsedirektoratet*), and of special importance for labour law etc. – the Labour Inspectorate (*Arbeidstilsynet*), and the Labour and Welfare Service (*Arbeids- og velferdsetaten*) (NAV).

II. The Counties

41. Norway is divided into nineteen counties (*fylker*), which again are divided into a different number of municipalities.

42. Each county is governed by a county council (*fylkesting*) consisting of representatives elected on political basis, every fourth year. The county council elects a smaller body, the county committee (*fylkesutvalget*) as well as a county mayor (*fylkesordfører*) and they deal with the daily political questions.

43. The county officer (*fylkesmannen*) is appointed by the King-in-Council, and is the head of the civil administration of the county. The county administration deals with matters of importance for the region, such as general planning, and cooperates in joint projects in the economic, social and cultural fields. The county officer has some controlling functions within the local communities, and as a part of the administrative procedure, certain cases decided by the local authorities may be appealed to the county officer.

44. Further, certain parts of the administration is, on the county level, organized through special bodies, e.g., the county farming board (*fylkeslandbruksstyret*), the county physician (*fylkeslegen*), the county road officer (*fylkesvegsjefen*), etc. It may also be noted that the secondary schools that provide three years further education, after ten years of primary school are run and administered by the county.

45. The labour inspectorate is, on this level, for practical reasons organized by districts. Some counties are therefore one district, and the border of the different districts does not always follow the border of the county.

III. Local Administration

46. Norway consists of 430 municipalities (*kommuner*) of different size and population. Each municipality is governed by a municipal council (*kommunestyre*) which is elected, on political basis, every fourth year. All inhabitants reaching the age of 18 during the year of election have the right to vote. Each council elects an executive board (*formannskap*) which consists of one-fourth of its members, as well as its mayor (*ordfører*). In addition, every municipality has a number of civil servants dealing with daily administration.

47. Certain parts of the administration on a local level are organized through special bodies under the central or county administration, e.g., the police authorities, and over the years certain administrative fields are transferred from the municipalities to the central or county administration, and vice versa.

IV. Administrative Procedure

48. It seems inevitable that the Norwegian welfare society should avoid the power of a growing bureaucracy. When a field needs greater public attention, it is usually necessary to build up an adequate administration or administrative body to cope with the tasks and lead the development in the desired direction. Over the last century, it has been considered necessary to engage the public to a continuously greater degree. Today, public authorities are involved or may influence to a considerable extent almost all parts of economic, social and cultural life.

49. This growing power of the bureaucracy might endanger the legal safeguards and rights of the citizens. To counteract this trend, it was in the 1960s considered necessary to establish the Ombudsman for Civil Administration (*Sivilombudsmannsembetet*, 1962), and *inter alia* to enact a Public Administration Act (PAA) (1967) as well as an Act on Access to Documents in Public Administration (1970, revised 2006).

50. The PAA 1967 gives private parties specific rights under administrative procedure. A private party must be informed before an administrative case is decided (section 16). It is an obligation for the public body to see to it that the case is as well prepared as possible before a decision is made, and to present certain information to the parties for possible comment. Sections 17, 18 and 19 regulate the rights and limitations for the parties to demand knowledge about the documents of the case, and sections 24 and 25 the rights and limitations of parties in demanding information about the reasons for the decision made. The parties or others with a legal appeal interest, e.g., an organization, have the right to appeal to the superior administrative body (section 28).

51. As regards appointments to the public service, it may be mentioned that exceptions are made as regards the right to demand knowledge about the documents of the case. Applicants are, however, entitled to knowledge of the names of all other applicants, their age, education and practice (cf. Regulation of 15 December 2006 No. 1456, sections 14–19).

52. The Act on Access to Documents in the Public Administration, 2006, which repealed the previous Act of 1970, basically entitles anyone – private parties as well as the press, mass media in general as well as others – to have access to the documents of a specific case, journals and registers (section 3). There are, however, quite a number of exceptions from this basic point (internal documents, statutory duty of secrecy, etc.), *inter alia* documents related to the proper execution of personnel management of the central or local government in question (section 23). Documents on appointments or promotions in the public service are also excepted. That exception, however, does not apply to lists of applicants. Information about an applicant may be exempted from public disclosure if so requested by the applicant (section 25).

§7. Ombudsmen

I. The Ombudsman for Civil Administration, Ombudsman for the Armed Forces and Parliamentary Ombudsman for the Civilian National Service

53. These ombudsmen are all appointed by the Parliament, report directly to Parliament, and are organs of Parliament's oversight and supervisory activities. The Ombudsman for Civil Administration is, in general, the most important, but the first ombudsman to be established – as early as 1952 – was the Ombudsman for the Armed Forces.

54. The activities of Norway's Parliamentary Ombudsman for Civil Administration (*Sivilombudsmannen*) are based on an Act of 22 June 1962 (cf. also (since 1995) the ConstA section 75 l). The ombudsman is elected by Parliament for four years. In principle, the ombudsman may be removed sooner by vote of two-thirds of the Parliament, but that has not happened so far. The ombudsman must have the same qualifications as demanded for a judge of the Supreme Court.

55. The duty of the ombudsman is, as the representative of the Parliament, to endeavour to ensure that the public administration does not commit injustice against any citizen (section 3 of the Act). The ombudsman may deal with cases either at the request of a person or on his own initiative (ex officio) (section 5). Anyone who considers himself to be unjustly treated by the public administration may file a complaint with the ombudsman, who will decide whether the complaint gives sufficient reason to be dealt with.

56. The ombudsman has only the right to express an opinion in the matter. Should the ombudsman be of the opinion that a decision is invalid or clearly unreasonable, a statement to this effect may be given (section 10). Further, the ombudsman may, if the circumstances justify, advise a public body that compensation be paid unless a new decision can rectify the matter. Also, the ombudsman may inform the ministry in question about possible inadequate rules of acts and administrative regulations. The opinions expressed by the ombudsman are published every year as a part of the annual report to Parliament – often referred to as *Somb* (Annual reports of the Ombudsman for the Civil Administration to the Parliament) – and are considered as an expression of how the law should be understood, as regards, e.g., civil servants.

57. The Parliamentary Ombudsman for the Armed Forces (*Ombudsmannen for Forsvaret*) and the Ombudsman's Committee (*Ombudsmannsnemnda*) are elected by the parliament for a period of four years, according to decisions of the Parliament since 21 April 1952. The committee consists of seven members, of which the chairperson is the ombudsman. The ombudsman has to safeguard the rights of all members of the armed forces, privates and officers alike – before, during or after time of service – and is an organ of Parliament's oversight and supervisory activities. In his role as independent military oversight mechanism. the ombudsman inspects military units home and abroad. The ombudsman may address or take actions on his own initiative in any matter which comes to his attention. Anyone who feels that he or she has been wrongly, unjustly or unreasonably treated can bring his or her case before the ombudsman, and request him to investigate the matter. The ombudsman reports to the Parliament.

58. The Parliamentary Ombudsman for the Civilian National Service (*Ombudsmannen for sivile vernepliktige*) and the Ombudsman's Committee for the Civilian National Service (*Ombudsmannsnemnda for sivile vernepliktige*) have been established, since 1957, in the same way as the Parliamentary Ombudsman for the Armed Forces (*Ombudsmannen for Forsvaret*) and the Ombudsman's Committee (*Ombudsmannsnemnda*), and are also elected by the Parliament for a period of four years.

II. Other Ombudsmen

59. The following ombudsmen are appointed by the King-in-Council or other state organs.

A. The Equality and Anti-discrimination Ombudsman

60. The Equality and Anti-discrimination Ombudsman (*Likestillings-og diskrimineringsombudet*) shall – together with the Equality and Anti-Discrimination Tribunal – work to promote genuine equality irrespective of gender, ethnicity, national origin, descent, skin colour, language, religion or belief in all areas of society. In the sphere of working life, the ombudsman shall also work to promote equal treatment irrespective of political views, membership of an employee organization, sexual orientation, gender identity, gender expression, disability, accessibility or age.

Furthermore, the ombudsman shall work to promote equal treatment and to prevent discrimination against disabled persons. The ombudsman shall also work to promote equal treatment irrespective of homosexual orientation in the housing sector (cf. the Anti-Discrimination Ombud Act of 10 June 2005, No. 40, section 3). The ombudsman is appointed by the King-in-Council for a period of four years, which may be extended once only.

B. The Consumer Ombudsman

61. The Consumer Ombudsman (*Forbrukerombudet*) shall, in the interests of consumers, seek to prevent market abuses, and – together with the Market Council – assist in the implementation of the provisions of the Marketing Control Act (MCA) of 9 January 2009 (cf. the previous MCA of 16 June 1972). The Consumer Ombudsman is not appointed by the Parliament, but by the King-in-Council, for six years at a time (cf. MCA, section 32).

C. The Children's Ombudsman

62. The Children's Ombudsman (*Barneombudet*) shall promote the interests of children in society (cf. an Act of 3 March 1981 No. 5). The Children's Ombudsman is not appointed by the Parliament, but by the King-in-Council, for four years at a time (cf. section 2).

D. The Patients Ombudsman

63. The Patients Ombudsman (*Pasientombudet*) works to meet patients' needs and protect their interests and legal rights in respect of the health service, and to improve the quality of the health service (cf. the Patients' Rights Act (PRA) of 2 July 1999 No. 63, section 8-1). There must be a Patients Ombudsman in every county, appointed by the state – the Directorate of Health – for an unlimited period of time.

E. Student Ombudsmen

64. The system of Student Ombudsmen should also be mentioned. According to the Education Act (EA) section 9a-5 on student participation in school environmental activities – designed in accordance with the provisions regarding safety representatives pursuant to the WEA – the appointed student ombudsmen of the Students' Council are to safeguard students' interests in relation to school authorities. The Students' Council consists of pupils only (EA sections 11-2 and 11-6).

65. The arrangement concerning safety representatives may be mentioned in this context, and will be dealt with below (*see* paragraphs 1265 et seq.).

§8. Boards, Councils and Committees

66. There are a number of boards, councils and committees, which are given assignments of giving advice or providing announcements. Some of them are even assigned to mediate between private parties, or between private parties and the public administration. These boards represent, in many ways, the passage from voluntary or administrative decisions to the traditional hearing of civil disputes in a court of law.

67. In general, a solution by a decision of a board, council, committee, etc. may not only be stipulated by law or public regulations, but may also be stipulated by agreement by the parties involved (in which case solution by arbitration may be achieved), or by collective agreement. Solution by a private council may even be agreed upon, as a supplement to solutions by a public council, e.g., the Council for Corporate Democratization (a public body) and the Council for Industrial Democracy in the Drilling and Contractor Vessel Industry (based on the collective agreement between the parties) may be mentioned.

68. Among the voluntary established councils may be mentioned the Financial Appeals Board (*Forsikringsklagenemnda*), and the Bank Board of Appeal (*Bankklagenemnda*) (the Bank Board of Appeal is from 1 July 2010 a part of the newly created Financial Appeals Board). Also the Package Board of Appeal (*Pakkereisenemnda*) can be mentioned in this context (cf. the Package Tours Act (of 25 August 1995 No. 57) section 10-1).

69. Within the area of working life, the Social Security Court (*Trygderetten*) plays an important role. The decisions of the Social Security Court may be appealed to the Court of Appeal, and not to the Court of First Instance (cf. the Act on Appeal to the Social Security Court (of 16 December 1966 No. 9) section 23).

70. Of significant importance as regards collective agreements and collective labour law are the Technical Calculation Committee (*Det tekniske beregningsutvalg*) (cf. paragraph 1530 below), the Contact Committee on Incomes Policy (*Regjeringens Kontaktutvalg*) (cf. paragraph 383 below), the Board on Extended Application of Collective Agreements (*Tariffnemnda*) (cf. paragraph 1502 below) and the National Wages Board (*Rikslönnsnemnda*) (cf. paragraph 1601 below).

71. Further may be observed the Dispute Resolution Board (*Tvisteløsningsnemnda*), which deals with certain labour disputes. Questions related to leave of absence and disputes concerning preferential rights for part-time employees pursuant to WEA section 14-3 are resolved by the Dispute Resolution Board (cf. section 17-2). Also disputes related to part-time employees who in the past twelve months have regularly worked in excess of agreed working hours, and have the right to an employment position corresponding to the actual amount of work during this period (cf. the new section 14-4a in the WEA (in force from 1 January 2014)), shall be resolved by the Dispute Resolution Board (cf. the WEA section 17-2(1)). A decision made by the Dispute Resolution Board may be brought before a court of law, pursuant to normal procedure. Here may also be mentioned advisory councils for vocational education and training (*yrkesopplæringsnemnder*). Cases concerning approval of training establishments, loss of approval and the quality assurance system for vocational education and training shall always be submitted to the council (cf. EA section 4-8(2)).

72. In this context should also be mentioned the Supervisory Board for the Supervision of Prisons (*Tilsynsrådet for tilsyn med fengsler*) pursuant to the Act of 18 May 2001 No. 21 section 9. There is also public supervision of psychiatric hospitals, etc.

§9. The Court System

I. Survey

73. Unless otherwise regulated, legal disputes may be brought before the ordinary courts. These may decide any case as far as the legal and constitutional questions are concerned, as well as legal questions in administrative matters, based on the facts of the case. Special courts are prescribed for certain cases only.

74. The general courts are the Supreme Court, the Courts of Appeal and the Courts of First Instance. In addition may be mentioned Arbitration Courts, and the Labour Court (*see* paragraphs 87 and 1494 et seq.).

II. The Supreme Court (Høyesterett)

75. Each case is usually decided by five judges (until 1939, seven judges), but certain cases may be decided by all the judges of the court in a so-called grand chamber (*in plenum*). A special committee of the court (*Høyesteretts ankeutvalg*, previously *Høyesteretts Kjaeremaalsutvalg*), consisting of three members, will decide whether an appeal from a lower court is accepted to be brought before the Supreme Court for consideration.

III. The Courts of Appeal

76. There are six Courts of Appeal (*lagmannsrett*): Hålogaland, Frostating, Gulating, Agder, Borgarting and Eidsivating. Civil cases are decided by three professional judges. In addition, two lay judges (*med-dommere*) take part in the decision, if so demanded by one of the parties or the court so decides. If the parties and the court agree that lay judges are not necessary, the court may deal with the case without lay judges (cf. WEA section 17-7(4)). In certain cases, the lay judges must have specialist knowledge, e.g., in maritime cases, including cases regarding the Ship Labour Act (the former Seamen's Act (SA)). As regards labour law cases, the lay judges are appointed from persons with knowledge of labour life (cf. WEA section 17-7).

IV. The Courts of First Instance

77. There are now seventy Courts of First Instance (*tingretter*). Civil cases are decided by one professional judge, but if so demanded by the parties, two lay judges shall also participate. In certain cases, e.g., regarding the Ship Labour Act, two lay judges with special knowledge participate. As regards labour law cases, the lay judges are appointed from persons with knowledge of labour life (cf. WEA section 17-7).

V. The Conciliation Council

78. There is a Conciliation Council (*Forliksråd*) in every municipality, consisting of three members, elected by the municipal council for four years. The Conciliation Board can hear cases that can be brought by writ of summons to the district court pursuant to the provisions on general procedure or small claims procedure in the Dispute Act. The procedure before the Conciliation Board helps the parties to achieve a simple, swift and cheap resolution of the case through conciliation or judgment (cf. DA section 6-1(1)). Before an asset claim can be heard by the district court, it is heard by the Conciliation Board. However, this does not apply if, among other things, the amount in dispute is at least Norwegian Kroner (NOK) 125,000 and both parties have been assisted by a lawyer, or if out-of-court mediation pursuant to DA Chapter 7 has been attempted (cf. DA section 6-2(2)). Cases concerning family matters or cases against a public authority are not brought before the Conciliation Court. Additionally, the Conciliation Board does not hear other cases, in respect of which it is provided by statute that conciliation before the Conciliation Board shall not take place (cf. DA section 6-2(1)). In this connection the WEA section 17-1(3) may be mentioned, as the provision stipulates that claims which are subject to negotiations pursuant to section 17-3 or that have been reviewed by a Dispute Resolution Board pursuant to section 17-2 shall not be subject to mediation by a Conciliation Board.

VI. Arbitration

79. In general, the parties may agree in writing on arbitration, if they have the right to dispose of the matter. The decision of an arbitration court has the same effect as a decision of an ordinary court, but can be appealed against only if the parties have so agreed.

80. Employees may not in advance enter into an agreement which states that a dispute concerning dismissal, etc., shall be brought before an arbitration board. A hearing before an arbitration board may, on the other hand, be agreed upon as soon as the dispute is a fact and has commenced. Additionally, the employer may enter into a written agreement with the chief executive of the enterprise to the effect that disputes in connection with termination of the employment relationship shall be settled by means of arbitration (cf. WEA section 15-16(1)).

VII. Right to Appeal

81. Usually, a decision of a Court of First Instance can be appealed only to a Court of Appeal, and then to the Supreme Court. But on certain conditions, a decision may be appealed directly to the Supreme Court, e.g., where the decision is of importance beyond the presented case.

VIII. Independence of the Courts

82. It is a principle of the Norwegian Constitution that courts must be independent from the administration and the Parliament.

83. It is, however, with small constitutional exceptions, a practical question whether the legislation should lay down a rule that certain cases are to be decided by the general courts or by a special court.

84. It is also a practical question whether certain cases should be decided by the general administrative authorities, with right to appeal to the courts, or by the courts themselves – and whether the courts should be given certain administrative tasks in addition to deciding cases.

85. To a certain extent, all these possibilities are used in the Norwegian court system.

IX. Special Courts, Administrative Bodies, Etc.

86. Some cases shall be dealt with by special courts, e.g., the Labour Court, the House Rental Court, the Guardian Court, etc.

87. In other cases, an administrative body decides the case, e.g., the Price Council may forbid an enterprise to refuse commercial connections with another enterprise or a consumer. The Price Council may e.g., assume that the refusal will hurt the public interest or will have an unreasonable effect on the other party.

88. Further, the Social Security Court (*Trygderetten*) will decide appeals regarding Social Security legislation, but, in the sense of administrative law, this 'court' is considered an administrative body, and the legality of its decisions may be tried by the ordinary courts. The decision of the Social Security Court will, however, have to be tried by one of the Courts of Appeal, and not by a Court of First Instance.

89. Certain cases, especially in the field of family law, are decided by the courts or by the administration if the parties so agree (e.g., divorce cases), and an adoption is granted by administrative authority, but repeal of the adoption relationships must be decided by a court. On the other hand, the courts carry out certain administrative tasks, e.g., registration of commercial firms, division of inheritances or bankrupt estates, etc.

X. The Labour Court and Other Courts Dealing with Labour Law Cases

90. Norway has only one Labour Court (*Arbeidsretten*), which deals with questions regarding collective agreements – e.g., their interpretation – provided that one of the parties to the collective agreement has brought a case before the Labour Court. In addition, the Labour Court deals with questions regarding the legality of industrial actions – e.g., strikes, lock-outs, etc. (cf. LDA section 33(2)). Boycotting acts (BoyAs) are dealt with by the ordinary courts. The parties may agree that disputes regarding the interpretation of a collective agreement, as well as questions regarding compensation caused by violation of a collective agreement, are to be decided upon by a court of arbitration (cf. LDA section 33(4); *see also* below paragraph 1494).

91. Other labour law questions are dealt with by the ordinary courts, i.e., questions regarding the interpretation of an employment agreement, unfair dismissal, etc.

§10. Some Vital Statistics

I. Composition of the Population

92. Age-wise, the Norwegian population is distributed in such a manner that the total number of young people is lower than the number of the middle-aged population. At the same time, the oldest part of the population is increasing.

Figure 1 Population at 1 January 2009

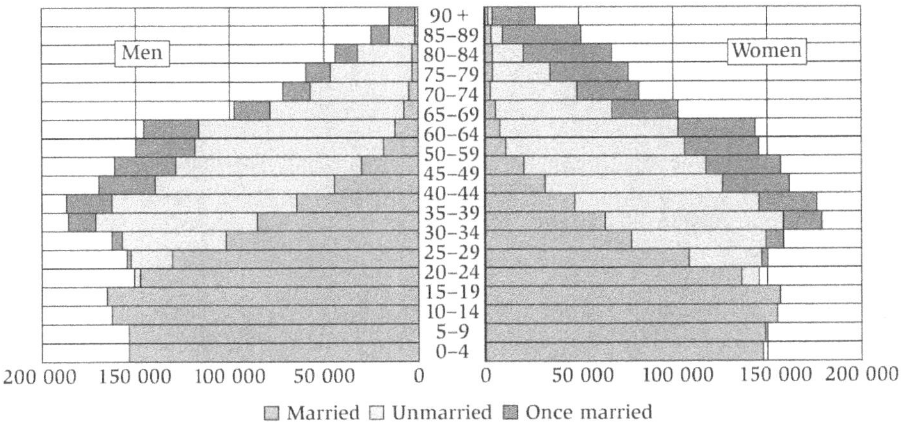

Source: Statistics Norway – official statistics about Norwegian society since 1876, www.ssb.no.

II. The Total Workforce

93. The total workforce, comprising self-employed as well as employees, in 2008 was 2,524,000 persons (of which 2,447,800 are employees).[1]

III. Some Main Branches

94. The total workforce carried in 2008 out activities in the following main areas:[2]

(a) Agriculture and forestry 59,400
(b) Fishing and fish farming 14,400
(c) Oil and gas exploitation 41,300
(d) Mining 4,300
(e) Industry (total) 298,100
(f) Electricity and water supply 13,100
(g) Building and construction 189,400
(h) Wholesale and retail trade, etc. 375,600
(i) Hotel and restaurant services 78,600
(j) Shipping, foreign trade 53,100
(k) Transport, other than shipping 118,900
(l) Post and telecommunications 37,100
(m) Financial services and insurance 48,800
(n) Business services 322,800
(o) Public administration and defence 159,400
(p) Education 187,900
(q) Health and social services 502,800.

IV. Immigration

95. The total number of immigrants in Norway is about 459,000 persons (2008), of whom 161,000 are from EU/EEA/EFTA, North America and Oceania, 52,000 from Eastern Europe outside the EU, and 246,000 from Africa, Asia (including Turkey) and Latin America:

- From Asia, the number of immigrants was (2001) from Pakistan 24,350, Vietnam 16,300, Iraq 13,400, Iran 11,700, Turkey 11,400, Sri Lanka 10,900, India 6,400, Afghanistan 2,100 and from other countries in Asia 22,400.
- From Africa, the number of immigrants was (2001) from Somalia 11,000, Morocco 6,000, Ethiopia 3,200, Ghana 1,400, Gambia 1,100 and from other countries in Africa 9,000.

---

1. *Statistical Yearbook of Norway 2008*, Tables 209 and 211.
2. *Statistical Yearbook of Norway 2008*, Table 211.

- From North America, there were 8,200, from Chile 6,600, from the South-and Mid-Americas 5,100.
- From Oceania, there were 1,000.
- As regards Europe, the largest number of immigrants, 41,900, are from the Scandinavian countries – Sweden 22,800 and Denmark 19,100. From Great Britain 10,800, Germany 10,000 and from other countries of Western Europe 24,600. From Yugoslavia 14,300, Bosnia-Herzegovina 13,200, Poland 6,700, Russia 4,400, and from other countries of Eastern Europe 10,500.

96. Net immigration to Norway has increased from 13,000 (2004) to 39,400 (2007). Over most recent years, a large number of workers from Poland have come to Norway, and also workers from Lithuania, Germany, Sweden and various other countries.

V. Asylum Seekers and Refugees

97. In this connection, it may be mentioned that a number of persons have come to Norway as refugees, and applied for asylum in the country.

98. As per 2008, over the years, totally about 115,000 people have the status of refugees, of whom about 73,700 have been granted Norwegian citizenship, and about 58,700 have foreign citizenship.

99. The number of persons applying for asylum varies considerably from one year to another. In 2007, about 6,500 people applied for asylum, while (per 31 October 2008) about 11,500 persons have filed such applications – of which about 7,300 were admitted, and about 3,400 rejected. The majority of the applicants came from Asia (about 2,500) and Africa (about 1,800).

VI. Full-Time and Part-Time Work: Men and Women

100. Out of the 2,524,000 employees 1,845 000 were working full-time (73.1%) and 674,000 part-time (26.7%); 359,000 of them were long part-time (14.2%) and 315,000 short part-time (12.5%).[3] Male employees (1,332,000) worked full-time 86.6%, long part-time 5.5%, and short part-time 7.7%. Female employees (1,192,000) worked full-time 58%, long part-time 23.9% and short part-time 17.9%.

101. Fewer women and more men are today working part-time than ten years ago, but many women working part-time wish to work more. Since 1972, weekly working hours for men have been reduced by about five hours, while weekly working hours for women over this period have been reduced with about one-and-a-half hours.

102. Compared with other countries, a large part of the adult population is at work in Norway. That is first of all due to the fact that a large proportion of the Norwegian women are working as self-employed or employees. As such, seven out of ten women and almost eight out of ten men are working. Thirty years ago, less than

3. *Statistical Yearbook of Norway 2008*, Table 209.

half of the Norwegian women were working as self-employed or employees. Men are about as active in the working life today as they were in the middle of the 1970s.

VII. Unemployed

103. The percentage of unemployed varies over the years.[4]

Table 1 Percentage of Unemployed

Year	*(%)*
1985	2.6
1990	5.2
1995	4.9
2000	3.4
2005	4.6

104. As per third quarter 2008, the unemployment rate was 2.5%, and as per 10 December 2008, 45,180 people were registered unemployed. In the first quarter of 2010, the unemployment rate was 3.7%.[5] In December 2013, the unemployment rate was 3.6%.

105. From the beginning of the 1970s and until the low point in 1983–1984, the unemployment rate was stable, a little below 2% of the workforce. In 1993, the unemployment rate was rather high, at 6%.

VIII. Public Administration

106. As regards public administration, it may be divided between state and municipal administration, where approximately the following number of persons are working.

Table 2 Number of Employees within the Public Administration

State administration	727,500
Of which defence	30,100
Municipal administration	457,000

107. It should be observed, however, that it is quite difficult to draw a distinction between state and municipal administration on the one hand, and other activities of public bodies on the other hand (*see* paragraphs 107 et seq.).

4. *Statistical Yearbook of Norway 2005,* Table 223.
5. www.ssb.no/arbeid/main.shtml.

§11. The Relationship Between the Private and the Public Sectors

108. The Norwegian economy may be characterized as a combination of private and public activity and enterprises, according to what is politically considered appropriate. To a certain extent, therefore, there is no clear distinction between the public and the private sector. Consequently, it is not always necessary to make it clear whether the activities carried out are of a private or public kind, as regards the question of whether private or public law is to be applied, because the same law may apply in any case. In other cases, it is necessary to draw a distinction. It is, however, necessary to bear in mind that over time the distinction between public and private tasks has not been drawn along the same lines.

109. Of course, basic activities – such as defence, the police, the national bank and the core of the central administration – are public tasks, and belong in the public sector. On the other hand – clearly in principle – production and distribution of goods and services belong in the private sector. But when there is a question of meeting the basic needs of the society, that is a question of public interests in addition to the private interests involved. Especially, it is politically necessary for a welfare society to have a system that can meet the needs of the population for welfare services, e.g., as regards schools and education, hospitals and nursing institutions for the sick, the disabled, the elderly persons, and so on.

110. Furthermore, it is a question whether activities within e.g., the cultural sector should be considered a task for the public, such as theatres, opera, radio and television, and so on. The further question is, however, whether such institutions should be run by private firms or by public bodies.

111. In Norway, private and public activities in these fields run more or less side-by-side – the majority of the institutions are, however, run by public bodies – and private institutions are to quite an extent entitled to contributions from public budgets as regards their expenses. It is even the case that special tasks for the public authority is delegated to private associations.

112. In a labour law context, it may be mentioned that the NHO, represented by the Norwegian Business and Industry Security Council (NSR), pursuant to the Act on Civil Protection (ACP) (of 25 June 2010 No. 45, sections 23 and 29) – previously the Civil Defence Act (CDA of 17 July 1953 No. 9) sections 48 and 41 and regulations regarding protective measures concerning industrial enterprises etc. of 29 November 1996 No. 1092 section 1, is instructed to organize and inspect protective measures instituted by a number of given industrial and craftsmanship enterprises, etc. The protective measures regard management, fire safety measures and sanitary measures, among other things.

113. In addition to defence and the police, it is considered a public task to run primary and secondary schools, as well as universities – and to quite an extent also kindergartens. Similar is – to a large extent – the case as regards hospitals and other health institutions. As regards national railways, that is in general considered a task for the public (NSB), as to a large extent also are local trains, as well as the national radio and television company (NRK). Production of electricity and water supply was previously considered a task for the public, but in this sector, there is now room for private companies as well. The postal services should also be mentioned in this regard.

Also, there are private radio and television stations. It should also be mentioned that the state owns about one-third of the land – and all over – the whole country. The supply of corn has been considered an important task for the public – there used to be a corn import state monopoly, which no longer exists. Based on political principles and considerations, the retail sale of wine and spirits is still a task for the state-owned monopoly only. Production of arms, iron and coal was once also considered a task for the state, and the state is today deeply – through a company (Statoil) – involved in the petroleum sector. Another example is the consulting activities of the state. Furthermore, the state has important tasks as regards financial operations based on the income from *inter alia* the royalties from petroleum activities, and is also involved in some of the Norwegian banks.

114. In general it seems fair to say, that as far as public activities shift from covering basic needs of the society to activities of a more mercantile kind, the characteristics of public activities more or less vanish. In recent years, the trend has therefore been, that such activities should be carried out by a separate body – a company – wholly or partly owned by the public authorities in question (state, county, municipality). Therefore, such activities may be organized as a joint stock company, or by special Act, giving the unit the status of a separate legal body, e.g., as regards the hospitals. In such cases, the public legislation will usually not apply, unless otherwise is stipulated. In such cases, therefore, the employees will not have the legal status of civil servants, but of ordinary employees.

§12. Underlying Social and Cultural Values of Society and Their Effect on Freedom of Association, Discrimination, Guaranteed Income, Etc.

115. As already mentioned above, the large majority of the Norwegian people and politicians have for a great many years agreed on the basic and major lines of Norwegian post-war foreign and domestic policy. In this period, there has been little social unrest, and political and economic stability is the dominant part of the picture.

116. A significant degree of homogeneity characterizes the population. This applies to a large extent to the ethnicity of the population, even though immigration always has made its mark. Just as important is the homogeneity of language and culture. To some extent, this homogeneity is under a certain amount of pressure. Substantial, however, is the homogeneity of the national education system, especially considering the ten-year-long compulsory primary and secondary school, which commences in the year that the child is 6 years of age. During the education, the educational plans and curriculum are essentially the same all over the country. A majority of children even make use of the day care system, from when they are 1 year of age, and the right to attend day care is regulated in legislation (cf. Day Care Institution Act (of 17 June 2005 No. 64) section 12a). Many young people continue with more extended education through secondary education at an advanced level (three years). The right to such extended education is regulated by legislation. Many people go even further with their education and become students at universities and colleges. The standard of education may therefore be characterized as high.

117. Statistics show that, during the year of 2007, 249,815 children attended day care, 616,388 children attended the compulsory primary and secondary school, while 228,363 youths were studying secondary education at advanced level. In the same year, approximately 219,464 students were studying at universities or colleges.[6]

118. Education is an important prerequisite for the individual's participation in society. Further, education will be important to prepare the individual for the working life. Based on this view the Human Rights Committee on Human Rights in the Constitution, appointed by the Parliament in 2009, has designed a proposal for revision of the Norwegian Constitution which includes a new provision (section 109) regarding the right to education. The proposal was delivered to the Parliament in December 2011.

119. There are no great differences concerning wages between people living in the cities and in the countryside, and between different districts, mostly due to active district politics and district development and funding. The differences in wages between the different parts of the population are also relatively small, but apparently have now started to increase. Differences in wages are deliberately levelled through taxation politics and throughout the system of transfer by legislation concerning social and welfare measures. There is, evidently, a significant interaction between taxes, social security and other forms of social measures.

120. In addition, it should also be mentioned that the majority of the Norwegian households live in dwellings, row houses or self-owned apartments. The politics of home ownership has for a long period of time been deliberate, and is based on a broad political consensus.

121. The relatively high standard of economic welfare within the population is evident from, e.g., the amount of cars per person. The same goes for holiday homes, and boats, access to the Internet within working premises, schools and homes, mobile phones, etc.

122. Traditionally, organized working life has had a strong position within the area of labour life, and the right to organize also holds a strong position. The same goes for the principle of non-discrimination based on religion and philosophy, ethnicity, skin colour, gender etc. Still, one may ask how far the principle of non-discrimination reaches, or has been developed, within all these different areas.

123. Finally, it can be mentioned that the freedom of religion is stated in the Constitution (cf. the Constitution of the Kingdom of Norway section 2). Traditionally, Lutheranism has been deeply rooted within the population, but with many shades, and in recent years, there has been a growth in the humanistic movement, together with an increase within the Catholic Church. The number of Muslims is significant. There is currently being held a rather lively political debate on what the relationship between the state and the church should be. On the 21 May 2012, the Parliament amended the Norwegian Constitution which resulted in a division between state and church. The Christian Lutheran Church is therefore no longer the official state religion of Norway.

---

6. *Statistical Yearbook of Norway 2007,* Table 157.

Chapter 2. Definitions and Notions

§1. Definition of Labour Law: What It Comprises

I. The Difficulties in Defining Labour Law: A Functional Approach

124. As will be dealt with below, the term 'labour law' does not, per se, constitute – as part of the legal system – a clearly in advance defined unit. The different legal themes of labour law are – all of them – also dealt with in other parts of the legal system. Therefore, it is not possible – by deduction based on a 'judicial logical' basis – to reach the conclusion that labour law has a specific content, or that the term 'labour law' should be limited in a certain way. That is, unless – in advance – a postulatory basis for such a deduction is set up.

125. When the themes of labour law are to be indicated, and distinctions drawn between labour law and other branches of law, it is necessary to make a number of choices, based on considerations stemming from the realities in question. Thus, it is necessary to decide which topics ought to be brought together and dealt with in a labour law context. The same will apply as regards the question of what weight each topic should be given, as well as how comprehensive and detailed the discussion of each topic should be. In this regard, it seems reasonable to take into consideration whether a topic is well suited to enlighten more general labour law questions, whether it is a question that frequently arises in practical life and whether the specific topic is thoroughly dealt with in other connections.

126. To indicate and define what labour law comprises, including distinctions as regards other parts of the law, thus implies, as a whole, no more and no less than deciding upon a number of systematic and practical questions of appropriateness.

127. Against this background, and in order to emphasize the connection and interaction between the rules of the different kinds of law, it seems to be practical and appropriate, and perhaps even pragmatic – when labour law is to be dealt with in a more comprehensive connection – that the basis should be a functional approach.

128. Based on a functional approach, it may be said that labour law comprises law and regulations regarding employment relations in the broadest sense. Thus, labour law embraces, *inter alia*, the rules on conclusion, content and termination of employment contracts, collective agreements, employees' right to co-determination, working protection, working environment and labour inspection, the public employment service, labour disputes, and the negotiation and settlement of disputes.

II. The Relation Between Labour Law and Other Branches of Law

A. *The Relation to Private Law*

129. It is obvious that the employment agreement – the contract between the parties, the employer and the employee – constitutes the basis for a number of important questions in the legal relationship between these parties, including conclusion and termination of their agreement. Already, therefore, it is evident that labour law will necessarily have to deal with questions that by nature are of a private law kind.

1. Contract Law

130. Thus, it is possible to approach labour law on a contractual basis, and thereby deal with the rights and duties of the parties in their contractual relationship. Thereby, labour law questions may be dealt with and compared to other kinds of contract. Such systematization is frequently used as regards contract law. An employer's right to make deductions from wages earned by the employee may, i.e., be compared with the general and specific rights of creditors and debtors to contra account. Previously it was not unusual for the rights and duties of an employment relationship to be dealt with in a separate part of a textbook on contract law, etc. Historically, such parts may in many ways be seen as a transitional stage to the present situation, with labour law as a separate part of the law.

131. Today, general contract law principles should, however, be applied with due regards to the specific circumstances of labour life, upon which labour law is based, as these have been expressed through the dynamic development of labour law and legislation, collective agreements and other practice of labour life, where *inter alia* social considerations are of importance. Thus, general contract law principles may – more or less – be modified because of the specific circumstances that have to be considered in a labour law context.

2. The Law of Associations

132. The legal relationship between the organizations of labour life and their individual members constitutes a basis for a number of questions concerning wages and working conditions as regards the employment relations for the members. This aspect of the law of associations gives a further basis for the private law as regards labour law, and – in addition – collective agreements play a most important role in a variety of sectors in labour life. The binding effect of collective agreements upon the members of the organizations, possibly also for non-members, as well as the use of industrial action (strikes, lock-outs, etc.) raises a number of basic labour law questions, which ought to be dealt with in a labour law context.

133. The important role of organizations in today's labour life has as a consequence that at least some aspects of the legal relationship between organizations and members should be dealt with in a labour law context – such as the employee's right, and possibly also duty, to be a member of a trade union; exclusion, suspension, fines for misconduct, union jurisdiction, etc. In addition may also be mentioned the legal relationship between superior and subordinate associations and federations of trade unions.

3. The Law of Companies

134. Important questions regarding the law of companies give labour law a further private law basis – in particular the rules on employee co-determination – which interferes with and influences management's decisions. In addition, important questions relating to labour law arise when the employer re-organizes the company, e.g., changes the kind of company, joins with another company (fusion), or leaves a company (fission), etc. Should the (formal) employer company be a part of a concern, it is further a question whether the whole concern (group of companies) may be considered as the (real) employer – in general, or as far as specific duties are concerned.

4. Other Private Law Aspects

135. Labour law also has connections with other aspects of private law, such as the law on torts and insurance, e.g., the compulsory insurance as regards accidents in connection with work at the workplace. It is also possible that compulsory insurance may be based on provisions stipulated in collective agreements. It may further be mentioned that also the law on tenants (*husleie*) has connections to labour law, e.g., as regards official residences (*tjenesteboliger*).

136. Further should also be mentioned the private law questions with regard to third parties arising from the employment relationship – such as possible direct responsibility for the employees when a third party suffers damage, e.g., as a consequence of a strike or lock-out. Again, it is a practical question, to what extent it seems appropriate to deal with such questions in a labour law context.

B. The Relation to Public Law

137. It is obvious that public interests are connected with labour life, and – consequently – there are connections between public law and labour law. In this regard, the term 'public law' comprises administrative law, as well as constitutional law, parts of international law, the law on court proceedings and the penal legislation.

1. Labour Exchange, Including Labour Life, Immigration and Work Permits, Etc.

138. It is in the interests of the society to counteract unemployment, e.g., through programmes related to the labour market – such as courses for professional training etc. – and through an efficient labour exchange service. Such activities are – undoubtedly – related to public law, and may as such be classified as administrative law, but are – indeed – also related to labour law. This pertains, even more, to the whole concept of an inclusive labour life.

139. Similarly, the law regarding immigration and work permits also has relations to labour law, e.g., the impact on the relationship between the parties if a work permit should not be granted, if it is withdrawn, etc. Even more important are the rights and duties of immigrant workers, and cross-border workers, as regards working conditions, etc. Further, these questions constitute an important part of the law on non-discrimination.

2. Security at Work, Working Environment, Etc.

140. Security at work and public inspection of the working environment in that respect is undoubtedly not only a part of public administrative law, but – indeed – also a traditional and basic part of labour law, at sea and ashore. The whole aspect of internal control, in order to ensure that the enterprise is operated within the provisions stipulated by the WEA and other legislation, is a central part of labour law, including, *inter alia*, the whole system of safety representatives and working environment committees. The role of the Labour Inspectorate in this regard is also important.

3. Social Security, Etc.

141. There is a close connection between labour law and the law on social security and welfare – and there is a considerable degree of overlap between these two parts of law. These questions are dealt with in detail below (*see* paragraphs 145 et seq.).

C. The Relation to International Law

142. As regards international law, it is sufficient to point out that a number of international conventions and other instruments stipulate rules and standards as regards labour relations. These are dealt with in more detail below (*see* paragraphs 417 et seq.). In this context, it is sufficient to emphasize that it would be most unsatisfactory should these international regulations not be dealt with in a labour law context, but be left to international law alone. The connection and interaction between international and national law would, in that case, be missing – and thereby important perspectives on labour law.

D. The Relation to Constitutional Law

143. Constitutional law is of importance on certain points of labour law, and should therefore be dealt with in a labour law context, and not solely in a constitutional law context. Of particular importance is the constitutional question of whether there are limitations on Parliament as legislator passing a specific Act in order to bring a legal strike or lock-out to an end – as well as the similar question as regards the King-in-Council passing a temporary Act with such a purpose. This problem is definitely not a constitutional question only, but also a labour law question.

144. Further, there is a constitutional question regarding the extent of employee co-determination – to what extent may legislation give the employees the right of co-determination, or whether the Constitution limits the legislator in this regard. In addition should be mentioned the prohibition against giving new legislation retroactive application – a prohibition that raise certain questions when new legislation on labour law is passed. Furthermore, it should be mentioned that the position of civil servants should be dealt with in a labour law context also and thereby give important perspectives on labour law in general.

E. The Relation to the Law on Court Proceedings

145. Again, quite important questions regarding labour law are closely linked to the law on court proceedings. In this connection, it is sufficient to mention the Labour Court as regards the interpretation and validity of collective agreements, as well as the legality of strikes, lock-outs, etc. Another example is the right of an employee who has been given notice of termination to remain in the position while the question of whether the termination was fair is being dealt with by the courts – and for such court proceedings, the employee is exempted from the obligation to pay court fees. It may also be mentioned that employees may demand that bankruptcy proceedings be commenced against the employer – e.g., in cases where wages are not paid – without having to provide security for the court's costs in that connection; this possibility makes the employees' claim more efficient, which is of practical importance. In these cases, the questions should of course be considered also in the light of the general law on court proceedings. But it would be quite unfortunate should such court proceedings questions not be dealt with in a labour law context as well, and thereby flesh out the substance of the rights of the parties involved.

F. The Relation to Penal Legislation

146. Even penal legislation has connections to important labour law questions. It is in this connection sufficient to mention that a company as such may be held liable for penalties for non-compliance with the rules and regulations on safety and working environment, that representative trade unions might be entitled to initiate criminal proceedings in such cases, and that illegal strikes, lock-outs, etc. are not subject to penalties. Such questions are of course of interest as regards the law on penalties in general, but – indeed – also in a labour law context.

G. Summing Up

147. When labour law questions are dealt with in connection with private law, public law, administrative law, constitutional law, international law, law on court proceedings or penal law, etc., it may be said that the questions are dealt with on the basis of a constructive system as regards the nature of the different rules. That method has the advantage that the specific labour law rules are seen in connection with the general principles as regards the different areas of the law. The disadvantage is, however, that the different sides of the specific area of the law – such as labour law – are not seen in a larger and more overall context. Therefore, the functional connection between rules with a different legal basis may not be focused on, nor the special considerations that lie behind the rules of labour law. Those considerations will be dealt with in greater detail below. Here should, therefore, only be mentioned that the subordinate position of an employee – which may lead to undue exploitation – is a concern that may not be fully considered in a 'pure' contract law setting. It may further be mentioned that the use of collective force – through strikes or lock-outs – which are basically legitimate means, and thus should be respected, might jeopardize the whole balance of society. Although the right to use collective force may, basically, be founded in contract law, the rules of contract law seem rather insufficient to cope with the core of the problems which may arise in such cases. The same may be said to apply as regards constitutional law, administrative law, penal legislation and so on.

148. On the other hand, a functional system may have the disadvantage that labour law is dealt with on an isolated basis, and considered as special law to a larger degree than is really the case.

149. In dealing with labour law questions, it is, therefore, necessary to be fully aware of this dilemma, and to have a good knowledge of the general law principles – as well as insight into the specific principles and rules of labour law. Indeed a challenge!

150. Concluding, and balancing these considerations, based on a functional approach, it may be said – as indicated above – that labour law should comprise law and regulations regarding employment relations in the broadest sense, and that it is important to enlighten the connection and interaction between the different parts and rules on labour law.

§2. The Relation Between Labour Law and the Law on Social Security and Welfare

I. Definition of the Law on Social Security and Welfare and What the Law on Social Security and Welfare Comprises

151. As there is no sharp distinction between public tasks and private activities, there is also no sharp distinction between the law on social security on the one hand, and labour law on the other hand. On the contrary, there is a close connection between social security law and labour law, and – in addition – a considerable degree of interaction between these two parts of the law (cf. paragraphs 149 et seq.). It should also be noted that the terms 'employer' and 'employee', generally, are understood in the same way as regards both of these two parts of the law (cf. paragraphs 192 et seq. and paragraphs 206 et seq.).

152. In the same way as regards labour law, the term 'social security law' per se is not necessarily clear, but depends on what should – from time to time – be considered as an appropriate definition. Today it seems fair to say, that the term 'social security law' should be given a quite broad and comprehensive meaning, including to a considerable degree also the law on social welfare.

153. Against this background, the law on social security and welfare may be seen as society's endeavours and objects to secure the needs of each member of the population, throughout the whole lifetime of the individual, from birth until death. Thus, the aim of the Social Security Act (SSA) is to give economic security during pregnancy, at birth and in a period of time after birth or adoption, at illness and accidents, in case of disability, unemployment, at old age and even as regards the funeral. Further, the social security system is based on membership, where – in principle – everyone living in the country is automatically a member.

154. Finally, the law on social security may be used as a tool in connection with the politics regarding the population. By maintaining good living conditions regarding children and families with children, tendencies concerning reduction of the population may be avoided. There may e.g., be given the right to extended leave of absence during pregnancy and after giving birth and the use of public economic funding systems during such leave of absence.

II. The Law on Social Security and Welfare as the Background for Labour Law Agreements and Arrangements

155. From this aspect, the law on social security and welfare constitutes an important platform for agreements and other arrangements as regards the different parties in a labour law context. Should it e.g., follow from the social security and welfare legislation that an employee is entitled to a minimum of wages for a certain period from the social security system during absence because of illness, it will not be necessary for the parties to an individual employment contract – or a collective agreement – to raise that question at all, and they may – possibly – limit their negotiations to the question of whether the employee should be entitled to further compensation from the employer or an independent foundation, etc. Consequently, from this point of view, the social security and welfare legislation mainly regulates the relationship between individuals and the public, while labour law mainly regulates the relationship between the parties to an individual employment contract or a collective agreement.

A. The Law on Social Security and Welfare and the Prevention of Misfortune

156. The aim of the law of social security and welfare is, however, also to prevent misfortune and in that connection to follow up and deal with situations where misfortune may occur, or has already happened. In this connection, it is sufficient to mention, for instance, that the health of the population is of importance for society, and that a number of measures are taken in order to achieve this goal, improve the health of the population – not at least as regards children, youth and elderly people – and to prevent illness arising and spreading. In this regard, the public health authorities play an important role. In a broader perspective, it may be held that annual vacations with pay will in the long run provide better health for the population as a whole.

157. Preventing misfortune is the aim in a number of other concerns, such as child welfare and welfare for the elderly, and the establishing of institutions with regard to these, and also as regards abolishing poverty and social misery, and giving social support to the poor.

158. Especially as regards labour law, should be mentioned the Labour Inspectorate, which has as an important task to prevent accidents at work. In this regard, it must also be mentioned that the social security and welfare system, as well as compulsory insurance, ensures that employees who have suffered because of such accidents receive compensation.

B. The Law on Social Security and Welfare and Efforts to Achieve Full Employment

159. As a consequence of attempting to prevent misfortune, it is important that persons who want to work can be employed and further, that they can contribute to the wealth of – and not be a burden to – the society. A public labour exchange is therefore of importance. In addition it is, however, also of the greatest importance to establish an inclusive labour life, so that all types of people can be included in this important part of the society – for example, the more or less disabled, the elderly, etc. – and thus contribute to the growth and well-being of the whole society. By seeing the possibilities of the individual person as a whole, in connection with possible contributions from the society through the social security system, it may be possible for the person in question to achieve employment and thus be included in working life. Similarly, it is important – for the individual as well as for the society – that a person who has been injured at work, or suffers from illness, should be able to continue being at work, if the workplace can be adapted to the new situation of the employee. The administrative reform in Norway – whereby labour exchange and social administration, since 2006, are united into a new administrative body, the Working and Welfare Administration (*Arbeids-og velferdsetaten* (NAV)) – is founded on this basic view. It should also be mentioned that an inclusive labour life is now explicitly mentioned as one of the aims of the WEA (cf. WEA section 1-1e).

C. The Law on Social Security and Welfare and the Strengthening of Trends in a Desired Direction

160. From another aspect, the social security and welfare legislation may also be seen as a possibility for society to strengthen and encourage certain trends into a desired direction, where labour law and social security and welfare legislation may walk hand-in-hand. The situation as regards families with small children – or who are about to have children – is illustrative. The rules of labour law stipulates that the working person – one or both of the parents – have the right to be absent from work in the last part of the pregnancy period, and for some time after birth – which should or may be divided between the mother and the father – and, later on, when the child is ill and must be cared for, within certain time limits. This right of being absent from work is – of course – important, but in practical life it is also of the greatest importance whether this absence leaves the family without income, or wages or other form of compensation is granted during such absence. To a large extent, the social security and welfare legislation stipulates that the family is entitled to wages or compensation, for periods that generally are synchronized with the labour legislation, and which makes the right to absence more effective. Similarly, absence for taking care of elderly relatives gives the same picture but for much shorter time periods.

161. Thereby, labour law and social security and welfare legislation give the authorities – especially the central authorities of the country – possibilities to encourage certain trends and strengthen a development, which is politically desirable. If the purpose is to encourage female workers' participation in labour life, without having as a result a drop in the birth rate, the above indicated will make it easier for women to have children, economically and otherwise, and – to some extent – the fathers will be encouraged to take part in the taking care of the child in the first year after the child's birth. In addition, establishing kindergartens for all children above the age of 1 year makes it in practical life possible for female workers to participate in labour life.

D. *Interaction Between Labour Law and the Law on Social Security and Welfare*

162. The interaction between labour law and the law on social security and welfare has already been mentioned. From a historical point of view, this interaction seems apparent, as important parts of today's legislation on social security and welfare are the results of developments within the labour law area, an illustrative example being employees' right to full wages from the very first day, during absence because of illness.

163. From a historical perspective, it may be said that there has been a long-lasting tendency to give employees a legal right to contributions of a social character – a tendency that may also be said to be based on a Christian and humanistic ethical tradition – and to be generous to those who suffer from illness, are poor for some reason, etc. In a labour law context, it seems that a great part of today's social security and welfare system is a further development of the rules that previously applied to an employment relationship, such as the duty of an employer to take care of employees who suffered from illness, were injured or elderly. Today, the system has been extended to include persons in situations that are not connected with an employment relationship. Still, however, employees are to a certain extent entitled to better contributions than persons in general. And this social security and welfare system has – to quite an extent – taken over the duties that previously were the duties of an employer. This system, financed through social security fees – from employers as well as from employees – is nowadays taken for granted by most people. Thus, employees are – so far – no longer dependent on the employer's discretion or economic ability as regards contributions after an accident, as regards pension, etc.

164. The situation as regards compensation for accidents at work is, of particular interest. Here, a compulsory insurance system is established, outside of and in addition to the social security and welfare system, and the expenses are paid by employers only.

165. Further, the situation as regards pensions is illustrative. To-day, employees are entitled to pensions from the social security and welfare system, and in addition a compulsory supplementary pension system is established, where employers and employees pay their contributions to an insurance company or other pension enterprise. The view, that employees through their employment contract may be entitled to pensions from a pension fund etc., as a part of their working conditions, was basically accepted in Decisions by the Norwegian Supreme Court (Rt.) 1928 p. 1028 (*Centralbanken*) (cf. also below paragraph 243), although the view that pensions – at least pension to the widow of an employee – should be considered as some gift *ex gratia* from the employer, was also expressed by the courts in the 1930s (cf. Rt. 1931 p. 297 (*Kvinnherad Sparebank*)). That view is probably now overruled (cf. Rt. 1966 p. 1509), which seems to be based on quite another attitude, and further, *inter alia* dictum of the Supreme Court Rt. 2000 p. 610 at p. 619.

166. Further illustrative is the situation as regards employees who suffer from illness. In cases of absence employees are entitled to their wages from the employer during the employer period – sixteen days – and thereafter from the social security and welfare system (cf. SSA sections 18–19). A system is, however, being established – through insurance – which will have as a result that employees will be treated by hospitals or other health institutions before other people; the employee will thus not have to wait in a health queue.[7]

167. The long term trend is, in other words, from employment-related rights and duties, to rights and duties in relation to the social security and welfare system – and again, but as additional rights and duties – back to employment-related rights and duties.

E. The Basic Amount of the Law on Social Security and Welfare

168. An important factor of the social security system is the basic amount (G), which is stipulated by Parliament, and at present (1 May 2015) amounts to NOK 90,068. In general, the amount is being adjusted every year, in connection with the budget of the state, to compensate for increased prices, etc.

169. In principle, this amount is the basis from which a person's pension and other contributions from the social security and welfare system are to be calculated, as well as in connection with some other pension Acts. The amount is, however, also used as a standard, upon which compensation for accidents is calculated – and in certain cases as a maximum for e.g., pensions (e.g., 12 G), and for the calculation of the wages that an employee is entitled to during annual vacations, according to the law (6 G), and even as regards succession duty for gifts before the death of the donor (one-half G). Changes in the basic amount may therefore have quite incalculable consequences. In any case, the basic amount is undoubtedly of importance also as far as labour law is concerned.

F. Summing Up

170. Undoubtedly, labour law and the law on social security and welfare overlap to a considerable degree. The focus of these two parts of the law is, however, rather different. To an extent, it seems fair to say, that – from a labour law point of view – the law on social security and welfare serves as a platform for the agreements and arrangements that are concluded between the parties of labour life.

7. Indeed – as Comrade Napoleon and co. proclaimed (George Orwell, *Animal Farm* (1945)) – all animals are equal, but some are more equal than others.

§3. Definition of Labour Law and of Concepts Which Are Most Frequently Used: Employee, Employer, Enterprise, Etc.

I. The Employment Relation: Some Introductory Remarks

171. As indicated above, labour law should comprise law and regulations regarding employment relations in the broadest sense.

172. When the term 'employment relationship' is to be defined, the meaning which the term normally has in legal contexts will be the starting point. With this modification, an employment relationship may be defined as a contractual relationship whereby one of the parties (the employee) places her or his personal labour at the disposal of the other party (the employer). Normally, this is done in return for a specified compensation, so that the contract is based on mutual obligations. However, the work may also be carried out gratuitously, although this is rather unusual.

173. Thus, the contribution to be made by the employee is his or her personal labour, and – basically – the employee does not bear the risk that the work provided will lead to the result intended by the employer. To a certain degree, the employee's rights may nevertheless depend on the results of the work – work carried out poorly may provide just cause for dismissal – and as regards piecework, the wages may depend wholly or partly on the number of units produced, etc.

174. Due to the fact that an employee places his or her personal labour at the disposal of the employer, the employment contract entails a more or less distinct subordinate relationship for the employee, so that the employer is given management authority which also imposes a duty of loyalty on the employee. However, the management prerogative as well as the duty of loyalty is subject to considerable limitations.

175. Thus, employment law rules and regulations will apply when the employer and the employee enter into an agreement to the effect that an employment relationship is established. Furthermore, employment law may also – to a greater or lesser extent – apply when employment is to be established in the future, or is being established. Similarly, employment law may apply when this is specifically stipulated, for instance by statutory provision, collective agreement or as a result of an agreement between the parties.

176. To some extent, the distinction between an employment relationship and other legal relationships will follow the definition of the term 'employee', e.g., as regards the distinction between an employee and an independent contractor (cf. paragraphs 261 et seq.). It is, however, most important to emphasize that an employment relationship is necessary if a person is to have the status of an employee – e.g., where work is carried out as a part of a family relationship, as member of an association, as partner of a company, and so on. The term 'employment relationship' is important to emphasize; the nature of the legal relationship between the parties is the basis for application of labour law rules and regulations.

II. Basis of the Employment Relationship

A. The Employment Contract

177. A basic condition for the application of rules and regulations of labour law is – unless special circumstances should indicate something else – that the relationship between the parties (employer and employee) is based on a written, oral or de facto agreement. Further, this agreement must imply that the employee places his or her ability to work at the disposal of the employer in order to carry out more or less specified tasks. This condition is usually expressed so that the employee must be employed by the employer (cf. e.g., WEA section 1-8(2), which defines the employer as 'anyone who has engaged an employee to perform work in his or her service').

178. Should the relationship between the parties not be based on an agreement, the rules and regulations of labour law will only apply to the extent that there is a special basis for this, for example a separate statutory provision, collective agreement, the parties' agreement or other special basis.

B. Members of Parliament, Members of County Councils, Mayors, Etc.

179. Persons who, according to law, are elected or appointed to a special task, an office, etc., are not employees – nor civil servants – and consequently do not fall under the Civil Servants Act (CSA), the WEA, the Holiday with Pay Act or other employment legislation. This applies, *inter alia*, to members of Parliament, members of county councils, mayors, public trustees and guardians.

C. Work Carried Out by Prisoners in Prisons

180. Similarly, work carried out by prisoners in prisons etc. (Decisions by Courts of Appeal and District Courts (RG) 1951 p. 892 Hålogaland), or imposed according to the legislation on social services (Decisions of the Labour Court (ARD) 1994 p. 16), or according to the legislation on defence, does not constitute an employment relationship.

D. Work Carried Out Based on Membership of an Association

181. Further, work carried out based on membership of an association does not constitute an employment relationship, because the dominant basis follows from the relationship to the association, e.g., for a person elected as a leader of a trade union (Rt. 1995 p. 2018).

E. Owners of Enterprises, Elected Members of the Company Board, Shareholders, Etc.

182. The owner of an enterprise is of course not an employee of the enterprise or the elected members of the board of directors etc. (with exceptions to a certain extents for employees elected by their fellow employees as their representatives to such a board; their position as board members should primarily be considered as a position of trust, and not a position following the employment legislation (cf. Rt. 1995 p. 2018)).

183. On the other hand, an employee may very well be a shareholder, and in principle the position of shareholder and the position of employee are separate. Thus, unless otherwise agreed upon, the employment relationship may be terminated, without obligation for the company (the employer) to pay to the employee the value of the shares, even if it was a condition of employment that the employee bought shares in the company for a stipulated amount.

184. It could also be the case that one or more of the owners are also employed by the enterprise. As employees, they are subordinate to decisions made by the management of the enterprise, e.g., the board. Should the underlying company agreement between the owners stipulate that one or more of them must work in the enterprise, decisions of the board must be kept within the frames stipulated in the company agreement. The latter could possibly be altered according to the principles of company law, but not according to the employment law principles (cf. e.g., Rt. 1957 p. 1047 and Rt. 1952 p. 658, also Rt. 1952 p. 967 and Rt. 1966 p. 648).

185. More complicated is the situation where a person holds the majority of the shares, is perhaps also the director of the company with limited liability, perhaps even the captain of the only ship owned by the company. In Rt. 1929 p. 640, the Supreme Court held, that the captain as a seaman was entitled to maritime lien in the ship for wages, etc. – which seems reasonable, provided the wages are within normal limits – because a ship will necessarily need a captain, and the position of the creditors is therefore not weakened compared to what would be expected. As regards claims on the social security system, the Supreme Court found that a subordinate employment relationship was not established for a person holding almost 55% of shares and who also was a member of the board, and the director of the company (cf. Rt. 1986 p. 1322 (*Norsk Staalpress*)). It could perhaps be argued that another result could have opened the door for speculative arrangements to the disadvantage of the social security system. Similarly, a person who held all the shares of the company, was the one and only person of the board, as well as a director, was not considered entitled to the position as employee as regards the legislation on transfer of enterprises (WEA (1977) section 73 A, now WEA (2005) section 16-1), when the petroleum company terminated the contract with his company and turned the petrol station over to its daughter company 'Tiger' (cf. RG 1999 p. 1607 Borgarting (*Esso*)).

F. The Significance of the Purpose and the Period of Time Spent on Work Activities

186. The purpose and time of the activities may also have significance when deciding whether the relationship between the parties falls within the borders of labour law. Activities with the only purpose of teaching or training will in principle fall outside these limits (cf. e.g., Rt. 1962 p. 1179 and ARD 1980 p. 48); in both cases, the activities were of a short duration. Outplacement of school children for introduction to labour life does not in principle constitute an employment relationship, but if the relationship turns into a more long-lasting situation, labour legislation may apply (cf. Rt. 1982 p. 1022).

G. *Work Carried Out by Family Members*

187. It should also be mentioned that work carried out by family members, in that capacity, in principle does not constitute an employment relationship. The legal relationship between family members is, in reality, based on their common basic community of interests related to their home and children, and the subsequent formal and traditional maintenance obligation. This will, for example, be the case where family members, especially the father, mother or child, are performing the usual chores at home such as maintenance of house and home, cleaning, childcare, etc. The case will nevertheless be somewhat different for work not related to the home, such as work carried out in a store or a small craft business run by the father and/or the mother. Unless the family member may be regarded as a co-owner, one must assume that a regular working relationship normally exists.

188. Correspondingly, one must assume that the above-mentioned thesis is also applicable for visitors and others who live in the home, if the work carried out exceeds what may reasonably correspond to the value of board and lodging.

H. *Work Carried Out as an Au Pair*

189. Work carried out as an au pair is based on the fact that a person will visit a family 'as a daughter or a son of the family'. An au pair may obviously come from somewhere else in Norway, but is usually from another country. In order to obtain a residence permit it is a condition that the purpose of the stay is cultural (cf. Immigration Regulations of 15 October 2009 No. 1286 section 6-25). Pursuant to the immigration authorities' standardized contract for au pairs (Norwegian Directorate of Immigration (UDI), www.udi.no), the au pair has the right to participate in tuition and leisure activities, to have twenty-five vacation days every year, to be treated as a family member and to have the opportunity to participate actively in the daily family life, among other things. Working hours shall normally not exceed five hours on a daily basis or thirty hours on a weekly basis, and shall be thoroughly stipulated for each and every day of the week. An au pair shall be given the opportunity to have a separate room in the house, to receive a minimum allowance of NOK 4,000 monthly, besides receiving free board and lodging. This allowance, and the value of free board and lodging (in 2010 it amounted to approximately NOK 108 per day) is also taxable.

190. In a labour law context, an employment relationship does not exist as long as an au pair's working hours, duties and remuneration do not exceed what usually is the ratio of what a housewife's son or daughter normally carries out and receives. Protection measurements – which normally involves that the weaker party's legal position need to be ensured – may indicate that this framework should be drawn fairly tightly. This is because an au pair in most cases is a stranger to the country, and is usually a relatively young person – aged between 18 to 30 years. Chores, working hours and remuneration, which are not limited to the family-based framework, indicate that an employment relationship exists. The borderline between the family-based framework and an employment relationship will necessarily have to be somewhat discretionary. Some factors may, on the other hand, be decisive in the estimation of the relationship's legal character: more chores that have to be carried out, the more working hours that are arranged, and the more thoroughly these factors are regulated, the stronger is the connection to an employment relationship and not a family relationship. The size of the allowance will also be of importance in this assessment. Thus, it may hardly be doubted that an au pair's relationship to a family, which is based on UDI's standardized contract for au pairs, and includes up to thirty working hours per week – which is equivalent to 75% of a normal working hours week (forty hours) – will have to be characterized as an employment relationship.

191. However, it should be mentioned that Oslo City Court (18 February 2008 TOSLO-2007-130127), stated that an au pair cannot be regarded as an employee, among other things. The statement is an obiter dictum, which means that the statement was not necessary for the conclusion, due to the fact that the court found that objectively justifiable reasons for dismissal did exist in the case in question.

192. As a starting point, the WEA should, therefore, be applicable to the au pair's working relationships. Regulations of 5 July 2002 No. 716 (cf. WEA section 1-5(2)), on the other hand, provide special rules for employees who perform housekeeping chores, supervision or care in the employer's home. Should the au pair's employment wrongfully be brought to an end, there therefore is no specific time limit for legal proceedings, and the au pair has no right to remain in his or her post while the case is being tried by the courts, nor is he or she able to require that an unfair dismissal with notice or a wrongful summary dismissal should be found invalid by the courts, but is entitled to compensation for economic and non-economic loss, as other employees (cf. also paragraphs 551 and 1080 below).

I. Nuns, Monks, Priests and Salvation Army Officers

193. Work is sometimes also performed as part of a calling, to such an extent that the work characterizes the entire life situation of the individual. Particularly severe is the situation for nuns and monks, who may devote their entire lives to the religious institution they belong to, such as a religious order, etc. To the extent that they perform work beyond what is necessary for their own subsistence, etc., it must presumably be assumed that their situation also represents an employment relationship. Nuns who perform work as part of the operation of a Catholic hospital are thus considered to be covered by the WEA's provisions on maximum working hours (cf. Labour Council Annual Report 1940 p. 10).

194. Similarly, the assumption also is that the Catholic priests are in an employment relationship with the church they belong to. Thus, the courts have held that the question of whether an ordering of a priest from a church in Norway to a community in Poland was legitimate or not could be tried by the Norwegian courts (Rt. 2008 p. 1529). The relationship between the priest and the Picpusorder in Poland was, however, to be taken in particular consideration, *inter alia* when the question later on was to be decided, whether the ordering was contrary to obligations stipulated in the Working Environment Act as regards termination of an employment relationship. The Court of Appeal characterized the attachment to the Picpusorder in Poland as the main employment, from which the employment contract in Norway was derived. Thus, that question was decided in the negative (cf. LB-2008-142425 Borgarting). Similarly, Salvation Army officers – who hold a special position within the Salvation Army – have a right to a written employment contract pursuant to the WEA. Their promise to the Salvation Army will not in itself be sufficient.

J. Pupils, Persons on Compulsory Military Service, Prisoners, Patients at Health Institutions, Etc.

195. For certain categories of persons who carry out work, it is explicitly stipulated by law that parts of the labour legislation shall apply. Thus, WEA section 1-6(1) stipulates that pupils, persons on compulsory military service, prisoners, patients at health institutions etc., are considered employees as regards rules and regulations concerning health, environment and security at the workplace. In such cases, it seems most correct to characterize the legal construction as quasi-employment relationships.

K. Enterprises That Have No Employees

196. In this connection, it may also be mentioned that some labour legislation shall apply, even for enterprises that do not employ any employees at all (cf. WEA section 1-4), which stipulates that even special regulations may be issued in that regard. Thus, the Regulation of 10 January 1986 No. 17 stipulates to what extent the rules of WEA apply to sole proprietorships in the building and construction industry – mainly as regards safety, health and the working environment.

III. The Collective Agreement: Introductory Remarks

197. A collective agreement is an agreement 'between a trade union and an employer or employers' association respecting conditions of employment and wages or other matters relating to employment' (cf. LDA section 1(c)). A collective agreement is thus a 'framework agreement' providing standards for what an employment contract may regulate regarding working conditions in employment relationships to which the collective agreement applies, or an agreement which regulates the relationship between the parties of the collective agreement.

198. The parties to a collective agreement are always a union or other employees' association on the one side and either an individual employer or an employers' association on the other (cf. LDA section 1(c)).

IV. The Term 'Employee'

199. The WEA defines an employee as 'anyone who performs work in the service of another' (cf. WEA section 1-8(1)). Several other statutory provisions contain similar definitions, e.g., the LDA, section 1(1), as well as the SSA. As per the latter, it is a part of the definition, that 'wages or other remuneration' is compensation for the work being done. That provision must probably be seen in connection with the fact that contributions from the social security and welfare system basically compensate for loss of wages. It should be observed, in general, that the terms 'worker' and 'employee' are synonymous, and are dealt with as synonymous terms in this monograph.

200. The wording of the definition of the WEA may convey the impression that commencement of the position is an essential part of the definition 'employee'. However, this cannot be unconditionally relied on.

201. The term 'employee' does not include situations where a person is taking on an assignment and carries it out on his or her own account and risk, such as for instance contracts for services. In these situations, the person is obliged to provide a certain work result while employment contracts refer to the employee's labour, not to any specific product.

202. However, it is not always clear whether the relationship should be classified as employment or an agreement with an independent contractor. If so, a concrete assessment of all circumstances of the contractual relationship must be made (cf. Rt. 1990 p. 903 and Rt. 1994 p. 1064).

203. Important factors will be whether the person executing the work is entitled to use co-workers of his or her own choosing and account, who procures and pays for maintenance of the operational factors, and whether it is allowed to carry out assignments for other principals while the contractual relationship between the parties is in force. The greater independence the contractor has in these respects, the less reason there is to subject the contract to the rules of labour law. However, the fact that the employees must, for example, provide their own tools or their own tractor for the job, or that he or she is reimbursed for expenses on account, does not necessarily prevent the relationship from being an employment contract (ARD 1968 p. 36 (cf. also ARD 1991 p. 140 and ARD 1996 p. 91)). The Supreme Court stated in 2013 (Rt. 2013 p. 354) that a person working as a caretaker for a family with particularly burdensome care needs, looking after a severely disabled child, was to be considered as an employee and not an independent contractor. The person had been engaged for the work based on four independent fixed time contracts, which originally were not considered as employment contracts. Thus, she was not entitled to holiday pay according to the contracts. The Supreme Court found, based on an overall assessment, that:

- The caretaker was not entitled to use subcontractors in order to perform the work tasks.
- She had no influence on the working hours and what work tasks that should be done.
- The work had to be done in the home of the family, with the tools and remedies that the family had placed at her disposal.
- The caretaker was reimbursed for the expenses she had in connection with the work.
- She was not responsible for the work results. The caretaker performed work that the municipality was responsible to perform according to the social care legislation, and therefore the municipality was responsible for the work results.
- The caretaker was paid salary on a monthly basis, based on submitted timesheets.

- She had worked for the family for about two months in 2008, and in certain periods from January 2009 until August 2010. This indicated a working relationship of a certain stable character.

However, one factor indicated that she was to be considered as an independent contractor; the fact that she worked for several principals at the same time. Nonetheless, the overall assessment indicated that she was considered as an employee, and she was entitled to holiday pay.

204. Other factors which are relevant to the assessment include the site of the work to be carried out, the duty to follow instructions on job execution, working hours and overtime, terms of settlement, the duration of the contract and any agreed periods of notice, etc. However, it must be noted that the principal subject to many contracts for service may also issue binding instructions on job execution, control the time spent on the work, etc.

205. It is not necessarily decisive that settlement is not paid until the job is completed, so that only a suitable advance is paid for work completed, or that remuneration is paid according to a certain price per unit produced (piece rate) or a lump sum (a job price contract).

206. Sometimes, the employer has a rather limited opportunity to issue instructions, for example because the employer may not have the necessary professional know-how, or because the employee according to the employment contract is entitled to a very independent position. This may be the case with highly qualified scientists or artists, whose work performance will, and must, to a considerable degree depend on the employee's personality and individual focus. In spite of such factors, the relationship may nevertheless be regarded as an employment contract. The Supreme Court has found that for stage directors the contract must be linked to the director personally, and not to the staging as a product of the labour, even though the contract concerns specific, time-limited assignments with a salary stipulated as a lump sum, and with at least a theoretical opportunity to carry out other assignments at the same time (Rt. 1958 p. 1229 (cf. also Rt. 1990 p. 903)).

207. For persons carrying out industrial homework at an agreed unit price, the Supreme Court has held that they are also entitled to a holiday allowance, at least if 'it concerns a permanent employment relationship of a not insignificant extent, and the work was carried out on a regular basis' (Rt. 1968 p. 725). Similarly, an athlete and a coach have been considered as employees and therefore fall under the regulations which provide protection against unfair treatment. The fixed annual remuneration was to cover ordinary living expenses and therefore had the character of wages, and the athletic association had the right to management and instruction (Rt. 1992 p. 534 (cf. also ECJ C-415/93 (*Bosman*)). Further, the contract between a football club and the professional football players is interpreted on the basis of the WEA (cf. Rt. 2012 p. 168).

208. On the other hand, if the relationship between the parties has been very vague and of an incidental nature – sales under demonstrations in private homes ('home-parties') – the Supreme Court has stated that an employment relationship was not established with regard to the regulations of the WEA and the Holiday with Pay Act (Rt. 1984 p. 1044).

209. In principle, it is not decisive whether an employer has deducted taxes from the employee or contractor, whether the employer or contractor has been registered in the register of employees or of enterprises, whether value added tax has been calculated, whether the employer has paid the employer's national insurance contributions, etc. (cf. e.g., Rt. 2007 p. 1458 (diver)). However, in cases of doubt the courts have placed a certain emphasis on how the parties have acted in the situation, e.g., whether holiday or sickness payments have been made (Rt. 1990 p. 903).

210. The overall evaluation of whether an employment relationship exists will not only be made in relation to the circumstances of the relationship between the parties, but also on the basis of the object of the different regulations subject to which the distinction between an employee and an independent contractor are of importance. Since the regulations may have quite different objectives, the classification may be different in relation to different regulations. One can therefore not assume that the term 'employee' will have the same meaning in all relations. Here, as elsewhere, the primary task is to interpret the specific rule of law to be applied. As regards regulations based on the necessity to protect the employee, it is reasonable to emphasize to a larger extent those facts that are connected with the prerogative of management, than the factures that are related to equipment and other means to carry out the work (e.g., Rt. 2007 p. 1458 (diver)).

211. Thus, it is conceivable that a person will not be considered as an employee in respect of the rules on value added tax, contributions to the social security system, tax withholding, etc. (cf. e.g., Rt. 1981 p. 872), but must be considered as an employee in respect of the Holiday with Pay Act or collective agreements stipulating rules relating to employees' rights. On the other hand, the responsibility as employer for torts caused a third party by the employees will, for a law firm, extend even to the partners of the firm, cf. Rt. 2015 p. 475, but it must be assumed that the internal relationship between the partners and the law firm will, at least usually, not be regulated by the employment legislation, e.g., as regards termination of their relationship etc.

212. The judgment in Rt. 1984 p. 1044 (home-parties) should also be noted. Here the Supreme Court did not place any emphasis on the fact that tax deductions had been made, that the employer's national insurance contributions were paid and the fact that the salesmen had been registered in the social security system, because this had to be done also for persons not engaged under contracts of employment, as long as they were not self-employed.

V. The Term 'Employer'

213. The WEA defines an employer as anyone who has engaged an employee to perform work in his or her service (cf. WEA section 1-8(2)). Several other statutory regulations contain similar definitions, e.g., LDA section 1(b).

214. The WEA, other Acts and regulations, as well as employment relationships as such, impose a number of obligations on the employer. Thus, it is the duty of an employer to ensure that the working environment of the enterprise is fully satisfactory (cf. WEA sections 2-1 and 4-1). Similarly, the employer may terminate the employment relationship by means of dismissal or summary dismissal, but it is also the employer who will be responsible for possible unfair or unjustified terminations (cf. WEA sections 15-12 and 15-14).

215. On the other hand, the employer position implies a managerial prerogative – to manage, delegate and control the work (*see* paragraphs 239 et seq.).

216. The term 'employer' of the WEA is based on a functional view on the employer position. Thus, *inter alia*, it is to be considered who in practice has acted as, and has performed, the functions of an employer. Furthermore, it is stated in the *travaux préparatoires* to the WEA that the responsibilities of an employer may lie with more than one person or enterprise, if special circumstances are present, for example where others in fact have acted as employer and exercised employer's functions.

217. In many situations, it is not difficult to decide who the employer is, for example when a small company is owned and operated by the owner himself (sole proprietorship). If the enterprise is operated by several people jointly, they will all be employers in relation to the employees, and they will among other things have joint liability for the employees' wage claims (cf. Rt. 1993 p. 955).

218. If it is a corporate body that owns and operates the enterprise, the corporate body will be the employer, while the functions of the employer will be exercised by the organs of the corporate body or others who can act on its behalf. Thus, it is the relevant private limited company, cooperative society, foundation, state corporation, etc. which will be the employer.

219. It should be emphasized, however, that it is of importance that it is stated in the employment contract who the employer is (cf. Rt. 1993 p. 490, Rt. 1993 p. 955, and also Rt. 1997 p. 623 and Rt. 2006 p. 420). That question may be of specific importance where two or more companies start a common enterprise together, e.g., by starting and running a centre together. In Rt. 1997 p. 623, the Supreme Court found that such an inter-municipal centre was itself the employer. Thus, the employees at the centre did not have a priority right to be engaged in any of the seven participating municipalities in their capacity as employer. The Supreme Court emphasized that all vital employer functions were vested with the board of the centre, which also had exercised those functions.

220. As already indicated, the situation on the employer's side could be rather complex, and the facts of Rt. 1993 p. 490 are illustrative (*see* paragraphs 472 et seq.).

221. Furthermore, it must be assumed that the legislative concept of 'employer' is a relative one.

222. The responsibility for ensuring that the employee receives wages and other benefits pursuant to the employment contract will normally lie with the party which has concluded the employment contract, even if the employee has carried out work for a third party and subject to that party's instructions and management, as is the usual situation for hired-out employees. Normally, the third party would therefore not be responsible for the employee's wage and other claims which arise in this connection (Rt. 1985 p. 957, Rt. 1985 p. 977 and Rt. 1999 p. 509). However, if the third party has acted to ensure his or her own interests, has in reality had control over the party which in the first place did conclude the employment contract (the 'original' employer), and in this connection has had work performed, paid wages, etc. that party might also have employers' responsibilities (cf. Rt. 1937 p. 21, comp. Rt. 1995 p. 270 and Rt. 1995 p. 584).

223. As regards the employer's obligations concerning a fully satisfactory working environment, the general rule is that this responsibility lies with the party who is actually in a position to instruct and supervise. This responsibility may therefore lie with the enterprise in which the employee carries out the work (Rt. 1985 p. 941 and Rt. 1982 p. 645). The same must supposedly apply to the employer's liability to pay compensation when the employee's actions have resulted in injury to a third party (Rt. 1963 p. 622). In this connection should also be observed WEA section 1-4(3), which states that regulations provided by the Ministry may stipulate that the provisions of the Act shall wholly or partly apply to anyone legally responsible for building assignments or his or her representative (cf. Regulations issued on 3 August 2009 No. 1028, and previous Regulations of 21 April 1995 No. 377).

224. It should further be observed that WEA section 14-6(1) a) stipulates that the written employment contract shall, among other things, state the identities of the parties, so that it states who the parties to the employment agreement, the employer and employee, are. The person stated as employer in an employment agreement, concluded by the employer or by someone acting on the employer's behalf, must be regarded as employer and be the responsible party as regards legislation, collective agreements and the employment contract itself. However, the statement in the contract of the identity of the employer does not – as such – prevent other persons or companies from having an employer's responsibilities in different relations.

VI. The Term 'Employer' When a Company Is Part of a Group of Companies

A. *Introduction*

225. In companies that are part of a group, the employer's liability pursuant to the regulations of the WEA concerning protection against unfair dismissal etc., will not always be limited to the company in which the employee is employed (cf. Rt. 1990 p. 1126 (*Wärtsilä*), *see also* Rt. 1989 p. 231 (*Exploration Logging*), Rt. 1993 p. 345 (*Matherson-Selig*) and RG 1994 p. 688 Haalogaland (*Norsk Jern Eiendom*)). Upon dismissal on the basis of curtailment of operations, etc. the employer must, however, not necessarily treat the different independent parts of the company group as a whole (cf. Rt. 1992 p. 776 (*Sparebanken Nord-Norge*) and Rt. 2015 p. 1332). It should be mentioned that seniority in the whole company group will not necessarily be decisive, because other factors may outweigh the relative importance of seniority. Should regulations regarding health and safety have been violated, it may – when the penalty is stipulated – be taken into consideration that the individual company is part of a group (Rt. 1995 p. 278 (*Block Watne*)).

226. Similarly, the employee's obligations may also reach further than only applying towards the company which is the formal employer. Thus, the duty of loyalty may also include the group management and is not necessarily limited to the subsidiary (cf. Rt. 2003 p. 1614 (*Telenor*)). Also, the overall evaluation of transactions carried out in Rt. 2006 p. 71 (*SAS-Braathens*) may be seen as a consequence of a basic company-group consideration.

B. Considerations

227. The question may be raised, if a group of companies should in these regards be considered as a whole – as *one* employer – wholly or to a certain degree, especially where the group is operated as an economic unit. It may be argued that the choice of company form – whether the company should be established as a number of smaller companies, with one holding company, or established as one large all-encompassing company – is a choice for the owners exclusively, where the employee side has no say. It may further be argued that it is necessary to divide the economic risk, and that it might be advantageous for tax reasons, to have separate legal units (companies). Furthermore, where a group of companies is operated as an economic unit, the basic and far-reaching decisions are often made by a board of directors of the parent company or a holding company, with quite direct consequences for the subsidiaries in question and their employees. The case could be that the deciding company of the group finds it useful to increase investments and production in two of the subsidiaries, and to phase out the third subsidiary by simply not keeping the equipment of that company updated. The basic argument could be, that the responsibilities as employer thereby would be placed to the decision-making company, so that responsibilities and realities of the economic interests of the decision would be united. Thus, the situation of the employees would not be different in a group consisting of a number of subsidiaries, from in a large all-encompassing company. In addition it could be added, that it is – generally – more difficult for employees to find other work, than it is for other creditors – as bankers, suppliers, etc. – to adjust or discontinue their economic relationship with a subsidiary being phased out.

228. Should the group be considered as one employer, the group as such would have the responsibility of maintaining a fully satisfactory working environment, as well as different subsidiaries. Should it be necessary to reduce the workforce in one of the subsidiaries that company would have to ensure that the termination of the employment relationship is fair, and that other suitable work is not available – as is the case where a division of a large all-encompassing company must reduce its workforce. The next step would be to see whether other suitable work is available in other divisions of the large all-encompassing company – and the same principle could be applied to the concern with its underlying subsidiaries. It may be noticed that it would in practice be insufficient to limit this responsibility to the parent company, especially if the parent company is holding company with a small administration of just a few employees.

229. The above line of argument is built on the basis that there is a superior managing company of the group as a whole. Should that not be the case, there is no reason to consider the group as a whole as regards these questions. However, if a company has determining influence over one or more other companies, it would be fair to assume that this company had a greater influence on the decisions made in one or more of the other companies. In such a case, however, the company with determining influence should have the opportunity to prove – and have the burden of proof – that it has not exercised any superior influence on the decisions made in one or more of the other companies.

230. Such a determining influence may have been established in different ways, e.g., by establishing new companies as new activities are started, by fusion, or through purchasing another company, and so on. Thus, the historical background may give some guidelines as regards the question of whether there is a superior managing company, which has exercised its superior influence. As regards cross-owned companies, such companies should probably be considered as having determining influence over each other – e.g., two companies owning 50% of each other – because the important decisions will require that the two companies agree, as regards questions like large investments, closing down of parts of the activities, or all the activities of one of the companies and so on.

231. Considerable weight should also be given to the question, of whether employees have, as part of their duty, an obligation to work for one or more of the other companies of the concern, if so decided or requested by the company with which their employment contract has been concluded. Should their employment contract explicitly state that the employee has such an obligation, should – similarly – considerable weight be given to such an obligation. In both cases, the group of companies has acted in such a way that the employees are employees of the group, and not of just one of the companies (cf. Rt. 1989 p. 231 (*Exploration Logging*), where the employees had a duty to move internationally between the different companies of a multinational group of companies).

232. Another example from practical life may also be mentioned – also from the petroleum and shipping sector – where it seems fair to assume that the whole concern (group of companies) should be considered as one employer, at least for most legal purposes: The concern was organized with a mother company with three subsidiaries, which again had one or more subsidiaries. Within shipping and oil exploitation, the different activities of these companies referred to: (a) administration and management of the concern as such, with land-based personnel, (b) oil-drilling activities and operation of permanent installations, with offshore personnel, (c) oil drilling, transportation and construction, and operation of mobile platforms, with offshore personnel, (d) construction and consultant activities, with land-based personnel, and (e) services related to drilling of wells and production of oil, with offshore and workshop personnel, and personnel at base. The boards of the different companies were one and the same, so that one board was elected and functioned in all of the different companies of the concern. Seniority was calculated for work in all the different companies as one company, common shop stewards were elected for the different companies and there was a common working environment committee, a common safety representatives system, common rules of proceedings and common collective agreements for the companies. The employees were rotated and moved from time to time between the different installations, depending on level of activities, capacity and competence, and there was an extended rotation of the employees between the different companies. As a whole, the activities of these companies were interwoven to a large extent.

233. Thus, the Council for Industrial Democracy in the Drilling and Contractor Vessel Industry approved on 7 November 2008 the application for joint employee representation in the joint board for the different companies of the concern.

234. Even though a group of companies is seen as a whole, with ensuring employer responsibility, a certain question arises regarding the event of transfer of ownership of enterprises, in this connection transfer of ownership of one of the companies within the group. Employees that are transferred to the new employer, supposedly have the right – in accordance with the general principle regarding transition of rights and duties (cf. WEA section 16-2(1)) – to keep the seniority which they had before the time of transfer, calculated according to the practice of the group of companies. Through such an interwoven work and rotation duty within the group of companies, there supposedly can be assumed that employees that object to transfer of the employment relationship to the new employer keep their seniority in relation to the other companies within the group.

235. More difficult is the question of which of the employees who may object to transfer of the employment relationship to the new employer has the right of reservation, when one of the companies within the group is transferred. This question may arise regarding the companies' employees with tasks relating to data, accounting, etc. The group of companies may have their own data and accounting company, with employees that do their work within all the other companies of the group, at the same time as the employees work in one of these companies, and in the data or accounting company.

As regards Rt. 2012 p. 983 (*Drill Rig*), the facts implied that employees who had been hired out ('seconded') and worked for several years 'had such a connection to the rig' that they were entitled to continued employment after the transfer of the rig to another company; although the employees were under the obligation to move to other working sites according to decisions of their employer ('seconding company'); the question as to whether the employees might object to the transfer of their employment relationship was, however, not dealt with by the Supreme Court.

C. Proposed Legislation and Summing Up Case Law

236. In Official Norwegian Reports (NOU) 1996: Six 'Employees' position in group of companies, etc. the committee considered the above questions, and suggested an addition to WEA (1977) section 4 (now WEA (2005) section 1-8(2)) in order to clarify the definition of the term 'employer'. According to the proposal, any other company that could exercise determining influence over the employer should furthermore be regarded as employer. It was also suggested, that where determining influence may be exercised by a group of companies, or by companies connected to such a group, all of the companies connected to the group of companies should be regarded as employer. These suggestions have later on been considered on different occasions, also when the WEA (2005) was adopted, but has so far not resulted in any change of the legislation.

237. It should be noted, however, that the view is expressed in the *travaux préparatoires* to the WEA that it would not be contrary to the present term 'employer', For inspection to take place with parent companies, should these – actually – be considered to have acted as employer. Further, it is also stated that age limits may not be stipulated arbitrarily, and that different age limits within the same company or group of companies for the same kind of work or profession would indicate arbitrariness.

238. Summing up, the main tendency of the practice of the Supreme Court seems to be that employment relationships are connected to the group of companies as such – especially where the employees are not solely connected to the individual company – as was the case in Rt. 1989 p. 231 (*Exploration Logging*), and also as regards Rt. 1990 p. 1126 (*Wärtsilä*) – compare also Rt. 1992 p. 776 (*Sparebanken Nord-Norge*) and Rt. 1993 p. 345 (*Matherson-Selig*). However, a more general view in this regard seems to have been the basis for Rt. 1985 p. 941 (OIS) and Rt. 2003 p. 1614 (*Telenor*). Perhaps it may be said that the general tendency of the Supreme Court seems to be that the basic realities should be considered decisive, and not the formal constructions made unilaterally by the deciding bodies of a group of enterprises.

VII. Managing the Enterprise on Behalf of the Employer

239. As stipulated in WEA section 1-8(2), the provisions of the Act relating to the employer correspondingly apply to those managing the enterprise on behalf of the employer. The provision is primarily of importance as regards the regulations on safety, working environment, etc. In private limited companies, such responsibility will therefore lie not only with the board of directors and the managing director (cf. Rt. 1990 p. 419), but also with others with management functions, depending on the extent of their independent authority in respect of technical and commercial matters (Rt. 1984 p. 773). Hence, a manager of a power station has been assumed to have such responsibility (Rt. 1985 p. 185) because he was the highest-level site manager and had a right to instruct other employees, as also a construction manager (Rt. 1983 p. 196), a manager of a construction site (Rt. 1982 p. 878) and construction site engineers (Rt. 1988 p. 692 and Rt. 1990 p. 419).

240. These responsibilities are to be defined in more detail through the internal control system for the individual enterprise (cf. WEA section 3-1(3) and the Regulation on internal control of 6 December 1996 No. 1127). *See also* paragraphs 1251 et seq. below.

VIII. The Term 'Enterprise'

241. The term 'enterprise' is not defined in the WEA. The term is used in several provisions of the Act, and in quite different senses. The further content of the concept must therefore be decided on the basis of an interpretation of the specific provision in which the term is used.

242. In the *travaux préparatoires* to the WEA is expressed the view that the legal person being the employer, will usually be identical with the enterprise of the employer, and that – in practical life – an enterprise will be what in common language is an enterprise. These remarks are, however, of a more descriptive than an analytic character, and give little guidance for a further analysis of the term 'enterprise'.

243. The term 'enterprise' includes both industrial companies, transport businesses, building and construction firms, business companies, public administration and intellectual activities. It is not decisive whether the business is run for profit. Thus, the term is comprehensive and includes, among other things, businesses with a non-profit purpose such as schools, homes for the elderly and hospitals, research institutions, etc. How the business is organized – as a foundation, private limited company, company with liability, etc. – is in this connection not decisive.

244. In several provisions of the WEA, the term 'enterprise' is used as a description of the operational activities that are led by the employer within an organizational framework, which may be geographically limited to a greater or lesser extent. Thus, an employer with extended activities may operate several enterprises. In situations where an employer operates several enterprises and a statutory provision uses the term 'enterprise', the question of whether the term comprises all activities that the employer is engaged in, or the term is limited to that part of the employer's local activities which within an organizational framework constitutes an operational unit, must be decided on the basis of an interpretation of the specific provision. Upon interpretation, proper regard must, of course, be to paid purpose of the relevant provision.

245. It may be observed that the Supreme Court, Rt. 1992 p. 776 (*Sparebanken Nord-Norge*) based a decision on the view that each branch of a savings bank had to be evaluated separately, on the basis of the quite considerable geographical area covered by the bank, with regard to the question of whether the employees were entitled to continue in their positions while the court proceedings took place (cf. WEA (1977) section 61 No. 4 and now WEA (2005) section 15-11(1) and (2)). The Supreme Court took also into consideration that the bank had recently implemented mergers of a number of local banks.

IX. The Management Prerogative

A. *Introductory Remarks*

246. The management prerogative may be defined as an employer's right to manage, delegate and control work – as well as the right to conclude and terminate employment contracts – within the limits of the employment law regulations. In that respect, the management prerogative is a necessary consequence of the employment contract itself and the employee's subordinate position and duty of loyalty towards the employer.

247. This management prerogative has never been absolutely 'free'. It is subject to many and extensive limitations as a result of statutory provisions and collective agreements, in addition to the employment contract itself. Further, the tendency has, for quite some time now, been towards further restrictions on the management prerogative.

B. *The General Principle of Fairness*

248. Furthermore, decisions made on the basis of the management prerogative must be kept within the limits that follow from the general principle of fairness. This standard may be seen as a consequence of the employees' subordinate position in relation to the management, owing to the fact that the management's decision-making may have quite significant consequences for the employees involved. If these decisions are to be accepted by the legal system, they have to be based on a proper and respectable basis, and not made on the basis of arbitrariness, random ideas, vengefulness, etc. on the employer side. Today, the principle of fairness must be characterized as a general principle of labour law.

249. Cf. Rt. 2001 p. 418 (*Statoil-Kaarstoe*) where the Supreme Court stated that the management prerogative:

> was also limited, however, by more general principles of impartiality. Exercising the employer's management prerogative requires certain standards as regards procedure, a justifiable basis for the decision must have been established, which must not be arbitrary or based on irrelevant considerations.... The decision in question was a following up of an organizational change. Such a decision is not...a breach of the general norm of impartiality.

Rt. 1989 p. 231, ARD 1980 p. 42 and ARD 2003 p. 14 may also be observed. Further may be mentioned Rt. 2011 p. 841, stating that the transfer of a school inspector from one school to another required just cause and fair considerations.

C. Alteration of Long-Lasting Practice and Streamlining Conditions for All EmployeesC. Alteration of Long-Lasting Practice and Streamlining Conditions for All Employees

250. It is also recognized as legitimate for the employer to unilaterally alter a long-lasting practice by the enterprise, in order to bring the practice in conformity with developments within the trade and to resolve a dispute between two groups of employees, in order to improve the working environment (cf. Rt. 2008 p. 856 (*Theatercaféen*)). The alterations implied that tips (gratuities) received from guests at the restaurant were supposed to be divided equally between the waiters and the chefs, and should no longer only go to the waiters. The dispute between the waiters and the chefs had escalated, and had been in progress for a long period of time, with negative consequences for the working environment, and meetings as well as negotiations between the employer and the employees' representatives had led nowhere.

251. Streamlining the conditions for all the employees may be considered objective and fair, and a formal notice of termination may be considered unnecessary (cf. Rt. 1959 p. 515 (*Insurance Agent*); possibly otherwise Rt. 1985 p. 507 (*Agents Council*)).

D. Alteration of Pension Schemes, Etc.

252. The pension scheme of an enterprise may also be unilaterally altered by the employer with effect for the future (*ex nunc*), provided that the employees do not have individual rights in this regard, limiting or excluding the right to alterations. Such individual rights may have been specified in their employment contract, or in an addendum etc., in which case the employer will not be entitled to make alterations without the consent of the employee; minor practical alterations probably excepted. The managing director may, e.g., have such an agreement with the company, which may not be changed unilaterally even in case of major economic difficulties for the company (cf. Rt. 2000 p. 610 (*Oslobanken*; insolvency)), or because of the fact that the retired person later on is also entitled to pension from public funds, etc. (cf. Rt. 1973 section 821 (*Dreyer*)). Further, specific pension schemes etc. may be stipulated in a collective agreement, in which case unilateral alterations may not take place until the agreement has expired, usually after a period of two years. Pension scheme rights was dealt with in the Labour Court case No. 36/2012 – *Norwegian Air Shuttle ASA (NAS)*. The case concerned the question of the effect from the alteration of a defined benefit pension scheme to a defined contribution pension scheme in Norwegian Air Shuttle ASA (NAS). The pension scheme alterations did not succeed in establishing sufficient compensation for employees who were entitled to a pension in accordance with the Pilot Agreement (a collective agreement between the Confederation of Norwegian Enterprises (NHO)/NHO Aviation/NAS and the Confederation of Vocational Unions/Parat/NPU). The question was whether NAS was obliged to maintain a defined benefit pension scheme, or whether it could be changed to a defined contribution pension scheme with a special compensatory scheme for pilots. The Labour Court stated that NAS was obliged to maintain the defined benefit pension scheme, according to the Pilot Agreement. The alteration was therefore in violation of the collective agreement and NAS was required to restore a tariff-related pension scheme.

253. Additionally, alterations may not be given retrospective effect (*ex tunc*) (cf. Rt. 1928 p. 1025 *Centralbanken*; held that insolvency did not have the effect that the pension fund in favour of the employees, which had been established to a sufficient degree, became a part of the bankruptcy estate, which would have wiped out the employees' rights to pensions with retroactive effect (cf. also Rt. 1934 p. 77 *Haugesunds Sparebank*; otherwise, however, Rt. 1934 p. 70 *Moss Privatbank*).

254. For pension schemes comprising all the employees of the enterprise – or a group of the employees – it is held as a general principle that the employer may unilaterally make alterations (cf. Rt. 2010 p. 412 (*FokusBank*) and Rt. 2008 p. 1246 (*Statoil*), also Rt. 2002 p. 1576 (*Hakon*)). Thus, the question is not whether alterations may take place, but to what extent, and under what conditions, alterations may be decided and be given effect. Therefore, an overall assessment of all relevant circumstances is required; such as the reasons for the alterations – which will have to be fair and objective – the degree of employee contribution and co-financing of the pension scheme, the costs involved if the present pension scheme should be upheld, whether the expectations of the employees were justified or not, whether information to and consultations with the employees' representatives did take place, etc. Further, it should be investigated whether certain employees would suffer especially negative consequences of the possible alteration – e.g., because of the fact that the age of one or more of the employees is almost the age stipulated in order to be entitled to the pension benefits – and whether special compensation in that regard has been considered (which was the case in Rt. 2010 p. 412 (*FokusBank*). It seems, thus, that these questions have to be decided according to a legal standard – whether the alterations seem to disproportionate (cf. also the Contract Conclusion Act (CCA)(1918) section 36).

255. It may finally be observed, that Rt. 2010 p. 412 (*FokusBank*), as well as Rt. 2008 p. 1246 (*Statoil*), seem to be decided on the facts that the legislation on pensions schemes etc. were changed quite drastically, in order to strengthen the economic security of the pension enterprises as regards future obligations, that it would be most expensive, and unforeseen, to upheld the original pension scheme; in addition – as regards Rt. 2008 p. 1246 (*Statoil*), the basic amount (which was the basis for the calculations of this pension) was also principally changed by the Parliament (*Stortinget*) to an unforeseen extent. It was thus held, that the pension should no longer be calculated to a specific amount, but according to the yields of the pension fund, which the Supreme Court assumed would secure the value of the pensions (Rt. 2008 p. 1246 (*Statoil*) paragraph 69). Rt. 1957 p. 219 (*Chassis Factory*) may also be mentioned; no obligation to upheld a pension scheme, as the price-regulating authorities did not grant the enterprise permission to include these pension costs when stipulating prices for its products.

256. Perhaps the observation should be made, that the costs connected to a collective pension scheme necessarily will add up to a larger amount than the costs for one individual employee – simply because of the fact that a collective pension scheme will include a number of employees. Thus, when pension costs increase, the increased costs will add up to an amount which may, in general, seem quite significant for the enterprise (although the increased costs per capita may be lower – perhaps considerably lower – than for a pension scheme in favour of an individual employee), which again may have as consequence that it may be easier to obtain legal acceptance of the view, that such changed costs will justify alterations of the pension scheme, than would be the case for an individual pension scheme.

257. As regards Rt. 2002 p. 1576 (*Hakon*), the Supreme Court held that the employer was entitled not to upheld any pension scheme for the future; the employer had established the pensions scheme unilaterally, had fully paid the contributions, the employment contract had no reference to the pension scheme, the employees had just been given information about the fact that the enterprise had a pension scheme; thus, held that the employees had no justified expectations that the pensions scheme would be upheld in the future.

E. Non-discrimination

258. The management prerogative is also limited by comprehensive requirements for the equal treatment of men and women. These requirements do not only apply in connection with advertising of vacant positions, appointment and conclusion of employment contracts. They also apply throughout the entire employment relationship, for example as regards training and competence development and leave of absence in connection with education (cf. WEA section 13-2 and the Gender Equality Act sections 2 and 5). Furthermore, the requirement for equal treatment will apply in relation to consecutive claims arising from the employment relationship, such as claims regarding termination of the employment relationship, claims in relation to preferential right to a new appointment, as regards pension entitlements, etc.

259. Direct and indirect discrimination on the basis of political views, membership of a trade union, sexual orientation, disability or age is also prohibited (cf. WEA section

13-1(1)). The same applies to discrimination on the basis of ethnicity, national origin, descent, skin colour, language, religion or belief (cf. the Ethnicity Anti-Discrimination Act (ADA) section 6, *see* paragraphs 245 et seq. and also paragraphs 1214 et seq.). The prohibition on discrimination applies not only in relation to employees but also to self-employed persons and contract workers (cf. WEA section 13-2(2)).

F. Protection Against Discrimination

260. Protection against discrimination comprises all aspects of employment, such as advertising of vacant positions, appointment, relocation, promotion, training and other forms of competence development, wages and working conditions and termination of employment (cf. WEA section 13-2(1); cf. also Rt. 2011 p. 1755 (*Gate Gourmet*); an agreement between the employer and the trade union, that the members of the union – but not non-members – should have priority to be re-appointed, held invalid). It should be observed that this enumeration is not to be regarded as exhaustive. This protection applies not only to employees but also to self-employed persons and workers hired from employment agencies or others (cf. WEA section 13-2(2)).

G. Employee Co-determination

261. The principle of employee co-determination has not only been an issue in employee representation in decision-making bodies, councils and committees of the enterprise, but has also – to some extent – resulted in the decision-making process being transferred to the employees, e.g., such as 'partly autonomous groups' and other kinds of changed organization of the work process.

262. Through corporate committees and new job design, the new types of co-determination have provided employees with greater influence on the decisions of the enterprise. Today, the rules and regulations give little room for decisions made unilaterally by the employer personally or by a corporate committee without allowing employees to take part in the decision. On the other hand, it is clear that in order for a company to be functional, it must have a management that can make decisions, also regarding matters that affect the employees. The reality in corporate democratization is that the decision-making process has been collectivized also in this respect, making it more appropriate now to speak of the management authority of corporate management, rather than of the management authority of the employer, since corporate management still has a management authority within the framework of legislation, collective agreements and employment contracts.

H. Establishing Positions and Appointing Employees

263. Unless restrictions follow from statutory provisions, collective agreements or in another manner, the management is free to decide which positions are to be established and filled. A collective agreement's listing of certain positions and their wage levels is not considered as a contractual obligation to establish or fill such positions, but only a provision on wages to be paid if the management has reason to establish the positions (ARD 1966 p. 26). Similarly, an employer may stipulate the tasks and purpose of the position (Rt. 1986 p. 1250).

264. In the whole, there is a tendency in the regulations towards imposing a duty on the employer to rely on justifiable criteria in employment, and it would hardly be too daring to assume that a standard of objectivity applies in connection with appointments in private companies. Within the public sector of working life, requirements for objectivity in connection with appointments follow from general principles of administrative law and regulations.

I. Instructions Regarding Behaviour at Work, Etc.

265. Basically, the management prerogative implies that the employer may instruct employees as regards the use of company emblems, attire, etc., and give instructions regarding how the employees are to dress at work (cf. Court Decisions on Norwegian Labour Law (NAD) 1988 p. 467 Haalogaland Court of Appeal, concerning instructions to cafeteria staff not to wear leather skirts at work). Such instructions must, however, be kept within what is considered proper and objectively justified and may not offence the integrity and dignity of the employee (cf. the WEA section 4-3(1)). Within these limits, the employer may also instruct regarding the length of hair, beards, the use of make-up, etc.

J. Safety Standards and Control Measures

266. It follows of the management prerogative that the management may decide the safety standard when work is to be carried out in the enterprise. The safety standard thus stipulated may be higher and more ambitious than the standard stipulated by public authorities according to law and regulations etc., and it is a duty of the employees to follow the standards stipulated by the management. Thus, a pilot may not object to the safety margins stipulated by the management of an airline (cf. Rt. 2003 p. 1702 (*SAS*)).

267. Further, and a consequence of the management prerogative, the management may decide what control measures are to be implemented. This is presumably relied on in the WEA Chapter 9 where, on the basis of fundamental requirements with regard to objectivity and proportionality, limitations on the management prerogative are stated.

268. Pursuant to section 9-1, control measures may only be implemented 'when such measures are objectively justified by circumstances relating to the enterprise', they must not involve 'undue strain' on the employees and such measures must be in compliance with the provisions of the Personal Data Act (PDA). Regard for protection of the privacy of the employees is essential. The provision lays down a legal standard, and establishes by law limitations which previously had a non-statutory basis.

269. Additional limitations with regard to the employer's access to control measures may ensue from a different legal basis, such as an employment contract, staff rules and collective agreements. A more far-reaching access to control measures cannot, however, be agreed or based upon the consent of the employee. Thus, the statutory provision is invariable. It must be noted, however, that the limitations of the PDA are modified if the employee has given consent.

270. In connection with the question of the employer's control of email and other forms of data communication, it must be noted that the employer, on the basis of the management prerogative, may decide that the employees are not entitled to make use of the company's data systems for private purposes. The employer may therefore set up technical solutions, which prevent such use, possibly also so that private emails are automatically deleted or returned to sender. The prohibition itself does not give the employer a right to make himself familiar with the content of such private notifications, but it may be a factor, which points in this direction (cf. Rt. 2002 p. 1500).

271. Before a decision is made in relation to implementation of control measures, the employer is obliged to discuss the need for such measures with the employee's elected representatives. Before the measures are implemented, the employer must provide the affected employees with information concerning the purpose of the control measures, practical consequences of the control measures and the assumed duration of the measures (cf. section 9-2 of the WEA).

K. Working Hours, Etc.

272. Within the framework of legislation, collective agreements and employment contracts, it is the company management that determines the working time, hereunder the place of attendance (cf. Rt. 2001 p. 418), use of flexible working hours, overtime work, night work, work on Sundays and public holidays, shift work arrangements, and the time for employees' holidays.

273. Should, however, the employment agreement specify at what time work has to be carried out – e.g., 'late work' at a hospital where the category of workers in question usually work on a rotation basis – the employer may not, unilaterally, transfer the employee to work on other times of the days, or according to the rotation arrangement at the enterprise, etc. (Rt. 2009 p. 1465 (*Nurses*). That would be to change a significant part of the employment agreement. On the other hand, it is held that the employer was entitled to stipulate an adjustment of the working time – prolonging the time of work with fifteen minutes per day, with economic compensation, in order to coordinate the working time of a group of employees with the working time for the other groups of employees at the enterprise – according to the management prerogative (cf. Rt. 1985 p. 78 (*Architects*).

L. The Legal Nature of the Management Prerogative and the Court's Re-examination and Re-assessment: Basics and Limitations

274. The courts may not only re-examine whether a decision has a justifiable basis, but may also through this re-examination assess whether the various factors have been weighed against each other in a reasonable manner. It will be of significance how far-reaching the decision being re-examined is – re-examination will be more thorough for a dismissal (*see* e.g., Rt. 1984 p. 1058) and when an employment contract due to other reasons is terminated after a considerable time (Rt. 1991 p. 872) than regarding a promotion (*see* e.g., ARD 1982 p. 264), an internal transfer (*see* e.g., ARD 1986 p. 165) within the same area of the production plant, while a transfer to another unit at a different geographical place was examined rather thoroughly (cf. Rt. 2011 p. 841) or regarding qualification requirements etc. upon appointment (cf. Rt. 2000 p. 1800, Rt. 1986 p. 1250 and Rt. 1991 p. 872).

275. It should be underlined, however, that the core of the management prerogative relates to questions and considerations regarding the activities of the enterprise, and how these ought to be carried out. Such decisions may relate to what products and services the enterprise should carry out at any time, and consequently also decisions as regards extensions, reductions – or even closing down – of the activities of the enterprise, as well as changes of these activities. These decisions will, again, necessarily have consequences as regards how many employees are required or desired, as regards their qualifications, training, updating of skills and knowledge – as well as concluding and terminating employment agreements – and further the organization of the cooperation between the employees in the different connections, as well as what means of production and equipment should be used, the place where the work should be carried out, and so on and so forth. When deciding such questions, the management, or the representatives of the management, will necessarily have to take into consideration prognoses as regards the expected developments – which may be more or less well founded – as well as the development which is or seems to be desired or expedient, etc. These considerations are usually – to quite an extent – founded on economic and mercantile principles, but may also be founded on considerations of a more policy-based kind, e.g., the wish to maintain activities in a certain branch or at a certain place, although it might be more profitable to close down, reduce activities or move the production to another place. Considerations of this kind are – anyway – basically not of a legal nature, and the legal evaluations will, therefore, apply only to a limited or perhaps even no degree. As regards questions related to the activities of the enterprise, the role of the courts will be limited to an evaluation of whether the procedure stipulated by law and agreements have been followed by the management, but 'in principle, it belongs to the prerogatives of the management to decide on closing down or continued activities of the enterprise' (cf. Rt. 1989 p. 508 (*Norsk Jern*)). However, otherwise may be stipulated in the employment agreement (cf. e.g., Rt. 2012 p. 168 (*Football player*)), where the employer's right to terminate the employment contract required that the economy of the football club had failed considerably, compared to a 'realistic' budget; in such a case, it is a legal question whether the budget was realistic or not, a question which the Supreme Court (dissenting 3–2) decided in the affirmative.

M. The Management Prerogative: Agreed Extensions and Limitations

276. The management prerogative follows, as mentioned, as a consequence of the employment agreement – as an integrated part of this agreement – but is therefore also limited by the frames of the employment agreement. Further, it follows from this basic principle, that the management prerogative may be regulated, stipulated, limited and extended, by the employment agreement.

277. The question then arises, to what extent an employer may obtain a more excessive management prerogative by the employment agreement with the employee/employees – and thus obtain the right to unilaterally make decisions to a larger extent – than an employer is entitled to, as per the general principles of the management prerogative. That question is closely related to two further, underlying questions; that is, how an employment agreement should be interpreted, and further (below paragraph 260), how the stipulated conditions of an employment agreement may be altered, e.g., when alterations are necessary because of the development that has taken place, or is about to take place.

278. Thus, it must be emphasized, at least for time-unlimited employment agreements, that the basic question is not whether an employment agreement may be altered – unless otherwise agreed – but whether the alterations in question may be stipulated unilaterally by the employer, based on the principles of the management prerogative – or by an agreement with the employee/employees in question altering the previous employment agreement; such an agreement may be the result of a notice from the employer to the employee/employees in question terminating the employment relationship – possibly combined with an offer of continued employment on revised conditions – and an acceptance of this offer by the employee/employees concerned. The basic principle is, however, that continued employment on altered conditions requires an acceptance from the other party, and without such an acceptance the employment relationship is terminated when the time of notice has expired; during the time of notice, the employment relationship continues on the conditions that the parties previously had agreed upon. Further – at least in principle (cf. paragraph 279 below) – notice of termination may not be given for just a part of the agreement, but must be given for the whole employment relationship; and the other party may choose to accept the termination, in which case of course, the relationship ceases at the end of the time of notice.

279. As regards the interpretation of employment agreements in this regard, the question seems to be approached on a basic assumption that the employer has not resigned from the right to make alterations, based on the management prerogative. Thus, agreed limitations as regards the management prerogative will have to be expressed relatively clearly in the employment agreement (cf. e.g., Rt. 2009 p. 1465 (*Nurses*), paragraph 256 above). Otherwise, the general assumption will apply, in practice not at least in cases where the particulars of a question has been further regulated in a separate agreement, scheme etc., constituting an addendum to the employment agreement (as is often the case as regards pension schemes (cf. the decisions mentioned paragraph 242 above, further Rt. 2000 p. 1193 (*Coop Svalbard*) may be mentioned; cf. also Rt. 1999 p. 163 (*AKAN*), held that stipulated guidelines as to how misuse of alcohol should be dealt with did not prevent the employer from terminating the employment agreement with immediate effect; Rt. 2010 p. 202 (*Nye Kystlink*), held that hiring a seaman above the age of 62 years did not limit the right of the employer to terminate the employment because the age of the employee was above the pension age of 62 years (paragraph 281 below); Rt. 1985 p. 78 (*Architects*) on working hours stipulated in the staff rules (paragraph 256 above) are other examples). On this background it is not surprising that quite general reservations in the employment agreement are referred to, also by the Supreme Court, justifying alterations made by the management prerogative, that such references to stipulated conditions will apply 'as stipulated at any time' as regards staff rules, pensions schemes, bonus regulations, etc. (cf. *inter alia,* Rt. 2010 p. 412 (*FokusBank*) paragraph 48).

280. It may be useful to remind and emphasize that the right to make alterations based on the management prerogative, or possible such extended right according to the employment agreement with reservations and references to supplementary documents, per se is not sufficient. This right is limited (cf. paragraph 257 above); a sufficient objective and fair reason is required; the alterations may not be disproportionate, and the questions must have been dealt with properly and in due course before a decision is made; further, the lawfulness of the management's decision may be decided by the courts. Thus, the interests of the employee/employees should thereby be secured, and possible misuse of the management prerogative prevented.

281. It is, however, not always quite clear, whether a decision is within the limitations of the rights following from the management prerogative, or whether a decision is so far-reaching that the terms of an employment agreement are substantially changed. If the latter is the case, the decision is in reality a notice of termination of the agreement, and in order to be valid, it is then required that the employee is given written notice, with the necessary details as regards the right to negotiations with the employer, time-limits for bringing a possible case before the courts, right to remain at work while proceedings take place, etc. Are these requirements not met, no time limit will apply for bringing the case before the courts (cf. WEA section 17-4(3), Rt. 2008 p. 1319 and paragraphs 1031 et seq. below). The question is, however, whether the missing formalities will have the effect that the decision will be considered invalid, should the court conclude, taking into account that the employer would have the burden of proof, that the result would have been no different, if formalities had been observed. In such an event, it may seem too formalistic to consider a decision invalid; on the other hand, it may be rather difficult to conclude in advance that formalities would have no effect; further, such a solution might give the employer a strategic advantage; in addition it is of importance that prescribed procedure is being observed, and that things are thus kept straight, so that uncertainties are avoided.

X. Employer Responsibilities for Other Than His or Her Own Employees

A. Presentation of the Problem and Basic Starting Points

282. Any employer is of course responsible for his or her own employees for any claims arising from their employment. Similarly, every employee is committed to his own employer, for example in terms of duties, loyalty, etc. The basis for these rights and obligations must be sought in the upper and subordinate relation arising out of the employment relationship – the managerial rights, decision-making and right to instruct the employee – which summarily may be described fairly as employer functions.

283. To the extent the employer functions are applicable to several enterprises, or are shared among several enterprises, the legal position of employer could apply to others than the enterprise which the formal employment contract specifies as the employer. With respect to this issue, the fundamental point of view is that the responsibility for the legal dispositions are submitted to that or those companies where the real decisions are made, as well as to enterprises that claim to have rights in relation to the employees, pursuant to the employment contract. Besides, the point of view does increase the efficiency of the protection that follows from the mandatory rules of law, such as the requirement for a fully satisfactory working environment, discrimination and job security, etc. The point of view also indicates that the concepts of employer and employee will be mandatory in relation to the mandatory provisions.

284. Illustrating is Rt. 2012 p. 983 (*Drill Rig*); the Supreme Court held (paragraph 103) that a person out placed on an oil-drilling rig according to a 'secondment' agreement was entitled to the same rights and duties as the ordinary employees of the oil-drilling company, when the rig was transferred to a new owner; should the formal 'seconding' employer still have the position as employer, the formal employer would have to:

> maintain most of employer functions. The more the real relationship between the oil-drilling company and the 'seconded' person has the character of an ordinary employment relationship, the easier that will be the conclusion, at least so that the 'seconded' will be entitled to those rights that the ordinary employees are entitled to.

This is the similar principal view that previously was expressed, *inter alia,* in the *OIS* case (cf. below paragraph 267).

285. The question of responsibility for other than its own employees, so that more than one employer will be responsible to the employee, arises partly by hiring in and hiring out of employees. Responsibility as an employer can also arise because an enterprise makes use of employer functions in relation to an employee in another enterprise, as the case might be in a group of companies. Moreover, responsibility as an employer may also arise in relation to a self-employed (independent contractor), where the underlying realities indicate that an employment relationship exists, even though the relationship should be formalized as a single mission, as the case often is between a larger enterprise and a sole proprietorship. Besides, any company has to make sure to organize its own activities so that work is organized and conducted in such a way that other than the company's own employees are assured a fully satisfactory working environment (cf. WEA section 2-2(1) a). The company is also committed to working together with other employers in order to ensure a fully satisfactory working environment (cf. WEA section 2-2(1) b). The responsibility to coordinate the individual business's environmental, health and safety rests with the enterprise that can be considered as the main enterprise (cf. WEA section 2-2(2)).

1. Hired Employees

286. When using hired employees, the employee will be employed with the company that hires out the employee, e.g., a recruitment agency, and it will often have been agreed that the employee shall do certain specific tasks in another company. According to the WEA, hiring of employees can take place in the same extent that employees can be employed on a time-limited basis (temporary employment), (cf. WEA section 14-12 together with WEA section 14-9(1) letters a) to e), and section 14-13). By the Act of 24 April 2015 No. 20 which entered into force 1 July 2015, the employer is now allowed to employ temporarily for up to twelve months on a general basis, cf. WEA section 14-9(1) subsection f). Thus, no particular reason is required in order to conclude a temporary employment contract according to this provision. However, the same Act made it clear that hiring of employees may only take place in the same extent that employees can be employed on a time-limited basis according only to WEA section 14-9(1) letters a) to e), cf. the amended section 14-12 first sentence. Thus, this rule disables an employer to hire in an employee on the basis of the new section 14-9(1) letter f).

287. The terms 'hiring in' and 'hiring out' are often used interchangeably. Seen from the hirer out's side there is talk of leasing out an employee to perform work for a user company, while from the user company's side there is talk of hiring in a worker to perform the relevant tasks. According to the WEA, the terminology used is 'hiring in' (cf. sections 14-12 and 14-13).

288. The use of hiring of employees will often mean that a company, whose object is to hire out labour, enters into an employment contract with the employee. The company, such as a recruitment agency, thus has employer responsibilities for those employees who are hired out. As an employer the recruitment agency will be responsible for wages, holiday pay, sick pay, tax deductions, etc., even though the individual employee is to perform his or her work with the contractor (user company). And in practice, the employee will receive his or her current instructions on the work performance from the contractor.

289. The contractor that makes use of hired employees, i.e., the user company, will also have obligations in relation to the employees, and it will be obvious that the user company also has employer responsibilities. This illustrates not only that the term 'employer' is of a relative nature, but it also illustrates that employer responsibilities may be incumbent to several companies, (cf. Rt. 1985 p. 941).

290. Illustrative is the *OIS* case (Rt. 1985 p. 941), where a criminal case was filed against the Oil Industry Services (OIS) Ltd. The case was filed because OIS had not ensured that the necessary basic training (cf. WEA (of 1977) section 14, paragraph (h)), had been granted for twelve employees who found themselves on the accommodation platform *Alexander Kielland* when it was wrecked. OIS claimed that the company was not to be considered as an employer because these workers were not employed by the company.

291. The OIS management had employed 220 workers. Of these, 50 were hired from member companies. OIS had in 1979 signed a cooperation agreement with Phillips Petroleum Company Norway. The agreement entailed among other things that OIS would be contractually responsible to Phillips, and OIS would have their own safety service in the field. On the basis of the agreement with Phillips, OIS entered into an agreement with individual member companies as subcontractors concerning the various categories of benefits and services. In relation to Phillips, OIS were responsible for the work performance. The OIS management ensured the coordination of the various operations. The OIS gave notice to the individual member companies about the work that should be performed, and the number of employees needed in the coming period, and what qualifications these employees should have. Member companies was supposed to provide the necessary labour and provided compensation, take care of taxation, social security, social spending, etc., on behalf of their employees. During the work offshore, all personnel under the agreement with Phillips was to be considered as

OIS-people, including foremen, general foremen and superintendents who led the work on the relevant platform. Even the people who carried out the management functions, were regularly recruited from member companies because OIS had only a limited number of persons employed in their service.

292. The Supreme Court concluded that OIS had to be regarded as an employer, and pointed out that, in terms of OIS and its relationship to the member companies, OIS was responsible for the distribution of both activities and responsibilities … . The cooperation…had, among other things, as one of its key points that OIS took over the member companies' responsibilities for ensuring that individual employees were given necessary information about the hazards of working on the platforms. This is also stated in the organizational structure of OIS, and the court recognizes that OIS has taken over this part of the employer's responsibilities regardless of whether employees were formally employed by the member companies and paid by them. Also supervision with the work offshore was part of the responsibilities that OIS had to perform, although here they used people from member companies.

293. The Supreme Court added:

> According to the contract with Phillips … all personnel during work offshore were to be considered as OIS-people. In relation to Phillips, OIS was responsible for the work performance. These factors, together with the work and responsibilities as the Court of First Instance has pointed out, constitute typical elements of the autonomy that comes with the employer position.

294. Furthermore, the Supreme Court noted: 'As far as this matter is concerned, I will not fail to remark that it may be that more companies in an "umbrella organization", such as the one OIS is a part of, in certain relations – in view of the specific conditions – will be regarded as an employer.'

295. WEA section 14-13 regulates hiring of employees from companies, whose purpose is not to hire out employees. As a general rule, hiring of employees is kept within the same framework as the WEA provides for temporary employments (*see* section 14-9). Hiring from companies whose purpose is not to hire out employees is only permitted when the employee is permanently employed by the recruitment agency. The use of hired employees may supersede the rules concerning for employees of the user company in the same way as the case may be by extensive use of temporary employees.

296. If an employee is hired in from a recruitment agency, whose purpose is to hire out employees, on a basis that involves that the terms in WEA section 14-12 is not fulfilled, it follows from section 14-14 that the employee will be able to file a claim demanding a verdict from a court of law that stipulates that the employee is employed with the user company. Such a verdict may be given, unless such a stipulation could be regarded as obviously improper. Moreover, the employee will also have the opportunity to file a claim for compensation.

297. In the Supreme Court case Rt. 2013 p. 998 the question was whether the employee, who was hired in by Statoil ASA should be deemed permanently employed at Statoil ASA or whether performed work as a part of a contractual relationship. The Supreme Court stated that the borderline between hiring in employees and a contractual relationship must be drawn after a comprehensive assessment. The decisive factor must be which of the parties (the employer/principal) was responsible for the management and outcome of the work performed. After a concrete assessment of a number of factors, the Supreme Court found that the disputed work, as was the delivery of internal corporate mail services, was conducted as part of a contract. Thus, the employee was not entitled to be regarded as permanently employed with Statoil ASA (cf. the WEA section 14-12(4)).

298. In another case (Rt. 2013 p. 1730), the question was whether an employee who was employed by a company (YIT), whose main object was not to hire out personnel (cf. the WEA section 14-13) was entitled to permanent employment in the user company (Statoil ASA). The employee worked the entire period of his employment in a full-time position for Statoil ASA. The hire was initiated and justified by the hiring company's needs and the employee had no position in YIT to go back to. The Supreme Court found that the hire did not fall within the scope for WEA section 14-13. Thus, the hire could not be considered to have sufficient legislative basis in this provision. The employee was therefore entitled to permanent employment with the user company (Statoil ASA) pursuant to the WEA section 14-12(4) (cf. section 14-9(5)). The previous WEA section 14-9(5) stipulated that employees that have been temporarily employed (or hired out (cf. 14-12(4)) for more than four consecutive years should be deemed to be employed on a permanent basis. By the Act of 24 April 2015 No. 20, in force from 1 July 2015, it is now stated in WEA section 14-9(6) that continuous temporary employment may not excess a period of four years when the employment contract is based on (and also the basis on which the employee is hired in on by the user company) section 14-9(1) letter a) (work of a temporary nature). In addition, continuous temporary employment may not excess a period of three years if the contract is based on section 14-9(1) letter b) (for work as a temporary replacement for another person or persons). The result of this is that there is both a four-year rule as well as a three-year rule, regarding continuous temporary employments based on the legal basis of the temporary employment contract. The four-year rule will only apply when the basis for the temporary agreement is solely based on section 14-9(1) letter a). The three-year rule will apply when the basis for the temporary agreement is based on letter b. The latter also applies if there is an agreement based on both letter a) and b).

299. By the Act of 22 June 2012 No. 33 new provisions in the WEA are adopted regarding the principle on equal treatment of hired employees from recruitment agencies regarding different aspects of working time, breaks/rest periods, vacations and holidays, as well as wages and other forms of compensation. The provisions are adopted on the basis of the implementation of Directive 2008/104 EC of the European Parliament and the Council of 19 November 2008 on temporary agency work.

300. Hired employees should at least be ensured the conditions that would apply to employment with the user company, to the specific areas listed above during the complete hiring period. The principle on equal treatment includes also posted employees (cf. WEA section 1-7) who are hired by recruitment agencies in other countries. Furthermore, the hired employees should have access to general goods and services provided by the user company, for example access to the company canteen and transport provided by the company and corporate day care centre. The provisions are included as the new section 14-12a of the WEA.

301. To ensure that the principle on equal treatment is being complied with, there has been introduced an obligation for the using company to provide with necessary information to the recruitment agency, so that the recruitment agency can fulfil the requirement of equal treatment to the employee, *see* the new section 14-12b in the WEA. Moreover, a duty for the recruitment agency to provide necessary information to the employee is introduced, so that the employee is able to assess whether the requirement of equal treatment are fulfilled. In addition, it is required that the recruitment agency shall provide information to the user company regarding the conditions under which the hired employees are actually given to the areas covered by the equal treatment principle. This is particularly relevant if the employee representatives within the user company choose to use the right of access to the hired employees' wage and working conditions that are covered by the requirements of equal treatment, *see* the new section 14-12b, fifth subsection.

302. In addition, the new section 14-12c in the WEA states that the user company shall be jointly and severally liable with the recruitment agency for the hired employees' right to receive wages, holiday pay and any other compensation covered by the principle of equal treatment. However, the principle on joint and several liability does not apply when the user company is bankrupt.

303. Similar requirements introduced in the WEA on equal treatment and measures to ensure compliance with these requirements are also included in the Civil Service Act, *see* the new section 3B, 3C and 3D.

304. The new provisions take effect from 1 January 2013 with the exception of the Civil Service Act section 3D, the WEA section 14-12c on joint and several liability, which enter into force on 1 July 2013.

2. Formally Recognized as Self-Employed (Independent Contractors): Employees in Reality

305. If the self-employed, which are formally called self-employed, in reality conduct work as employees the labour law rules will apply, with the effect that the principal has to be regarded as an employer.

306. In this context, it is illustrative to notice the ruling in Rt. 2007 p. 1458. The Supreme Court concluded that:

> the way the employment relationship was organized show certain characteristics that are typical in ordinary employment relationships. I assume that [A] was totally under the company's management with respect to the assignment. He was thus subject to the management's instructions with regard to what was done, where and when this should be done, and the way the job was performed…It must also be assumed that it was his personal effort, he got paid for, and not a concrete result. It was thus the company and not [A] which had the risk of the outcome of the work. In reality [A] had to have been in a relationship to the company that indicate a need for a legal protection of such a character as provided by the WEA.] … [After this, I must conclude that the real relationship, consisting of [A] and the company, increasingly have more of a character of an employment relationship other than by an independent contract relationship.

307. The case concerned the application of the WEA's (of 1977) penal provision in connection with a diving accident. A company used a boat to ferry supplies and personnel in connection with the laying of a water main. There was also diving from the boat. The work consisted of installing the cable that was laid on the seabed, along with the wire that led to the surface. During the dive, one diver ran out of air, and he did not succeed in returning to the surface. After some time of searching, he was found on the seabed. He was taken to hospital where he died five days later.

308. The Supreme Court considered, among other things, whether the diver (A) was considered to be an employee or as self-employed. The Supreme Court noted that the WEA (1977) section 2(1) was applicable to 'any business that employs employees'. An employee is in section 3 No. 1(1) defined as 'any person who performs work in the service of another person'. This meant that if the diver were to be regarded as a self-employed, the WEA would not be applicable.

309. There was no written agreement between the diver and the company. Whether the diver was to be regarded as an employee in the legal sense had to be based on a 'comprehensive assessment of the specific circumstances of the case'. The diver was registered with a sole proprietorship in the business register, and he was also registered in the VAT register. He got paid by the number of hours, an hourly rate of NOK 250 excluding VAT, and he estimated sales tax. There was no tax deducted or contributions paid to the social security and the employment relationship were not recorded in the employer/employee register. These were matters that clearly pointed in the direction of the diver being self-employed.

310. The Supreme Court stated further: 'That payments formally was provided in a form that is typical when using self-employed may not be decisive for how the relationship between [the diver] and the company shall be classified if the facts also shows that it actually existed an employment relationship.'

311. It often occurs that a self-employed person is hired in by a recruitment agency, which in return hires the person out to another company, where the person conducts his or her work. This is fairly normal in the petroleum business area. In such cases, the reality could indicate that the recruitment agency was the employer, or even also the user company.

312. In this context, the ruling in Rt. 2002 p. 996 (*Norsk Teknologi*) may be mentioned. In this case, an engineer that was hired out from an engineer-services agency in order to conduct a time-limited job related to offshore installations. The court concluded that, in the light of the Norwegian taxation rules, the engineer had to be considered as an employee in relation to the engineer-services agency, and not as a self-employed person.

3. Self-Employed/Independent Contractors Who in Reality Are Not Employees

313. It is incumbent upon employers to ensure a fully satisfactory working environment for contractors who are genuinely independent, and therefore cannot be regarded as employees (cf. WEA section 2-2(1)). This obligation is incumbent upon the employer when an independent contractor performs tasks related to the employer's activity or facility. The contractor performs the work within or near the area where the employer conducts its physical activity or has its facility.

314. The prohibition against directly or indirectly discrimination on the basis of political views, membership of a trade union, sexual orientation or age shall also apply to the employer's choice and treatment of self-employed (cf. WEA section 13-1(1) and section 13-2(2)). This prohibition will also apply to their enrolment and participation in a trade union (cf. section 13-2(3)).

4. Organization of the Employer's Own Enterprise

315. In general, employers are obliged to organize their own activities so that other than the employer's own employees have a fully satisfactory working environment when carrying out work in relation to the employer's activity or facility (cf. WEA section 2-2(1)). This applies not only to independent contractors, for example, but also to employees of a transportation company, when these are on the employer's site to deliver goods to the employer's business.

316. In cases where the employer's business is located next to other businesses – such as shops at shopping malls, businesses in industrial parks or office buildings, etc. – the provision also applies. The general view is that the employer will be responsible if the employer's business involves a working environment risk for other businesses, including their employees.

5. Obligation to Cooperate with Other Companies to Ensure a Fully Satisfactory Working Environment

317. Employers are obliged to cooperate with other companies in order to ensure a fully satisfactory working environment (cf. WEA section 2-2(1)). This obligation is incumbent upon the main business, as will be the case for a main contractor to subcontractors in the construction business. If no company can be considered as the main business it will be agreed in writing who will be responsible for this coordination, or if not possible, this will be determined by the Labour Inspectorate. However, it is a condition that there are more than ten employees working at those businesses in the context in question (*see* paragraphs 1251 et seq.).

6. Group of Companies: Company Relations

318. The WEA is based on a functional concept of the term 'employer', so it should be emphasized in practice who has acted as an employer and exercised employer functions (*see* Proposition No. 49 (2004-2005) section 6.2, p. 76). In a group of companies, the parent company could be held responsible for the dismissal of the managing director of the subsidiary company (Rt. 1990 p. 1126 (*Wärtsilä*)), when estimating the sentencing for violation of the WEA it may have to be taken into account that each company is part of a group (Rt. 1995 p. 278), the staff may be obliged to perform work in all the subsidiaries covered by a worldwide group, and thus be considered as employees of the company group (Rt. 1989 p. 231 (*Exploration Logging Norway*)). The employee duty of loyalty of a group of companies is not necessarily limited to the subsidiary company that is the formal employer, but can also be extended to include the corporate management of the parent company (cf. for example (Rt. 2003 p. 1614 (*Telenor*)).

7. The Client Requires That the Contractor Shall Make Specific Arrangements in Relation to the Contractor's Employees

319. The question of responsibility for persons other than own employees may also occur in the relationship between clients and contractors, and can also occur in other cooperative relationships between independent enterprises.

320. For example, it could happen that client (A) requires that the contractor (B) shall take a certain specified person (C), employed by the contractor (B), out of all work related to the mission and perform work within the client (A's) activities. The mission may be, for example security activities at A's facilities, or it can be a mission in which employees at B are made available for A to perform work at A's facilities, instructed and led by A, as will be the case on a regular basis when employees are hired out. In the former case, B will perform the contract according to A's instructions, but instructions will regularly be provided by B to C. In the latter case A's instructions regularly go directly to C; however, B is usually kept informed. Alternative methods can also occur.

321. Where the principal/client intervenes directly in the managerial rights which the contractor has in relation to its employees, the reality is that the client carries out the employer functions directly in relation to the contractor's employees. Contractor employees must be able to hold the client responsible as an employer, based on the fundamental principle that responsibility for legal dispositions is placed on the company that makes the real decisions. Responsibility could also be justified by a predictable safety consideration, where the degree of fault could be taken into account (cf. Rt. 2001 p. 501 (*TollpostGlobe*) on liability for improper boycotts). The reality will be that the client must prove justifiable basis for the orders given to the contractor, and otherwise be responsible as an employer to its employees.

Chapter 3. Labour Law: Special Characteristics, Challenges and Perspectives

§1. Labour Law: Special Characteristics

I. Mandatory Legislation

322. One of the main characteristics of labour law is the subordinate position of the employee – the employee is, traditionally, the weaker part in the employment relationship compared with the employer – and not only has a weaker bargaining position, but is also exposed to possible undue exploitation and hazardous conditions, especially as regards the performance of the work agreed upon. In general, this is probably still the case, although the employees' right of co-determination as regards the decisions of the management may be said to slightly differentiate these positions. Consequently, legislation that to a large degree is mandatory is one of the main characteristics of labour law. Thus, the individual employee may not renounce her or his rights, as provided by the law, unless the law stipulate otherwise.

II. A Certain Collective Freedom to Renounce Mandatory Legislation by Collective Agreement

323. It follows from the purpose of rules and regulations stipulated in order to make sure that the employees' security and health is being taken care of, that such legislation cannot be renounced by agreement. As regards circumstances that are more focused on the employees' well-being and welfare on the work place, the question becomes, however, somewhat different. And the need for absolutely mandatory legislation is not so pressing when it is not the individual employees that negotiate, but their organizations – in such cases, the relative strength between the parties becomes more equal. It is therefore a clear tendency to the effect that otherwise mandatory legislation may be departed from by collective agreement – and to a larger extent for the great organizations than for the smaller ones. Thus, it is illustrative that WEA section 10-12(4) stipulates that a trade union with more than 10,000 members may conclude a collective agreement as regards working hours, almost without any of the limitations regarding working hours that are stipulated in the Act. In other cases, consent from a public authority is required, in order to secure that an arrangement stipulated by agreement has a standard equal to what is prescribed by law. A catchword for this enlarged freedom on a collective basis could be collective freedom of disposition.

III. Penalties

324. As regards the rules and regulations on safety and working environment, it is characteristic that non-compliance with such legislation is generally subject to penalties, based on the view that it is of public interest – and not just in the interests of the parties, employer and employee – that such legislation is respected. Further, a company as such may in this regard be held liable, and fined, even in cases where no single person may be held responsible for the non-compliance of the legislation (cf. e.g., Rt. 2012 p. 770, Rt. 1995 p. 278, Rt. 1990 p. 419, Rt. 1982 p. 878 and Rt. 1982 p. 1022).

IV. The Collective Element

325. To a large extent, labour law is characterized by the collective element. The expanded freedom for agreements and arrangements concluded on a collective basis with regard to mandatory legislation has already been mentioned above. Similarly, it is mentioned above that the decision-making process in enterprises of a certain size has been collectivized. First of all, however, the collective element is particularly prevalent by virtue of the fact that wage and working conditions are, to a large extent, agreed upon on a collective basis, by collective agreements concluded between the organizations of labour life. Basically, also the terms of a collective agreement must be invariable, unless otherwise stipulated in the collective agreement itself. Should the individual employee be allowed to freely agree to terms other than those stipulated in the collective agreement in question, much of the purpose of the collective agreement would be defeated. However, the invariability as regards the terms of the collective agreements will apply not only as regards renouncements of the disadvantage, but also as regards renouncements in favour of the individual. Thus, the nature of the invariability as regards the collective agreements has another character than the invariability that usually applies to legal provisions.

V. Human Factors: Employees Are Human Beings

326. Characteristic of labour law is also that human concerns are of great importance – indeed, one should not even consider anything else – based on the simple fact that every employee is a human being. It follows from the very basis of the employment agreement itself that the employee has the obligation to personally carry out the work, while at the same time the working situation can easily influence tFhe individual's entire life situation.

327. Thus, already the necessity of good and confident collaboration between the company and the employees is expressed in the Basic Agreement LO-NHO (BA) (2014) section 9-1, and WEA section 4-3(1) stipulates that the work shall be organized in such a manner that the integrity and dignity of the employees is taken into account. It is further stipulated that the working situation should be arranged so that the employees have reasonable possibilities for occupational and personal development, and that the employee – as far as possible – shall be given opportunity for variation and to see the connection between the different tasks (cf. WEA section 4-2(2)).

328. It may further be mentioned among other rules based on the view that human concerns are of the most importance, that an employee is entitled to be exempted from working overtime for health reasons and for weighty social reasons, and – in general – when the work can be postponed or performed by others without detriment to the enterprise (WEA section 10-6(10)). Likewise should be mentioned the right to leave of absence to care for a sick child (WEA section 12-9), and to take care of close relatives during the terminal phase of their life (WEA section 12-10). Collective agreements often stipulate that employees may be entitled to short leave of absence for other welfare reasons, such as the death and funeral of close relatives.

329. Human concerns are also to be taken into consideration when deciding whether there are sufficient reasons for summary dismissal because of serious breach of duties, or to give notice of termination to an employee with a long period of service in the enterprise. Finally, as regards certain employment relationships – seamen and domestic servants – it should be mentioned that the employer has an obligation to take care of the employee in case of illness.

330. Against this background and from this perspective it may – to a certain extent – be said, that one of the main purposes of ILO, that 'labour is not a commodity' has been achieved, perhaps particularly as regards regulations on employee safety and the quite extensive requirements for ensuring a fully satisfactory working environment. The system established in this regard has had – and still has, indeed – an important role, where the functions of safety delegates, working environment committees, the Labour Inspectorate, the social security and welfare system, shop stewards and the trade unions, and others, constitute important parts of the totality.

VI. Involvement of Public Authorities

331. Characteristic of labour law is also an extensive involvement of public authorities, as will be dealt with below under paragraphs 347 et seq.

§2. Labour Law: Some Challenges

I. Often Politically Controversial Reforms

332. The special characteristics of labour law are apparent even upon examination of its scope. It encompasses not merely the contractual relationship between two private parties, the employer and employee. It also encompasses the personal welfare of individuals, while they are at work, and beyond. In general, an essential part of employees' welfare and living conditions is to quite an extent influenced by their employment situation. Furthermore, basic organizational and economic interests are interwoven with questions regarding wages and working conditions. Therefore, questions on labour law are often of a sensitive political nature – perhaps even controversial as well as central. Furthermore, the state may have the most significant interests involved at many levels.

II. A Dynamic Part of the Law

333. As labour law regulates questions of quite a different character, it also reflects the many, in part conflicting, interests and trends that are involved. Thus, labour law is a dynamic part of the law, and the labour law of today is a result – so far – of conflicting interests in an ongoing evolution. Depending on the relative strength of the different groups involved, the development may go in one direction first, and then in another. As regards some parts of labour law, the rules reflect to a certain degree solutions built on compromises, and the rules of labour law are not developed to the same extent for all the different parts of working life.

III. Labour Law Reforms: Expectations and Concerns in Practical Labour Life

334. It should be particularly noted, when reforms of labour law are being prepared, that the public and political debate may be rather intense, and that the involved parties may have high expectations as well as worries as far as the reform is concerned. The WEA of 1977 represented an important and quite thorough reform of labour law, but as regards the effects of the Act, the expectations were to an extent unrealistically high. The introduction of regulations on whistle-blowing from 2007 may serve as another example, and further the introduction of additional pensions for employees in 2006. Of course, legislation cannot per se be anything more than a formal framework for the relationship between the parties involved. How their relationship will function in practical life will, to a large degree, depend on circumstances, which the legislation can influence only to a modest degree. Thus, in this connection it may be mentioned, that the law cannot per se create a fully satisfactory psychosocial working environment. The law may prescribe that the working environment be fully satisfactory, also in that regard. But such a working environment will, necessarily, have to be realized by the parties and persons involved through, *inter alia*, their mutual ability and willingness to collaborate. Certainly, the law may prescribe sanctions, should the working environment not be fully satisfactory. Such sanctions will, however, as such be of a negative nature – which in practice must be implemented towards reluctant persons in a company, management and perhaps employees as well – and cannot replace the positive approach of persons at different levels, which is absolutely necessary for a fully satisfactory psychosocial working environment. The situation as regards non-discrimination and equality legislation, as well as the recently passed rules on whistle-blowing, seem basically to be very much the same.

IV. Implementing Reform into Practical Labour Life

335. Therefore, law reforms of this kind require that the reform is followed up by means other than the judicial system. In that connection, the parties of labour life have an important role, because the challenge is to create a positive attitude to law reform. Thus, it might be said that after the enactment of the reformed law and the political discussions have come to an end, the further discussions, disagreements and solutions will have to take place between the parties to labour life, in order to implement the rules of the law to the practical realities. The scene of the discussions is therefore changed. On this next scene, the organizations of labour life – employers' associations as well as trade unions – will then have the leading roles, but individual company managers and as well as the employees at the different levels will all have their part in this connection. Only in this way may the law achieve its intended aims. Should that not be the case, the law may not fulfil its purpose, but an unfortunate attitude to the rules of the law may also be the result, perhaps even mistrust and frustration regarding the whole system, which may be most unfortunate for the general climate in the labour life – the seeds of social unrest could be encouraged – perhaps combined with a general mistrust of labour law as such. The connection between law and non-judicial attitudes and measures can in this field not be exaggerated.

§3. Labour Law: Perspectives

I. The Superior Position of Employers and the Subordinate Position of Employees: Perspectives in the Knowledge-Based Society

A. Points of Departure

336. The obvious points of departure are, as mentioned above, that labour law relates to human labour, that human labour cannot be separated from the human being, that the employment agreement constitutes an obligation for the employee to personally carry out the work, that the employment agreement constitutes the basis for the employer's right to make use of the employee's working ability and capacity, and that all kinds of production require that the work to be done must be organized in some kind of a production process. The consequence of this organization is a subordinate position for the employees and a corresponding superior position for the employer, and those who act on behalf of the employer.

B. The Basic Tension and Dilemma: The Principle of Equality Between Persons

337. A consequence of the employment relationship is therefore a – more or less limited – superior and subordination relationship between persons. In a society based on the philosophy of equality between persons, a tension will necessarily arise

– and persist – between the basic principle of equality, and the labour law-related principle of subordination and obedience.

C. *Easing the Subordinate Nature of the Employment Relationship: Employee Co-determination and Corporate Democratization*

338. In many ways, the developments of labour law may be seen as an expression of the way that these two competing principles have been balanced against each other – in line with developments in the community otherwise, and the general trends from time to time prevalent in the social, cultural, technological and economic spheres. It may probably be said that at least since the 1950s the trend has gradually been towards achieving equality to a greater degree – thus easing the subordinate nature of the employment relationship. This trend is particularly apparent in the various ways of employee co-determination in the decision-making – corporate democratization as a whole – which today may be said to be a marked feature in Norwegian working life and labour law.

D. *The Subordinate Nature of the Employment Relationship and the Knowledge-Based Hi-tech Labour Life*

339. Along with this development of corporate democratization should also be observed, and emphasized, the transition from the industrial to the post-industrial society, which perhaps is best characterized as the knowledge-based society. A continuously increasing level of education in the society has taken place, perhaps especially since the 1970s. At the same time, the general life of society – and of working life in particular – has become more and more based on advanced technology with, e.g., personal computers, the Internet etc. Perhaps one should even talk about the hi-tech society. A consequence of the increased level of education is, *inter alia*, that employees' background is based on a development of their ability of independent thinking and understanding – through primary schools, for many through secondary schools, and for some even studies at university levels – and, during their working life – supplementary or additional education through participation in courses, part-time studies etc., perhaps even paid for – partly or in full – by their employer. Employees' knowledge and experience are in many ways the most important resource, and in many companies employees are referred to as colleagues – perhaps even as participants of a team. Against this background, the basis is also established in such a way that it may easily appear as right and reasonable that the employees raise questions as regards the management's planning and the development of the enterprise – on special issues or in general. It may even be the case that the employees are required, as a part of their tasks, to raise possible counter-considerations or concerns. Consequently, these developments tend to shake the very basis of the principle of the employees' subordination and obedience. These basic problems are evident as regards questions related to the employees' freedom of speech, and as regards whistle-blower questions. However, these questions are also present in regard to the employment relationship in general – e.g., as regards how employees and management associate, whether the dignity of an employee has been respected, whether a reprimand is justified, etc.

II. Building on and Developing Further the Principle of Collaboration versus Confrontation

A. General Remarks

340. Another perspective is the development of the basic principle of collaboration between the parties to labour life, and even between these parties and the public authorities. This development is easily observed not only on a collective level – i.e., between the main organizations on the employer and the employees' side – but also between management and shop stewards at the different enterprises, particularly at enterprises with a certain number of employees.

B. The Principle of Collaboration on the Collective Level

341. On the collective level, this basic principle of collaboration – without abandoning, if necessary, the principle of a right to confrontation and conflict – dates back to the beginning of the previous century. In the 1920s, the question was – again – discussed with intensity within the Norwegian Federation of Trade Unions, which adopted this principle. In this regard, the first Basic Agreement (1935) is an important milestone. Since 1945, and during the 1950s, and again in the 1960s, the main parties in Norwegian labour life – LO and NAF (today NHO) – have built and developed further their relationship on this principle. Here, part B of the Basic Agreement (1966) – the Agreement on Collaboration – is another milestone. Still further, as a result of the common project of collaboration between these main parties, this principle is formally agreed upon, worked out in more detail, and is since 1974 – *inter alia* with its new forms of employee participation in decision-making – incorporated in the Basic Agreement, section B, as later amended.

C. The Principle of Collaboration at the Individual Enterprise Level

342. Most individual enterprises, at least over a certain size, are covered by collective agreements, which stipulate in more detail how this principle is to be applied. Further, WEA section 8-1 stipulates that enterprises employing regularly at least fifty employees shall provide information and discuss with the elected representatives of the employees, issues of importance for the employees' working conditions (cf. paragraph 297 and paragraph 1348, on corporate democratization and employee co-determination).

D. The Principle of Collaboration and the Principle of Confrontation and Open Labour Conflict

343. A consequence of this development is that the principle of collaboration is usually applied, while the principle of confrontation and use of open labour conflict – strikes and lock-outs – is in practice reserved for the main questions, where negotiations and mediation on collective agreements do not have as result that such an agreement is concluded.

E. The Principle of Collaboration and Relation to Public Authorities

1. The Principle of Collaboration, Mandatory Legislation, Internal Control, the Labour Inspectorate, Etc.

344. A similar tendency, i.e., to apply a principle of collaboration, is also apparent as regards the relation between public authorities and the conditions of labour life. As mentioned below (*see* paragraph 382) collective freedom to renounce by agreement, from otherwise mandatory legislation, is recognized to a certain degree especially as regards the regulation on working hours. In addition may be mentioned that the principle of enterprises' internal control (cf. WEA section 3-1), may be applied so that the enterprise itself ensures, that the provisions stipulated by law or regulations are being followed. Thus, the Labour Inspectorate may concentrate on the question of whether the system applied by the enterprise is satisfactory in this regard. This may be more efficient than the traditional inspection, especially as regards complicated processes, which require very specialized knowledge, which the Labour Inspectorate may perhaps not even have at its disposal.

2. The Principle of Collaboration and Three-Party Arrangements

345. Even more apparent is the principle of collaboration as regards three-party arrangements, i.e., arrangements where the employers, the trade unions, as well as public authorities participate. The Agreement on Inclusive Labour Life (2010–2013) is such an example – on certain conditions enterprises may engage persons, or allow employees certain rights, e.g., as regards absence because of illness, and receive certain benefits or compensation from the public.

346. In this regard should finally, but not least, be mentioned the coordinated settlements on collective agreements. Here, the employers' associations, the trade unions associations, other associations, as well as public authorities discuss – and possibly agree – the economic and other frameworks as regards negotiations and conclusions of collective agreements for – usually – a period of two years. Such discussions take part through the Technical Calculation Board and thereafter through the Contact Board. These boards play a central role in this connection. If a settlement is reached, the public authorities agree to make use of certain means as regards e.g., taxes, duties, and/or contributions connected to the social security system – e.g., when elderly workers retire. The AFP arrangement is in this connection an illustrative example: under certain conditions workers above the age of 62 may retire, and receive their pension until they reach the age of 67, which is the general pension age as per the SSA. Their pension between 62 and 67 years is partly paid by funds established by the parties in labour life, and partly by the state through the social security system.

III. Use of 'Quasi-collective' Agreements for Groups Other Than Employees

347. As regards employment relations, the system of using collective agreements must in practical life – undoubtedly – be considered as quite a success. It is a clear tendency that collective agreements are used by other groups of employees than perhaps was the case before, e.g., employed lawyers and other jurists, medical doctors, architects, etc.

348. It may also be the case, that employees and employers are organized within the same 'umbrella' organization, where collective agreements are concluded between these parties' sub-organizations.

349. It may also happen that one and the same agreement applies to employees as well as independent professionals, e.g., for employed lorry drivers as well as independent drivers with their own lorry, etc. In such a case, the Labour Court stated that it could deal with the case as a collective agreement, as it would be sufficient for the competence of the court that some of the persons in question were employees (cf. ARD 1991 p. 140 (at p. 170)).

350. Further, there is a clear tendency for the collective agreement model to be transferred and used by groups other than employees and employers – in fact, to quite an extent. This may be the case for independent professionals, such as practicing doctors, with regard to e.g., the municipality or county, as regards contributions from these public health authorities to the doctor, per patient treated. This system is also being used by others within the health system, such as physiotherapists, psychologists, etc. It is not unusual for negotiations with the association for such groups of individual professionals on the one side, and the municipality or county on the other side, to take place before such contributions are stipulated.

351. It may further be mentioned that for sectors such as farming (agriculture), 'reindeer-farming', etc., framework agreements are concluded between the state on the one hand, and the independent farmers' associations – or reindeer-owners associations – on the other hand, regarding contributions to the individual persons, e.g., per produced unit (e.g., per litre milk, meat etc.). The final decision is made by the Parliament, after negotiations between the parties.

352. Even as regards retired persons, negotiations take place between their associations and the state, before a final decision is made by the Parliament, which, e.g., may be of great importance as regards the amount of pensions.

353. It may also be mentioned that it is not unusual for a branch organization to conclude an agreement with another organization, e.g., a consumer organization, as regards what terms should apply and; 'agreed documents'.

354. In such situations, it may be proper to characterize the agreement as a 'quasi-collective' agreement. It is – obviously – not a collective agreement in a labour law context. Thus, the consequences of a labour law collective agreement will not apply – such as the superior and binding effect of the collective agreement *vis-à-vis* the individual's agreement (the principle of indispensability), or the obligation to maintain peace for the agreed period (the peace obligation), nor the mechanisms that are established in order to settle disputes, and so on. However, the by-laws of the association, combined with provisions in the quasi-collective agreement, may to a certain extent lead to more or less the same results, and it may be agreed upon in such an agreement that possible disputes are to be solved by arbitration.

355. An agreement between two individual parties – where both or at least one of them are members of an organization, which is a party to such a 'quasi-collective' agreement – will be a valid agreement, even if that agreement is not fully in accordance with the terms of the 'quasi-collective' agreement; the terms of the 'quasi-collective' agreement will not automatically replace the diverging terms of the individual agreement, partly or wholly. The party or parties of the individual agreement may, however, be subject to sanctions according to the by-laws of the association, e.g., fines, exclusion, etc. As regards labour law, however, the collective agreement will automatically replace the diverging terms of an individual employment agreement, at least where the collective agreement includes both of the parties. That very strong position that is given to the collective agreement in the labour legislation is unique, compared with other contractual relationships operating with framework-agreements, etc.

356. Should a 'quasi-collective' agreement have expired, and negotiations for a new agreement stranded, different actions are possible, e.g., farmers may stop deliveries of milk to the main production chains, practicing doctors refuse to treat their patients with the exception of emergencies only, etc. It is probably a condition that such an action may take place only after a fourteen days' notice is given, because the action probably is to be considered a boycotting action, as the supply to third parties (supermarkets, consumers) necessarily will be the effect of the action. In such cases, where negotiations are stalled, it must probably be assumed that their employed colleagues – e.g., employed doctors in health institutions etc. – are entitled to give notice of, and eventually carry into effect, a sympathy strike in order to support the claims presented by their independent colleagues (cf. paragraph 1491 below).

357. It must be observed, however, that there has also been a tendency in recent years towards an individualizing of rights and duties of employees to a larger degree – more independent of a collective level. It may be said that the collective element is under some pressure towards a larger degree of freedom for the individual employee to agree to conditions different from the usual. This tendency may be observed, e.g., as regards the legislation on working hours, where the individual employee may agree – to some extent – to working hours different from the main rules of the legislation. The recent decisions on trade union fees for unorganized employees may also be seen from this angle (cf. *inter alia* Rt. 2008, p. 1601 and paragraph 1452 below).

IV. Interaction Between Regulation by Collective Agreement and Regulation by Law

358. The important role of the associations of employers and the employees' associations (trade unions), and thereby the important role of the collective agreements as an instrument of regulation not only of wages, but also other working conditions – as well as conditions prior to and post of an employment relation – has already been described implicitly. Therefore, it is hardly surprising that collective agreements are trending – generally – to regulate other and new parts of these issues. Already mentioned are the collective agreements on the employees' codetermination as an illustrative example, and the AFP arrangements, as further examples may be mentioned collective agreements on application of new technologies in the enterprises, and prolonged annual vacations with pay. It is a clear trend that important labour law questions find their solution through the collective agreements, which thereafter are – with possible amendments, of course – transferred into labour law legislation.

V. Competing Trade Unions: New Constellations

359. There seems to be a trend towards a larger degree of competition between the different trade unions for membership among the employees. It may, in general, be said that the trade union movement was for quite some time united – mainly under the Norwegian Federation of Trade Unions (*Landsorganisasjonen i Norge*) – and that this was the dominant picture until about the 1970s. Of course, within such a large main association, there were different opinions. Such questions were, however, mainly resolved within the association. That picture is now more complicated. There are now four main associations the Norwegian Confederation of Trade Unions (*Landsorganisasjonen, LO*) (cf. also paragraphs 1453 et seq. below), the Academics (*Akademikerne*), the Confederation of Vocational Unions (*Yrkesorganisasjonenes Sentralforbund, YS*) and the Confederation of Unions for Professionals (*Hovedorganisasjonen for universitets- og høyskoleutdannede,* UNIO), and in certain areas of the labour life there are some independent trade unions, which are not members of a superior main association. There is, perhaps, a tendency towards a larger number of trade unions, possibly also towards an additional number of main associations.

360. It may be said, also, that – generally speaking – the Norwegian Federation of Trade Unions (*Landsorganisasjonen i Norge*) has had, and has, a rather close connection to the political 'left' – in particular the Labour Party – while the other main associations seem not to have the same clear political profile. It may, however, not be said that in Norway there is a tradition for a trade union movement with a Christian Democratic political profile.

361. It may also be added, that – to a certain extent – in practice the new trade unions, their representatives and their members, have not had the same training and knowledge of rules and traditions as regards labour law, etc., as generally is the case as regards representatives and members of the established trade unions. These differences have caused some difficulties in practice, but perhaps not to the same extent today as previously.

362. It should be added that in a few areas of labour life there have for quite some time been two different trade unions – especially as regards foremen, and bus drivers and others – with more or less the same percentage of the employees in that area. Thus, the questions arising from two or more competing trade unions are not new but seem now to be coming more to the surface, as the size make these questions more apparent.

363. The situation where two or more competing trade unions are involved with questions concerning wages or working conditions, and in negotiations and agreements in that connection, raises a number of legal questions. For example, will all these trade unions have the right to negotiate with the employer or employers' association; will they all have the right to negotiate separately, or only jointly, or may the law stipulate that these rights are limited to just to the largest organization, or to those that represent more than half of the affected employees, and so on. Similarly may be raised the question, of which main associations may – and should – be given the right to participate in the discussions at a central level, e.g., as regards the Technical Calculation Board and the Contact Board. It may be observed, that rules of the LDA do not particularly deal with these questions. In the following, some of these questions will be dealt with below.

364. It may finally be observed, that similar questions may appear on the employer side, but do not seem to have caused the same practical complications.

VI. The Relationship Between Trade Unions and Their Members

365. Finally, concerning the position of the trade unions, some trends should be mentioned as regards the relationship between trade unions and their members. Although on the outskirts of labour law, this relationship is closely linked to the right and the freedom to organize, and has at the same time practical implications as well as legal consequences for the individual employee who chooses to be or not to be a member of a trade union.

366. The freedom to organize is now a part of the Norwegian Constitution, cf. section 101, as amended since 14 May 2014. This constitutional freedom includes the right to form, to join and to withdraw from at trade union, as well as regards other associations. Previously, the right to organize was not stipulated by any general act, but followed from common law and the principles of international law, cf. *inter alia* the ECHR (1950) section 11, and further the constitutional obligation for public authorities to respect and secure the human rights, cf. previously section 110 C of the Constitution, now replaced (since 2014) by the corresponding section 92 of the Constitution. Thus, the freedom to organize is now specifically covered by the Constitution, and therefore strengthened, as this freedom can be repealed or amended only by following the time-consuming process stipulated in the Constitution, and a majority of at least two-thirds of the members of the Parliament (Stortinget) is also required, cf. section 121 of the Constitution. It is a duty for the State to ensure that this freedom is covered by legislation, general principles of law etc. A violation of this freedom between individuals may have as consequence responsibility for possible economic loss. That would be the case, should an employer, e.g., require that an applicant for a vacant position should be and remain unorganized. Such a condition would be contrary to WEA section 13-1, cf. also section 13-4 (1) and 13-9.

367. Furthermore, the larger trade unions in particular have a structure which implies a distance as well as a superior/subordinate relationship between the bodies that constitute the management of the trade union and the individual members. Therefore, it is of importance to underline – with parallel to the situation as regards public administrative law, as well as labour law – that the position of the individual members is based on the principles of the law on associations as well as other law, that decisions of a trade union must be kept within the limitations which follows from the law, that decisions of a trade union must not be arbitrary, but probably must be based on fair preparations and considerations, e.g., as regards the question whether the trade union should take part in or otherwise support a court case which a member wants to raise, because the employment relationship of the member has been terminated, that questions regarding rights and duties in this regard may be brought before the courts by the members, and that it is not an act of disloyalty if a member should choose to bring such a case before the courts.

368. There seems to be a tendency to strengthen and clarify the legal position of employees, as regards their right to become and to remain membership, as well as their position as members, e.g., as regards their right and freedom of speech on labour and trade union matters. There is, however, also another tendency which should be observed in this connection, as the trade unions seem to extend their activities to other fields than just questions connected with the collective agreements. Trade unions may, because of their size, obtain favourable conditions for their members as regards insurance of their members with possible family members on a collective basis, as regards purchasing of petroleum products for their cars, homes etc., travelling and hotel accommodation in connection with vacations, perhaps even as regards shopping in a certain chain of supermarkets, and so on and so forth. The difficult question in this regard is, to what extent – if any – a trade union may stipulate that the members are obliged to participate in and make use of such a collective arrangement. Should e.g., the members be obliged to have their homes insured in one specific insurance company – at quite a reasonable premium – or would that be going too far as regards matters on the personal level, which have nothing to do with the employment relationship? And further, should such arrangements be constructed so that a member may make reservations ('contract out'), or is it in this regard of importance that the member must adhere to the arrangement ('contract in')? The legal situation is somewhat uncertain (cf. also paragraph 1447 below).

369. There is a clear interdependence between increasing demands for security on the job and the increase in the standard of living. Parallel to this is the strengthened position of the individual relative to the employer, and – in general – relative to the government services. The call for increased protection of the rights of the individual is a timely demand. Much continues to be uncertain about how far the demand for security of individual rights extends to trade unions.

370. A consequence of the strong position of the trade unions is that the individual members often feel that they must pursue their own claims through the union – for example where the member feels entitled to higher wages than the employer pays. If the union will not pursue the claim, the member can easily feel disappointed and be abandoned by his or her peers. A negative response from the union can be more difficult to accept than an ultimate reduction in wages by the employer, and the individual can get the impression that the employer and the union are playing on the same team. In establishing union policy, it is important through the dissemination of information to protect against the frustration and feelings of powerlessness by individual members. Otherwise, favourable conditions can easily be created for new competing unions. From a legal point of view, however, a union is normally able to assess whether or not there are good grounds to pursue a member's grievance.

371. A potential subject of tension is the relationship between permanent employees and persons who have not yet obtained permanent work, as well as substitutes and part-time employees. Through regulations providing protection against dismissal and seniority systems and rules regarding employees preferential rights to new positions, security is provided for those permanently employed, but at the expense of others, among them the young. It is customary to employ a substitute when a permanent employee takes a leave of absence, for example, for further education or training. However, substitutes and short-time employees do not always accrue rights of the nature described, thus there is a certain danger that a lower class within the workplace develops, made up of people with fewer rights than those permanently employed. At the same time, stronger rights for those permanently employed create a certain rigidity within the workplace – as is evident in the conflicts between the principles of seniority and the enterprise's need to retain those best qualified through the curtailment of operations, efficiency measures and the like. The dilemma one faces here is how far to go in protecting permanent employees against notice of termination at the expense of other groups. It is not easy to know today whether or not society is about to reach its limits regarding this problem.

372. In this connection, it should be mentioned that there has been a rather strong movement towards part-time and short-term employment as alternatives more flexible than traditional year-round and full-time employment. This is partly a recognition of the fact that the traditional working arrangements are not possible for each employee throughout their professional working life. Nevertheless, if part-time employees over a longer period of time, also take on a large amount of extra shifts, or have to work overtime for their employer on a more or less regular basis, this indicates a need for an increased employment position percentage for employees on part-time contracts. Consequently, and as a preventive action against extensive usage of part-time employees combined with extensive extra working shifts and overtime work, a new section 14-4a has been introduced in the WEA in 2014 (in force from 1 January 2014). This section states that part-time employees who in the past twelve months have regularly worked in excess of the agreed working hours, have the right to an employment position corresponding to the actual amount of work carried out during this period, unless the employer can demonstrate that the need for additional work no longer exists. This is important, especially for those employees who over a longer period of time have been working a large number of working hours in excess of the agreed part-time employment contract, and wish to be appointed on full-time basis. This has been the case for women, especially women carrying out work within the healthcare sector. It should be noted that this section does not have retroactive effect, meaning that an employee who wishes to claim the right of an increased employment position may only do so from 1 January 2015 at the earliest.

VII. The Collective Labour Law Perspective

373. Labour law bears an imprint of collectivity. Its development clearly proceeds in the direction of including new areas of the working relationship within regulation through collective bargaining agreements. The collective bargaining agreements on employee participation in decision-making, new technology implementation, and production organization are examples of the most recent developments. Also worth mentioning are the progression of new groups of workers that are going over to collective bargaining agreements – including groups that represent such 'non-labour' professions as, for example, lawyers, doctors and architects. Even where both employees and employers are organized within the same 'umbrella organization', in practice one finds examples of collective bargaining agreements between the parties' sub-organizations. There is also a tendency to use the collective bargaining form of agreement familiar from labour law in work situations in which the 'workers' do not have an employment relationship with their counterparts, although these are not considered to be collective bargaining agreements for labour law purposes. An example of this is the community agreement on doctors' contracts with municipalities about the operation of private general practices.

374. Today, the unions have a dominant voice in the establishment of wages and working conditions. The main points of these conditions are decided by collective bargaining agreements to which the unions' individual members are bound. In no other contractual setting is the general agreement into which the unions enter given so strong a position relative to individual contracts.

375. Central to this development is the relationship between the individual employee and the trade unions. Traditionally, the individual seeking employment stands in a weak position relative to the employer and basically has to be content with the wage and employment terms offered. The subservient position of employees together with the proliferation of greater concentrations of labour and capital provided the basis for the establishment of the trade unions. Parallel to this development is governmental activity aimed at protecting the employee against injuries in the working environment.

376. On the other hand, it must be noticed that recently there has been a non-insignificant tendency of to a larger degree individualizing the employees' rights and duties, moving further away from the collective level. This may also be formulated to the point where the collective element is under pressure in favour of a greater amount of individual freedom of disposition. The provisions concerning working hours in the WEA are to a certain degree characterized by this tendency.

Chapter 4. Historical Background

377. Modern labour law is based on long social traditions. Certain invariable rules on worker protection are found already in the old Norwegian *Lagting* laws, including, among other things, provisions that the worker could be sick for a certain number of days without the master having the right to reduce his or her wages. And the previous provision in section 11(2) of the SA (repealed by the Act of 21 June 2013 No. 102 (Ship Labour Act), that a seaman has a right to leave when circumstances have arisen of a welfare nature, and another qualified man can be procured in his place, is found in Magnus Lagaboete's *bylov* (city law) of 1276.

378. With larger economic units and a greater concentration of labour, came the need for more detailed rules on workers' legal status. First came the Sea Act of 1561, with rules directing the shipmaster to care for sick or injured seamen, and it provided detailed rules on various issues concerning hire. After the mining industry started to flourish at the end of the 1600s, provisions were set forth in the Mining Act of 1683 on sick pay and medical help for injured miners. There was also a ban on the truck system, where workers were paid in kind while the employer controlled the prices. The Act also established a public agency – the *Bergamtet* – to help workers protect their rights. From the mining activity also came the forerunner of the collective agreement, entered into in 1634 between the copper works at Kvikne and the farmers driving the copper from Kvikne to Trondheim.

379. In this pre-industrial period, the status of craftsmen was, of course, of utmost importance. In 1682, rules were issued concerning periods of notice, entitlement to job references, etc., and apprentice contracts, rules which remained on the books as long as until 1839.

380. However, the legal status of servants in the country declined. In 1619, they lost their old rights regarding sickness, and persons who left their duties unduly forfeited a year's wages.

381. The pattern created by seventeenth-century legislation remained until the late nineteenth century. But with this pattern important developments took place that largely enhanced the status of workers, chiefly servants in cities, seamen and miners, but to some extent also servants in the country. Here we also find the forerunners of the modern enrolling system for seamen (1723) and public employment service.

382. Developments in the first half of the nineteenth century are characterized by the breakthrough of liberalism, manifested, among other things, by the Craft Act of 1839, which broke entirely with the guild system and made the craft industry far more open than previously. Nevertheless, the Act stipulated detailed rules on guilds and on the legal relations between master, journeyman and apprentice; with respect to labour law, the Act must therefore be characterized as traditional. Also case law reflects the breach between the new, liberal ideas and strict statute regulation. Among other things, prerequisites in the employment contract on the scope of the employee's duties are given relevance, even against explicit rules of law, in a Supreme Court judgment from 1845: a girl who was taken on as a housemaid left her post when ordered to work in the barn. For this offence, she was sentenced to the pillory for two hours pursuant to an ordinance from 1754 stipulating that no servant in the country could excuse himself from 'certain types of work'. However, the Supreme Court reversed the judgment and acquitted her, although she was ordered to pay all legal costs (Rt. 1845 p. 404). The decision also illustrates a major social inequality: the prosecutor's salary was set at NOK 16, while the girl's annual wage was NOK 20 and a pair of boots.

383. The pauper laws of 1845 ordered the employer to provide for servants during illness for up to four weeks, and the Exchequer to defray expenses for sending shipwrecked seamen home. A basic social view was also manifested in the interpretation of ship owners' obligations to sick seamen (Rt. 1850 p. 289 and 1857 p. 301), and the same applied to miners (Rt. 1853 p. 769). The Sea Act of 1860 improved seamen's status in several areas, including the right to wages during sickness and injury, and it stipulated that no signing-on articles could commit the seaman for a period of more than two years.

384. The second half of the nineteenth century was characterized by the breakthrough of industrialism and establishment of the first trade organizations and collective agreements. In 1866, the craft industry was totally liberated, no longer requiring craft examination. One result was that masters were no longer willing to hire apprentices and assume all the responsibilities that went with this, but only 'casual' workers, so that the old social bond between master and employee nearly disappeared. The far more liberal employment conditions ensuing in the craft trade corresponded to the situation in factory enterprises which were now proliferating, and where labour law regulation was sparse. Life was hard for factory workers, though for many it was better than the cotter's life they came from. Hence, it is not surprising that the first trade unions, which emerged in the 1870s, were formed within the earlier craft trades. The first collective agreements were also entered into here. The labour movement grew relatively fast, though not without resistance, first culminating in the formation of the Norwegian Federation of Trade Unions (LO) in 1899. The employers' corresponding organization, NAF (Norwegian Employers' Confederation) was established in 1900.

385. The lack of labour law regulation of factory conditions contrasted sharply with the situation in the mining industry and shipping, which had elaborate rules. However, towards the end of the nineteenth century there were so many factories that legal regulation became necessary. Working hours in bakeries became regulated in 1885, and with the Factory Supervision Act of 1892 came the ban on child labour, restrictions on working at night and on weekends, regulations stating that workers' life and health should be protected as much as feasible, and rules on government labour inspection. The workday for youths between the ages of 14 and 18 was limited to ten hours. In 1984, the Act relating to accident insurance for factory workers was passed and craft-trade legislation became stricter.

386. The passage of the LDA of 1915, with the establishment of a separate Labour Court and a public mediation authority, in many ways marked a change of view on workers' right to organize and on collective agreements. The same year, working time in industry was limited to ten hours per day, and a maximum of fifty-four hours per week. Already in 1919, working hours were again reduced, this time to eight and half hours per day and no more than forty-eight hours per week. Said provision remained in effect until as recently as 1957, when the forty-five-hour work week was passed (replaced by forty-two and half hours in 1968 and forty hours through the WEA of 1977).

387. The scope of worker-protection legislation is constantly expanding. It currently embraces not only industry workers, but also employees in commerce and office establishments, in public administration, the transport sector, etc. In 1948, separate laws were passed for domestic help and farm workers, replaced by the current Act of 1963 relating to the conditions of employment for domestic servants and the Farm Worker Protection Act of 1958. In 1985, employment and working conditions in forestry and aviation were incorporated into the rules of the WEA. Separate seamen's laws were enacted in 1923 and 1953, replaced by the current Seaman's Act of 1975, which, through the amendment of 1985, largely approximated the rules of the WEA. The legal status of civil servants was regulated in a comprehensive Act of 1918 which, however, only applied to civil servants in state government. The Act of 1918 was repealed through the Civil Service Act of 1977, which in turn was replaced by the current Civil Service Act of 1983. In 1933, civil servants were given the right to negotiate with the state on wage and working conditions, but not until 1958 was the collective agreement system adopted also for the state and civil servants.

388. The right to a fourteen-day holiday was initiated with the Worker Protection Act of 1936. In 1947, a general Act was passed relating to holidays, replaced by the current Holiday Act of 1988, stipulating four weeks plus one day of holiday.

389. The Act of 1920 relating to worker committees in industrial enterprises and the provisions relating to worker's share capital in 1929 opened the possibility for workers to have a say in the affairs of the enterprise. However, these arrangements had only limited significance. Far more important was the passage of the first BA (today NHO) in 1935, which acknowledged the shop steward system and thereby the basis for the joint committees which the parties later agreed on. In 1966, the Cooperation Agreement in part B of the Basic Agreement was adopted, with rules on works councils, department councils, works conferences and joint councils, which still form the general basis for the current Basic Agreement. In 1972, the Companies Act was amended, giving employees the right to be represented on the board of a new corporate committee – the corporate assembly – in major limited companies. These rules were carried out in the current Companies Act of 1976, and are now found in the Companies Act of 1997 and other company-related legislation.

Chapter 5. Role of Government Institutions in the Shaping and Administration of Labour and Industrial Relations Policy

§1. Introduction

390. The degree of government influence within the area of labour life is significant. A 'classic' liberal point of departure relates to the situation between the employee and the enterprise; from the management's point of view, the ideal is to make as good use of the labour force at hand as possible. Bearing in mind that the employer has a different position and is more experienced when negotiating the terms of labour – whereas the employee in most cases cannot afford being unemployed and has no other choice but to agree on what the employer has to offer – the need of governmental (regulatory) influence is essential. In these situations, the need of government regulation systems can be summarized with the key words protection and safety considerations. It comes down to protection of the employee from the hazards that occur in connection to the workplace, from work accidents and occupational diseases, etc. From an economic perspective, such regulation systems can be explained by the fact that society cannot afford to exhaust the recourses of labour, because it would be too expensive in relation to the national social budget. Based on the more human terms, it cannot be accepted that production will take place at the expense of reasonable security measures for the protection of employees' lives and health.

391. Protective and safety considerations are also relevant in connection to the contract of employment itself. An example illustrates this: the employer should not have the opportunity to, unconditionally, withhold some of the employee's wage because the employee has to pay the employer compensation for damaging a machine at work. The employee is depending on his or her wages to cover his or her daily needs and those of the family, and this represents a need that must be prioritized. A different example relates to regulation systems concerning termination of the contract of employment, and especially regulation systems that provide protection against unfair dismissals.

392. The 'classic' liberal point of departure is modified by the growth and strength of trade unions, among other things. The reason for this is that negotiations and the development of working conditions will take place between somewhat fairly equal parties.

393. The challenge is thus to find the most appropriate balance between the freedom of the parties on the one hand, and regulation systems concerning the working conditions on the other hand. This relates both to contracts of employments and to what can be determined through collective agreements. It also relates to working conditions in general.

§2. Workplace, Etc.

394. This item refers to the concrete outer limits of the work place – e.g., the size of the premises, heating of the premises, supply of light and air – technical equipment, the goods that are processed, and so on. Other factors such as work pace, the process of production itself, working hours and breaks can also be mentioned in this connection.

395. Rules concerning working conditions in general, which can be found both in the labour legislation and in different regulations, are to a certain extent thoroughly regulated in detail, due to considerations regarding protection of employees from work hazards and occupational diseases.

396. An important factor in current labour legislation, which also has been the principle in working environment legislation since 1977, is that both physical and psychosocial aspects of the working environment shall be seen in context with one another. This principle is also based on the wish to promote work satisfaction. According to the WEA section 1-1(a), the purpose of the Act is 'to secure a working environment that provides a basis for a healthy and meaningful working situation'.

397. Safety and protection considerations – in a narrow sense – are not necessarily in an opposite position to welfare and satisfaction considerations – in a broader perspective. In both cases, the underlying contemplations rely on social considerations. Still, based on the resources that public supervisory authorities have at disposal at any given time, it entails that certain tasks – such as protection against accidents and health-related problems – need to be prioritized before tasks based on welfare considerations.

§3. Safety Considerations and Welfare Considerations: Connections and Differences

398. Public agencies, such as the Norwegian Labour Inspectorate and the Norwegian Ship Control Authority (*Skipskontrollen*), need as a starting point to be in total control of circumstances regarding safety and health issues concerning the employees, through legislation that cannot be dispensed with by agreements between the parties. If there is a need for different arrangements other than those prescribed by the legislation, this has to be accommodated by rules that allow exemptions. Rules that allow exemptions should also be able to prescribe necessary conditions.

§4. Supervision and Collaboration

399. Within the area of supervision – concerning questions regarding supervision of safety regulations, and making sure that the rules are complied with by the parties – the starting point has to be that this is something that public authorities need to be in total control of. There might on the other hand be minor risks involved if some of the responsibilities of supervision were handed over to trade unions, and even to the individual employers and their employees. Collaboration between the public supervisory authorities, trade unions and the local employees' elected representatives will in most cases result in obvious and major practical advantages. It will be impossible for the Norwegian Labour Inspectorate to be present at all places at all times, and certain circumstances of greater importance relating to safety measurements can easily be missed. A condition for this collaboration to work properly is that the employee's elected representatives are able to attract the public supervisory authorities' attention if the employer does not fulfil, or does not wish to fulfil, the demands in accordance to safety regulations. In addition, public supervisory authorities need to have the power to intervene whenever they find it necessary.

400. A control system based on collaboration between locally elected representatives and labour supervisory authorities is based on old traditions. Since 1977, this system has developed further, and is now based on provisions concerning working environment committees (cf. WEA Chapter 7).

§5. Prior Agreements Given by the Public Supervisory Authorities Regarding Their Administrative Powers

401. One may ask whether public supervisory authorities by entering into prior agreements are precluded from giving new or altered prohibitions or orders, for as long as the prior agreement applies. This question may be of practical importance when an establishment of a new work plant is being planned and there is no way to avoid the fact that running the plant will result in a certain degree of contamination, e.g., air contamination.

402. An approval given in advance may not, in itself, interfere with the fact that a new resolution may be given containing additional prohibitions. An example in this connection relates to WEA section 18-9, after which any person wishing to erect a building or to perform construction work that will or may foreseeably be used by an enterprise subject to the Act, shall obtain prior consent from the Norwegian Labour Inspectorate. It is stated in the *travaux préparatoires* to the WEA in connection to the said section that:

403. If the Norwegian Labour Inspectorate has given their consent, it does not, however, indicate that the authority has vouched for the fact that all circumstances in connection to the enterprise, covered by the consent, are in accordance with the relevant legislation. Even though the Norwegian Labour Inspectorate has given its consent, the authority has to be able to give instructions regarding safety or environmental measurements later on, if this should be required for being in compliance with the relevant legislation.

404. As a condition for the public administration to enter into agreements concerning how it will exercise its very own administrative powers, there is a general assumption that the relevant facts need to be ascertained with a relatively high degree of certainty, in advance. In addition, the legislation or relevant regulations must not preclude the opportunity of entering into such agreements.

405. On the other hand, there clearly are some limitations as to what public supervisory authorities can agree on. For as long as the subject concerned is based on safety and protection measurements, due to considerations regarding the lives and health of the employees, the assumption needs to be that such a prior agreement cannot be entered into, with binding force, by the public administration. The risks involved seem considerably minor when entering into such agreements in circumstances characterized by welfare considerations. The development we have had here in Norway in direction of wider collective freedom of disposition – see the below – seems to be based on such a distinction. As far as the principle of contract is accepted, when it comes to organizational collective agreements, it also seems adjacent to assume that the principle of contract can be accepted in relation to situations where public authorities are one of the parties. Especially, when it comes to agreements fixed on a time limit, this thesis seems applicable; it might also include agreements containing provisions stipulating that negotiations will take place in particular and specified situations. This could probably also result in a more flexible system, given that agreements would be a supplement, or even an alternative, to public regulations and individual prohibitions and orders. The agreement concerning the including labour life – to which the state is a party together with a number of other organizations and associations – may be of illustrative significance in this connection.

§6. Welfare Considerations: The Collective Freedom of Disposition

406. As regards the factors of the working environment that first and foremost relate to work satisfaction and welfare, it may be held that the need of invariable labour legislation is not necessarily of such great importance as is the situation regarding circumstances related to safety and protection. The situation may be that certain circumstances give the enterprise good reasons for allowing employees to choose between increased wages, instead of introducing certain welfare measurements within the enterprise. The question that arises in these situations will generally be whether the employees, through their respective trade unions, should be given the opportunity to enter into collective agreements with the enterprises concerning such circumstances. If the employees, or their respective trade unions, are able to foresee the long-term effects of the various alternatives, there is a lot to be said for the fact that the labour legislation should enable the parties to make such a choice. This represents, briefly, the basis of the collective freedom of disposition.

I. Working Hours

407. Chapter 10 of the WEA, which mainly concerns the arrangement of working hours, illustrates certain aspects of the collective freedom of disposition. Due to safety and protection considerations there clearly needs to be a limit to the extension of the working hours. This was also stressed in the *travaux préparatoires* to the former Work Protection Act of 1915, which stated in section 23 that the normal working hours might not exceed ten hours per twenty-four hours and fifty-four hours per seven days (cf. Ot.prp.no. 35 (1914) p. 97).

408. According to the current WEA section 10-12(4), the collective freedom of disposition is maintained. Throughout the years, the legislation has developed from relatively strictly stipulated working-hour arrangements to gradually, and to a larger extent, accepting collective freedom of disposition. Today the individual employee is even given the opportunity to enter into agreements with the employer that to some extent deviates from the normal working hours (cf. WEA section 10-5(1) which stipulates that the employer and the employee may in writing agree that the normal working hours may be arranged in such a way that, on average, during a period not exceeding fifty-two weeks, they are no longer than prescribed by section 10-4, but that the total working hours do not exceed ten hours per twenty-four hours and forty-eight hours per seven days). In addition, the employer may enter into similar agreements with the employees' elected representatives, within certain specified limits.

409. Since 1968, the labour legislation has made it possible for the major trade unions to enter into collective agreements regulating working hours which derogate from the stipulated arrangements. This relates to collective agreements that are entered into by trade unions that represent more than 10,000 members. However, there are certain limits stipulated in the legislation which the collective agreements may not exceed.

410. Many of the provisions concerning working hours in the WEA stipulate that exemptions may be arranged, but only with a given consent of the Norwegian Labour Inspectorate, e.g., WEA section 10-5(3) and section 10-6(6). Before the Norwegian Labour Inspectorate makes its decision, the working-hour arrangements must be discussed with the employees' elected representatives. When making its decision, the Norwegian Labour Inspectorate will attach particular importance to the health and welfare of the employees.

411. Outside the scope of the WEA, regulatory systems concerning working-hour arrangements in other areas of labour life also have a liberal attitude as to whether different arrangements can be regulated by entering into collective agreements. However, this does not apply to the same extent in all the different areas. *See* e.g., the Ship Safety and Security Act (SSSA) of 19 December 2007 No. 9 section 24.

II. Holiday with Pay Act (of 29 April 1988 No. 21)

412. The Holiday with Pay Act also recognizes the collective freedom of disposition (*see* section 10(6) which prescribes that 'rules in this section concerning the calculation of holiday pay from employers may be departed from in a collective agreement'). Moreover, as far as circumstances regarding distinct welfare measurements are concerned, the collective freedom of disposition is recognized. The provisions expressed in this Act may be departed from, through collective agreements, without having to be given the consent of public authorities. The reason for this is that the Act stipulates certain terms, or limitations, which collective agreements have to be in accordance with, and cannot exceed.

III. Act Relating to 1 and 17 May as Official National Holidays (of 26 April 1947)

413. According to section 3 of this Act, trade unions entitled to submit recommendations pursuant to the LDA section 11, may enter into collective agreements that depart from the provisions of this Act. The reason for the establishment of this system was mainly because the trade unions wanted to be able to agree on a more practical settlement, which the legislation then in force did not allow.

IV. The Former Act Concerning Employment Conditions for Teachers in Upper Secondary Schools (Repealed by Act of 11 June 1993, No. 30)

414. The former Act concerning Employment Conditions for Teachers in Upper Secondary Schools (of 21 June 1974 No. 55) section 22 stipulated that 'terms and conditions of employment, dismissal and notice, suspension, retirement and other legal relationships affecting senior appointments and teaching appointments were to be stipulated by law', but such an Act was never passed. No law regarding these circumstances has yet been provided by the government. However, a collective agreement (*Rettsvilkaarsavtalen*) was entered into (on 1 January 1976) by the Norwegian Ministry of Church and Education on the one side, and a number of trade unions representing teachers on the other side. Today, the WEA covers some of these circumstances.

V. The Former Act of 27 June 1947 as Regards Placing and Engagement of Seamen (Repealed by Act of 12 December 1988, No. 77)

415. According to the Act as regards Measures to Promote Employment of 27 June 1947, section 19, the placing and engagement of seamen should be conducted in accordance with certain stipulated rules. The rules could be developed in fuller detail by collective agreements between the principal organizations of the shipowners and seamen. The collective agreement had to be subject to the approval of the King-in-Council.

416. In general, there is nothing wrong with the legislation demanding a 'double-track-system', in the sense that the parties can enter into a collective agreement, which also has to be approved by the public authorities. It should be observed, however, that regulation by collective agreement was to be the principal solution, and regulation through decisions by public authorities was to be subsidiary.

417. By a decision of the King-in-Council of 17 June 1949 an agreement entered into on 31 May 1949 (between the Employer's Association concerning Shipping, the Employer's Association concerning Whaling, the Norwegian Employers' Confederation, the Shipowners' Association and the Norwegian Seamen's Union) was approved. The agreement stipulated guidelines for the placing and engagement of seamen. However, over the years this system turned out to be superfluous, and not appropriate, and also had certain unfortunate consequences. Thus by an Act of 16 December 1988, No. 77, the whole system was repealed. Today, as regards placing and engagement, the same legislation applies to seamen as to other employees (cf. the Act on Labour Market Activities of 12 December 2004, No. 76).

§7. Collective Agreements

418. This section refers to governmental influence in relation to the collective agreements in general and government influence in relation to the establishment and content of such collective agreements.

I. The Traditional Position

419. Over a long period of time the traditional position regarding trade unions representing the employees' interests on the one hand and associations representing the employers' interests on the other hand, has been that the parties themselves should resolve questions in connection to payment and working conditions. Public authorities were supposed to maintain a relatively passive position in this relation: only establishing a certain regulation system stipulating the measures that needed to be considered when the parties did not succeed in agreeing on such conditions through negotiations, resulting in labour disputes. In addition, public authorities should be able to intervene and mediate between the parties.

II. Current Legislation

420. The current legislation in Norway is based upon this traditional position. Both the LDA and the Labour Disputes Act for the Public Sector (LDPS) stipulate provisions concerning the establishment of public mediation, and the deadlines that shall be met by the parties before labour disputes can take place. Moreover, the provisions also stipulate other terms, e.g., that collective agreements shall be drawn up in writing, the time of validity of collective agreements and conditions regarding termination (*see* paragraphs 1411 et seq.).

III. The Economic Effects of a Collective Wage Payment Settlement

421. In this section, we shall briefly deal with the economic effects of a collective wage payment settlement. Most of the payment settlements take place during springtime or early summertime.

422. The main collective wage payment settlement between LO and NHO directly includes approximately 470,000 employees. In addition, the result of the main payment settlement is given an almost automatic effect to an almost equal large amount of employees that to some extent are members of LO, but are working in enterprises that are not included in the agreement with NHO, and to another extent are employed in NHO-enterprises, but that are not members of LO. The settlement within the public sector, which also takes place in the spring, includes approximately 680,000 employees. These settlements are often coordinated together with the settlements regarding the employees within the sectors of the counties and municipalities.

423. Negotiation and settlement as regards collective agreements for seamen engaged in foreign trade or employees working within the service sector, take place at other times of the year. An important factor in this regard is that also other working groups have been given their wage increases, or wage developments, partly based on the results from the revisions and negotiations. This relates not only to farmers and fishermen, but also to a number of other professions.

424. Increased expenses within economic and business life will have to be compensated by higher prices, in order to maintain or increase their own income. This increase in prices will easily be 'consumed' by the increased wages that payment settlements provide for the employees. Due to tax progression, the employees' increased wages will be 'consumed' by the public administration with a higher percentage than would normally apply. And when the public administration uses the larger taxation revenues, they seize an increasing part of production.

425. The development throughout the years between 1970 and 1972 illustrates what is described above. In those years, employees' wages increased nominally by 10%. The price index concerning the general consumption increased by 6.5%. The tax progression and increased member fees to the national insurance brought the increased taxes up to approximately 2%. The actual wage increase was therefore minor to the individual employee, approximately 2%. As a matter of fact, for some employees there were no increases at all, some even suffered a minor recession.

IV. The Need for Collaboration Between Public Authorities, Trade Unions and Employers' Associations: The Organization of Collaboration

426. An establishment of collaboration between public authorities, trade unions and employers' associations seems somewhat inevitable. From an organizational point of view, such collaborations will not necessarily involve a loss of the right to negotiate within collective agreement relations. From a government point of view, collaboration does not necessarily involve handing over administrative powers to organizations within an important area of economics. This also seems to apply to other organizations within the economic life.

427. Such collaborations can be illustrated with an example. The Contact Committee on Incomes Policy (*Regjeringens Kontaktutvalg*) was established in 1962. Today, the prime minister is chairman of the committee which includes national unions such as LO, the Confederation of Vocational Unions (YS), the Confederation of Unions for Professionals (Unio), the Federation of Norwegian Professional Associations (*Akademikerne*), the Confederation of Norwegian Enterprise (NHO), the Enterprise Federation of Norway (Virke), the Employers' Association Spekter, the Norwegian

Association of Local and Regional Authorities (KS), the Norwegian Farmers' Union (NFU) and the Norwegian Farmers' and Smallholders' Union (NBS). The committee does not have a formal authorization. Through meetings, the committee serves as a forum providing mutual orientation to the involved parties. These orientations seek to coordinate wage settlements in time, meanwhile debating whether the government should assist in the settlement.

428. An important factor in this connection is that wage negotiations, due to economic necessity, need to be coordinated and debated in context with other political aspects, e.g., income tax as well as national insurance and prices policy.

V. Coordination and the Right to Negotiate

429. The economic necessity of coordination does not reach further than keeping the wage negotiations within certain limits, e.g., that a certain percentage of total economic growth is passed on to the wage earners. How this percentage should be distributed among the different groups of wage earners will still be up to the organizations within labour life to find a solution to, in a traditional manner – through negotiations, or if necessary through labour disputes.

430. Besides, the entire point behind this coordination lies within the economic sector, even though collective agreements also contain provisions concerning other circumstances. As far as provisions regarding economic circumstances are concerned and provisions regarding additional payment benefits to the ordinary wages (such as additional payments due to seniority, nuisance bonus, travel and daily allowances), this can be calculated and coordinated within a given economic framework. The same applies to other provisions within the collective agreements, which mainly concern economic aspects, e.g., the amount of holiday pay, pension and early retirement schemes, etc.

431. Other provisions within the collective agreements have less or nothing to do with economic aspects, such as provisions regarding dismissals, lay-offs, the right to organize or duty to do so, etc. Such non-economic aspects can also be negotiated between the organizations of labour life, or problems related to these aspects may be resolved through legislation provided by government.

VI. Relations Between the Public Authorities and the Free-standing Organizations

432. Within the area of labour life, a coordinated wage settlement presupposes the existence of centralized bargainers, or at least that certain parties have a dominant position. In this regard, the Norwegian conditions are of a rather simple nature, in the sense that LO and NHO are the dominating parties. Both of these main organizations will to a large degree make a contribution to the fact that the individual associations follow a centralized and coordinated arrangement. However, there are other organizations and associations besides LO and NHO.

433. In relation to the freestanding organizations, there is a possibility that the public authorities will choose to make use of compulsory arbitration. Previously there was at least in principle also a possibility, provided that certain conditions were fulfilled, that public authorities might connect settlements involving the freestanding organizations to the settlements obtained by the main organizations, when such settlements were to be decided by the members of the different organizations by ballot. Since 2012, such ballots will require the consent of all organizations involved.

VII. Compulsory Arbitration

434. Compulsory arbitration needs to be decided through legislative provisions – or a provisory ordinance. In situations where the State Mediator has not succeeded in bringing the parties to a voluntary solution and a labour dispute is threatening an area within labour life in which society cannot allow an open dispute, compulsory arbitration has its main purpose. In a number of occasions, provisions enabling the use of compulsory arbitration have been carried out, both in legislation and in provisional ordinances. During the Second World War, compulsory arbitration was carried out through a provisional ordinance, and the following Act regarding compulsory arbitration applied until 1952, now the Wage Board Act (WBA) of 27 January 2012 No. 10. Usually, the special Acts and Ordinances stipulate that the conflict be settled by the National Wage Arbitration Board, but it may also be stipulated that the conflict be settled by a special board with a different composition. Thus, in 1966, in connection with negotiations on the wage settlements, a labour dispute was about to take place between the Norwegian Nurses Organization (NSF) and the Norwegian Association of Local and Regional Authorities (KS). By a special Act of 21 June 1966, the dispute was ordered to be settled by compulsory arbitration or by a board especially appointed by the King-in-Council.

435. Even though compulsory arbitration should not be used on a general basis, it does not imply that it does not have its purpose within a system that is based on negotiations and labour disputes. An interesting example in this regard is the provisions stipulated in the LDPS sections 29 and 30. According to these provisions, questions regarding 'adjustments' and 'regulations' of posts covered by the State Pay Regulations are to be determined by the State Wage Panel or a specific committee, if the parties cannot come to an agreement. This is an example of disputes which must not be solved through compulsory arbitration.

§8. The Individual Contract of Employment

436. The object of the legislation within different areas of labour life, especially concerning the individual contracts of employments has partly been protection of the employees by introducing invariable provisions, e.g., provisions regarding protection against unfair dismissals. In addition, the object has partly been to introduce provisions of which the purpose is to supplement the contract of employment if the contract itself does not contain certain provisions. This has been done because of the wish to ensure that employees are given certain minimum rights. In other respects, public authorities generally maintain a relatively reserved role. The actual entering of contracts of employments takes place between the parties and they agree on which conditions are to apply, within the limits stipulated in the legislation. It is up to the employee himself or herself, or possibly through the trade union, to ensure that he or she is given the rights stipulated in the legislation.

I. Different Forms of Encroachment by Public Authorities

437. As stated above, public authorities maintain a relatively reserved role when it comes to the actual contracts of employments. This seems to a large extent to work well, especially given the position that trade unions have. On the other hand, the position of the different trade unions is not equally strong within all the different areas of labour life.

A. Apprentices

438. Apprentices represent a relatively vulnerable group of employees. Their legal position is regulated in the EA (of 17 July 1998 No. 61) Chapter 4. Apprentices and training candidates are employees of the training establishment with which they have a contract of employment and placement, with rights and obligations pursuant to legislation and collective agreements. When the apprenticeship or training period is over, the contract of employment also ceases to apply (cf. EA section 4-2(2)). The training establishments need to be approved by a public authority (cf. EA section 12-1 and the following sections).

439. In general, apprentices are employees of a rather young age. The contracts are often entered into on a long-term basis, during which the employees are given an adequate education within a subject by doing practical work combined with theoretical apprenticeship training. This group of employees has a considerable need of having their legal position strengthened, partly because of their age and partly because of their dependent relationship with the employer. If the employer does not fulfil his or her obligations, this can cause the apprentice a considerable loss, both economically and in connection to circumstances regarding his welfare.

440. Already at the time of entering a contract of employment, public authorities show their engagement. According to the EA (of 17 July 1998 No. 61) section 4-5(2) and in accordance with regulations issued pursuant to the section, the contract be concluded in writing on a form established by the ministry. The section also stipulates what the contract shall contain at a minimum. For the contract to be valid, it has to be approved by the county authority (the Apprenticeship Board) and be given a signature, which represents the county authority's approval.

441. The apprenticeship contract may not be amended or rescinded in any other way than in accordance with the EA section 4-6. Only with the consent of the county authority may the contract be rescinded both by the training establishment and by the apprentice if, e.g., the other party is guilty of serious breaches of his or her duties connected with work, or the apprentice or training establishment proves to be incapable of continuing the apprenticeship.

442. The Act also establishes an internal control system that is supposed to ensure that the apprentice is given the appropriate training, which he is entitled to according to the apprenticeship contract. In accordance with section 4-7, one or more representatives for the employees shall assist the training supervisor(s) regularly to ensure that the training establishment fulfils its obligations in accordance with the EA and its regulations. The training establishment is to make an annual report to the county authority about the training provided for apprentices.

443. The EA does not provide any provisions which give the apprentices the right to assistance by public authorities if a conflict arises during the period of contract, e.g., a claim for compensation due to insufficient training. However, it seems clear that the Apprenticeship Board may provide some guidance to the individual apprentice, due to the central position this board has in these contractual relations. According to the PAA (of 10 February 1967) section 11, the administrative agencies have, within their sphere of competence, a general duty to provide guidance. The extent of this guidance must, however, be adapted to the situation and capacity of the administrative agency to undertake such activity. Even though the provision does not apply directly in conflicts between private parties, there are many indications that this provision should be applied analogically.

B. Seamen

444. The public authorities have also been strongly engaged in relation to contracts of employment concerning seamen, even though the actual contractual relationship is thoroughly regulated by the Ship Labour Act (of 21 June 2013 No. 102). According to the Ship Labour Act section 3-1(4), the Ministry of trade, industry and fisheries may prescribe by regulation the information to be contained in the contract of employment and the contract form.

445. Today, the need of public control with the contracts of employments regarding seamen is hardly of great importance anymore. According to the *travaux préparatoires* to the previous SA (of 30 May 1975 No. 18), it is stated that these provisions have been provided in order to ensure that Norway complies with commitments pursuant to the ILO Convention No. 22 (cf. also the Maritime Labour Convention of 2006 (MLC) (cf. Ot.prp.nr 36 (1970-1971 p. 64)).

C. Contracts of Employment That Require Approval from Public Authorities

446. There are many examples within the labour legislation which require that the contract of employment shall be given approval by public authorities in order to be valid. The object of such a system seems to be that the public authorities shall be able to ensure that the individual contract of employment does not derogate from provisions provided by the legislation or regulations.

447. As mentioned above, the apprenticeship contract illustrates a contract of employment, which requires such an approval. Another example relates to the situation when someone is taking on the lease of a farm. Leases are not regarded as contracts of employments, because the lessee is running the farm for his or her own account and at his or her own risk. According to the Act related to leasing of a farm (of 25 June 1965 No. 1) section 4, the landowner should submit the lease to the council committee concerned with questions of land and forest use.

D. Public Statements

448. Public pronouncements are one of the mildest forms of encroachments on the contract of employment given by the public administration, judicially speaking. When giving such pronouncements, the public administration does not make individual decisions relating to the rights or duties of one or more specified persons. Thus, there is no need for any legal authority in these circumstances. On the other hand, such pronouncements may have great importance for the parties concerned.

449. Within certain areas of labour life, and the labour legislation, public authorities are instructed to provide guidance and to give pronouncements. According to the Holiday Act of 1988 section 13, the Norwegian Labour Inspectorate is instructed to give advice in matters concerning the Act. As mentioned above, the apprenticeship board may provide guidance to the individual apprentice.

E. Contracts That Are to Be Submitted to Public Agencies

450. Current labour legislation contains a number of provisions, which stipulates that agreements between the parties shall be submitted to the proper public agency. Here can be mentioned that the LDPS section 11(2) stipulates that a copy of a collective agreement shall be sent to the State Mediator not later than a fortnight after the signing of the agreement. The purpose of submitting collective agreements to the State Mediator is to ensure that the State Mediator has a total overview concerning the collective agreements. A similar duty is, however, no longer prescribed by the LDA (2012) (cf. previously the LDA (1927) section 3 No. 1). Another example relates to the establishment of staff rules (cf. WEA section 14-17). According to the WEA section 14-18, rules drafted pursuant to section 14-17 shall be submitted to the Norwegian Labour Inspectorate not later than three months after the enterprise commences operations. The purpose is to make it possible for the Norwegian Labour Inspectorate to ensure that staff rules are established in a lawful manner and that they do not contain provisions contrary to the Act (cf. WEA section 14-19).

§9. Provisions Concerning Application of Conditions Pursuant to Collective Agreements Regarding Employees Who Are Not Legally Bound by the Collective Agreement

451. In a number of situations, it would be appropriate to make conditions pursuant to a collective agreement applicable also to employees who are not legally bound by the collective agreement, e.g., because the employees are non-union members.

452. An example relates to the WEA section 10-12(4). A collective agreement can be entered into, in accordance with this section, which to some extent departs from the provisions of WEA Chapter 10. Such an agreement will then establish a different arrangement of working hours, other than the arrangement according to the provisions regarding normal working hours. If such an agreed arrangement of working hours should only be applicable to the organized employees, it would be very difficult to carry out the collective agreement in practice. For this reason, WEA section 10-12(5) stipulates that if a collective agreement has been entered into (pursuant to sections 10-5, 10-6, 10-8, 10-10, 10-11 or 10-12(4)) and a majority of the employees are bound by the agreement, the employer may make the provisions of the agreement concerning the working hours applicable to all employees who perform work of the kind covered by the agreement.

453. In addition, the Act relating to 1 and 17 May as official national holidays, section 3(2) stipulates a similar possibility for making collective agreements applicable to employees who are not union members.

454. Provisions pursuant to collective agreements have, also prior to these legislative provisions, been made applicable to non-union members, the authorization for such applications was found partly stipulated within the individual contracts of employment concerning non-union members, partly stipulated within the collective agreements themselves, and partly because the collective agreements have been applied as supplementing provisions.

455. The starting point is that there exists a collective agreement. The collective agreement may – as regards employees – in practice, rest upon a majority decision within the trade union, even though this does not always have to be the case. This does not, however, give rise to any problems in particular, just because of the fact that the minority of organized employees are also legally bound by the collective agreement. In this case, the approach to the problem does not diverge from the problem concerning the legal position of the minority pursuant to collective agreements in general. As members of a trade union, the minority have been given the opportunity to give their influence, especially by giving their vote.

456. However, when the collective agreement is expanded, in the sense that non-union members also are included in the agreement, this implies that they are legally bound by the provisions contained in the agreement, without being given the opportunity to have any influence on the matter. The non-union members should therefore be safeguarded against being put in a more unfavourable position than other employees, unless just grounds within the working conditions should indicate a different approach (cf. also the WEA sections 13-1 et seq. and Rt. 2011 p. 1755 (*Gate Gourmet*) paragraphs 71 et seq.).

457. As mentioned above, it is up to the employer to decide whether the collective agreement shall be expanded to also apply to non-union members or not, according to the WEA. As far as this matter is concerned, the Act establishes a system where the employer is basing the decision by virtue of the management prerogative. However, there can be reason for considering it to be somewhat doubtful whether this is an appropriate system: there already exists a collective agreement with the employer as one of the representing parties. Unless otherwise stipulated or agreed upon, the general rule is that the conditions pursuant to the collective agreement will be applicable to all contracts of employment that are subject within the scope of the agreement. Thus, it will be contrary to the collective agreement if the employer applies conditions in relation to the rest of the employees other than those applicable to organized employees.

458. As for as the legislative provisions stipulate that the decisive factor is whether a majority is legally bound by the collective agreement, this may entail that a minority decides the majority's conditions. On the other hand, this situation may also occur in collective agreement relations in general; insofar as these circumstances are concerned the legislative stipulated access to expand the collective agreements' scope of applicability does not represent a problem of major significance.

Chapter 6. Sources of Labour Law

§1. Introduction

459. The sources of labour law are rather complex. They consist of a few articles of the Norwegian Constitution, international conventions and recommendations, legislation with appurtenant regulations, collective wage agreements, staff regulations and other company rules. Case law, custom and other practice in employment relationships must further be noted, in addition to what has been agreed between the parties in the individual employment contract.

460. When reference is made to the Industry agreement (IA) (*Industri overenskomsten*) in the following, it is because this generally has been normative in relation not only to collective agreements on wages and other working conditions in the private sector, but also in the public sector.

§2. International Conventions, Etc.

I. Basic Position

461. The basic position in Norway regarding the interaction between international law and Norwegian national law is dualism. This means that international and national law is seen as two separate legal systems with different origins. In Norway, national law has precedence. Therefore, agreed treaties and conventions pertaining to international law will only be enforceable within the national law system after being correctly implemented by the Norwegian authorities (cf. also paragraph 426 below).

462. Norway is not a member of the EU but may, as an EFTA state, be bound to implement large parts of EU legislation into national law through the EEA Agreement. In addition, Norway also implements numerous other treaties and agreements from the EU outside the scope of the EEA Agreement (cf. paragraph 420 below). A directive from the EU is not binding for the EFTA states until it has been included in the EEA Agreement by the EEA Committee. A party in the EEA Committee can, in theory, use a right of veto to refuse a directive. However, if the directive regards a subject relevant to the EEA Agreement, such a refusal would probably have a major negative political impact on the relationship between the country and the EU, as well as the other EFTA states. Thus, Norway has only once made use of the right to make reservations, in 2012, as regards the post directive (Directive 2008/6/EC of the European Parliament and of the Council of 20 February 2008 amending Directive 97/67/EC with regard to the full accomplishment of the internal market of Community postal services).

463. When passed by the EEA Committee, the directive only binds the EFTA states as an international obligation to implement the regulations further into domestic law. The single domestic legal effect a directive under the EEA Agreement has when it is not correctly implemented, is that the Norwegian government can be liable for loss private persons suffer as a consequence of failed implementation. Only when the EU directive is correctly included in the EEA Agreement and later implemented into domestic law, is it enforceable in Norway. Most of the EU directives are implemented by transformation, which means that the directives are translated and adjusted before being passed as binding acts and regulations. This process makes the directives appear as a natural part of the Norwegian law system. The directives can be transformed as a whole or they may only require small changes in already existing national Acts. In the case in which national law already is in conformity with the new directives, a mere declaration of legal harmony can be sufficient. Concerning a Norwegian refusal of implementation of a part of the EEA Agreement, the situation would be similar to that described above regarding refusal to pass an EU directive.

464. Council Directive 2000/78/EC establishing a general framework for equal treatment in employment and occupation, prohibits discrimination based on religion, belief, handicap, age or sexual orientation, and is not a part of the EEA Agreement. The priority provision in the EEA Agreement Act (EEAAA) section 2 will supposedly not be applicable, because the directive is not a provision 'that applies in order to fulfil Norway's commitments pursuant to the EEA agreement'. According to Norwegian law, the directive is still implemented, due to an independent evaluation (cf. Ot.prp. nr.104 (2002-2003) p. 14). Regarding the question on how one, within Norwegian law, should relate to the development of law, e.g., the practice of the European Court of Justice in this regard depends therefore on what has been the Norwegian legislator's – Parliament's – intention and assumption. This question will have to find its answer in accordance with Norwegian law (cf. Rt. 2010 p. 202 (*Nye Kystlink*)).

465. The consequence of this principle is, therefore, that the Norwegian courts will have to consider the questions related to the interpretation of the equal treatment directive on the basis of the same legal sources that would apply, as if the question had been presented to the European Court of Justice. Thus, the assumption of the legislator that the legal situation at that time would not be altered, may not necessarily be upheld (cf. Rt. 2012 p. 219 (*Helicopter Pilots*) paragraph 46, and further Rt. 2011 p. 609, Rt. 2011 p. 964 (*Gjensidige*), and Ot.prp.no. 104 (2002-2003) p. 30).

466. In Rt. 2010 p. 202 (*Nye kystlink*), the Supreme Court held (paragraph 56) that the question on whether Norway's seamen's legislation was in accordance with the directive had to be evaluated by the Norwegian courts 'on independent grounds based on the same sources of law, which would apply if the question was brought before the European Court of Justice'. The valuation concerning whether the age limit of 62 years for sailors was objective and reasonably motivated in accordance with the directive Article 6 No. 1, had to be done on the basis of a group approach (paragraph 65). It was up to the legislator to evaluate whether the considerations regarding the ship's and the crew's safety were sufficiently strong enough to motivate the especially low age limit, and in this relation the state has, according to the practice of the European Court of Justice, a wide margin of appreciation. Since, in this situation, the case concerned a directive that Norway was not, pertaining to international law, obliged to implement, the Norwegian courts had to be especially reluctant in putting aside the evaluation made by the legislator (paragraphs 68 and 70). The dismissal of the sailor, based on the grounds of reaching the age limit of 62, was thereby not invalid. *See* further Rt. 2012 p. 219 (*Helicopter Pilots*), below paragraph 1066.

467. Norway has ratified a considerable number of conventions in the field of labour law, and the ILO Conventions must be mentioned. A number of other international conventions also contain regulations which are of importance in employment relationships. In the following, a few of the most significant regulations will be mentioned.

468. The ECHR (1950) Article 11 determines that everyone has the right to form and to join trade unions. A corresponding regulation is set in the International Covenant on Civil and Political Rights (ICCPR) (1966) Article 22. The European Social Charter (1961, revised in 1996) sets out several comprehensive regulations within the range of employment legislation and social law, the International Covenant on Economic, Social and Cultural Rights (ICESCR) (1966). Furthermore the International Convention on the Elimination of All Forms of Racial Discrimination (CERD) (1966), and the Convention on the Elimination of All Forms of Discrimination against Women (CEDAW) (1979) should also be noted.

469. In addition to the above-mentioned conventions, the EEA Agreement (1992) is of considerable importance to employment relationships.

II. The Relationship Between International Law Commitments in International Conventions and Norwegian National Law

470. Traditionally, there is a presumption that Norwegian legislation is in accordance with the regulations of international conventions and other international regulations that Norway is bound by. As regards the employment law area Rt. 2001 p. 248, Rt. 2001 p. 1413 and Rt. 1986 p. 1250 are illustrative.

471. Still, it might happen that Norwegian regulations are passed which are in breach of the regulations in a convention, and that the Norwegian regulations are so distinct that neither on the basis of harmonization nor the presumptive principle it will be possible to interpret the Norwegian regulations in such a manner that they comply with the relevant convention. In such a case, it is the traditional view, that the Norwegian courts must apply the Norwegian regulations (cf. ARD 1990 p. 118 and Rt. 1997 p. 580 (the *OFS* case)). In the latter case, the Supreme Court expressed this traditional view in an obiter dictum. In that case, a provisional act had been issued that the industrial conflict should be settled by the National Wages Board, banning the use of strikes, lock-outs etc. The Federation of Offshore Workers' Trade Unions argued that the provisional act was not in accordance with the international conventions on the right to strike (cf. *inter alia* ECHR Article 11 and ILO Conventions Nos 87, 98 and 154). The Supreme Court held, however, that there was no international obligation for Norway to limit the right to make use of industrial actions when essential public interests were at large; thus, there were no conflict between the international obligations and Norwegian law. The European Court of Human Rights (EctHR) did also find, considering the facts of the case, that the Norwegian provisional act had been held within the limits of the essential services principle (cf. application No. 38190/97 of 27 June 2002, underlining that 'the national authorities have a wide margin of appreciation in the area under consideration', but also, that this 'power of appreciation is not... unlimited').

472. However, it may be stated in Norwegian legislation that the Norwegian regulations are to comply with international law. A practical and important example is the Act regarding the EEA Agreement of 27 November 1992 No. 109 (the EEA Act), which in section 1 states that the provisions in the main part of the agreement concerning the European Economic Cooperative Area shall apply as Norwegian law. Furthermore, it is stated in section 2 that statutory regulations which implement Norway's obligations subject to the agreement 'shall, in the event of conflict, take precedence over other Regulations that regulate the same matter'.

473. In this connection, section 92 of the Norwegian Constitution should be noted. According to this provision, it is 'an obligation for the authorities of the country to respect and safeguard the Human Rights, as expressed in this Constitution and in treaties binding for Norway on human rights'. The wording of this section could lead to the conclusion that this obligation to respect and secure the human rights is limited to such rights that are *both* expressed in the Constitution, *and* in for Norway binding treaties, but that interpretation of section 92 would have as consequence that the whole provision is superfluous and unnecessary. Section 92 repealed in 2014 the previous section 110 C, which since 1994 stipulated the obligation to respect and secure the human rights, and that further provisions to implement this principle could be stipulated by law. The purpose of section 92 is to strengthen the position of the human rights, and an attitude towards a more restrictive view than previously on the human rights can therefore not be the basis of the interpretation of section 92. In other words, section 92 should be understood so that it is sufficient that the human right in question is *either* expressed in the Constitution, *or* follows from one or more international treaties binding for Norway. Thus, the obligation to respect and safeguard the human rights is the paramount and direct part of this section of the Constitution, and legislation to this effect will have to be held within the frames that follow of the human rights, a view which the present writer has expressed also previously, as regards section 110 C of the Constitution.[8] It should be observed, however, that the general opinion previously was that the general obligation to respect and safeguard the human rights depend on the legislation that has implemented the human rights; a view which has as consequence that the Norwegian legislation will not necessarily have to be in accordance with the human rights, even if that question should be brought before Norwegian courts.

474. By the Act on Human Rights of 21 May 1999 No. 30, section 2, is stipulated that specifically enumerated human rights conventions are a part of Norwegian law, and superior to other legislation (cf. section 3). Those conventions are the ECHR, the ICESR, the ICCPR, the Convention on the rights of the child, and CEDAW (cf. also paragraph 1418 below).

475. Other conventions are implemented by other legislation – such as the Lugano Convention – but without formal status superior to other legislation.

8. Jakhelln Henning, 'Menneskerettighetene, Grunnlovens §110 c og arbeidsretten (Human Rights, Section 110 c of the Constitution Act, and Labour Law)', in Njål Høstmælingen (ed.), *Gjennomføringen av internasjonale menneskerettigheter i norsk rett* (1995), Torkel Opsahls minneseminar 1995, p. 151–178; reprinted in Henning Jakhelln: *Arbeidsrettslige studier* (Studies on Labour Law) (2000) p. 1720–1742.

476. From a practical point of view, it seems fair to say, that in this way the human rights are in general taken well care of in Norwegian law, and it is considered important that legislation is kept within the frames of the human rights conventions. As regards collective labour law, and the use of specific ad hoc legislation prohibiting starting or continued use of industrial action by strikes and lockout, the relation between international law and human rights on the one hand, and internal Norwegian law on the other hand is, however, brought to the surface – and is still a most live question in Norwegian labour law to-day.

477. From a principle point of view, however, the formal technique – to implement human rights by specific legislation – is qualified to strengthen the attitude and impression of human rights as limited to those fields of law where the legislation has expressed the view that human rights apply – the positivistic approach – which may even lead to the antithetic view that human rights do not apply elsewhere. The general view, that human rights are fundamental and superior to national law, and should be safeguarded ex officio by public authorities – and not in the least by the courts – may in this way be brought out of focus and into the background, and may in addition have as consequence that the question will arise, as to whether or not the human rights specifically mentioned in the Constitution should be interpreted and understood in the same way, as human rights in the different conventions.

478. Therefore, and from this angle, it may – as is still the opinion of the present writer – be raised the question, whether the passing of the Act on Human Rights (1999) was a major mistake, because this act applies only to the specifically mentioned conventions and is therefore not given as an act of a general nature. Therefore, a better approach to these questions would be to simply state in the act that is ‘an obligation for the authorities of the country to respect and safeguard the Human Rights’. Furthermore, it should also be stipulated in the act that the interpretation of the Conventions on Human Rights by Norwegian Courts should be based on the same principles as those applied by the International Courts, e.g., the ECtHR.

III. The Significance of Legal Opinions Expressed by the EFTA Court

479. The opportunity which Norwegian courts have to submit questions to the EFTA Court (cf. the Courts Act section 51a), is a part of the EEA Agreement.

480. In Rt. 2000 p. 1811, the Supreme Court elaborates its view like this: ‘The statement from the EFTA Court is advisory, but at the same time I find that the statement must be given considerable emphasis.’ Further, cf. Rt. 2013 p. 258 (STX Norway Offshore), section 93-94, the Supreme Court emphasized that it had thus the authority, as well as the duty, to decide to which degree a statement of the EFTA-Court should be followed; provided, however, that specific circumstances did apply, and did not follow completely the opinion of the EFTA-Court.

IV. International Recommendations

481. International recommendations are recommendations to individual countries regarding which regulations ought to be relied on in national laws and regulations.

482. If a reference to the recommendation is made during preparation of Norwegian legislation, the regulations of the recommendation will be a relevant factor in the interpretation of the Norwegian regulations.

§3. Legislation

483. The legislation concerning labour is not gathered in one simple Act, but in a number of different Acts. The most important of these is the WEA of 17 June 2005, No. 62.

484. In addition to the WEA there are a number of rights and obligations in employment relationships that are regulated by separate legislation. Amongst the most important are the Holiday Act, the Act regarding salaries in connection with temporary redundancies, the Gender Equality Act, the Sexual Orientation Anti-Discrimination Act, the Ethnicity Anti-Discrimination Act, the Anti-Discrimination and Accessibility Act, legislation concerning safeguarding of salary claims, etc. the Employee Inventions Act, the Religious Communities Act (RCA) (which gives employees right to time off for religious holidays), the regulations of the National Insurance Act (*inter alia* concerning medical benefits, benefits upon sickness and childbirth, adoption and children's sickness, during unemployment and rehabilitation, entitlements for retirement pension, disability pension and payments due to occupational injuries, funeral benefits, etc.), the Act regarding occupational injury insurance, the Act concerning 1 and 17 May as public holidays and the regulations of the Contract Act regarding the validity of agreed non-competition clauses.

485. In many employment relationships agreements concerning collective insurance schemes for the benefit of the employees have been entered into. Such insurance agreements are regulated by the Insurance Contracts Act (ICA) of 16 June 1989 No. 69, especially Chapter 9 and Chapter 19. Regulations concerning the employees' right of co-determination are *inter alia* included in the company legislation, for instance the Companies Act/Joint Stock Public Companies Act (cf. also section 110(2) of the Norwegian Constitution).

486. Some employment relationships fall outside the WEA, for instance sailors and other employment on board ships (cf. WEA section 1-2(2)(a)). Here, the Ship Labour Act of 21 June 2013 No. 102 will apply. The Ship Labour Act is to quite an extent harmonized with the provisions of the WEA.

487. As regards certain other employment relationships, there are specific provisions in separate legislation, but so that the regulations of the WEA will otherwise apply. This applies to employees employed by the state, to which the CSA of 4 March 1983 No. 3 provides a number of special regulations concerning the relationship between the state and its servants. Employees in county administrative or municipal service are, however, covered by the regulations of the Working Environment Act.

488. The CSA does not comprise employees in public companies which are demerged as separate legal entities (cf. in this connection also the Act concerning state-owned enterprises of 30 August 1991 No. 71 section 4). Employees in the state's public sector enterprises are on the other hand comprised by the CSA, but a number of the public sector enterprises have in the recent years been demerged as individual legal entities.

489. As regards the legal status of apprentices, Chapter 4 of the Training Act should be noted. The chapter provides regulations regarding, *inter alia*, probationary periods and contracts of apprenticeship, of changes to the apprenticeship and termination of the apprenticeship contract.

490. Senior public servants are characterized by the fact that the basis for their position is laid down in the Constitution, which has no regulations concerning the position of other public civil servants.

491. Legislation concerning collective agreements and the use of labour disputes is more clearly set out than legislation concerning individual employment contracts. The regulations of collective agreements concerning salary and terms of employment are in practice of major significance in many employment relationships.

492. The LDA of 27 January 2012 No. 9 provides regulations regarding collective agreements and their legal effects for employment agreements where the employer and the employee are bound by such an agreement, and regulates the right to initiate labour disputes (strikes, lock-outs and other labour disputes), mediation and regulations regarding the Labour Court.

493. The LDA also includes county council districts and municipalities. With regard to the state, these questions are regulated by the Public Services Disputes Act of 18 July 1958 No. 2. In this connection must also be noted the Boycott Act of 5 December 1947 No. 1, which however is not limited to employment relationships. Furthermore, the WBA of 27 January 2012 No. 10 must be mentioned, which gives the parties jointly the opportunity to bring an unsolved dispute of interests before the National Wages Arbitration Board.

494. By an ad hoc Act or interim legislation, unsolved disputes of interest are often referred to be solved by the National Wages Arbitration Board, which then acts as compulsory court of arbitration in the relevant dispute.

495. Finally must be noted the Act relating to general application of collective agreements, etc. of 4 June 1993 No. 58. Some wage agreements are extended to make them generally binding for all workers within certain sectors and geographical areas.

496. The Board on Extended Application of Collective Agreements (*Tariffnemnda)* may therefore make a decision to the effect that a nationwide collective agreement wholly or partly shall apply to all employees who perform work of the kind which the agreement regulates, as regards the salary and working conditions of the individual employee, (cf. paragraph 1505 below).

§4. Regulations

497. Regulations play an important role in addition to legislation. In many situations, the legislative clauses only set up a framework for how the employment shall be, while the more specific content of the clauses will be amplified through supplementary regulations. In practice, it can therefore be just as important to know what the regulations contain, as what the law itself lays down. However, the extent of regulations is comprehensive. In addition, regulations are amended frequently, so that a detailed review of the regulations' content will be outdated quite quickly.

§5. Collective Agreements

I. Introduction

498. Together with legislation and appurtenant regulations, collective agreements are of significance both in relation to the mutual rights and obligations of the parties in an employment relationship and as regards the relationship between the parties of the collective agreement itself. On the side of the employees, the party to a collective agreement is always a union, while the party on the side of the employer may be a single employer or an employers' association (cf. the LDA, section 1(8)).

499. In practice, collective agreements are often entered into between a trade union and an employer's association/union, on behalf of the employees and the employers that are members of the unions. The collective agreements that are entered into between the main organizations in working life and the agreements entered into by the government are of particular importance. Norwegian working life is in many ways dominated by two main organizations, LO (*Landsorganisasjonen i Norge*) and NHO (*Næringslivets Hovedorganisasjon*). In addition to these organizations, there are a number of nationwide organizations, for both employers and employees.

500. A collective agreement is characterized by establishing the content of the individual employment contracts that are or will be comprised by the collective agreement, to the effect that salary and working conditions beyond the framework of the collective agreement may not be agreed upon. So far, the regulations of the collective agreement are invariable. In addition, a labour dispute with the aim of changing the salary and working conditions stated in the agreement may not be initiated during the period where the agreement is applicable. Thus, the collective agreement imposes an obligation on the parties of the agreement and employers and employees who are comprised by the agreement, to keep the industrial peace. It is also characteristic that the regulations of the agreement and the labour peace obligation in principle will only apply for the period stated in the agreement itself. In practice, collective agreements are often entered into for a period of two years.

501. The parties of the collective agreement are, as an obvious starting point, bound by the legislative limitations of the contractual freedom. If a collective agreement is contrary to invariable legislative provisions, it will therefore be invalid.

II. Characteristics of the Collective Agreement

502. The fact that individual agreements entered into in a field of law must be in compliance with a framework agreement which the parties' organizations have entered into is not unique to employment law. Similar arrangements are common in many areas. However, the statutory principle of invariability distinguishes the collective agreement from other framework agreements. Members of the organizations may not derogate from a collective agreement by which they are bound, any such agreement is invalid (cf. the LDA section 6). In other fields of law, the individual agreement will usually be binding upon parties, even if it is in breach of the regulations of the framework agreement, and it will be up to the individual organization to take action against a member who has breached the framework agreement in this manner.

503. The invariability of the collective agreement will also have to be given considerable emphasis as regards copyright questions. In that regard, it should probably be assumed that collective agreements will have the same standing as – and no further copyright protection than – acts and regulations etc. (cf. the Copyright Act of 12 May 1961 No. 2 section 9 and the Bern Convention on protection of literature and works of Article (1886, as later amended) section 2(4)).

§6. The Individual Employment Agreement

504. The individual employment contract is the agreement between the employer and the individual employee, where the employee undertakes to – usually in return for remuneration – perform work for the employer. In the WEA section 14-6(1) is stated the minimum requirements regarding the content of the written contract (cf. paragraphs 1471 et seq.). Legislation, regulations, collective agreements and company regulations indicate the further content of the employer's and the employee's rights and obligations pursuant to the employment contract. In this manner, the employment contract is supplemented by the underlying rules of law and general principles of contract law, unless the parties have agreed upon something else.

505. Within this framework however, it will be decisive what the parties have agreed, for example with regard to extent of the work, working hours, etc. It must nevertheless be emphasized that the underlying legislation to a considerable extent is invariable, so that it will apply even if the parties have agreed something else, or that they may only be deviated from in favour of the employee.

§7. Staff Rules

506. Staff rules may also contain regulations which are of importance for the employment relationship. Industrial, commercial and office enterprises employing more than ten persons shall have staff rules for those employees who do not hold leading or supervisory positions (cf. the WEA section 14-16).

507. The staff rules shall contain the necessary code of conduct, rules relating to working procedures, conditions for appointment, dismissal with notice and summary dismissal, and rules relating to payment of salary.

508. At enterprises bound by a collective agreement, the employer and the elected representatives of the employees may establish staff rules by written agreement (cf. the WEA section 14-17(1)). If the enterprise is not bound by a collective agreement, the staff rules may be drafted by the employer on the basis of negotiations with the employees' representatives. However, in order to be valid, the rules must be approved by the Norwegian Labour Inspectorate (cf. section 14-17(2)).

509. The staff rules have priority after invariable statutory provisions, collective agreements and special conditions agreed upon between the employer and the individual employee. Thus, the staff rules are a relatively low-ranking source of law, which is illustrated by Rt. 1985 p. 78, where the Supreme Court did not find it necessary to consider the regulation of working hours stipulated in the staff rules, because the working hours regulation had been altered properly through regulations and managerial decisions.

§8. Common Law and Practice

510. Common law and practice will often be significant for the further content of rights and obligations in employment relationships, when nothing else has been agreed or follows from other regulations. This especially applies when existing practice is unambiguous, and has persisted for a long time. If the practice is not clear, or is based on special circumstances, it will, however, not carry the same significance.

511. On a somewhat different level is the legal development which is a result of customary practice as regards collective agreements, especially between the main labour organizations. The provisions of the collective agreements may form norms, also outside their actual scope, to the extent that they express what is common in the particular type of employment relationship. This applies in particular if the collective agreements cover a broad scope of working life and have been applicable for a long time. This is the situation for several provisions in the BA between the LO and NHO.

§9. Case Law

512. Within employment law case law is an important source of law, both with regard to areas regulated by statutory provisions, by collective agreements and as regards areas of non-statutory law. Significant rules of law are developed and defined through case law, not infrequently in such a manner that case law has led to subsequent legislation based on individual cases and results of case law.

513. An employer's obligation to offer, as far as possible, an employee who is dismissed due to curtailed operations or rationalization measures other suitable work in the enterprise, is now stated in the WEA section 15-7(2). But already on the basis of the general requirement of just cause (cf. now the WEA section 15-7(1)) the Supreme

Court held that this duty was an integral part of this requirement (cf. Rt. 1966 p. 393 (*Papyrus Paper Mill*)).

514. The further content of the regulations of the WEA regarding protection against dismissals, etc. is moreover a typical area of employment law where the significance of case law is especially apparent. The same correspondingly applies for the opportunity to make use of labour disputes, implement a boycott, etc. In the main, case law is of major significance for the further content of a number of regulations in the area of employment law, even if not to the same extent in all areas.

Chapter 7. International Private Labour Law, Conflicts of Law, Choice of Law

§1. Issues Concerning Employment Contracts Involving More Than One Country: Legal Sources

I. Introduction

515. As far as jurisdiction is concerned, it may be noted that Norway has ratified the Lugano Convention of 2007 on jurisdiction and the enforcement of judgments in civil and commercial matters, with nine appendixes. By an Act of 19 June 2009 No. 79, amending the Disputes Act (2005) the convention, with its appendixes, are implemented to the Norwegian legal system, and given status 'as law', with effect since 1 January 2010 (cf. the Disputes Act section 4-8). – The previous Lugano Convention (1988) was ratified by Norway and implemented 'as law' by an Act of 8 January 1993 No. 21.

516. It needs to be pointed out in this regard that Norway is a party to the EFTA Agreement. One may also note that the EU Court's interpretation of similar provisions pursuant to the Brussels Convention has been taken into consideration within the Norwegian case law (cf. Rt. 2002 p. 404 (*Scarabeo*), due to considerations regarding harmonization of these rules (cf. also Rt. 2004 p. 981 (*Agrimann*), where the Supreme Court stated (paragraph 22) that 'especially the practice of the EU-Court will be of importance when Norwegian courts shall decide on the interpretation of the Lugano Convention'). Further, Rt. 2011 p. 1034 (*TUI Fly*) should be mentioned; the Supreme Court simply observed (paragraph 18) that the decision of the Court of Appeal (CA) 'was built on the general legal views of the decision of the EU Court great chamber in the *Koeltzsch* case (C-29/10 of 15 March 2011)'; thus, the appeal was rejected.

517. Because Norway is not a member of the EU, the EU Regulation of the Council (EC) No. 44/2001 of 22 December 2000 on jurisdiction and the recognition and enforcement of judgments in civil and commercial matters, Norway is not legally bound by the regulation.

518. The legal questions regarding jurisdiction are dealt with in greater detail under paragraphs 471 et seq.

519. Norway does not have a general act regarding matters concerning choice of law. Because Norway is not a member of the EU, the country is not covered by the Rome Convention of 19 June 1980. Questions regarding choice of law matters therefore need to be solved by general private law principles concerning choice of law. As far as employment contracts are concerned, this implies that the actual choice of law needs to be determined by a holistic assessment on where the working relationship does have its closest ties. This is also the point of departure in the Rome Convention (cf. Articles 4(1) and 6(2)). Considerations concerning harmonization therefore imply that within

Norwegian case law there needs to be taken into account the development of the case law in the EU.

520. As regards this general view, should in particular be observed Rt. 2011 p. 1034 (*TUI Fly*); the Supreme Court referred to the decision of the EU Court great chamber in the *Koeltzsch* case (C-29/10 of 15 March 2011), which dealt with the choice of law question; observed that also the jurisdiction questions had been taken into consideration (paragraphs 16 and 18); concluding implicitly that the development of the case law in the EU would have to be of particular importance, also as regards the choice of law considerations.

521. Further, it follows of the *Koeltzsch* case – as well as of Rt. 2011 p. 1034 (*TUI Fly*) – that there may be a connection, and perhaps even an interaction, between the developments of the jurisdiction questions and the developments as regards the choice of law questions, as – in both of these aspects – the special position of the employees will have to be taken into specific consideration.

522. The legal problems related to choice of law are dealt with in greater detail under paragraphs 495 et seq.

523. In March 2002, the Brussels Convention was partly replaced by a regulation concerning rules regarding choice of law (the regulation does not yet apply in Denmark: Regulation of the Council (EC) No. 44/2001 of 22 December 2000 on jurisdiction and the recognition and enforcement of judgments in civil and commercial matters). The rules regarding individual employment contracts are stated in part 5, sections 18–21, which to a large extent are in accordance with the rules stated in the Brussels Convention. In this regard, the EU Court's practice regarding the rules pursuant to the Brussels Convention will still be of relevance. The current situation is therefore that there are two sets of rules within the EU system; the Brussels Convention in relation to Denmark and the Regulation concerning choice of law in relation to all the other EU States.

524. In the following, the legal problems concerning matters related to jurisdiction and choice of law, which is attached to individual employment relationships, will be dealt with. To some extent, these matters will also be dealt with in relation to collective agreements. The legal problems related to matters regarding public law will only be dealt with briefly.

II. The Complexity of International Labour Relationships

525. More and more often, an employment relationship may have connections to more than one single country. In such cases, it has to be decided which country's law shall apply and which country's courts and other authorities will have jurisdiction to make decisions as regards the employment relationship.

526. An employment relationship involves not just the two parties – i.e., the employer and the employee – but may also involve interests of a collective kind, such as the interests of trade unions, employer associations, and so on. Further, interests of a public nature are usually involved, such as safety regulations and social security, tax legislation, etc. Thus, questions may, as regards jurisdiction and which country's law to apply, be rather complex – and even more complex as the questions may have to be considered in a different manner, both as regards jurisdiction and applicable law, as well as interests of individual, collective or public kind in these regards.

527. Furthermore, per se, the international employment relationship may be rather complex. It may be e.g., that a company in Norway hires an employee living abroad, to carry out a particular job in Norway or in a third country, or in different countries as required by the company. Similarly, a company with the head office in a foreign country may hire an employee living in Norway to do a job in Norway or in one or more other countries. The situation can be further complicated by the company's having subsidiaries in the foreign countries in which the job is to be carried out, so that the employee will be working under the management of the subsidiary in question. In such cases, special employment contracts may even be drawn up between the employee and the individual subsidiary, in addition to the original and basic employment contract with the head office. Furthermore, the company entering into the employment contract may have joint venture agreements with other companies in different countries, and the employment contract may stipulate that the employee shall work at the other companies and perhaps even under their management.

528. As regards jurisdiction and applicable law questions, it seems necessary that this complexity of the international employment relationship be taken into consideration. Thus, it is a question e.g., whether an employment relationship to a multinational group of companies should be considered as a unity, covered by the law and jurisdiction of one specific country – or whether each assignment to different countries should be considered as independent employment relationships in this regard. Should the first question be answered in the affirmative, it may further be a question – should the group of companies have more than one company operating in the country – whether a decision against one of these companies may be given effect also against the other companies of the group, and – possibly – against the parent company.

III. The Importance of Establishing Who the Employer Is

529. It follows from the complexity of the international employment relationship that it may be difficult to decide which company is responsible – on the employer side – as regards claims and duties arising from the employment relationship. It is therefore of significant importance that the employment agreement clearly indicates, which company shall have the employer status, with the obligations deriving from that status. This is of particular importance if such responsibilities shall rest upon a company other than the company which has concluded the employment contract. Should this question not have been clarified, or perhaps even omitted, the position of the employee would be most difficult, should the employee not have the right to hold at least the company, which did conclude the contract responsible for such claims. The employee may have little or no knowledge of the relationship between the different companies involved, and cannot be expected to have such knowledge. Whether recourse may take place between the companies involved on the employer side will depend on the underlying conditions between these companies. Further should be remarked, that it may follow from the circumstances of the case, that other companies may also be held responsible.

530. The complexity on the employer side is illustrated in Rt. 1993 p. 490 (*Reksten Management*). In this case, a seaman demanded a war risk bonus from Reksten Management a/s for service aboard a ship in the Persian Gulf in 1987-88. The seaman had originally been employed with the Norwegian shipping company Viking Supply Ships. In 1986, the ship was flagged out to Panama where the owner was Offshore Support Service International Inc. That company was wholly owned by Norske Skips a/s Excelsior of Norway. The ship was hired out on a bareboat charter to Spector Shipping SA of Panama, which in turn was owned by Scan Tugs AB of Sweden. A management contract was concluded between Spector Shipping SA, Reksten Management a/s of Norway and the parent company of Reksten Management a/s, Maritime West a/s of Norway. According to this agreement, Reksten Management a/s was to be manager for the ships belonging to Spector Shipping SA, and Maritime West a/s manager for Spector Shipping SA. Between the seaman, Viking Supply Ships and Reksten Management a/s was concluded an agreement that the seaman would terminate his employment with Viking Supply Ships, but should continue his work on board the ship. However, the new employment agreement did not indicate the name of the employer. The basic question was, in the opinion of the Supreme Court, whether Reksten Management a/s had made it sufficiently clear, that (Reksten Management a/s) should not be the employer, and that the employer was to be another company, for which Reksten Management a/s acted as their authorized agent only. It was of the greatest importance that it might be difficult for the individual employee to draw definite conclusions about his employment, based on the information on the contractual relationship between the different companies. For seamen, information about the employer relationship is especially important when employment is to be concluded with a foreign employer, considering the consequences thereof as regards the enforcing of their rights. On this basis, the Supreme Court held Reksten Management a/s liable for the war risk bonus.

IV. Choice of Law and Choice of Jurisdiction Agreements: Advantages, Hesitations and Restrictions

531. The parties may have stipulated in their employment agreement that possible disputes arising from their employment relationship are to be tried by the courts of a particular country, and also, that the law of that country – or another country – shall apply. Such agreements may clarify possible uncertainties as regards the jurisdiction and choice of laws questions. Thus, the purpose of their agreement may be most legitimate.

532. However, the choice of jurisdiction question, as well as the choice of law question – especially if those questions are linked together – may imply consequences as regards the legal position of the parties, and thereby the realities of their contractual relationship. Thus, a formal equality between the parties may, in fact, have as consequence that the position of one of the parties is weakened. That may in particular be the case, should one of the parties have a weaker position than the other party, as regards negotiations on the terms of their employment agreement – which in general may be the case as far as employees are concerned. In addition, as regards choice of jurisdiction questions, interests of a public nature are also involved. Thus, as far as these questions are concerned, the freedom of the parties is not, and should not be, without limitations.

533. In general, three principles seem to apply as far as these restrictions are concerned.

534. As regards jurisdiction, the principle of forum non conveniens seems to apply, so that the possibilities of an employee to bring a case before a court should be reasonably fair, as regards claims based on the employment relationship. As regards choice of law, it seems that the law chosen must have sufficient connections to the parties or their employment relationship.

535. As regards choice of law, it must be kept in mind that the labour legislation of most countries stipulate – at least to some degree – invariable regulation in order to protect the position of the weaker party, usually the employees. The effect of such invariable regulations might be weakened considerably should a choice of law agreement lead to the result that invariable regulations would not apply. Such an effect would be contrary to the very nature of such invariable regulations. Thus the principle seems to be that – in spite of a choice of law agreement – such regulations will still apply. In other words, the position of the weaker party will be no different than it would have been without the choice of law agreement.

536. In addition, the principle of *l'ordre public* will apply, e.g., the jurisdiction as regards the legality of industrial actions, such as strikes, lock-outs, etc.

537. Regulation of the right to a labour dispute – *inter alia* strikes and lockouts – touches on essential public interests as well as the interests of the respective employer's association and labour union and their members. The legality of a labour dispute in Norway would therefore have to be decided according to Norwegian law, regardless of what the parties have agreed on (cf. the principle of *l'ordre public*).

538. On the other hand, this question need not be decided by a Norwegian court, e.g., the Norwegian Labour Court. There is no reason to assume the parties could not agree to settle the matter in a foreign court, although the foreign court would then have to decide the matter according to Norwegian law. The public interests do not apply with the same force when it comes to interpreting a wage agreement. It must therefore be assumed that the parties may agree to settle the matter of interpretation in a foreign court and according to foreign law.

539. It is thus in order to point to the principle of *l'ordre public*. The Norwegian Supreme Court has in several cases, in which the rules concerning choice of law points to the foreign legislation based the application on Norwegian legislation by using the principle of *l'ordre public*. This principle, as a point of departure, does however not reach any further than establishing that foreign legislation does not apply in the individual situation. It does not follow from this that the Norwegian legislation will apply. In addition, it is generally agreed on the fact that the courts shall be rather careful when applying the principle. Therefore, it is not given that the principle can be used in order to state the reasons for excluding foreign rules regarding the use of industrial action. Which rules shall apply must therefore be determined pursuant to the rules of international private law.

540. As a point of departure, one may assume that some rules pursuant to the LDA are internationally mandatory, in the sense that some nationally mandatory rules are regarded as so important that they are given international impact. Views in the same direction is somewhat implied in ARD 1995 p. 214, and in foreign and later Norwegian literature. This way of dealing with this legal problem also complies with the system within the Rome Convention (cf. Article 7), and in that way also with the legal situation in Europe in general.

541. In ARD 1995 p. 214, the Labour Court declared that it agreed with the parties as to 'the mandatory rules regarding arbitration etc. pursuant to the Labour Disputes Act' must be assumed to apply in the relationship between the parties. On the other hand, this question will not necessarily have to be determined by a Norwegian court of justice, e.g., the Norwegian Labour Court. There is hardly any reason to assume that the parties should not have the possibility to agree on the question being determined by a foreign court of justice. The foreign court of justice would, nevertheless, have to determine the question on the basis of Norwegian legislation. The public interest does not manifest itself with the same strength when dealing with the question on interpretation of a collective agreement. Therefore, one needs to assume that the parties may enter into an agreement stating that a question regarding the interpretation shall be determined by a foreign court of justice, and on the basis of foreign legislation.

542. The Norwegian Labour Court, ARD 1993 p. 11, has dealt with the question whether the legality of notified termination of employments, required before a strike may take place, was to be dealt with by the Swedish Labour Court and according to Swedish law, as stipulated in the collective agreement. The Norwegian Labour Court found that this question could be settled by the Norwegian Labour Court, and in accordance with Norwegian law, taking into account, *inter alia*, that 'it follows of a natural understanding that...the legality of such a notice of termination should be dealt with by the Norwegian Labour Court, as it concerns Norwegian employees whose employment is connected with Norway and who are organized in a Norwegian trade union'. However, this decision can hardly be said to be built on the opinion that questions concerning the legality of the use of strikes, lock outs, etc. necessarily must be dealt with by a Norwegian court. The decision on the case stipulated the reservation that the dispute could be dealt with by a Norwegian court, should the question be raised whether the application of Swedish law would be contrary to indispensable Norwegian law. On the other hand, the decision was built on the view that Norwegian law on the obligation of the parties to maintain peace during the period of the collective agreement (cf. LDA (1927) section 6, now LDA section 8), was indispensable also as regards the choice of law. Thus, the decision seems to be based on the view that a foreign court will have to apply Norwegian law, as regards this question. The Labour Court also remarked that Swedish law was not completely in accordance with Norwegian law. Finally, the Labour Court stated that the interpretation of the collective agreement was to be dealt with by the Swedish Labour Court. The decision implies that the provisions of the collective agreement on jurisdiction and choice of law were considered valid.

V. Jurisdiction and Choice of Law as Regards Legislation of a Public Nature

543. In general, legislation based on interests of a public nature are limited to the territory of the country and – depending on the law of the country – to the territorial waters, continental shelf, economic zones, ships registered in the country, and so on. Thus, the safety regulations based on Norwegian laws, such as the WEA, the Ship Safety Act etc., do not apply to work carried out in a foreign country, nor the territorial waters of such a country. Similarly, foreign legislation of public nature does not apply to work carried out in Norway, and the Norwegian public authorities may choose not to apply such legislation. However, otherwise may be stipulated in special legislation, which again may be based on a treaty between two or more countries, e.g., on mutual cooperation between the states and the public authorities involved as regards safety regulations at workplaces. Further, it may be stipulated in an employment agreement that the safety regulations of a certain country shall apply when work is carried out in a foreign country. The parties may e.g., not be sure whether the legislation of a foreign country is fully satisfactory, and prefer to stipulate the level of safety at work in their agreement. In such cases, the safety legislation of the country chosen by the parties has a contractual basis. Thus, it may be a breach of the contract should the standards of the chosen legislation not be followed, which again may e.g., justify employees not carrying out their work until the situation has been rectified.

544. Unless otherwise stipulated in the legislation of the country where the work is carried out, the authorities of that country must, however, apply the legislation of that country, regardless of what may be stipulated in the employment contract between the employer and the employee. Thus, the safety standard of their contract will in practice usually imply that – between the parties – a higher safety standard shall apply. Whether the public authorities of that country may contribute to the effect that such a higher standard be applied – through inspection, decisions, etc. – will depend on the legislation of that country.

§2. Jurisdiction of Norwegian Courts

545. According to the Disputes Act of 17 June 2005 No. 90 section 4-3, disputes in international matters may only be brought before the Norwegian courts if the facts of the case have a sufficiently strong connection to Norway.

546. If no venue can be established pursuant to section 4-4 (i.e., provisions concerning ordinary venue) and 4-5 (i.e., provisions concerning venues which may be elected by the claimant) of the present Act but the case is still subject to Norwegian jurisdiction, an action may be filed with the Oslo District Court (cf. the second subsection of section 4-3).

547. In order for Norwegian courts to try a case, the facts of the case must imply that the case has sufficient attachment to Norwegian conditions. However, the requirement of sufficient attachment to Norwegian conditions may vary from one branch of law to another. In labour jurisprudence, the requirement of sufficient attachment to Norwegian conditions is apparently fulfilled if the place of work – the place where, according to the employment contract, the employee will usually be carrying out his or her work – lies in Norway. A work place aboard ships registered with the Norwegian Domestic Ship Register or the Norwegian International Ship Register (NIS) will have the same standing as the above.

548. However, exceptions must supposedly be made for cases in which the work in Norway is of a purely temporary and casual nature (cf. the Disputes Act (2005) section 4-5(4) and the Lugano Convention Article 19). Should a group of travelling repairmen, employed with a foreign shipyard, work a few days on board a Norwegian ship, the attachment to Norwegian conditions will be of a very brief nature, and Norwegian courts will usually not be considered to have jurisdiction to decide a dispute arising from the employment relationship between the travelling repairmen and their foreign employer. This applies, unless a dispute may be established within the frames that follow from the Regulation of 16 December 2005 No. 1566 on employees which are sent abroad (cf. section 4). A statement in Rt. 1978 p. 1547, where a lawsuit regarding an employment contract was dismissed, may in this regard be observed. The Supreme Court observed, *inter alia*, that the case 'did not have any attachments to Norwegian conditions beyond the fact that it regards an employment relationship on the Norwegian continental shelf. Both the plaintiff and the defendant are foreigners, and have their home jurisdiction abroad'.

549. As regards seamen, claims following their employment on board the ship – e.g., as regards wages etc. – are usually secured by maritime lien, which may justify arrest of the ship; thus, the Maritime Act (1994) section 73 (cf. the Dispute Act (2005) section 4-5(5)), stipulate that the Norwegian courts will have jurisdiction where the ship is in a Norwegian port.

550. As regards migrant workers it should be observed that Norwegian courts to a certain degree may have jurisdiction (cf. regulations of 16 December 2005, No. 1566, section 4).

551. The fact that the employee resides or has an address in Norway will per se hardly constitute sufficient attachment, but when other factors are also involved, the case might have sufficient attachment to Norwegian conditions:

- The employee's residence is, on the other hand, pursuant to the Act of 12 June 1987 No. 48 related to the NIS, section 6, sufficient in order for a sailor/seaman to file a case against the shipping company 'by a court of justice in the country in which the employee has his or her residence'. Whether such a case may be filed by the court concerned depends, on the other hand, on the procedural rules pursuant to the country's own legislation. The Norwegian provision is established in connection to the special condition which apply in employment relationships on board such ships, and with regard to the principle on forum non conveniens (cf. the *travaux préparatoires* to the Act mentioned above (Ot.prp.nr.45 (1986-1987) p. 23)); 'the seaman would, if other principles applied, be without the possibility to get a claim against the employer tried before a court of justice, if the employee is located in a distant country'.
- Illustrative is also Rt. 1936 page 900, where an English shipping company, with a ship registered in England, signed on a number of Norwegian fishermen for Greenland fishing during the 1934 season. The fishermen were signed on in Norway with contracts written in Norwegian. They were signed on by the local English consul and the Norwegian shipping officer while the ship lay in port in the Norwegian town Aalesund. A contract in English was then also signed by the fishermen, but that was not to replace the previously established individual

contracts, which remained the basis of the legal relations between the parties. Besides the fishermen, the dory masters, fishery workers, dory foremen, fishery master and expedition leader were also Norwegian. A dispute arose between the fishermen and the shipping company, resulting in a cessation of the fishing activity. Later, the shipowners filed for damages against the fishermen. The city court found that the case could be tried because of its many attachments to Norway (Nordic Maritime Law Reports (NDS) 1935 p. 33 Bergen), which the Supreme Court implicitly agreed to. As mentioned above, it follows from the general venue principles that the case could be brought against the Norwegian fishermen – provided that the case had sufficient attachment to Norwegian conditions, as stated by the city court in its arguments (cf. today the Disputes Act (2005) section 4-3(1) and (2); previously the Civil Procedure Act (1915) sections 17 and 18).

- RG 1984 p. 139 (Gulating Court of Appeal) may also be mentioned. A British citizen who had been hired in Britain, wages paid by the English company, carried out work in Norway as an engineer for a period of three years, possibly five years. The engineer, who had been given notice of termination, claimed that the dismissal was unfair, as well as the right to continue in his or her position while the case was processed before the court (cf. now WEA section 15-11, previously WEA (1977) section 61(4)). The decision seems to be based on the fact that the employer had a permanent representative in Norway. The Court, referring, not quite aptly, to the Civil Procedure Act section 28 (cf. now the Disputes Act section 4-4(4)), stated – rightly – that the case would have to be tried in Norway 'regardless of which country's material law that would be applied'.

552. When it follows from the employment contract that the employee is obliged to carry out work in different countries, and thus has an international obligation to move, the question arises as to whether legal action regarding employment relations can be instituted in Norway if the employee has worked there for a non-temporary period. It seems obvious that the case should be based on the fact that working in Norway to such an extent constitutes sufficient attachment to Norwegian conditions, and that legal action should be allowable in Norway. It may also be important to the employee to have access to take legal action in Norway rather than having to file suit in, say, a remote country. The employer will generally be better equipped to overcome any disadvantage this might entail, compared with the disadvantages the employee would generally suffer in having to bring a case before a foreign court:

- Rt. 1989 p. 231 is in this context significant. Here, the Supreme Court found that an employee's obligation to carry out work in different countries, in accordance with the employment contract with an international group of companies, could be decided by Norwegian courts. The dismissal issue was previously settled in earlier rulings, (cf. Rt. 1988 p. 476 (NAD 1988 p. 586), and the corresponding case and parallel ruling by the Interlocutory Appeals Committee of the Supreme Court (NAD 1988 p. 696) (cf. also Rt. 1987 p. 1412 (NAD 1987 p. 953)). The case concerned an American citizen who in 1982 was employed as a geologist with an American oil company with its head office in Houston, Texas, USA. In March 1982, he was transferred to London, and in September 1985, he was transferred again to the company's division in Stavanger, Norway. In October 1986, he was informed that he was to be transferred back to Houston. The employee claimed that this constituted a dismissal and brought action against the oil company's Norwegian subsidiary, claiming damages and that the dismissal be ruled invalid. The CA found that the action should be allowed because the Norwegian subsidiary was the formal employer. The employment was not temporary, and the job protection rights pursuant to the rules of the Working Environment Act are perceptive. The Interlocutory Appeals Committee of the Supreme Court set aside this ruling (cf. Rt. 1987 p. 1412 (NAD 1987 p. 953) in that the CA had not taken a stand as to whether the company's decision to transfer could be considered as a resignation or dismissal pursuant to the rules of the WEA. In a new hearing before the Court of Appeal, the court found that an employment relationship did exist between the geologist and the parent company in the USA and the Norwegian subsidiary, with an extensive international obligation to move. In other words, it was neither a resignation nor a dismissal, and the case had to be dismissed by the City Court, which at that time could act in its capacity as a local labour court. The Interlocutory Appeals Committee came to the same conclusion (cf. Rt. 1988 p. 476 (NAD1988 p. 586)). In the hearing of the material issue (cf. Rt. 1989 p. 231), the Supreme Court agreed that the Norwegian subsidiary was rightly sued, and that the rules of the WEA applied.

- Also, the decision in Rt. 1985 p. 1319 (NAD 1984-85 p. 782) is based on the fact that legal action in such cases might be institutable in Norway. Two British citizens had entered into employment contracts with a British multinational company. The employees would be working at the company's various foreign divisions pursuant to instructions by the company, and the employments were to be regulated by British law. Separate employment contracts were drawn up in Norway. When the employees later received dismissal notices, they brought action pursuant to the rules of the WEA, demanding to continue in their jobs. The city court dismissed the case; but was overruled by the Court appeal and the Supreme Court; one could depart from the law only in the event of a short-term employment in Norway.
- Additional reference is the ruling by the Stavanger City Court of 27 November 1987 (NAD 1987 p. 1051). Five British citizens living in Great Britain had worked on the Norwegian continental shelf pursuant to an employment contract with the British parent company. The English parent company terminated the employment contracts for the Norwegian subsidiary as well as for the parent company itself. The city court found that the employment contracts regulated the employments during the work in Norway. The subsidiary would have to be deemed the real employer of the employees regarding work on the Statfjord Field.
- The Gulating Court of Appeal's ruling of 5 July 1988 (NAD 1988 p. 837) has a different tendency. An American citizen had taken action against the Norwegian subsidiary of an American parent company, claiming damages for unfair dismissal. The subsidiary ran its operations from Stavanger and the plaintiff had worked for more than two years in Norway before he was ordered to be transferred from the American parent company. The city court dismissed the case. The court stated that: 'It is assumed that such a dispute, which concerns the understanding and scope of the main contract, must be judged according to American law and decided

by American courts. It has no connection with Norwegian conditions or Norwegian working-environment law.'

553. When an obligation to work internationally is incumbent on the employee, a further issue arises in respect of the Dispute Act (2005) section 4-5(4) (cf. also the Lugano Convention, Article 19(2)a, whether work in Norway – for a non-short-term period – can be deemed 'the place where the employee usually carries out his or her work').

554. In such cases, it may be argued that the entire employment should be considered as a whole, and thus – should the employee have worked for two or three years in each of the different countries – that none of these countries are the place where the work is usually carried out. Should this interpretation apply, a lawsuit would have to be instituted in the country where the place of business is located, from which the employee was employed. The provision that stipulates that legal actions must be instituted in the country where the place of business is located and from which the employee was employed, has a solid argument in respect of work which is carried out for a short-term period in the country in question. The longer the employee works in the country, the stronger becomes the attachment to that country. Consequently, it can also be claimed – on most solid grounds that when the employment in a country lasts longer than a short-term period – that the country should, in this connection, be deemed the country in which the work is usually carried out, although the work period in the country must be considered temporary in respect of the employment as a whole, and the court practice seems to be based on the latter view.

555. In the Supreme Court case Rt. 2002 p. 404, a drilling manager was hired to work on moveable drilling rigs. The drilling manager was a British citizen and had his residence in Scotland. He was employed with a Swiss company (*Saipem Services AG*), which was run by the Italian Saipem SpA. Saipem Services was a subsidiary company to Saipem SpA. The companies had a mutual branch in Stavanger. The drilling manager was hired on the drilling rig called 'Scarabeo 6' from December 1997. The employment contract contained provisions regarding the employee's obligation to move whenever needed. On 16 March 2001, he was informed that he was about to be transferred to another working location, abroad. His wages pursuant to the Norwegian employment contract would consequently stop from 21 March 2001. The drilling manager would not accept the wage-stop. The Supreme Court found that the provision pursuant to the employment contract regarding the jurisdiction, which was stipulated to be in Zurich, had to be put aside, due to the fact that the contract was entered into before the dispute had commenced (cf. the Lugano Convention (1988) Article 17 No. 5).

556. Another case worth mentioning is the Gulating CA of 16 May 2002. A project manager was hired in June 1999 in a shipbroker company in Bergen. He commuted from June 1999 to April 2000 between Bergen and Houston, where the shipbroker company's registered company was situated. The court found that the stay in Houston was of a temporary nature, and that the company in Bergen was stated as the employer on the employee's working visa in the USA. He was, during his stay in Houston, still formally employed with the company in Norway, and the management in the head office in Bergen had both formal and actual influence in regard of important decisions related to his employment contract.

557. Especially, as regards employees working in an international airline, should be mentioned Rt. 2011 p. 1034 (*Tui Air*), where a pilot, working for a Swedish airline with a branch at Oslo airport (Norway) was given notice of termination because of loss of license caused by illness. He had Oslo airport as his station, with ID card, checked in and out, carried out necessary work on the ground, checked weather information, took necessary telephones etc. The CA held that Oslo airport mainly was his in- and out-checking place and thus the basis for his activities. The airline could thus be sued in Norway. The decision was concurred with by the Supreme Court, *inter alia* with reference to the *Koelizch* case (C-29/10) (cf. paragraph 465 above).

558. Similarly, the Supreme Court decision of 17 June 2014 *(Ryanair 2)* and Rt. 2013 p. 1589 (Ryanair) should be observed concluding that the Irish airline could be sued in Norway by a cabin service agent, an Italian citizen who claimed that she was entitled to a permanent employment contract with Ryanair. Her employment had been terminated because she was still in the probationary period of one year according to her contract: while in Norway, a probationary period may not exceed six months (cf. the WEA section 15-6). She was contractually and mainly located at Rygge Airport (Norway) and had to live no more than one-hour travelling time from the airport. She had not performed any other work of a significant character, in any other states. The majority of her work was performed during flights, but she returned to Rygge Airport, which was considered the main base for the employment relationship. Rygge Airport was therefore considered to be place that she habitually carried out her work, cf. the Lugano Convention Article 19 No. 2 a).

559. The Borgarting CA decision 21 December 2011 (*Ryanair 1*) may also be mentioned, where a 'cabin services agent', Hungarian citizen, since 2008 had worked at the Hahn airport at Frankfurt (Germany); worked since January 2010 at Rygge airport (Norway) as 'base supervisor'; that assignment was limited in time until 1 October 2010; received notice of termination on 25 October 2010 with wages for two more weeks. The CA held, that the airline could be sued in Norway; as Rygge airport was the centre of his activities; he received all instructions at Rygge, started and ended his journeys there, and the aircrafts of the airline were stationed there. Further, the employment contract stated that he had an obligation to live within a distance from the airport of one hour, and some of his activities had to be carried out on the ground.

560. The jurisdiction of Norwegian courts can also be limited by rules of international law (cf. section 1-2 of the Disputes Act, where this is explicitly stated). Thus, Norwegian courts can scarcely try issues regarding the legality of foreign management decisions, or public officers' legal status in respect of a foreign state. Similarly, legal actions may be dismissed because of the immunity of the public servant by virtue of international law, or by a special provision pursuant to a convention:

- As an illustration Rt. 2004 p. 402 may be mentioned. A local chauffeur hired by the South-African embassy in Oslo, filed a case against the South-African state before the Oslo City Court, claiming the dismissal from his post to be found invalid. All the courts rejected the filed case. The Supreme Court stated in its reasons that the activities run by a foreign country's embassy lies within the core of a states' exercise of its authority, and therefore there need to be evident limitations as far as regards the recipient country's right to exercise its jurisdiction in cases concerning hiring and dismissing of embassy personnel. There had evidently been a development from an almost absolute rule on immunity to a restrictive theory on immunity. Due to lack of more detailed legislation on the question concerned, it had to be established that a distinction existed between acts characterized by exercise of authority, and acts of a more private law nature. A judgment stating that the dismissal was to be regarded as invalid, with the right for the employee to re-enter into the contract of employment, would be incompatible with the general principals regarding state immunity, pursuant to international law.

- Legal proceedings instituted by an Italian citizen employed with the Italian Institute of Cultural Affairs in Oslo regarding termination of employment pursuant to a ruling by an Italian court, were disallowed in a ruling by the Oslo City Court of 27 May 1983 (NAD 1981-83 p. 634). The Institute had to be considered a department of the Italian embassy and thus protected by immunity through international law. The Institute of Culture had some income from Italian language courses and from translating textbooks and literature, to the amount of roughly NOK 50,000 a year. The city court found that this did not entail that the Italian state was thereby operating a business activity in Norway. It did not concern business activity for financial purposes and with an eye to financial gain. One had to consider the Institute's cultural activity as a whole, and the income was insignificant in this respect. The Institute of Cultural Affairs was thus conducting an activity under international law from the side of the Italian state.

561. Both of the judgments mentioned above relate to employees hired by an embassy. The legal situation is presumably the same when it comes to employees within the military services:

- Furthermore, one may note the dismissal ruling by the Eidsivating High Court 29 May 1989 (*Kayiambakis v. the United States of America*) regarding proceedings following dismissal from employment with the US Element/ Department of the Air Force at Oesteraas outside Oslo. The plaintiff was employed in a civilian job as shop assistant in the US Element shop which carried duty-free items reserved for personnel with duty-free privileges. The court found that international law immunity does not apply when the matter concerns a foreign country's business activity in another country. However, the business operated by the US Element had to be considered a support measure for the international law activity in which the USA participated through the Allied Forces Northern Europe within the framework of the NATO treaties.
- Likewise, Norwegian personnel within the military services – e.g., under international operations – would not be able to file a lawsuit against the Norwegian state before a foreign court of justice regarding their working relationship. Such a lawsuit would need to be raised before a Norwegian court of justice.

§3. Choice of Law

I. The Employment's Closest Ties

562. Principally, the choice of national law with respect to multinational employment should be founded on a holistic evaluation of where the employment has its closest ties. This general basis in Norwegian international private law was originally formulated by the Supreme Court in Rt. 1923 II p. 58 (the *Irma-Mignon* case) in a case concerning choice of law in a ship collision. There is apparent general agreement on the theory that this general principle is also applicable with regard to individual employment contracts. It is especially significant that also the EC Convention of 19 June 1980, relating to choice of law in respect of contractual obligations, is based on this general principle (cf. Article 4(1)), and renders said principle applicable to individual employment contracts (cf. Article 6(2)).

II. No Single Criterion Decisive

563. Since the choice of law must be made on the basis of a holistic evaluation of where the employment has its closest ties, it cannot be decided on the basis of a single criterion such as residence, nationality, the place where the employment contract was entered into, place of work, language of the employment contract, the parties' conduct during the period of employment, the parties' more or less stated assumptions as to choice of law, etc. However, these factors will be included as criteria in the holistic evaluation, which raises the question of how much weight to assign each factor. Here, however, the emphasis will vary according to whether an employment contract has been entered into, whether the formal requirements have been fulfilled, the content and interpretation of the employment contract, and compliance with the employment contract. Furthermore, factors regarding invariable rules of law will raise particular difficulties.

564. On these complex issues, which concern the relationship to the laws of other countries, the logical thing is to give special consideration to how the issues are treated internationally. Major emphasis should therefore be placed on the rules set forth in the EC Convention of 1980 (cf. also the paragraph 466 above), taking additionally into account that the legal picture with regard to Norwegian international private law in the context of labour law, must be considered sparse, among other things because these issues have been treated by Norwegian courts in only a modest number of cases.

III. Objective and Subjective Factors

565. An employment's ties to a particular country will follow in part from the parties' affiliation with the country in question, through residence, citizenship, place of registry, etc., and in part from factors such as that the work is carried out and/or administrated from the country. These factors may be characterized as objective, and have the litigious benefit of lending themselves to objective stipulation. In addition, rules of public law – in practice, particularly rules related to place of work – might be so comprehensive and thorough as to appreciably influence the employment, and hence should be stressed when choosing which private law to apply. However, the parties might additionally have more subjective attachment to the country, e.g., because they feel more attached to that country for various reasons. These subjective bonds may be more difficult to demonstrate legally – the parties might also have different interpretations – and their interpretation might contradict the objective factors. Consequently, basing the choice of law on objective circumstances or on subjective factors becomes an essential issue.

IV. Agreements on Choice of Law

566. The importance of the parties' assumptions regarding choice of law depends on the parties' right to enter into an agreement on choice of law. In other words, if the parties have full access to enter into an agreement on choice of law, then there is also reason to stress their assumptions expressed more or less in that respect. One may then say that the choice of law is based on the principle of litigant autonomy, which makes it logical to stress the parties' hypothetical wishes. And if the parties have little or no access to enter into an agreement on choice of law, then there is much less reason to place emphasis on their assumptions. The principle of litigant autonomy is then weakened correspondingly.

567. It is basically apparent, then, that the litigants do not have an unlimited right to enter into an agreement on which country's law to apply with regard to an employment contract. Consideration of the employee must supposedly entail that the employment must be reasonably attached to the country of the law chosen:

- An arbitration case can also be understood as implicitly entailing an agreement on choice of law. In this connection, we may note the judgment by the Interlocutory Appeals Committee of the Supreme Court recorded in Rt. 1980 p. 886, where the employment contract stipulated that any dispute should be settled by the courts in Texas, USA. Actions before Norwegian courts were therefore denied, because there was no 'basis for dismissing the clause in a case such as this'. There are judgments by the lower courts and other information not referred to in the Supreme Court Reports, such as the fact that the employment contract had been entered into with an American citizen while that employee was working in Wyoming. The employee came from the USA to work on the Norwegian continental shelf, and the employment contract was entered into for a limited period of eighteen months. The company's head office was in Texas, while the subsidiary was registered in Bermuda. These facts seems to imply that the employment had a reasonable attachment to Texas.
- The Sandefjord City Court judgment of 12 November 1992 (unpublished) (case No. 91/482A, *McClurev.Ross Drilling Co. a/s*), may also be noted; an American citizen who had lived in Norway for more than ten years was employed in June 1991 as a tool pusher/assistant tool pusher at Ross Drilling Co. a/s, Sandefjord,

to work aboard the British-registered oil rig *Sovereign Explorer*. The owner of the oil rig was an English company: Scotdril Offshore Company. According to the operating agreement between Scotdril Offshore Company and Ross Offshore a/s, Ross Offshore a/s was to procure assignments for the rig, provide the crew and operate it on the account of Scotdril Offshore Company. Ross Drilling Co. a/s was a subsidiary of Ross Offshore a/s with the sole function of employing a crew and hiring out the crew to Ross Offshore a/s. Shortly after his employment, the tool pusher was given notice, and he brought action for unfair dismissal against Ross Drilling Co. a/s before Sandefjord City Court, referring to the fact that the employment contract stipulated, among other things: 'All legal matters in connection with the employment shall be settled on the basis of Norwegian law. The parties accept Sandefjord as the appropriate venue.' The City Court deemed itself competent by virtue of the agreement on venue and of section 36 of the Civil Procedure Act 1915 (the provision is now to be found in the current Dispute Act 2005 section 4-5), and the fact that there was no objection regarding the City Court's jurisdiction. The validity of the agreement on choice of law had to be settled according to Norwegian and not British rules, and on the basis of a holistic evaluation. The City Court stressed the fact that everyone involved had the strongest ties to Norway: the employment contract was signed in Norway and concerned exploration drilling on the Norwegian continental shelf, with an employer – both parent company and subsidiary – registered in Norway, and with an employee with a longstanding domicile in Norway, although he was an American citizen. The parties had also agreed that Norwegian law should be applied. The only affiliation with Great Britain was that the oil rig was registered in Britain, and it would be 'highly irregular for a rig manned by the defendant to be regulated by national laws other than those regulating the three other' Norwegian-registered rigs owned and operated by Ross Offshore a/s. In the total assessment, one also had to take into account the fact that the employee's protection from dismissal was weaker according to British than Norwegian law.

568. Also, according to Article 6(1) and (2) of the EC Convention (1980), the principle of litigant autonomy is departed from with regard to individual employment contracts, since an agreement on choice of law cannot deprive the employee of the protection following from the invariable rules of the country's law that are applied in lieu of an agreement on choice of law. If it is found that the employment is most closely related to Norway, the employee may, according to this provision, apply the invariable Norwegian rules on e.g., dismissal protection, validity of an agreed competition clause and validity of an agreement limiting the employment to a specific period, right to overtime pay and to special remuneration for work on 1 and 17 May, right to holiday and holiday pay, etc., unless the Norwegian rules must be interpreted restrictively, e.g., so that they do not apply to work conducted outside Norwegian borders. Although application of Norwegian rules is not mandatory, the rules may nevertheless apply if the employment contract is to be interpreted as meaning that the parties have assumed that these rules will apply.

569. Against this background, it should probably be concluded that the above objective circumstances be given more emphasis than the parties' subjective relations.

V. Considerations Behind the Connecting Factors

570. It would be appropriate to take a closer look at the considerations favouring emphasis on the individual factors that apply when determining the country to which the employment is most closely connected.

A. Place of Contract

571. It would appear logical to first consider the place where the contract was entered into – the place of contract – when also other factors point in the same direction. In part, it may be somewhat incidental whether the contract was closed in one country or the other; the same concerns the country where e.g., the letter of appointment is drawn up, or the signing on or enrolment has taken place. Nor is the place of contract a particularly guiding factor when the contract is entered into through correspondence between persons who happen to be in different countries. Per se, the language in which the contract is drawn up is also apparently a factor of less importance, although it may become significant if other factors point in the same direction.

B. Citizenship

572. By itself, the parties' citizenship will often be a relatively peripheral element compared with others that weigh more heavily with respect to the employment. Moreover, an employer might have employees with different citizenships, and it would readily create an unmanageable or confused situation if employees working at the same place were to have their employment regulated according to the laws of different countries. The citizenship factor becomes somewhat stronger if both the employer and employee have the same citizenship, but this component is still so peripheral to the employment relationship that it can hardly be given any emphasis worth mentioning.

C. Domicile

573. The parties' domicile (residence), on the other hand, is a factor which should be given significance, particularly because the parties will generally have a stronger economic and other attachment to the domicile country than the countries of which they are a citizen. If the parties have their domicile in the same country, it will be significant if they entered into the employment contract under the condition that the law of the domicile country shall apply. This is particularly applicable when the parties have little or limited knowledge of the rules of law of the country in which the work is to be carried out.

574. If the parties have their domicile in different countries, the logical thing would be to place considerably greater emphasis on the employer's domicile than on that of the employee, because the employer may have employees with domiciles in different countries and hence it would create an unmanageable or confusing situation, and hence inconvenience, if employees working at the same workplace were to have their employment regulated according to the laws of different countries. Placing the emphasis on the employer's domicile simplifies matters. In addition, the employer's functions and decisions relating to these functions will normally be made by the employer or his or her representatives at the employer's domicile. Such decisions will normally touch on key issues throughout the employment period, not only the employment contracts signing and termination through notice or dismissal, but also the continuous control, management and apportionment of the actual work, including decisions to alter or shut down operations. These factors make the employer's domicile a factor of far greater importance than the domicile of the employees. If, however, the employee is working in the country of his or her own domicile, then the employment must be deemed to have closer ties to said country.

575. Should the citizenship or domicile be changed, the employment linkage at the time of entering into the employment contract must basically be given the greatest importance. Normally, change of citizenship will not be rendered any importance worth mentioning. However, for practical reasons the employee might move to the place of work as part of fulfilling the employment contract. If this results in a permanent arrangement, not only a temporary stay, the importance of the original domicile will diminish.

576. Also significant is where the employer's operations shall be considered to have their domicile, especially if the enterprise is organized with a parent company and subsidiary registered in different countries, or if the enterprise has its head office in one country and branch offices or division offices in other countries. In choosing law with regard to individual employment contracts, one should supposedly emphasize the place where the enterprise exercises its central employer functions. One should also consider whether the contract is entered into with the parent company or subsidiary, or with the head office or branch office. Furthermore, one should stress whether the parent company or head office has been directly involved in the execution of the work through somewhat frequent contact with the employees or through other control measures, whether it has taken part in managing the work, taken a stand on various personnel issues such as e.g., training, leave of absence, holiday scheduling, etc., or if these functions have essentially been delegated to the subsidiary or branch office, so that the activity of the parent company or head office at that time has been confined to more general guidelines and directives. However, this is only a point of departure, and the employer-domicile factor can be enhanced or weakened by other factors such as contract place, employees' domicile, work place, duration of the employment, etc.

577. If the employment contract stipulates that the employee will be working in different countries, separate employment contracts might be drawn up for the job that is to be executed in each country. For example, the employment contract may have been signed with the parent company in an international group of companies obliging the employee to work at the group's various subsidiaries in other countries as stipulated by the parent company. In such cases, an employment contract might also be drawn up with the subsidiary in question for the period during which the employee will be working in the country where the subsidiary has its operations. By itself, such a special employment contract has little significance in respect of the question of where the employment has its strongest ties, e.g., when the employment contract is drawn up in consideration of the requirements of public authorities in the country in question. But the special employment contract can be an indication that the subsidiary is the body exercising the employer functions during the period the employee is working there, and this is a factor which reinforces the connection to said country.

D. *Significance of the Work Place*

578. One of the most important questions concerns the significance to be attached to the work place. Choosing the law of the country where the work is performed has the advantage that one can apply the same country's rules of public and private law relating to the employment. In that case, it will not be necessary to decide whether a rule comes under private or public law and – perhaps equally important – the rules of public law may have influenced those of private law in that country. In addition, labour legislation is largely compulsory, based on a desire to protect employees, in which case one cannot assign too much importance to the parties' wishes and assumptions. Doing so would indirectly constitute acknowledgement of a certain dispositional freedom in that field. Finally, it is significant that Article 6(2) letter (a) of the EC Convention 1980 presumes the law of the country in which the employee carries out his or her work. On that background, certainly the work place must be assigned considerable importance when evaluating where the employment has its closest ties.

579. As with weighting other components, the significance of the work place will increase if other factors point in the same direction, for example when the employer's domicile is situated in the country in which the work is carried out, while it will be weakened if other factors point in a different direction. If the employment contract is entered into in the parties' common domicile country, this, too, will have a bearing on the degree to which the employee has maintained his or her connection to his or her home country while performing the work in another country. This is particularly valid when the employment contract states that the connection with the home country will be maintained; the employee must, e.g., travel to the home country to discuss questions regarding work execution with the employer, or has a right to travel home during holidays, etc.

580. The connection following from the work place will also vary, depending on whether it is a short-term engagement in the country in question, e.g., if the employee is going to do one or more short-term assignments in the country or long-term work in the country. The real considerations behind the presumption regarding the law of the country of work become particularly applicable in long-term employment. Since the other factors may apply with lesser or greater force, and must be ascribed differential importance, no definite limit can be drawn as determining when an employment must be deemed to be of a short-term or long-term nature. As far as it goes, the basis must be what the parties have agreed concerning the duration of the employment, and not how long the employment has actually proved to last, or for how long the employee actually carried out the work. If the employment was originally agreed for a short period – e.g., two years – but later extended by one or two years, there may be reason also to consider whether the extension is made in the interest of the employer or the employee. An extension due to the employer's willingness to oblige the employee's special wishes to remain in a country, should therefore be given less importance as a connecting factor than when the extension is due to the employer's need to continue to have the employee in his or her employ in the said country. If nothing is agreed upon, as to the duration of the employment, it must be deemed to have lasted until notice is given, and the judgment would ostensibly have to be based on whether the parties originally intended a long-term or short-term employment.

581. However, a rule on the law of the work place is of little help if the work is to be carried out in different countries at the employer's choice, or according to an established rotation schedule or similar arrangement. The same may also be the case if the work is actually carried out in different countries even though it was not agreed in advance between the parties, but agreed from one time to the next. Furthermore, the connection to the country in question may be less for special employment than for regular employment; for example, if the employment entails that the employee must work in relatively isolated groups of persons on e.g., artificial islands, oil platforms, research or fishing stations in remote places, etc.

582. Against this background, one must assume that even when the work is to be carried out, and is indeed carried out, in a particular country, the relationship between the parties may be of such a nature that it would be illogical to apply the law of said country. For example, if a Norwegian enterprise employed an engineer living in Norway to supervise a construction project in a remote country for a five-year period as decided on a running basis by the enterprise in Norway, applying that country's labour law – with which perhaps neither the employer nor the employee were familiar – could hardly be deemed the most natural solution. Consequently, the work place (country) – especially in long-term employment – will be an important factor in the choice of law, but should hardly be considered decisive by itself, or assigned too much importance. True, caution must be exercised so as not to give too much consideration to the parties' subjective assumptions and circumstances, which is not to say that one should arrive at the opposite extreme by lending too much significance to the work place as the most objective connecting factor. Here, as in general, one must try to reach some sort of balance between the various factors, rendering importance also to the parties' more subjective factors.

583. There is hardly any reason to distinguish between a high-ranking and low-ranking job in this respect. The protection factor is probably stronger with regard to employees of lower than those of higher rank, but it is not given that the law of the work place provides better protection than e.g., the law of the employer's home country.

584. Regarding employees on board ships, etc. the general principle pursuant to maritime law concerning the law of the ships' home country ('the law of the flag') could be seen upon as related to the principle on the law of the place of employment. Nevertheless, it is just as appropriate that the country in which the ship is registered has a connection to the principle on the employer's domicile.

VI. Precedents

585. There are a number of Norwegian legal precedents on choice of law with regard to individual employment contracts.

586. In Rt. 1929 p. 433, the parties agreed that the matter of banning competition should be settled according to Norwegian law (cf. section 38 of the Contract Act). The case concerned a salesperson who worked in France for a Norwegian firm, and who later took employment with a competing firm. The Supreme Court decided the case based on the agreed choice of law.

587. In Rt. 1936 p. 900, English law was applied, in that 'hire aboard a ship must be judged according to the law of the flag'.

588. The judgment of 9 May 1968 in Drammen City Court, docket No. 70/65 A, 102/65 A and 97/65 A (unpublished): Norwegian employees were employed by an engineering yard in Drammen, and thereafter sent to Gothenburg to carry out various assignments for the company. The employees worked there from two to three months up to one year, and apparently left their employment after the period of employment in Gothenburg, so that the workers' entire employment period appears to have been in Gothenburg, at least essentially. The issue in the case was whether the firm was allowed to include holiday pay in the agreed hourly wage. The court stated:

589. It must be quite clear that this right to holiday pay is not forfeited if they… were sent to Sweden to carry out an assignment there. There can be no doubt that the holiday rules of Norwegian law must then also apply, in that said employees were employed in Norway by [A]'s firm in Drammen and were also employed in the same firm for the duration of the employment in Sweden.

590. ARD 1980 p. 10: three civil servants in Norwegian Telecom were transferred to Sweden for a period of between one and two years. The civil servants' right to overtime pay, calculated according to Norwegian labour rules, was complied with. Overtime amounted to approximately 200 hours per year per person. The court found that the civil servants must have assumed 'with good reason that Norwegian Telecom… had accepted' that the regular Norwegian working-hour provisions would apply during the work in Sweden.

591. RG 1982 p. 903 (Agder Court Appeal) concerned a claim for unfair dismissal. The employee was employed as a department manager at the firm's office in Dubai. The employment contract was entered into in Norway and was limited to a three-year period with renewal outside Norway with domicile in different countries, the last year in Dubai. He was a Norwegian citizen, had moved home to Norway where he had purchased a house, and he had also spent his holidays in Norway. The CA found no basis for indicating that upon being employed, he was 'definitely set on continuing to live in Dubai or anywhere else abroad'. On the employer's side, a partnership agreement between two Norwegian companies with business offices in Norway, and an Arab partner, was arranged but the entire share capital was Norwegian. The Norwegian companies were to handle the actual operation and supervise the employees, among other things. Hence the relationship would have to be 'equated with that of a Norwegian company in a more regular way running a business in another country through its own division in the country'. Against this background, the court found that the:

> close ties that both parties have to Norway make it natural to assume that, had the question arisen, they would have agreed to settle any disputes between them according to Norwegian law before Norwegian courts. In lieu of any other agreement, the alternative would have been the law of the place of work, and it is highly improbable that the parties had intended their relationship to be decided by a legal culture as alien as the one in Dubai.

592. In RG 1984 p. 139 the CA noted with respect to a choice between Norwegian and British law that the job assignment 'was assumed to be of a certain duration, at least longer than what one would call temporary', and that 'assumedly our main rule is that foreigners working in Norway come under Norwegian provisions of labour law, even when the proprietor of the enterprise is a foreigner living abroad, and the employee has the same citizenship as he or she has'.

593. NAD 1984-85 p. 552 (Eidsivating Court of Appeal): A, who was living in Denmark, was employed in 1960 with a Danish company. In 1977, he was transferred to the company's branch office in Norway. In 1979, the branch office was registered as a Norwegian company with the Danish company as sole shareholder. A was director of the Norwegian company. In 1983, A was given notice with immediate effect. A brought action against the Norwegian company, claiming damages for unfair dismissal and demanding that the case be settled according to the Danish Act relating to salaried employees. The court stated that it 'was improbable that [this] employment should be regulated by foreign private law. The factors invoked by A in support of applying Danish law are, according to the Court of Appeal, insufficient reason for agreeing a choice of law other than that one would naturally assume'.

594. In NAD 1984-85 p. 691 (Eidsivating Court of Appeal), a Norwegian weekly magazine entered into an agreement in Oslo with a journalist (a Swedish citizen), for the latter to be its permanent freelancer in the USA. The journalist was permanently residing in the USA. There was nothing that indicated that he at any time would join the weekly magazine's staff in Norway. After a couple of months, the magazine terminated the contract. The CA noted that the journalist 'has never been a Norwegian citizen and has never lived in Norway. It is quite clear that, according to the contract, the work was to be carried out in the USA. Under these circumstances, the court can establish no grounds for applying the rules of the Working Environment Act relating to dismissal protection'.

595. Rt. 1985 p. 1319 concerned employment lasting approximately five and three years. The Interlocutory Appeals Committee of the Supreme Court noted: 'According to the Court of Appeals' interpretation of the provision in WEA Section 61 (cf. Section 5 (cf. current WEA Sections 15-11 and 1-9)) one may deviate from the Act only in the event of short-term employment in Norway. The Committee agrees with this interpretation.'

596. RG 1987 p. 797 (Gulating Court of Appeal) concerned the dismissal of an American citizen employed by the group of companies' head office in Houston, Texas, USA. He was to work for the group's English company and its branch office in Norway, and worked over four years on a permanent installation on the Norwegian continental shelf. His residence for the entire period was in the USA, and his wages were paid to his residence by the head office in Texas. The majority of the City Court found that the English company was his employer, and 'having worked on the Norwegian continental shelf for more than 4 years, made him subject to the protection of the Norwegian WEA'. Genuine considerations indicated that employers on the Norwegian continental shelf should not be exempt from following the rules of the WEA also in these circumstances.

597. In NAD 1987 p. 1051 (Stavanger City Court), the court found 'that Norwegian labour-law provisions apply when regarding a job assignment of a certain duration, even if it concerns foreigners working in Norway for a foreign company'. The assignments varied from one-and-a-half years to nearly three years and, for some, almost four years. Furthermore, the employer had stated without reservation that the rules of the WEA would apply as indicated by both the collective agreement and correspondence with the Norwegian Labour Directorate. In the subsequent judgment of 21 January 1988 (NAD 1988 p. 255) in the same case, the City Court found that the employment contract's reference to 'applicable law' regarding the length of the period of notice would have to be interpreted as a reference to the law of the country in question, and applied the rules pursuant to the WEA.

598. NAD 1988 p. 705 (Oslo City Court) is also illustrative. Christiania Bank og Kreditkasse hired a few Norwegian citizens at Christiania Bank (UK) Ltd in London, with a letter from the London office for a period of three years. The issue in the case was whether the employees had been dismissed. The court found that it was an arrangement of a purely formal nature that they were employed in Norway and ordered to work in London, but both parties wanted this arrangement. They were not 'ordered' to London, and thus dismissals existed which could be tried according to the WEA. The choice-of-law issue, however, was not particularly discussed by the court.

599. Gulating CA judgment of 13 November 1992 (Interlocutory Appeals Committee case 92/1051): a French citizen on a leave of absence from his job in France worked at the French school in Stavanger as a librarian. The employment contract was in French and entered into at the French school's head office in Paris and signed by the librarian in Norway. The employment was limited to one year, but was later extended by an additional year, but no more than that. The librarian claimed that the time limitation was in violation of section 58(7), of the WEA (cf. current WEA section 14-9), and requested a temporary injunction. The request was granted in part (cf. Rt. 1991 p. 848 and Rt. 1992 p. 792). In the subsequent judgment, the CA found that the WEA was applicable because of the close connection to Norway. The librarian had:

> for a long time worked at an institution in Norway in a post particularly concerning the activity conducted in Norway. The French school has its own affiliated employees with a permanent work place there, and their employment contracts being entered into with a senior agency in France, which owns and operates the school is of no significance. Nor does it matter if the employment contract particularly concerns work at the French school in Stavanger, or if this is only one of several places in several countries where [she] could be assigned to work.

VII. Summary of Precedents

600. Generally, current practice in Norway has been to emphasize the parties' joint domicile in Norway when the employment abroad has been of short duration and when the employer's branch office abroad has had little independent decision-making authority in personnel matters, among other things, or when the matter concerns brief job assignments, etc., abroad. In these situations, Norwegian law has been applied, the place of work being given secondary importance.

601. In cases regarding long-term work in Norway for an international group of companies with a separate subsidiary in Norway, Norwegian law has also been applied. With a separate subsidiary, essential employer functions will – at least usually – lie with the subsidiary and not to the parent company. A domicile in Norway will strengthen the employer's ties to Norway, which will be additionally enhanced by long-term work in Norway.

602. Although the employer's enterprise had neither a branch office nor a subsidiary in Norway, and although the employer and employee had their domicile in the same foreign country, Norwegian law has been applied in a single decision in which the work in Norway was of long duration. However, there were other factors indicating application of Norwegian law: the contract was entered into in Norway and the employee was to work in Norway throughout his employment. The decision thus seems to harmonize with the views stated above on the significance of the place of work (cf. paragraphs 511 et seq.).

603. On the other hand, agreed venue abroad was accepted as grounds for disallowing the case in a short-term employment, if both the head office and subsidiary of the international group of companies were registered abroad, and the law of the ship's home country was applied if the ship owner conducted his or her business from that country.

604. Short-term employment was considered from two to three months, up to a year (Drammen City Court 9 May 1968), between one and two years (ARD 1980 p. 10), three years with renewals counting for one year at a time (RG 1982 p. 903 Agder Court of Appeal), three years (NAD 1988 p. 705 Oslo), dismissal 'shortly after the accession' (Sandefjord City Court 12 November 1992), summary dismissal after working a few months in the USA (Gulating CA16 May 2002).

VIII. Evaluation of Precedents

605. The premises in some of the decisions discussed above seem in part to be too indiscriminatingly characterized by the duration of the employment in Norway being a crucial factor, by the line between short-term and longer-term employment being determinable purely objectively, and by the other factors in choosing law having little or no bearing. Particularly pronounced are the premises in RG 1984 p. 139 Gulating Court of Appeal, but the same trend is also evidenced in the statement by the Interlocutory Appeals Committee of the Supreme Court in Rt. 1985 p. 1319. This way of deciding choice of law is technically simple because the only question that remains then is whether the employment can be characterized as short term or long term. However, the choice-of-law issue cannot be decided that simply (cf. paragraphs 511 et seq. on 'significance of the work place').

IX. Misgivings About Preferring Norwegian Law to Foreign Law

606. Present Norwegian case law might give the impression that Norwegian courts have a tendency to prefer Norwegian law to foreign law, by giving ties to Norway greater weight than ties to a foreign country. Such a trend – as far as it goes – can easily be explained by the fact that Norwegian courts are familiar with Norwegian rules of law and are used to applying Norwegian law, while foreign law may appear more unfamiliar and thereby uncertain. However, such reluctance to apply foreign law seems fundamentally questionable, particularly in a system where the decisions reached by Norwegian courts are acknowledged internationally. This system is established not least by the Lugano Convention, where a judgment by a Norwegian court concerning the litigants' employment may be precedential for the other countries embraced by this convention, and block actions in these countries on issues that the Norwegian court has decided or is hearing. This system is based on the assumption that the courts in the individual country are based on and apply the choice-of-law rules of the same material content. Otherwise, the party first bringing action could gain an advantage by choosing a court in the country that would apply the choice-of-law rule most benefiting that party, thereby obtaining a different and better result than a court in a different country would have arrived at. Hence, in this system, it would be more unwise for a Norwegian court to apply Norwegian choice-of-law rules favouring the application of Norwegian law than to apply international, generally accepted rules on choice of law. The rules following from those on choice of law in the EC Convention of 19 June 1980, must be characterized as internationally generally accepted rules on choice of law, and should – as stated above – also be applied by Norwegian courts, considering how these rules are put into practice by the EC Court and the courts in EC countries. Also significant in this context is that EC convention on choice of law was prepared on the principle that the law application rule in Article 6 on individual employment contracts basically may be applied to work performed outside the jurisdiction of any of the Convention states. On this background, it would supposedly also be practical, from the point of view of labour law, if the rules in the EC convention on choice of law were binding for Norway, e.g., as is the case regarding the Lugano Convention.

X. Rules That Apply According to the Rules on Choice of Law

607. According to Article 10 of the EC Convention, the law of the country which is applicable according to the rules or valid agreement on choice of law, shall be applied with regard to interpretation, fulfilment, effects of violation, other grounds for termination and the effects of an agreement's being invalid. Basically, the country's law will also apply with regard to formal requirements for entering into agreements; (cf. EC Convention, Article 9(1), which does not set forth special rules for employment contracts. If the parties are in different countries, it will suffice that the formal requirements are fulfilled according to the law of one of these countries (Article 9(2)). As for formal requirements for declarations of intention made pursuant to an existing agreement, the law of the country which is applicable according to the rules or valid agreement on choice of law, shall be applied; a declaration of an intention to fulfil the formal requirements in the country in which the declaration is given will suffice (Article 9(4). For example, notifying a notice or dismissal constitutes such a declaration of intention.

608. Formal requirements in this context must include one that (the declaration) is in writing, possible requirements as regards witnesses, but there is no particular requirement with regard to content, e.g., that the notification contain specified information (cf. (regarding Norwegian law) section 15-4 of the WEA).

609. The country's law that is applicable will also include the choice-of-law rules in that country, so that application of, e.g., Norwegian law will include Norwegian rules on choice of law.

XI. Procedural Issues Regarding Actions Before Norwegian Courts on Unfair Notice or Wrongful Dismissal Where Foreign Law Is Applicable

610. When it follows from the rules or valid agreement on choice of law that a foreign law shall apply, actions before Norwegian courts regarding the employment must basically be tried according to the ordinary rules of the Disputes Act 2005. If the action concerns the validity of a given notice, or legitimacy of a dismissal, judged according to foreign law, one may ask whether such an action shall be tried according to the ordinary rules of the Dispute Act or according to the special procedural rules set forth by the WEA for such actions, when Norwegian law is applicable.

611. Favouring the application of the procedural rules pursuant to the former WEA of 1977, was the fact that the courts with jurisdiction to try notice and dismissal cases would presumably be more familiar with the issues that would normally arise in such cases, and the presumably faster proceedings – the shorter appeals deadline, among other things – were deemed to be in the interest of the parties. However, according to the current WEA (of 2005) section 17-1(1) all city courts are now competent to try cases regarding legal proceedings concerning rights or obligations pursuant to said Act. The Courts of Justice Act and the Dispute Act shall apply in addition to the special provisions laid down in Chapter 17 of the WEA. Thus, there are no longer only certain courts that are competent to try notice and dismissal cases, and the presumption regarding these courts being more familiar with labour law cases no longer apply to the same degree. In addition, the appeal deadlines in these cases are no longer shorter than in other legal cases.

612. However, the procedural rules of the WEA constitute a system where procedural and material rules are interwoven. This particularly concerns the right to continue in one's post while the case is being tried by the courts, but it is also significant that action deadlines are in part calculated as of the end of the negotiation meetings, which in turn assumes the right by the employee to demand negotiations with the employer, etc. Application of the rules of the WEA must therefore be limited to the specific procedural rules, thus ignoring the material rules. This factor complicates the issue somewhat, but is in itself no crucial argument against applying the procedural rules of the WEA. Of crucial importance, however, is whether applying Norwegian or foreign law is questionable. This issue would have to be settled during the proceedings. It would be more economical for the case to continue in the same procedural form and before the same court, regardless of the results of this issue, while disallowing the action so it would possibly have to be brought anew would result in major complications.

Since the WEA stipulates the procedural mode for notice and dismissal cases, it should therefore be assumed that these procedural rules are applicable also with regard to the legality of giving notice and fairness of a dismissal as related to foreign rules of law.

613. For employees aboard a ship, etc., the general principle of maritime law regarding the law of the ship's home country ('law of the flag') may be viewed as a result of the principle regarding the law of the work place. But equally apt is the fact that the law of the country of registry is correlated with the principle of employer's domicile (cf. Jakhelln: 'Lovvalgspørsmål ved blokade av NIS-skip i utenlandsk havn', *Lov og Rett* 1989 pp. 321 et seq. particularly pp. 323–327 (cf. also Stein Evju: *Arbeidsrett* (2010) pp. 208 et seq.). Here, it is also expressed that exception to the choice-of-law rule is conceivable when the parties' only tie to Norway is that the work is conducted aboard a Norwegian ship; for example, when catering personnel aboard a Norwegian ship are employed by a foreign employer who has assumed the responsibility of running catering activity aboard the ship for his or her own account. Similarly, may be noted the judgment by Sandefjord City Court of 12 November, 1992, as well as the general statement of the Supreme Court (cf. Rt. 1939 p. 205 regarding loading and unloading workers working aboard foreign ships during the ships' stay in Norwegian ports: 'I believe there is no question that a Norwegian aboard a ship at a Norwegian dock must generally be judged according to Norwegian law, even if the ship is foreign.') The connecting factor for the ship in such cases is entirely of a brief and incidental nature.

Part I. The Individual Employment Relation

Chapter 1. Definitions and Notions

§1. Significance for Norwegian Individual Labour Law

614. In an international context, the following aspects are worth mentioning when dealing with Norwegian labour law.

615. The rules concerning job security, imply that a dismissal must be objectively justified, and offer quite wide access for a thorough re-examination of the employer's procedures. In addition, the employee has a right to remain in his or her position and receive salary after notice of dismissal have been given, provided that legal proceedings have been instituted within eight weeks. These rules imply that the employee will remain in his or her position until eventually the court finds it necessary to pronounce a verdict for the employee to resign.

616. Opportunity for the employer to enter into temporary employment contracts is rather strictly regulated. Temporary employment may be agreed upon e.g., when warranted by the nature of the work, or when working as a temporary replacement for another person. When the employment is entered into on one of these grounds, the general rule is that the employment is limited in time, that is to say up to a maximum of four and three years, depending on which of the grounds the time-limited contract is based on. But according to case law the limit is stipulated to be approximately two years, due to the fact that the court considered that the employee had fulfilled a continuously and vast need for permanent workforce on the employers hand. Thus, there was no legitimate ground for the employer to engage the employee on time-limited contracts.

617. The period of notice, which is stipulated in the legislation, is of relatively long duration, one month until expiry of the next calendar month.

618. The employment contract shall be in writing, also including amendments to the contract (cf. WEA sections 14-6 and 14-5).

§2. The Different Categories of Employee (Blue-Collar, White-Collar, Commercial Travellers, Seamen, Student Workers, Etc.)

619. In general, the WEA applies to most categories of employee. The WEA does not distinguish between blue-collar and white-collar employees. From this general principle, there are, however, some exceptions.

620. The employment relationship for sailors and other employees on board ships are regulated by the Ship Labour Act, and by the Ships Safety Act, as regards safety regulations, etc. For employees working in civil aviation – e.g., pilots and cabin crew – the WEA does apply.

621. The WEA also applies to petroleum activities at sea, on the Norwegian continental shelf, and to a certain extent also outside this area. The specific regulations on health, environment and safety regarding petroleum activities and certain plants onshore, of 12 February 2010 No. 158 should in this regard be observed. However, as regards petroleum activities carried out by ships – e.g., supply ships, diving ships, drilling ships etc. – the Ship Labour Act will apply.

622. Also, the WEA does apply to work carried out in the home of the employee, e.g., telework (cf. WEA section 1-5, as stipulated in more detail by the Regulation of 5 July 2002 No. 715).

623. Furthermore, the WEA does apply to work carried out in the private home of the employer – e.g., by a housemaid (cf. WEA section 1-5, as stipulated in more detail by the Regulation of 5 July 2002 No. 716). The Rules pursuant to the WEA are therefore in principle applicable also to an au pair's working relationship. In connection with WEA section 1-5(2) the Regulation of 5 July 2002 No. 716 exempts from the provisions pursuant to the WEA employees who perform housekeeping chores, supervision or care in the employer's home. For employment relationships of shorter duration than one month, or relationships where the weekly working hours not exceed eight, the provisions pursuant to the WEA still applies (cf. Regulations section 1(3)). The Regulations contain detailed rules on requirements for a written contract (section 2), the right to leave of absence during pregnancy, birth and adoption (section 3), the employer's and the employee's duties to ensure a fully satisfactory working environment (sections 4 and 5), working hours and leisure time (sections 6 and 7), the payment of salary, etc. (section 8). Termination of an employee must be in writing and have an objectively justifiable reason. Additional formal requirements are, on the other hand, not stated. The mutual notice period for dismissals are fourteen days (section 9), the employment contract can be terminated by reason of gross breach of duty, etc. (section 10), and claims for damages for wrongful termination of employment contracts may be brought before the courts pursuant to the standard procedural provisions (sections 11 and 12). There is therefore no specific time limit for legal proceedings, employees have no right to remain in their posts while the cases are being tried by the courts, and they may not require that unfair dismissals with notice or wrongful summary dismissals should be declared invalid by the courts (cf. also above paragraphs 183 et seq.).

624. The position of the chief executive of an enterprise (the managing director) is also regulated by the WEA, but certain special regulations should be observed. Thus, the chief executive may enter into an agreement with the effect that the protection against termination of the employment relationship pursuant to WEA Chapter 15 is relinquished, provided that the agreement secures him/her with an unconditional right to severance payment. The chief executive may also, subject to WEA section 14-19, be appointed for a fixed term, and subject to WEA section 15-16(1) the employer may enter into a written agreement with the chief executive to the effect that disputes in connection with termination of the employment relationship shall be settled by arbitration.

625. As regards public servants – employees working for the Norwegian state – their employment relationship is regulated by the CSA. However, the regulations of the WEA will apply, as regards safety regulations, the working environment, etc.

§3. Employment Contracts for an Indefinite Period

626. The general rule is that employment contracts are entered into for an indefinite period of time (cf. WEA section 15-3 concerning periods of notice).

§4. Temporary Employment Contracts

I. General Principles of Temporary Employment

627. In a number of situations, employment takes place in order for the employee to perform specific work of a passing nature, or to work only during a specific period of time. For example, a municipality employs a consultant in order to implement the celebration of the town's 150th anniversary, a department store employs a student to be Santa Claus during the month of December, or a worker is employed to install purchased machinery (ARD 1980 p. 105). In such situations the main rule is that the employment contract expires without further notice on expiry of the agreed period or when the specific work is completed (cf. the WEA section 14-9(5)). In such situations it is not necessary to provide a dismissal or any form of notice.

628. However, an employee who has been employed for more than one year is entitled to written notice of the date on which the employment will terminate, given not later than one month prior to the termination date. If the notice period is not observed, the employer may not require the employee to leave his or her post until one month after notice has been given.

629. If there were to be free access to enter into temporary employment contracts, this could easily result in a deterioration of the employees' protection against dismissal, and might also imply a concealed and extended probationary period. The WEA section 14-9 first paragraph therefore states that employees generally shall be appointed permanently, and pursuant to this establishes strict limits for temporary employment. Furthermore, it is stated that continuous temporary employment may not excess a period of four years when the employment contract is based on section 14-9(1) letter a) (work of a temporary nature)(cf. section 14-9(6)). In addition, continuous temporary employment may not excess a period of three years if the contract is based on section

14-9(1) letters b) and f) (for work as a temporary replacement for another person or persons, and as temporarily employed on a general basis for a period of up to twelve months).

630. Employment contracts which apply for a specific period of time, or for a particular work of a passing nature, may therefore only be agreed upon in the following situations:

(1) when the work is of a temporary nature;
(2) for work as a temporary replacement for another person or persons;
(3) for work as a trainee;
(4) for participants in labour market schemes under the auspices of, or in cooperation with the Public Employment Service (NAV);
(5) for athletes, trainers, referees and other leaders of organized sports; or
(6) for a period of up to twelve months. Such agreements may include up to 15% of the workers in the enterprise, rounded upwards, however, the agreement may always be made with at least one employee.

631. In addition, collective agreements may be concluded as regards temporary employment for specified groups of workers (cf. the WEA section 14-9(3)), and pursuant to section 14-10(1) the chief executive of a company may be appointed for a fixed term. Fixed-term appointments may moreover be agreed upon when deemed necessary as a result of an agreement with a foreign state or international organization.

632. The regulations are thus constructed as casuistic – as an enumeration of individual situations where there is access to temporary employment. However, the provision may not be interpreted antithetically or restrictively. The considerations that speak in favour of temporary employment may be so strong that a limitation of the duration of the employment must be accepted, and the expression 'nature of the work' will then be interpreted so that also such cases will be included by the concept. The opportunity to enter into temporary employment contracts in situations where it is not possible to appoint an employee with adequate qualifications (Rt. 1985 p. 1141) is illustrative.

633. Which limitations that ought to apply concerning the opportunity to enter into temporary employment contracts is a question, which is politically disputed, and has been so for a long time.

634. On the one hand are the regard for protection against dismissal and the risk of this protection being deteriorated by a wide access to temporary employment. On the other hand is consideration for the employers' need to be able to flexibly adapt the number of employees in relation to the workload at any given time. A strong protection against dismissal may result in employers being reserved with regard to new appointments, which again may have as a consequence that it becomes more difficult for young applicants to find work. The employers may instead try to fulfil their need for temporary labour through other means, for example by instructing already existing employees to work overtime.

II. Requirement for Written Agreements

635. Presumably it is not a requirement that the temporariness of an employment relationship is agreed in writing, but in the event of an oral agreement, the employer carries the burden of proof (cf. Rt. 2007 p. 129).

III. Work of a Temporary Nature, Etc.

636. Pursuant to the WEA section 14-9(1) letter a), temporary employments may be agreed upon when 'the work is of a temporary nature'. This wording was amended by the Act of 24 April 2015 No. 20, which entered into force on 1 July 2015. Before this amendment, the wording stated that temporary agreements could be agreed upon when warranted by 'the nature of the work and the work differs from that which is ordinarily performed in the enterprise'. The reason for this statutory amendment is that case law has stated that it is not an absolute requirement that the work that will provide the basis for temporary employment, in terms of content, must separate from the enterprise's regular work tasks. Thus, both differences in the nature of work that differ from the ordinary working tasks, and marked differences in workload will continue to be covered by the provision. In other words, the statutory amendment shall not be considered to cause any material changes, and previous case law relating to the provision will still be of relevance. The following description of the provision will therefore be based on the previous wording.

637. The expression 'nature of the work' is somewhat discretionary, but will in general imply that the work tasks must be of a time-limited nature. The *travaux préparatoires* refer in this connection to situations where the employee 'is only required to carry out a specific task', which is regarded to be included by this expression. The duration of the employment must therefore be given considerable emphasis. Likewise, it is of significance that the employer has a clear organization of temporary employments, so that temporary employment is limited to what is strictly necessary.

638. In cases of doubt, the parties' assumptions will also be given a certain emphasis. If the temporary employment has been extended, perhaps several times, this indicates that the work tasks are of an ordinary nature in the company. The condition that the work must differ from what is ordinarily performed in the company is a clarification of the concept 'nature of the work', but this does not prevent temporary employment in order to meet an extraordinary demand for labour due to seasonal variations, for example in connection with Christmas trade, within the tourism industry, in the fish processing industry, etc., even though such variations are normal and recur annually. Budgetary factors will generally not entitle the employer to use temporary employment, nor will the fact that the company is reorganizing:

- Construction workers hired to complete a particular building, special experts employed to carry out a particular assessment task, work of a strong seasonal character, and hiring by NRK (the Norwegian Broadcasting Corporation) of special staff to work on programmes are referred to in the legal preparatory work as examples of work which nature renders fixed-term work contracts appropriate.

- In ARD 1980 p. 69, the Labour Court decided that the nature of the work for a dramatist at a theatre was not of such a nature that the individual could be employed on a one-year contract that could be renewed, and that the fixed-term restriction was therefore not valid. The same must be the case for, e.g., actors, leading executives in a company, etc. but *see also* paragraphs 616 et seq. below.
- Similarly, Rt. 1992 p. 729 applies to the employment of teachers for one year at a time at a private school. Fixed-term employment period was partially due to the fact that the number of pupils at the school could change quickly. With the approval of the Appeals Committee of the Supreme Court, the Court stated that rapid changes in the number of pupils made it necessary for the school to be able to change the number of teachers, but 'it cannot be acknowledged that this makes it necessary to have one-year fixed-term contracts, because a reduction in activity due to reduced numbers of pupils would provide reasonable grounds for termination of employment'.
- The decision of Rt. 2001 p. 1413 must also be noted, in which the Supreme Court came to the conclusion that it was admissible to make a fixed-term contract for one-year temporary employment for international aid work clearing landmines for a humanitarian organization (Norsk Folkehjelp) (Norwegian People's Aid).
- The decisions of the Supreme Court in Rt. 2009 p. 578 and Rt. 2009 p. 179 are of particular importance, and are therefore dealt with in detail below (cf. respectively paragraphs 568–581 and 583–587).

639. In Rt. 2009 p. 578, the question was whether temporary employments over several years constituted the basis for permanent employment, either in pursuance of the previous four-year rule in WEA section 14-9(5) or the non-statutory doctrine from Rt. 1989 p. 1116 and Rt. 2006 p. 1158. (The four-year rule and a new three-year rule now follows from section 14-9(6), by the Act of 24 April No. 20 which entered into force on 1 July 2015.)

640. In Rt. 1989 p. 1116, it was assumed that in certain cases there was a limit to what could be agreed on between the parties concerning ongoing temporary employment, resulting in employees not being given the benefits of permanent employment. In this case, the employer had a large absence rate among employees on permanent employment contracts, which created a need for temporary employed employees. The absence rate was stable and predictable at all times, and the company had a large number of employees in its staff. The court emphasized that the temporary staff on a permanent basis, over a long time, had filled a general, large temporary employment need for the company, and that there were no special circumstances which indicated that these employees needed to work as temporary staff, without permanent employment contracts.

641. In Rt. 2006 p. 1158, it was emphasized that it was normal for some larger companies with a fairly steady and predictable demand for temporary workers that there might be an option to cover a fixed labour need by increasing the staff of permanent employees instead of temporary ones.

642. The Supreme Court pointed out that the four-year rule in the previous section 14-9(5) only stated the maximum time limit for temporary employment. Therefore, in line with previous case law an employee could still be considered a permanent employee of an earlier date than four years, and even three years, cf. the new section 14-9(6).

643. In Rt. 2009 p. 578, employee (A) worked in 2001 as trainee at Sanderud hospital. For four months in early 2002, he worked in a 14% position. The position as an intern student was during this time reduced to 86%. In addition, he worked a total of thirty-five extra work shifts. From April 2003 to 2004, A trained as a nurse. Besides the study, he worked extra shifts at the hospital equivalent to at 34% position in 2003 and a 41% position in 2004. After he received his certification as a nurse, the number of extra shifts increased. From 30 May 2005 and the rest of that year, he had a 100% permanent substitute contract.

644. In January 2006, A took a part-time course in psychiatry. He got a temporary job at the hospital in a 50% position to meet the demands of education practice. For budgetary reasons, A's position was funded with funds affiliated with temporary seats. The appointment letter stated, among other things, that A had leave of absence. It was stressed that the employment was temporary and linked to the curriculum. The temporary employment for 50% position was assumed to expire 2007. During the study period, A was working overtime and took extra shifts to a considerable extent.

645. In October 2006, A claimed that he filled the requirements for permanent employment at the hospital, but the claim was not granted. The hospital stopped giving A work shifts beyond what he had claimed in the temporary 50% position. A was sick in November 2006 and did not return to work at the hospital. In October 2007, A instituted legal action against the hospital, demanding permanent employment for 100% position and compensation and redress.

646. The Supreme Court found that the staffing at the hospital was good. The demand for substitutes was due to the fact that permanent employees in shifts could not work more than every third weekend. The nature of work required the use of temporary workers who knew the patients and procedures at the relevant records. The court could not see that there was any real alternative for the hospital to increase the staff, to carry out the work that A and other substitutes performed. The Supreme Court found that it was neither contrary to law nor to its purpose that the relevant labour demand was solved by the use of temporary staff. A was therefore not entitled to permanent employment on this basis.

647. Accordingly, the question was whether A was entitled to permanent employment in pursuance of the four-year rule in WEA section 14-9.

648. The Supreme Court found that only the temporary employment referred to in section 14-9(1) letter (a) and (b), was included when calculating the four-year rule. That is to say when 'warranted by the nature of the work and the work differs from that which is ordinarily performed in the enterprise' and 'for work as a temporary replacement for another person or persons'. Trainees and participants in labour market schemes, and temporary work as mentioned in subsection (e), should therefore not be included in this calculation. This applies whether the employee is in such work by the end of the four-year period or has had such temporary employment previously.

649. The next question was whether extra work shifts, overtime work and the position in which A had had 14% employment in parts of the observation period should be included in pursuance of the four-year rule.

650. The Supreme Court stated that:

> Subsequent temporary employment shall be considered if the requirement for 'continuous' temporary employment is met. I find no reason to go further into the question of whether the actual overtime work and extra work shifts had the sufficient scope and frequency to be considered as a continuous work on their own grounds. Crucial to me is that the work cannot be considered detached from the internship.
>
> Overtime work – which occurred 16 times during the year and a half, of up to two and a half hours each time – was in direct extension of the internship, and I find it clear that this must be considered as part of the internship. The 35 extra work shifts were random and scattered, and I cannot see that there was a sufficiently regular pattern in the shifts, other than that the work as an intern was the basis for this work.

651. However, it did not appear clearly whether the position of 14%, which A had in parts of the internship period, was related to the internship. The court found that the requirement of continuous employment was not met. The position of 14% could therefore not be included in the calculation in pursuance of the four-year rule.

652. As far as the period from April 2003 to the end of 2004 was concerned, when A studied as a graduate assistant, the court found it clear that this temporary work was included in the calculation pursuant to the four-year rule. Accordingly, the commencement of the calculation period pursuant to the four-year rule was after this the 1 April 2003.

653. The temporary replacement position for 50%, which A had while attending training, was classified as a temporary position pursuant to WEA section 14-9(1)(b) or trainee pursuant to the letter (c). The Supreme Court pointed out that 'the provisions must be interpreted with the intent that the Act's main rule in Section 14-9(1), first sentence, is that workers shall be employed on a permanent basis'.

654. The Supreme Court found that the substitute factor was clearly more prominent than the trainee element, in such a way that A must be considered to have had a temporary position in the sense of the four-year rule, even while he attended the education. When work in the 50% position had to be regarded as temporary and not as trainee work, there was no further question about the classification of extra work shifts – even this work had to be regarded as temporary. The Supreme Court concluded that the absence of a certain length because of illness had to be deducted when calculating the four-year rule pursuant to the previous section 14-9(5). A was therefore considered not to have been employed continuously in temporary positions for four years, and had no right to permanent employment. Two of the five judges dissented.

655. The previous WEA section 14-9(5), last sentence, has been amended and since 2010 involves that when calculating the employment period pursuant to section 14-9(5), second sentence, no deduction shall be made for the employee's legitimate absence. According to the Act of 24 April 2015 No. 20 this provision is now stated in WEA section 14-9(6). A new fourth subsection of WEA section 14-12 (cf. Act of 22 June 2012 No. 33, in effect from 1 January 2013) states that an employee's legitimate absence shall not be deducted when calculating the period of employment according to the four-year rule for hired employees. The provision thus establishes that the rule regarding non-deduction for legitimate absence is the same for hired employees as for other temporary employees.

656. In Rt. 2009 p. 179, the dispute was an issued request from the employer that the employee (A) should resign during the court proceedings (*see* WEA section 15-11, second subsection second sentence). The question was what significance it had for the right to require such dismissal that the employee had been moved to another position with the employer.

657. A was employed in 2002 in Bergen County as a teacher. In 2007, she was given notice of termination with effect from August 2007, based on alleged cooperation problems in relation to colleagues and superiors, as well as conflicts with students. In July 2007, A instituted a lawsuit against the county by the City Court. A claimed, among other things, that the dismissal was to be considered unfair and invalid. Bergen City Court acquitted the county. Before the court ruled A had acceded to the position of information officer at county…company Z. She was offered that position in a letter from the county where it said that the position was 'temporary', without further clarification on what the meaning of this expression was. The CA did not uphold the petition for the employee's resignation.

658. The Supreme Court stated as follows:

> The event was adapted to the difficult situation that had arisen, and A's need for facilitation. It is clear that the changes went beyond the employer unilaterally to decide by virtue of their autonomy.
>
> The CA has held that an employer's right to demand resignation pursuant to the WEA Section 15-11, second subsection second sentence, does not apply when the employee after termination is moved to a new position, which goes beyond what the employee in accordance with the original employment contract could be put to. Employers must instead announce a special notice from the new position, and then claim resignation from this.
>
> The Appeals Committee of the Supreme Court agrees with the CA that this must be the main rule. But in a situation, which in our case, the solution must still be another. The position of information officer in company Z was a preliminary and contract-based arrangement, pending the resolution of the original position's part. This new position was an alternative to A, so that she was left in a position with a content within the framework of the employer's managerial prerogative, which for health reasons she could not hold. In such a situation, it is the Committee's view it seems to be correct to judge the actual employment as a whole, not the individual position.
>
> The Committee notes that the right to remain in one's post do not apply 'if the court finds it unreasonable that employment should be maintained during the

> proceedings', *see* WEA Section 15-11, second subsection second sentence … The Commission cannot see that the interests of continuity is essential to prevent that in relation to Section 15-11, second subsection, to see the employment as a whole, in a case such as the present. This also follows from the travaux préparatories (Ot.prp.nr.49 (2004-2005) page 235), in which the Ministry show to the need for continuity 'in employment'. In this area, there is good reason to have rules that encourage flexibility for the employer.
>
> Accordingly, the County has the opportunity to petition for resignation in relation to the temporary position, as part of the court proceedings.

659. In Rt. 2006 p. 1158, an employee (A) had entered into an agreement with Akershus County to be 'temporary help with occasional serving/ indefinite working hours' in the ambulance service. The Supreme Court concluded that the system of temporary employment as practised was in contravention of the WEA of 1977 section 58A No. 1 (current WEA section 14-9 first subsection) concerning the temporary appointment.

660. The Supreme Court stated that:

> The question of whether a temporary appointment shall be set aside as contrary to Section 58A, has first of all a side to a company's needs – a real labour need will not be covered by temporary employment, but with a larger staffing of permanent employees. This means that for larger companies with a fairly steady and predictable demand for temporary staff, it normally may be that such a temporary post, such as in our case, may be illegal. Second, individual employees must have a sufficient attachment to the company in order to claim permanent employment.
>
> The ambulance service in Akershus included about 140 positions, and after the merger with Oslo, it was approximately 260. As I have explained earlier, the ambulance service in Akershus was divided into four regions, which were divided into two to four drives. Absence rate in Akershus in 2002 was as high as 27. It is not stated what the absence is due to, but I cannot see that it matters, provided that they are distributed evenly throughout the year. This distribution is illustrated by data on the costs of temporary use. Such information is only available for the years of 2004 and 2005, but should be representative also for the years before. For Akershus there was stable substitute cost of approximately NOK 500,000 per month, for Oslo at least NOK 400,000. Even if one divides the costs among the four regions in Akershus, they are fairly stable.
>
> The employment contract contained a number of detailed provisions, among other things, it was stated in section 5 that the Temporary Replacer / Extra Helper 'will be offered shifts when needed, and are free to accept or reject the shifts

offered'. In section 7, it was stated that the individual agreement for occasional duty 'is to be regarded as a time-limited employment contract that ceases when it / the agreed shift(s) is finished, cf. WEA Section 58A'. Furthermore, it was stated here that service as Temporary Replacer or Extra Helper 'does not give the right to claim permanent appointment in the County, or the right to permanent employment.

661. The next question was whether A had a sufficiently attachment to the ambulance service. The average time he served there was approximately 44% of a full-time – less in the beginning, more later on. With the exception of May 2002, when he had vacation, the service was spread over all months. No duty lasted fourteen months, and it was the employer who terminated the employment. A was therefore considered to have had a sufficiently attachment to the ambulance service in order to invoke that the general scheme of temporary use was contrary to the WEA section 58A.

662. By the Act of 24 April 2015 No. 20, in force from 1 July 2015, it is now stated in WEA section 14-9(6) that continuous temporary employment may not excess a period of four years when the employment contract is based on section 14-9(1) letter a) (work of a temporary nature). In addition, continuous temporary employment may not excess a period of three years if the contract is based on section 14-9(1) letters b) and f) (for work as a temporary replacement for another person or persons, and on a general basis for a period of up to twelve months). The result of this is that there is both a four-year rule as well as a three-year rule, regarding continuous temporary employments based on the legal basis of the temporary employment contract. The four-year rule will only apply when the basis for the temporary agreement is solely based on section 14-9(1) letter a). The three-year rule will apply when the basis for the temporary agreement is based on either letter b), or a combination of letter b) and f). The latter also applies if there is an agreement based on both letter a) and b), a) and f) or a), b) and f).

IV. No Qualified Applicants

663. According to the *travaux préparatoires*, the expression 'nature of the work' is assumed to include situations where the employee 'does not fulfil statutory required qualifications'. Likewise, it has previously been relied on in case law that the term 'nature of the work' would not prevent temporary employment, where it is not possible to fill a position with an applicant who has the qualifications required for the position. The question has been especially relevant within the health sector where, among other things, consideration for the patients must be emphasized. Temporary employment must however be limited to what is strictly necessary, be kept within fairly narrow timeframes and the required qualifications must be realistic and have a justifiable basis:

- In Rt. 1985 p. 1141, fixed-term employment of activators in positions that were normally regulated for occupational therapists at a county hospital were considered by the Supreme Court not to be in conflict with the previous WEA (1977) section

58 No. 7 second subsection. The Supreme Court cited consideration for the patients among other things and that the existing need was based on good reason along with the fact that the employment was limited to what was strictly necessary.

- The decision of 1985 must be seen in the context of a more recent decision in Rt. 1991 p. 872, where a licensed practical nurse was temporarily employed over a large number of years (12) as an assistant department manager at the county council's central institution for the mentally handicapped. The required qualifications in the staffing plan were motivated by the appropriate need to secure the best possible professional standards for the institution, but the Supreme Court characterized this requirement as being not very realistic and the institution had made systematic use of temporary contracts to solve a permanent staffing problem.
- An illustrative case is Rt. 1989 p. 1116, where a service worker worked as a substitute at the Statfjord field for two and a half years, in accordance with temporary worker agreements each time she went out to the field. Her service was not essentially different from the shift arrangements of permanently employed service workers. The Supreme Court found that she should have been considered as a permanent employee and the temporary staff arrangements the company practised in her case were in conflict with the provision pursuant to the previous WEA (1977). Even if there had been fluctuations, there had been a great deal of absenteeism amongst employees at the field throughout, especially among service workers. The situation had been stable and predictable for the company.

V. Officiating in Other Positions

664. The WEA section 14-9 and section 14-10 do not prevent an employee who is employed in one position in the company from officiating temporarily in another position within the same company. In these situations, the employee will have another position to return to, when the reasons which indicated officiating in another position are no longer present.

VI. On-call Agreements

665. Enterprises that have a need for labour during shorter periods of time often have lists of people who may be contacted to carry out work when there is a need for it. For instance, this is common within the hotel, restaurant and service industry, the tourist industry and the trade industry. In practice, the terms 'extra help' and 'on-call help' are often used for this category of workers.

666. The WEA does not contain any special provisions for such employment relationships. Thus, the question of whether there is access to limit the employment relationship to the duration of a specific assignment must be evaluated on the basis of the WEA section 14-9.

667. A question which arises in connection with temporary employment – and on-call agreements in particular – is whether each separate period of performed work is to be deemed as a separate and terminated employment relationship, or if the separate periods of employment must be seen in connection and as a continuous employment relationship.

668. As long as it concerns a single assignment of this kind, special circumstances must be present in order for the contractual relationship to entail rights or duties beyond the agreed assignment. In principle, neither the employer nor the employee will therefore be obliged to offer or to undertake one or more new assignments.

669. Correspondingly this must be relied on where one of the parties has had such an assumption, as long as this assumption has not been made known to and accepted by the other party, and other circumstances which indicate the opposite are not present.

670. If the parties have agreed that the employer may contact the employer in order to undertake assignments when there is a need for it, the employee will undoubtedly be free to assume or not assume the work, and in principle, the employer will not be obliged to contact the employee.

671. However, if the employer agrees with the employee that he or she shall be offered new assignments if the need should arise, the matter will be different. If so, the employee will not be obliged to undertake the assignment, but the employer has assumed an obligation to offer the employee available work and breach of this obligation may result in liability for compensation for the employer.

672. In practice, it is not unusual, however, that the relationship between the parties develops so that the employee – with greater or lesser regularity – performs work subject to the need of the employer. In such situations, it would not be adequate to only emphasize what the parties have expressly agreed, because it will often be expected that work will be performed unless special circumstances were to prevent this. The contractual relationship must therefore be evaluated on the basis of the whole situation which has gradually developed between the parties.

673. The connection with and the purpose of the WEA's provisions concerning protection against dismissal, including the limitations as regards the use of temporary employment, which follow from section 14-9 of the Act, must also be emphasized in order to avoid these provisions being undermined. For this reason, it cannot be relied on that what the parties have expressly agreed is necessarily valid (cf. the WEA section 1-9).

674. To summarize, it seems necessary to evaluate the various work tasks on the basis of extent, frequency and stability, so that emphasis is placed on the actual connection between the parties which the various assignments have established.

675. Whether the employee has been legally obliged to perform the individual work tasks has apparently not been made a major issue in those cases which have been decided by the Supreme Court, but are often mentioned as factors in lower court case law. On the contrary, the fact has been relied on – especially in Rt. 1989 p. 1116 and Rt. 1997 p. 277 – that an employer may expect that an employee will undertake the assignments. If the necessary continuity exists, the available case law from the Supreme Court does not seem to distinguish between cases where this continuity is a result of the employer's needs or the employee's interests. Nor would such a distinction be appropriate in order to promote the protection which *inter alia* the regulations regarding protection against dismissal are based upon.

676. If, on the contrary, the relationship between the parties has been more free, uncommitted and of an occasional nature, the necessary degree of continuity will not be present. An important factor in this connection will be whether the employee has been part of a rotation arrangement or such like, and whether the employee has performed work on a fairly regular or on an uncommitted basis.

VII. Trainee Work

677. In accordance with section 14-9(1) letter (c) of the WEA, temporary employment may be agreed upon concerning work as a trainee. This is work which is necessary for training purposes, for example in order to be accepted at a technical college or similar, or to become qualified during or following education.

678. In these situations, it may be agreed that the employment is to endure for a fixed period of time, but not longer than required by the purpose of training. If the normal training period is one year, a time-limited agreement for trainee work lasting for two years cannot be entered into, such a time limitation will be deemed invalid.

679. In Rt. 2009 p. 578, as mentioned under paragraphs 566 and 569, the Supreme Court said the following about the understanding of 'trainee work', as a starting point:

> Trainee work will normally be the nature of the work in connection with educational training or qualification within a subject area and will often be a starting point for further education.

680. In Rt. 2013 p. 1392, a so-called LIS doctor (a doctor who is attending a medical specialization programme after finishing the medical study at university) who was temporarily employed by a hospital, did not succeed in his claim for permanent employment. The Supreme Court found that the position as LIS doctor was covered by the scope of the WEA section 14-9(1) (c), even though the medical specialization programme normally takes more than eight years to complete. Emphasis was placed on a natural understanding of the term 'work as a trainee' and the fact that it was an established practice for temporary employment of LIS-doctors, which also to some extent had been approved by the Norwegian Medical Association.

VIII. Work as a Substitute

681. The WEA section 14-9(1)(b) also concerns temporary employment for work as a replacement for another person or persons. If so, the temporary employment contract must be based on an actual need for a substitute so that the substitute is performing work for another person who is temporarily absent, for instance due to illness, holiday, leave of absence, etc.

682. As regards the lawfulness it is not necessarily decisive that the duration of the temporary employment may be determined in advance or that it in advance is stated which person the substitute is working as a replacement for. Thus, it is possible to enter into temporary contracts with holiday substitutes even when it is not clear which individuals the substitute is to work for.

683. Within a large company, it is often the case that one or several employees are constantly temporarily absent, and there may be a need for a substitute who can fulfil the roles of the different employees. However, a temporary employment contract cannot be used in order to meet such requirements. In these situations, where the substitute regularly and for a considerable time fulfils a general and extensive need for temporary labour, the substitute will be comprised by the standard provisions regarding dismissals etc., which apply to permanent employees (cf. also Rt. 1989 p. 1116).

684. By the Act of 24 April 2015 No. 20, in force from 1 July 2015, it is now stated in WEA section 14-9(6) that continuous temporary employment may not excess a period of three years if the contract is based on section 14-9(1) letters b) and f) (for work as a temporary replacement for another person or persons, and temporarily employed on a general basis for a period of up to twelve months). The three-year rule will apply when the basis for the temporary agreement is based on either letter b), or a combination of both letter b) and f). The latter also applies if there is an agreement based on both letter a) and b), a) and f) or a), b) and f). If this provision is neglected, the effect is that the employee is deemed to be regarded as employed on a permanent employment contract.

IX. Labour Market Creation Programmes

685. Temporary employment may also be agreed for participants in labour market schemes (cf. the WEA section 14-9(1) (d)). The condition is that this is done under the auspices of, or in cooperation with, the Norwegian Labour and Welfare Service (NAV). For example, will sheltered workshops therefore be able to enter into temporary employment contracts with disabled workers. The fact that an employer receives contributions from the public authorities for employing individuals with difficulties on the labour market will however not entail that temporary employment can take place, unless the appointment is done in cooperation with the NAV, *see also* paragraph 626 below.

X. Fixed-Term Appointment of the Chief Executive of the Company

686. Pursuant to the WEA section 14-10, the chief executive of an enterprise may be appointed for a fixed term. This access only applies to directors on the highest level of executive management, with an extensive independent liability, which usually ought to include responsibility for budget and profit for the entire enterprise. In such positions, there are special and stringent requirements as regards leadership ability.

687. The WEA does not contain any provisions regarding the duration of such a fixed-term appointment, but it is assumed that the period of employment must not be so short that the director is not given an actual chance to show his or her abilities in the position. It is assumed that a probationary period may be agreed on fixed-term contracts and – if nothing else has been agreed – that dismissal may take place within the fixed-term period, if there is justifiable basis for it.

XI. Fixed-Term Employment as a Result of an Agreement with a Foreign State or International Organization

688. Appointment for a fixed term may also be agreed when deemed necessary as a result of an agreement with a foreign state or international organization (cf. section 14-10(2) of the WEA).

689. This access to temporary employment is caused by the practice, which has been followed by the joint Nordic institutions, on the basis of a decision in the Nordic Council of Ministers, so that employees are employed for a period of four years, with access to an extension of a maximum of four years.

690. The provision is general and therefore not limited to fixed-term employments in joint Nordic institutions, etc. But the provision is nevertheless limited to fixed-term employments, and does not provide general access to temporary employment.

XII. Athletes, Trainers, Referees, Etc.

691. In accordance with the WEA section 14-9(1) letter (e) temporary employment is allowed for 'athletes, trainers, referees and other leaders within organized sports', e.g., football players (cf. Rt. 2012 p. 168).

692. It seems to be assumed that solely administrative work connected to sports does not fall within the scope of the provision, and that the term 'other leaders' primarily includes 'sports managers'. Unless work tasks related to sports constitute a major part of the manager's work, it will probably not be possible to enter into a temporary employment contract in accordance with this provision.

XIII. Temporarily Employed on a General Basis for No Longer Than twelve Months

693. By the Act of 24 April 2015 No. 20 which entered into force 1 July 2015, the employer is allowed to employ temporarily for up to twelve months on a general basis, cf. WEA section 14-9(1) subsection f). Thus, no particular reason or legal basis is required in order to conclude a temporary employment contract according to this provision, and it may be used if the work tasks to be performed are both limited in time and/or are of a more permanent nature. The opportunity to conclude a temporary employment agreement according to WEA section 14-9(1) subparagraphs a) to d) applies as before. The government assumes that twelve-month duration will be a good solution for both the employee and the employer, when it first comes to being employed temporarily. The idea is that employees with no – or lack of – relevant work experience will be able to earn necessary experience with relevance for future and permanent employment and the employer will be given a relevant basis for assessing his or hers manpower needs.

694. However, there are given certain restrictions to this provision in order to counteract misuse. According to section 14-9(1) subsection f) only a quota of up to 15% of the workers in an enterprise, rounded upwards – however, always at least one employee – may be employed temporarily pursuant to this provision. The proportion of the workforce shall initially be estimated for the entire enterprise. It is the number of employees in the enterprise at the time the temporary employment contract is concluded that forms the basis for calculation.

695. In addition, WEA section 14-9(7) states a prohibition against engaging on a consecutive contract period pursuant to section 14-9(1) subsection f), when the first twelve-month period on such an employment contract has expired. If an employee who is temporarily employed pursuant to subsection f) does not get further employment when the contractual period expires, a quarantine period is initiated and imposes a prohibition against the employer to engage the same or another employee on a temporary employment contract pursuant to section 14-9(1) subsection f), for another period of maximum twelve months. The quarantine period initiates on the first day after the expiration of the contract period – either the actual contract period has been twelve months or of a shorter period – and if the employer and the employee at that time have not either entered into a permanent employment contract, or neither a temporary employment contract pursuant to WEA section 14-9(1) subsection a) to d). The quarantine period is always twelve months.

696. The quarantine-restriction only enters into force if the work that shall be performed during the consecutive temporary employment contract period (pursuant to WEA section 14-9(1) subsection f)) implies that the (same or another) employee is to perform 'work of the same nature' as has been carried out pursuant to the previous temporary employment contract period. According to the *travaux préparatoires*, the term 'work of the same nature' is somewhat discretionary, but will to a large extent depend on a specific assessment. The actually performed work tasks during the expired temporary employment period will be regarded as the basis of the assessment. But also work tasks that would have been natural to impose on the employee, shall be deemed to be covered by the quarantine provision. At what time of the day or night the work is performed is in principle not critical. Nevertheless, the actual organization of the work tasks may be a significant factor. The work tasks and the exact organization of a night working position may for example differ from how work tasks are organized in a daytime position, and may in practice mean that the work that shall be performed is carried out very differently. An example is a transport worker, hired to run one specific type of truck. The quarantine will normally also include the tasks of running both this and other types of trucks, or cars, to perform transport. But if transport missions differ from each other to the extent that the work tasks to be performed are to be assessed as very different, they will not necessarily be considered tasks of the same nature. Other elements in the assessment can be different levels of responsibilities and job levels. Also the education or skills required to perform the work will be of relevance.

697. Employers may regard units within the enterprise with at least fifty employees as a separate enterprise, cf. WEA section 14-9(7).This means that units within the enterprise of at least this size can be considered in isolation, and the rest of the enterprise is considered separately, in terms of the scope of the quarantine-restriction. It is a requirement that these units can – to some extent – be assessed as organizational independent units. Some examples are business areas within an enterprise or departments with at least fifty employees.

698. If the temporary employment contract pursuant to section 14-9(1) subsection f) continues to run beyond the expiration date (beyond the twelve-month limit) and the parties have not entered into a new employment contract on a different legal basis (or a permanent contract), the employee will be entitled to a permanent employment contract in accordance with the provisions of WEA section 14-11. This is the legal effect if the quarantine period is neglected.

699. If the employer neglects the restriction regarding the maximum proportion of the workforce in an enterprise that may be employed temporarily pursuant to section 14-9(1) subsection f) (the quota-restriction), the employee will only be entitled to a permanent employment contract if 'special circumstances' is recognized by a court law, cf. section 14-11(1) third sentence. Such 'special circumstances' may be recognized if the employer has engaged on temporary employment contracts on a general basis extensively and in excess of the quota-provision, or if the employer systematically or for some time has overstepped the quota-restriction. If 'special circumstances' are recognized, an employee could file a claim for compensation against the employer according to WEA section 14-11(2), and would be entitled to damages based on both economic and non-economic losses, if the damage conditions are met.

700. Furthermore, it is not allowed to enter into individual agreements on average calculation of working hours between an employer and an employee when entered into a temporary employment contract according to WEA section 14-9(1) subsection f), cf. WEA section 10-5(1) last sentence.

XIV. Collective Agreements Concerning Temporary Employment

701. According to the WEA section 14-9(3), national trade unions may conclude collective pay agreements with an employer or an employer's association concerning the right to make temporary appointments within a specific group of workers employed to perform artistic work, research work or work in connection with sport.

702. The opportunity to regulate temporary employment by collective agreement is reserved for nationwide labour organizations for these occupational groups. Nationwide labour organizations are trade unions that organize employees within occupational groups or sectors, independently of which company the employees work in or where in the country they live; trade unions on company level ('in-house unions') are not included, nor local trade unions. The collective agreement entered into does not, however, have to be nationwide.

703. The above-mentioned parties are regarded as well qualified to evaluate whether there is an actual need for temporary employment within the individual sectors.

704. If the collective pay agreement is binding for a majority of the employees within a specified group of employees in the enterprise the employer may, on the same conditions as mentioned above, enter into temporary contracts of employment with other employees who are to perform corresponding work.

705. A collective agreement concerning access to temporary employment will only be binding in relation to employment contracts, which are entered into after the collective agreement came into force.

XV. Termination of Temporary Employment Contracts

706. As regards temporary contracts of employment, these will in general expire on expiry of the agreed period or when the specific work is completed (cf. the WEA section 14-9(5)).

707. An employee who has been employed for more than one year is, however, entitled to written notification of the date on which he or she is to leave the post. What is decisive is whether the employee at the time of resignation will have been employed for more than one year. It is assumed that this concerns continuous employment.

708. Such notification is not equal to a notice of termination. The notification shall be given no later than one month prior to this termination date, and is deemed to have been served when received by the employee. The employer carries the burden of proof that notification has been given, that it has been provided at the correct time, and that notification has been provided in a satisfactory manner, so that the employer may rely on the employee having been made aware of the notification no later than one month prior to the agreed time of resignation.

709. If the time limit is not observed, the employer may not require the employee to leave the post until one month after notification has been given. This implies that the employment relationship exists, including both duties to perform work and to pay salary and other rights and obligations, until expiry of the period of notification. The employee will, however, be entitled to resign on the agreed date. The employee may not waive his or her right for such notification in advance.

710. Such notification may not be placed on equal terms with a dismissal. Notification must be given no later than one month prior to the time of resignation. This month must be calculated from the point in time which the employee received the notification.

711. The above-mentioned requirements with regards to notification does not apply to persons participating in labour market schemes (cf. section 14-9(1) letter (d)).

712. To what extent the employment could be terminated by dismissal prior to expiry of the agreed period or before the specific work is completed, was somewhat uncertain before the Act of 24 April 2015 No. 20, which entered in force on 1 July 2015, and depended on an interpretation of the employment contract (cf. ARD 1951 p. 186 and ARD 1981 p. 84, and further Rt. 2012 p. 168 (football player), where a limited right for the club, as the employer, to terminate the agreement because of unexpected economic difficulties was stipulated in the employment contract).

713. In Rt. 2012 p. 168, it is stated that in the absence of other relevant factors, notice to terminate the employment relationship, with effect before the stipulated time has expired, may not be given (cf. WEA section 14-9(5)). As far as a right to terminate the employment relationship by notice is stipulated, the usual regulations regarding the period of notice will apply (cf. WEA section 15-3), and – as regards notice of termination given by the employer – the general principle of fair and just cause will apply (cf. Rt. 2012 p. 168 (*Football player*) paragraphs 49 and 51). It may, however, follow from the employment agreement that the right to terminate the employment relationship before the stipulated time has expired is more limited than what follows from the general principle of fair and just cause (cf. e.g., Rt. 2012 p. 168 (*Football player*), where it had been agreed that such termination would require a substantial decline of the economy, compared to what would follow from realistic expectations regarding the economic development of the football club. The Supreme Court held (paragraph 73), *inter alia,* that it would 'clearly' not be sufficient cause, should the football club be retreated to a lower division, as such a risk would apply to every football club.)

714. By the Act of 24 April 2015 No. 20, it is now stated in WEA section 14-9(5) second sentence that 'during the temporary contract period the legislative provisions on termination of employments contracts applies'. This has the effect that temporary employments may be terminated by dismissal prior to expiry of the agreed period or before the specific work is completed, according to WEA Chapter 15. Thus, the usual provisions regarding the period of notice will apply (cf. WEA section 15-3), and – as regards notice of termination given by the employer – the general principle of fair and just cause will apply, cf. WEA section 15-7.

715. If employment continues beyond the agreed fixed-term period, the employment relationship will be comprised by the ordinary regulations concerning termination, which apply to the termination of permanent employment relationships.

716. An employee who is temporarily engaged and who, owing to circumstances relating to the enterprise, is not offered continued employment will have a preferential right to a new appointment in the enterprise unless the vacant post is one for which the employee is not qualified (cf. the WEA section 14-2(2)). It is not required that a notification as mentioned above contains information concerning this preferential right. If a temporary employee is dismissed, this is however different (cf. the WEA section 15-4(2)).

XVI. Termination of a Temporary Employment Contract Which Lasts beyond Four Years

717. For employees who have been temporarily employed for more than four consecutive years solely on the basis of WEA section 14-9(1) letter a), the provisions concerning termination of permanent employment relationships will apply (cf. the WEA section 14-9(5)). The same applies for temporary employment contracts exceeding three years if the legal basis for the employment is WEA section 14-9(1) letter b), both letter a) and b), a) and f), or a), b) and f), cf. section 14-9(6). This may also be expressed so that the employee is (automatically) regarded as permanently employed. Thus, the provision implies a set of maximum limits as to for how long an employee may be temporarily employed. When calculating the period of employment, no reductions shall be made for the employee's absence from work during this period (cf. also paragraph 582 above).

§5. Legal Proceedings

I. Legal Proceedings When the Employee Has Resigned

718. An employee who has resigned from his or her position and wishes to claim that an unlawful temporary appointment has been made may demand negotiations with the employer (cf. the WEA section 17-3(1)). An employee who wishes to claim negotiations must notify the employer in writing within two weeks. The time limit runs from the actual time of resignation (cf. the WEA section 17-3(2)).

719. Legal proceedings must be initiated in accordance with the section 17-4 of the Act. The time limit for initiating legal proceedings is eight weeks, or six months if an employee only claims compensation. The time limit runs from the conclusion of negotiations or from the actual time of resignation if negotiations are not conducted.

720. The right to remain in post while a case is pending (cf. the WEA section 15-11(3)) does not apply to temporary employees unless otherwise decided by the court.

II. Legal Proceedings When the Employee Has Not Resigned

721. If the employee has not resigned and a dispute arises whether a legal temporary employment exists, a lawsuit concerning such a dispute will be included by the WEA's provisions of procedure (cf. the WEA sections 17-1(1) and 17-4).

722. However, when the employee has not resigned there is no time limit for demanding negotiations or initiating legal proceedings.

III. Legal Proceedings When the Employee Resigns After a Dispute Has Arisen

723. If the employee resigns after negotiations have been demanded, or after legal proceedings are initiated, it must be assumed that the situation shall be handled in accordance with the provisions which apply when the employee has resigned (cf. above).

§6. Probationary Period

724. If the initial period of employment shall be a probationary period, this must be agreed in writing between the parties, and the length of the probationary period has to be clearly stated (cf. the WEA sections 14-6(1) letter (f), 15-3(7) and 15-6 letter (a)).

725. If the probationary period is not agreed in writing, the special provisions concerning termination during probationary period (cf. WEA section 15-6) will not apply. If so, the employment will be regulated by the ordinary provisions concerning protection against unfair dismissal (cf. WEA section 15-7).

726. A probationary period may also be agreed for temporary employment, something that amongst others can be relevant for fixed-term appointments subject to WEA section 14-10.

727. According to the CSA section 8 No. 1, a civil servant will automatically be employed on probation for the initial six months of employment, and it may only in special situations be agreed that a probationary period shall not apply.

728. The purpose of the probation period is that the employer for a time-limited period shall be able to test the employee's suitability for the position. During the probation period, a shorter period of notice applies, and unless otherwise is agreed in writing or stated in a collective agreement, the notice period is fourteen days (cf. the WEA section 15-3(7)).

729. During the probation period, the employee can be dismissed due to lack of suitability for the work, or lack of proficiency or reliability (cf. the WEA section 15-6). Termination during the probation period for reasons other than the aforesaid must be assessed according to the general rules regarding protection against unfair dismissal (cf. WEA section 15-7).

730. The employer cannot require that the standard of performance is ideal, but the employer may demand that the work performance is on an average level. The employer must, however, take into consideration the employee's lack of previous work experience. In general, the employer may place great emphasis on punctuality with regard to attendance, on whether the employee stays away from work when this is not authorized by the employer and whether the employee performs the assigned work tasks. On the other hand, the employee must be given a real opportunity to show his or her abilities in the position. For this reason, it will often be assumed that the employee shall receive particular instruction and training during this period. Under the evaluation of what constitutes adequate training, the previous work experience of the employee must be taken into consideration (cf. Rt. 1984 p. 337).

731. The decision in Rt. 2003 p. 1071 can be mentioned as an example. A general manager was dismissed during the probationary period, and the Supreme Court declared the termination void based on the fact that the employee had not been given sufficient opportunity to show his or her abilities in the position. Further, Rt. 1983 p. 537 can be noticed. An apprentice was given notice after approximately three weeks of employment, but had only received training and instruction for the first two days. The Supreme Court emphasized that the instruction had only been sporadic and occasional in character, and that the apprentice had not shown either lack of ability or lack of willingness to comply with the instruction given to him.

732. The employer is obliged to be alert in relation to, and try to solve cooperation problems, which arise during the probation period. An employee who is subject to a probation period shall receive adequate feedback in relation to possible mistakes, so that he may correct and adjust the work performance. Thus, a notice of termination should not come as a surprise to the employee.

733. The evaluation with regard to suitability for the work, proficiency and reliability will necessarily be based on the employer's discretionary decision. However, the courts can review the employer's assessment, so that the employer must be able to identify the basis for the termination. However, if the court finds it reasonable to rely on the facts of the matter, which the employer has relied on, it is assumed that the courts will be reserved with regard to re-examination of the employer's evaluation of whether the employee is suitable for the position. Thus, the employer's evaluation in relation to suitability, etc., will generally only be deemed invalid if it does not seem to be justifiable.

734. The special provisions concerning termination of employment subject to probation period only applies within the probationary period, which may not be longer than six months.

735. If the employee has been absent from work during the probationary period and the employer does not cause the absence, the employer may extend the agreed probationary period by a period corresponding to the period of absence. However, such an extension may only take place when the employee has been informed of this possibility in writing at the time of his or her appointment, and when the employer has informed the employee of the extension in writing prior to expiry of the probationary period.

736. An employee's absence from work in the probation period due to prison detention, and whether this absence constituted a right for the employer to dismiss the employee (cf. WEA section 15-6), was the case in Rt. 2011 p. 74. The employee was arrested on 5 November 2008 and released on 2 November 2008. The absence was approximately one month. In addition, the employee had overslept one morning prior to the arrest, resulting in him coming to work more than three hours late. More than one year later, the employee was acquitted from the charges against him. The Supreme Court stated that:

> the absence led to a reduction in time that is at the employer's disposal to test the employee's suitability for the work, his skills and reliability. In such a situation the employer alone cannot bear the risk for the employee's absence. If the absence is of such a length that the employer does not have a sufficient basis to evaluate the employee's suitability for the position before being permanently appointed, it may indicate that termination is valid. But in these cases there should be considered an extension of the probationary period, as an alternative to dismissal. It is not obtained information that the employee in the period up to imprisonment not fully adapted to the work, or that he did not work satisfactorily in accordance with the position's qualifications. The court finds that the employee on the termination day – in December 2008 – after five months of probation had been set up well in the job and proved that he could perform tasks in a satisfactory manner. Besides the incident when he overslept on 2 November, there was nothing to say on his reliability as an employee. On this basis the Supreme Court held the dismissal invalid.

737. Upon changes in the employment relationship, and in the event of transition to another position, it can be questioned whether a probation of any period may be agreed upon. In this connection, both consideration for employees' protection against unfair dismissal and consideration for flexibility in employment relations must be emphasized.

738. Based on these considerations, the Supreme Court has stated that a probation period cannot be agreed upon in relation to a substitute who has worked as a replacement for a period of more than six months, if the substitute is appointed to the same position or a position within the same enterprise which mainly is similar to the position in which the employee worked as a substitute (cf. Rt. 1996 p. 1026).

739. Furthermore, the Supreme Court has stated that an employee who has achieved ordinary protection against dismissal in one position, may be appointed subject to a probationary period in another position within the enterprise, as long as the employee were entitled to return to the former position (cf. Rt. 1997 p. 56).

740. Upon termination on the basis of curtailment of operations, the question may be raised whether an additional period of probation may be agreed if the employer offers the employee 'other suitable work' (cf. section 15-7(2) of the WEA).

741. Generally, the Supreme Court has expressed that the Act must be interpreted in such a way that an employer who in the event of termination due to curtailment of operations or other rationalization measures has other suitable work to offer the employee, as a main rule will be obliged to offer such work without imposing a probation period. However, this will not apply if a probation period is necessary in order to establish whether the position in fact may be regarded as 'other suitable work' in relation to the particular employee.

742. It is sufficient that notice of termination is given before expiry of the agreed probation period, or within the extended period of probation (cf. section 15-6(4) of the WEA). If notice is given after expiry of the probation period, the ordinary provisions on protection against unfair dismissal will apply (cf. Rt. 1992 p. 1188).

743. An employee whose employment has been terminated during the probation period, and who wishes to claim that the termination is unlawful, may demand negotiations with the employer and initiate legal proceedings subject to the regulations of the WEA sections 17-3 and 17-4.

744. In the same manner, the dismissal may be deemed invalid, and the employee may be entitled to compensation (cf. section 15-12 of the Act). The employee will however not be entitled to remain in the post while a dispute concerning whether the employment has been legally terminated is pending (cf. section 15-11(3)). An employee who is dismissed during a probationary period must therefore resign by expiry of the notice period, and claim for reinstatement in order to remain in post until the courts settle the case.

745. During the probationary period, an employee may not only be dismissed based on 'the employee's lack of suitability for the work, or lack of proficiency or reliability', but also on other justifiable grounds such as curtailment of operations, rationalization measures, etc. (cf. Rt. 1999 p. 1131). Thus, the access to termination in accordance with the ordinary provisions is not limited during the probation period. Even if such grounds warrant termination, the shorter period of notice will apply.

746. An employee who is dismissed during the probation period will not be entitled to remain in the post while a dispute is pending, regardless of the reason for the termination (cf. Rt. 1999 p. 1131) unless otherwise decided by the Court (cf. WEA section 15.11(4)).

§7. Written Contract Is Compulsory

747. According to the WEA section 14-5, all employment relationships shall be subject to a written contract of employment. In employment relationships with a total duration of more than one month, a written contract of employment shall be entered into as 'early as possible and one month following commencement of the employment at the latest'. In employment relationships of a shorter duration than one month or in connection with contract labour, a written contract of employment shall be entered into 'immediately'.

748. Section 14-6 of the Act provides detailed minimum requirements regarding the content of the written contract. The employer shall draft the contract in accordance with these requirements.

749. The contract of employment shall state factors of major significance for the employment relationship, including the identities of the parties and the place of work. If there is no fixed or main place of work, the contract of employment shall provide information to the effect that the employee is employed at various locations and state the registered place of business or, where appropriate, the home address of the employer. Further, the contract shall contain a description of the work or the employee's title, post or category of work, and the date of commencement. If the employment is of a temporary nature, its expected duration shall be stated and the specific legal basis for the temporary employment, cf. WEA section 14-9. Correspondingly shall any provisions relating to a probationary period of employment and information concerning any collective agreements regulating the employment relationship, be included.

750. Furthermore, the contract shall include regulations regarding the employee's right to holiday/holiday pay and the provisions concerning the fixing of dates for holidays, the periods of notice applicable to the parties, duration and disposition of the agreed daily and weekly working hours, length of breaks, the pay applicable or agreed on commencement and any supplements or other remuneration not included in the pay, for example pensions contribution, method of payment and payment intervals for salary payments. This type of information may, however, be given in the form of a reference to the Acts, regulations and/or collective agreements regulating these matters.

751. Subject to section 14-5 of the WEA, an employee is entitled to engage the assistance of an elected representative or another representative both when drafting and in connection with later amendments to the contract of employment.

752. It may occur that parties make an agreement that is in conflict with a non-negotiable legal act, e.g., that the employee will have no holidays. In that case, the contract will be invalid, and as the terms and conditions agreed are illegal, they are replaced by the rules of law. A similar situation may occur with regard to collective agreement provisions. It can even be envisaged that the work contract aims to promote a purpose that is not recognized by the legal system. The work contract may then be invalid due to conflict, with 'decency' (cf. Norwegian Law Book (NL) section 5-1-2). In that case, the parties cannot demand delivery with regard to entitlements and obligations in the contract.

753. Workers who had contributed to the building of a torpedo battery during World War II, in accordance with the employment contract with their employer, could not demand their wages paid by their employer. The Court of Appeal dismissed the case, as contrary to NL 5-1-2, as such work for the German occupying military forces was far beyond the obligations according to international law as regards the civil population of an occupied country (cf. Rt. 1946 p. 720).

754. If changes to the above-mentioned conditions of the employment relationship are implemented, these shall be included in the contract as early as possible and no later than one month after entry into force of the change concerned (cf. WEA section 14-8). This shall nevertheless not apply if the changes in the employment relationship are due to amendments to Acts, regulations or collective agreements regulating these matters.

755. The above-mentioned provision (section 14-8) does, however, only regulate the formal implementation of changes, not whether the employer materially may implement such changes. The question of whether the employer unilaterally may implement changes to the employment relationship must be determined on the basis of the employer's managerial prerogative.

756. The requirement of the WEA sections 14-5 et seq. with regard to a written contract of employment is not regarded as a condition for the validity of the employment contract. Thus, if a written contract of employment is not entered into, the employment contract will still be legally binding. The general principle stating that an oral agreement is binding also applies in relation to contracts of employment.

757. The fact that a contract of employment has not been made in writing may, however, indicate that the parties (the employer and the employee) have not reached beyond the point between advanced negotiations and the final, concluding agreement, and the burden of proof will rest upon the party claiming that a final agreement has been concluded (cf. e.g., Rt. 1965 p. 360 and Rt. 2004 p. 53). The similar will apply as regards changes of an employment agreement, e.g., when the question is, whether a prolongation of a temporary agreement should be interpreted as a continued time-limited agreement, or as a permanent employment (cf. e.g., Rt. 2007 p. 129).

§8. Ability to Conclude a Labour Contract (Minors, Others)

758. Appointment implies that an employment contract is entered into between the employer and the employee and this may – in the same way as for other agreements – happen orally, in writing or through an act of quasi *ex contractu*. In practice, it is not uncommon for an employer and an employee to orally agree that the employee is to commence employment on a certain date, and such an agreement will generally be binding upon both parties.

759. The question of whether the parties have entered into an employment contract or have not proceeded beyond negotiations must be decided on the basis of general principles of contract law. Under the assessment, it will be of significance whether a written contract of employment has been prepared. At least as far as leading positions are concerned, however, it can hardly be assumed that a final agreement has been reached on a purely oral basis without subsequent written confirmation. If the employee has commenced the work and the employer is aware of this and does not object it, this will be a strong indication that an employment contract has been entered into.

760. In order for an employer to be bound by an employment contract, this must be entered into by the employer himself, or by someone who by power of attorney may act on the employer's behalf.

761. Employees under 18 years of age must have consent from their guardian in order to be able to enter into an employment contract. If the minor has reached 15 years of age and commenced work that he may use to provide for himself, the minor may however terminate the employment contract and assume similar work. Subject to reasonable notice to the employer, the guardian may however elevate the employment contract entered into a minor who have reached 15 years of age, if he finds that the regard for the development and welfare of the minor render it necessary (cf. the Guardian Act of 22 April 1927 No. 3 section 32). In connection with contracts for apprentices, it is not necessary with the consent of the guardian (cf. the EA section 4-5(4)).

762. A person under guardianship may agree to undertake work, and may terminate the employment contract. The Public Trustees Office may, however, decide that only the guardian may enter into and terminate employment contracts, and that the guardian may revoke an agreement which the incapacitated has previously entered into.

763. In this connection must also be noted the prohibition in the WEA section 11-1, according to which children under 15 years of age or children attending compulsory education as a general rule must not perform work subject to the Act. However, this does not apply to cultural work or the like, to light work provided the child is 13 years of age or more and to work that forms part of their schooling or practical vocational guidance approved by the school authorities, provided the child is 14 years of age or more. The Ministry may by regulation issue further conditions for such work.

764. In general, persons under 18 years of age must not perform work that may be detrimental to their safety, health, development or schooling.

765. Furthermore, it is stated in the WEA section 11-4(2) that the Ministry may issue regulations concerning medical examinations where the work makes special demands on the health or physical characteristics of the employee, and subject to section 11-2 and section 11-3 special regulations apply concerning working hours for children and young people.

§9. The Interim Period Between the Conclusion of the Contract and the Commencement of Work

766. Commencement is normally the next step, subsequent to entering into the agreement. In accordance with the ordinary use of the word, commencement has taken place when the employee has presented himself or herself at the agreed time and place to carry out the work that has been agreed. Inevitably, a shorter or longer period will pass between entering into the agreement and commencement of the work, unless the employee starts working immediately. There arises the basic question of how the legal relationship between parties – and the relationship with the public – shall be judged in this interim period. Should the working agreement in this period be judged in terms of the legal working regulations, or will these not be applicable until commencement of employment has taken place.

767. The question of whether the legal employment regulations are applicable prior to commencement can probably not be answered generally. The legal regulations governing work regulate a range of different conditions, where very different considerations apply, so that the question must be answered in a much more nuanced way than with a simple point of view based on the commencement as the decisive demarcation. In other words, it is not given that the solution must be the same for protection rules, contractual rules, collective agreements, penalty regulations, legal process regulations, choice of law regulations, etc.

768. In the context of public law, commencement can hardly be considered a condition for applying the regulations of the WEA. For example, the public legal regulations behind the requirement for a fully appropriate working environment are such that it must be assumed that the Norwegian Labour Inspectorate has the expertise to intervene with an order applying to the workplace and the work to be carried out, regardless of whether the employer has any employee, or whether the work has commenced.

769. Also in relation to the WEA's regulation of private law, it seems that the meaning of commencement must be evaluated in the context of the actual consideration that applies in relation to the individual regulations. As a starting point, it must be possible to establish whether all the entitlements and obligation arising from a working relationship are realized on commencement.

770. Entitlements and obligations can, however, come into effect immediately on entering into the agreement. Thus, between signing the agreement and commencement there is more of a gradual difference than a difference on principle as regards which entitlements and obligations apply between the parties.

771. For example, it must be clear that any requirements for advertising and hiring pursuant to the regulations on equal treatment in the WEA, ADA and the Gender Equality Act are not restricted by any commencement requirement.

772. On the other hand, it seems evident, in relation to entitlements that are earned over time that the commencement also marks the start of the period during which contribution time is calculated.

773. The employee's general duty of loyalty towards the employer must also be considered as commencing as soon as the agreement is signed, to some degree perhaps even before this time. Thus, it would be in conflict with the duty of loyalty if the employee made public statements that were strongly critical and unfounded with regard to the employer's activities.

774. As regards the question whether a concluded employment agreement is valid or not, the Supreme Court has held that there is a difference between the situation before the employee has commenced the work, and after that time (cf. Rt. 2004 p. 76). Before the work has commenced, the general principles of contract law will dominate the picture; thus, the employer could bring the relationship to an end without fulfilling the formal requirements regarding a notice of termination according to the WEA section

15-4. Should, however, the employee have commenced the work, those formal requirements would apply (paragraphs 47–49).

775. Since there is a general principle of maintaining objectivity and relevance in labour law, this requirement will also apply to dispositions that are made in the interim period between hiring and commencement. This includes restrictions on the employer's right to manage during this period, while it must also be assumed that the employer will exercise his or her right to manage during this period.

776. This implies that the principle of fairness must also be the basis of cancellation or termination of the working relationship before commencement of the work, e.g., by giving notice that the employee's services will not be required.

777. It must probably be assumed that any compensation will be calculated in accordance with the regulations which normally apply in connection with termination of employment relationships (cf. in this regard the decision of the Supreme Court Rt. 2012 p. 983 (*Drill rig*) paragraph 115), and below paragraph 1080).

778. Compensation for non-economic loss will, however, probably not be granted, as such compensation – according to the general principles of contract law – does not follow as a consequence of a breach of an agreement, but requires special legal authority (cf. *inter alia,* the statement of the Supreme Court Rt. 2012 p. 983 (*Drill Rig*) paragraph 116).

Chapter 2. Rights and Duties of the Parties During the Employment Period

§1. Duties of the Employee

I. Obligation to Work

779. It follows from the employment contract that the employee shall place his or her labour at the other party's disposal and, in the terms of the previous SA (section 39) 'execute his or her service conscientiously'. The type of work to be performed by the employee depends on what is explicitly or implicitly agreed between the parties. For example, a person employed as a stenographer should not be required to drive company lorries. However, this only provides a point of departure. The further scope of the employee's duties must be determined on the basis of the terms of collective agreements, company rules and general practice in the enterprise and industry in question. In the case of extraordinary events such as emergency shutdowns, illness and accidents, the duties of the employee is extended in proportion to the extraordinariness of the event. However, legal strikes are not among the events entailing an extension of the employee's duties (Rt. 1927 p. 296 and Rt. 1936 p. 220). It is a different matter, however, if the strike is illegal (ARD 1945-48 p. 247 and ARD 1951 p. 140).

II. Duty of Loyalty

780. In the same way as in other contractual relationships, the parties in employment are obliged to act loyally with regard to the interests of the other party. An employment assumes a relationship of trust between the parties, and it follows from this that an employee has a general obligation to promote his or her employer's interests. Here is often mentioned the employee's duty of loyalty or duty of fidelity. This general duty of loyalty, which has not been generally expressed in legislation, has been formulated as follows by the Supreme Court (cf. Rt. 1990, p. 607): 'It must be relied on that there exists a general and non-mandatory duty of loyalty and fidelity in employment relationships.'

781. The duty of loyalty can to some extent be seen as a further specification of the content of the work obligation, and that therefore stricter requirements must be made for employees in management or executive positions than to employees in more subordinate positions (cf. for example Rt. 1997 p. 1128). For example it is beyond doubt that the employee is obliged to perform work in a conscientious and proper manner. It may thus be a breach of the employment obligation if a senior employee with control tasks to a large extent ignores breaches made by subordinate employees, for example by not taking any disciplinary action towards a subordinate employee who is constantly too late for work. In the same manner, it would be blameworthy if a senior employee were to instruct a subordinate to do something illegal, and thus creating a conflict between the relationship to the company and the relationship to the superior (cf. e.g., Rt. 1997 p. 1128).

782. It must also be noted that the duty of loyalty implies that the employee himself or herself must actively raise matters with the employer if it is doubtful whether a matter or a situation which involves the employee outside of the employment may cause difficulties in the employment relationship between the employee and the employer (*see* Rt. 1996 p. 1401).

783. Employees are also obliged to contribute towards any irregularities being revealed (cf. Rt. 1965, p. 763, compare in this relation also Rt. 1974 p. 990, and Rt. 1993 p. 300). If an employee refrains from contributing in this manner, perhaps either through fear of having to reveal his or her or her own blameworthiness or perhaps even criminal conduct, such omission in itself will be a breach of the duty of loyalty, and may possibly lead to dismissal or even discharge.

784. It may also happen that an employee is dissatisfied with an employer's management of the company, or for other reasons is not satisfied with the situation in the employment relationship. Such matters will have to be raised with the employer by the employee himself or herself, possibly through employee representatives, but does not justify an employee acting disloyally.

785. An employee must not be loose-tongued about matters concerning the enterprise, and may be punished if he or she reveals any company secrets, not only while he or she is employed, but also for two years after leaving the enterprise (cf. section 294(2) of the Penal Code (PC)). Violation of also other statutes relating to professional secrecy may result in criminal charges (cf. e.g., section 121 of the PC and Rt. 1989 p. 1363). Nor must the employee endeavour to promote his or her own interests at the expense of the employer's. Thus, a purchasing manager may not receive any payment, 'kickback' or other remuneration from a supplier to buy goods, even when the goods have a price and quality equal to that of other companies, as long as the employer has not agreed to the arrangement (cf. Rt. 1919 p. 747, and further the PC section 405 b and the Marketing Act section 6). Obviously, the employee must not compete with his own company while employed there (cf. e.g., Rt. 1918 p. 575), or prior to resignation violate the employer's interests in order to promote his or her own business interests (cf. e.g., Rt. 1990 p. 607).

786. On the other hand, he is free to compete once his employment contract has expired (*see* section 294(2) of the PC), unless the company has bound him or her to a so-called competition clause. However, being that such clauses can lead to idle labour, placing an unreasonable restraint on the individual's freedom, section 38 of the Contract Act has curtailed the validity of such clauses considerably cf. also section 34 (cf. section 41, of the Agency Act (No. 56 of 19 June 1992)). The employer must also apply the competition clause within the agreed deadline (Rt. 1990 p. 607).

A. *Employees' Freedom of Speech: Whistle-Blowing*

1. The Balance Between Freedom of Speech and the Duty of Loyalty

787. The question of employees' freedom of speech, the relationship between freedom of speech and the duty of loyalty, as well as the question of legal protection for whistle-blowers, has been the object of considerable attention also in a legislative connection.

788. The principal challenge is to state how the borderline between the duty of loyalty and freedom of speech shall be drawn. This limitation applies not only to the question of the legal relationship between the two parties in the individual employment – employer and employee – but is moreover, also of considerable significance for basic relations in society, as well as for the basic and general view of the employees' position in society and employment life.

789. The question of the legal position of whistle-blowers is connected to the conflict area between freedom of speech and duty of loyalty. Anyone who draws attention to blameworthy circumstances in a company is often called as a 'whistle-blower' (cf. the WEA section 2-4(1)). In practice there may, however, be a seamless passage from freedom of speech, which applies to general questions in society, as well as the company, to questions which concern circumstances within the individual company. An important factor concerning the whistle-blower's situation should be noted however: generally, enterprise employees who have spoken out concerning matters connected to the enterprise feel that they have done so exactly on the basis of the duty of loyalty.

2. More Specifically Concerning 'Whistle-Blowing'

790. Pursuant to the WEA section 2-4, an employee has a right to notify concerning censurable conditions at the enterprise, and pursuant to section 3-6, the employer shall facilitate internal notification if the circumstances in the enterprise so indicates. Breach of section 2-4 is subject to the penal provisions of sections 19-1 et seq. The regulations of section 2-4 and section 2-5 are exempt from the Labour Inspectorate's competence to issue orders and make individual decisions (cf. section 18-6(1)).

791. On a political legislative level – when in connection with the new WEA further improvements were to be made to aim for a fully satisfactory working environment, with special emphasis on the psychosocial working environment in order to work against harassment and discrimination – the regulations regarding whistle-blowing, and thus the regulations which shall protect the person who notifies, perhaps constitute one of the greatest challenges. This is because it is so important that the notification takes place – and that it takes place in due time, before the accident, illness, harassment or discrimination is a fact – with subsequent misery.

792. This basic principle is reflected in section 2-4, which also balances consideration for the duty of loyalty. Legitimate notification, where the requirement of an appropriate procedure is fulfilled, is not in breach of the employee's duty of loyalty. At the same time, it is also important that the company builds a culture in which it is natural for employees to notify circumstances, which seem to be problematic or unresolved.

793. The statutory right to notify pursuant to section 2-4 will apply regardless of whether restrictions to this right have been agreed upon or implemented (cf. section 1-9 of the Act). However, more far-reaching entitlements to notify may be agreed or laid down by other means. In addition, an agreement based on more far-reaching duty to notify than what follows from the statutory regulations will also imply a corresponding extended right to notify. If an employer were to initiate retaliation against an employee who notifies subject to such an extended right, the employer will be in breach of the employment contract.

794. The breach of contract may represent an independent basis for liability for the employer, but the special regulations in sections 2-4 and 2-5 regarding burden of proof and compensation will not apply. The same applies upon breach of promised anonymity.

3. Whistle-Blowing and Appropriate Procedure

795. The requirement that the employee shall follow an appropriate procedure implies that the employee must be in good faith with regard to the truthfulness of what is presented in connection with the notification. The evaluation shall be made on the basis of the understanding which the employee – based on his or her qualifications – had reason to believe at the time when the employee notified concerning the matter. An employee shall not make groundless or weakly founded allegations.

796. The evaluation of what due care the employee must have taken will, *inter alia*, depend on whether it concerns internal or public notification. It is assumed that 'internal notification only under special circumstances will fall outside the scope of the right to notify', and that 'the normal procedure in a whistle-blowing situation would be to report internally first'. This must imply that in cases of internal notification, the requirements with regard to the care of the employee in relation to the truthfulness of the basis for the notification are not strict. By internal notification is meant notification in accordance with routines developed by the enterprise, for instance in accordance with section 3-6 of the WEA, or to a responsible person in the company. According to the *travaux préparatoires*, it will always be acceptable to notify the safety deputy or employee representative. The same applies to notification to supervisory authorities or other public authorities.

797. It is not a requirement that internal notification be done first, if the employee has reason to believe that such notification will be aimless. It must be noted that the distinction between internal and external notification is not necessarily clear, for example with regard to group concerns (cf. Rt. 2003 p. 1614 (*Telenor*)).

798. Under the evaluation of justifiability, consideration must be given to the nature of the blameworthy circumstance. The matter will be very different if it is a question of corruption, environmental crime, etc. than in the event of an internal working environment problem. The regard to health, environment and safety in the enterprise, for users and recipients of the company's services, and to the society's interest in notification of censurable circumstances, shall be given greater emphasis than concern for the company's internal interests.

799. If the employee has acted in attentive good faith and considered whether notification should be given internally, to supervisory authorities or through media, it is assumed that the employee 'must have a broad margin of discretion with regard to choice of procedure'.

800. There will nevertheless be a certain basic requirement of due care with regard to the employee's choice of procedure. Thus, there may be a distortion of the question regarding whether it was a blameworthy matter in the company, to the question of whether the employee has shown sufficiently due care.

801. The burden of proof for whistle-blowing having taken place in breach of the clauses in section 2-4(1) and (2) rests on the employer, section 2-4(3), because in practice it will often be that the company has access to and overview of relevant circumstances in a completely different way than an employee may have.

B. Gifts and Similar from Business Associates

802. The requirement of loyalty also implies that employees may not receive gifts or other kind of payment from the company's business associates without the employer's knowledge. Thus, return commission (kickback) to a manager who purchased goods on behalf of the company is regarded to be in breach of the duty of loyalty, even though the company would not have received this commission and therefore had not suffered any economic loss (cf. Rt. 1919 p. 747).

803. For civil servants, the CSA section 20 stipulates a general prohibition against receiving gifts, etc. which may, or are meant, to influence the actions of a civil servant in the course of his or her duties. A reservation must however be made for customary gifts of insignificant value, for example when a teacher receives flowers from parents at the end of term as an appreciation of his or her efforts towards the pupils.

C. Competing Activities

804. It will also be in breach of the duty of loyalty if an employee operates or participates in a business, which competes with the employer's company. This applies in particular if the employee is to promote the employer's interests in a special area, but also in other situations. A journalist of a local newspaper was therefore rightly directed to discontinue his cooperation with NRK's district broadcasts, because the relationship had developed in such a way that it resulted in news in the newspaper not reaching the subscribers before the news had gone 'on air' through NRK (the Norwegian Broadcasting Corporation).

805. The requirement of loyalty will also be of significance in situations where an employee is in the process of establishing his or her own business, or transferring to another position in another company. It may be that the employee lets his or her present employer pay for training, at the same time as the employee has decided to leave the employer shortly after the training is completed. Such conduct would be in breach of the duty of loyalty. The same applies if the employee makes use of his or her knowledge of the employer's customers, for example so that the employee submits a competing tender while he or she is still employed with the employer.

806. From case law may be mentioned Rt. 1990 p. 607, where the executive director and the it-director both participated in establishing a competing enterprise, where after they gave their notices of termination; the Supreme Court held both of them responsible for the loss their employer had suffered. Further, immediate dismissal of the marketing director was considered justified (cf. Rt. 1993 p. 300); he had negotiated with the management of another enterprise in order to personally take over that firm, without informing his employer, and his employer had previously been negotiating with the other enterprise in order to take over the firm. Consultations with a possible customer and possibly start his own company, knowing that his employer might be interested in obtaining this order from that firm was, however, by the Supreme Court not considered a breach of loyalty (cf. Rt. 1960 p. 371).

807. Planning to start a competing firm with one or more of the other employees at the enterprise, without informing the employer of their plans, will of course be a significant breach of their loyalty obligations, especially if one or more of the employees in question hold senior or important positions at the enterprise (cf. e.g., RG 1989 p. 313 Eidsivating Court of Appeal).

D. Work During Spare Time

808. The duty of loyalty is also of significance in relation to the employees' work during spare time (extra sources of income). Thus, this applies to the extent of the extra work. As the employee is obliged to perform the work properly and correctly during work hours, he or she may not make arrangements for the spare time to such an extent that he or she cannot perform the ordinary work satisfactorily. This applies either the spare time activities consisting of pleasure or personal duties – for example partying or house-building – or economic activities, such as paid work. In other words, the employee's use of the spare time is subject to general limitations.

809. How far this limitation goes is dependent on several factors, for example common practice, and activities of a brief duration will be accepted more easily than long-term activities. In addition, the purpose of the free time activity will be of significance. It is easier to tolerate the fact that an employee comes to work tired and indisposed as a result of building his or her own house than from partying.

810. In Rt. 1959 p. 900 a welder at a shipyard was dismissed from his position because he had taken on extra work for another employer during his spare time. As a basis, the Supreme Court stated that 'the individual employee does in general have complete control of his spare time – including the opportunity to take on extra work during these hours – as long as the work does not represent such a strain on his work capacity that it affects his ordinary work'.

811. Furthermore, an employee cannot be engaged in other work, which is not compatible with those requirements of trust which his or her position necessitates. In practice, it is held that Revenue Officers are not entitled to take on accounting work or assignments with contractors in the municipality (cf. Rt. 1961 p. 1012). A public official who is to perform control functions towards citizens must accept limitations which are deemed necessary in order for the holder of the position to enjoy the necessary trust, and which ensures that the activities will be performed in an independent and objective manner without regard to personal interests. Correspondingly, employees of the Labour Inspectorate cannot operate or hold economic interests in a company subject to the authority of the Labour Inspectorate.

812. Usually, work in relation to additional occupations may not be performed during work hours (cf. Rt. 1983 p. 1481).

813. If an employee's additional work may be in conflict with the employer's interests the employer may, on the basis of the management prerogative, demand that the employee provides information of the type and scope of the additional work.

E. The Duty of Loyalty During the Period of Notice

814. The duty of loyalty also applies during the notice period. During this period, the employee may therefore not actively influence the employer's customers with a view to getting the customers to place future orders with him when he has become established. The situation may, however, be different if the employee does not go out actively, but for example upon request from one of the customers simply informs that the employment is about to cease, and that he or she will start up business of his or her own at a later stage.

815. In this connection, it can also be mentioned that upon resignation an employee is not entitled to take lists of customers or similar, or to make copies of such documents, for use in the employee's new capacity.

F. The Situation After Termination of the Employment Contract

816. Also following termination of employment, there are certain limitations regarding what information etc. the former employee may make use of. Subject to the PC section 249 No. 2, it is a criminal offence to make use of or make available to others business or trade secrets, unless two years have passed since resignation.

817. Furthermore, the employee may be subject to additional duties of secrecy towards the former employer, and breach of such obligations may entail liability for damages.

818. Breach of an agreed obligation to maintain secrecy may constitute grounds for dismissal, even if the employee has only been negligent (cf. Rt. 1937 p. 62).

§2. Duties of the Employer

I. Obligation to Receive the Work Effort

819. As a general rule, it must be relied on that the employer is obliged not only to pay the employee the agreed salary, but also to receive the work effort. The employer may therefore be liable for compensation if an employee in a critical way is left passive without work tasks. Partly it is unsatisfactory for the employee to be without work tasks; partly other employees will be given the impression that there are irregularities, and partly the employer may use such a rejection of work effort in order to provoke a notice of termination of the employment from the employee.

820. In this connection it is also relevant to refer to the WEA section 15-11 regarding an employee's right to remain in his or her post in the event of a dispute concerning whether the employment relationship has been legally terminated. However, if it is not possible for the employer to receive the work effort, the employer may be entitled to leave the employee without work (Rt. 1953 p. 607), but if so the situation must be assessed in relation to the regulations which apply in connection with termination of employment relationships (cf. in particular the WEA section 15-7 and section 15-14).

821. There exist no coercive means to ensure that the employee is given work, as running fines cannot be used to force someone to receive a work effort (cf. the Enforcement Act of 26 June 1992 No. 86 section 13-14 fourth subsection). However, this does not prevent the employee from being successful in a claim for a temporary injunction (Rt. 1989 p. 360), or a verdict subject to WEA section 15-11(1) to the effect that the employee is entitled to remain in his or her post while the case is pending.

822. The argument that the employer has fulfilled his or her obligations by paying the agreed salary to the employee and therefore is not directly obliged to receive the employee's work efforts, is not tenable where the salary is arranged in such a way that it is dependent on the employee's efforts, such as with piece-work and payments on commission basis. In these situations, the employee will normally not have agreed to settle for a guaranteed minimum salary. Furthermore, the argument is not tenable in relation to *inter alia* the WEA section 4-2(2) where it is stated that arrangements shall be made to enable the employee's professional and personal development through the work, and imposes on the employer obligations not being limited to payment of salary.

823. In this connection can also be noted that contracts of apprentices clearly are based on the employer having to provide the employee with such work that the apprentice may attain the necessary expertise. Otherwise, it would represent a breach of the agreement on the employer's side, and the employer is criminally liable upon gross negligence of the training obligation. In many employment relationships, it will be necessary to perform work in order to maintain the professional expertise and competence; this is pronouncedly so for pilots, divers, etc., but also applies to most other professions.

II. Training and Development of Competence

824. Training and instruction of the individual employee is a major part of an employer's obligations during the probationary period. Breach on the employer's side may entail liability for compensation (cf. for example Rt. 1983 p. 537).

825. Necessary training, practice and instruction also has a security aspect, and the WEA section 3-2(1)(a) and (b) therefore stipulates that the employer shall ensure that the employees receive that training, practice and instruction which is necessary in order to avoid accidents and health hazards. Here the employees' previous experience from corresponding work must be given considerable emphasis (cf. among others Rt. 1984 p. 337 and Rt. 1985 p. 941).

826. The employee's entitlement to training is especially marked as regards apprentice contracts. In accordance with the EA section 4-8, the employer is liable for compensation if the obligation is breached, and the employer is also criminally liable upon gross negligence of the obligation.

827. The need for training and competence development is, however, important in employment relationships in general, not at least as a result of the technological development and the adjustments which this development necessitates. As long as it is a question of training within the general development of the professional area, which is covered by the employee's obligation to work, so that it is a question of professional update of knowledge, it must be assumed that the employer will be obliged to ensure that such update can take place. Such an obligation is expressly stipulated in the EA section 10-8 as regards teachers and other employees at a school.

828. Likewise the employee will be obliged to participate in those measures, which the employer initiates in this regard. Where it is not a question of professional updating but of training beyond this, it is much more doubtful how far-reaching the employer's obligation is.

Chapter 3. Working Time, Annual Vacations, Holidays

829. Regulations regarding working hours are closely related to the employees' duties to carry out work. In order to protect the employees against excessive and inconvenient working hours, the WEA as well as other statutes and regulations, contain detailed provisions regarding the length of working hours and the time of day at which employees can be required to work. Correspondingly, there are special provisions regarding night work, work on Sundays and holidays, overtime work, etc.

830. The public interest underlying these provisions impels that the provisions generally are unalterable. Longer working hours than those prescribed by statutory provisions may be arranged by collective agreement or other agreements, but only within the limits prescribed by law (cf. the WEA section 1-9). On the other hand, the provisions do not prevent an agreement on shorter working hours.

831. Within the framework of the statutory provisions, the working hours may generally be stipulated in the employment contract. Thus, the employee is as a general rule obliged to carry out the work during such hours and at such part of the day as stipulated in the employment contract. In many employment relationships, the working hours are however also regulated by collective agreements – and possibly by collective agreements only – which may imply limitations to what the employer and the employee may agree upon.

832. In the following, only the provisions pursuant to the WEA will be dealt with.

§1. Briefly Regarding the International Basis for the Regulation of Working Hours

833. The regulation of working hours is also a major theme internationally. In order to see the provisions pursuant to the WEA in an international perspective, we therefore mention briefly some important international conventions and EU directives.

834. Norway has ratified the ILO Convention No. 14 (1921) regarding weekly time of rest in the industry, the ILO Convention No. 30 (1930) concerning the regulation of working hours in trade and office activities, the ILO Convention No. 47 (1935) on the forty-hour week, etc.

835. Also the European Social Treaty (ESP 1961) and the revised Social Treaty (1996) contain important regulations regarding working hours.

836. As regards EEC the working hour directive, Directive 2003/88/EF of 4 November 2003, must be noted. The directive sets up a framework for the organization regarding working hours, limiting national freedom as regards legislation etc.

§2. Questions Concerning Working Hours: A Politically Challenged Area of Law

837. Provisions regarding the length of working hours have been long existent in employment legislation. Each time the law has been revised, it has become clear that questions connected to regulation of working hours have been placed high on the political agenda. In particular, this regards questions concerning duration and calculation of working hours, the length of rest and spare time between work shifts, overtime work, placement of working hours in a twenty-four-hour period, passive service, etc.

I. The Concepts of Work and Off-Duty Time

838. Working hours is the time during which the employee is at the disposal of the employer, while off-duty time is the time during which the employee is not at the employer's disposal (cf. the WEA section 10-1). This is in accordance with Article 2.1 and 2.2 of the Working Hours Directive, and with previous law pursuant to the WEA (1977) section 46 No. 1.

839. In line with case law from the European Court of Justice, work of a passive nature shall be fully counted as working hours if the employee must remain at the place of work 'in case of the need to perform work', so-called standby duty.

840. Travel and walking time used from entrance door to place of attendance does not constitute part of working hours, unless there should exist special circumstances that indicate otherwise.

841. Rt. 2001 p. 418 (*Kaarstoe*) must be noted in this regard. There had been a reorganization at Statoil's plant at Kaarstoe, resulting in groups of employees being given altered places of attendance or turn-out locations which were further away from the gates leading in to the plant than earlier. The question was whether the extended travel and walk-time, which could constitute approximately 20-25 minutes each day, was included in part of the working hours in relation to individual employment contracts. The Supreme Court stated that the expression 'at disposal' must be understood in such a way that 'it presupposes that the employee is at the disposal of the employer in order to perform work tasks in accordance with the employment agreement', which meant that travel to and from work was not counted as work time.

II. General Clauses Concerning All Working-Hour Arrangements

A. *Regard to Reasonableness*

842. Pursuant to the WEA section 10-2(1), working hours shall be arranged in such a way that employees are not exposed to adverse physical or mental strain, and that they shall be able to observe safety considerations.

843. There is reason to emphasize that working-hour arrangements shall be arranged in such a way that these considerations are safeguarded. Therefore, it is not necessarily sufficient to base the working-hour arrangement on the fact that it is in compliance with the maximum limits of the Act.

B. Entitlement to Exemption from Night Work

844. The right to exemption from night work for an employee who regularly works during the night (cf. WEA section 10-2(2)), is based on EU's working hours directive. An employee who regularly works at night are entitled to exemption if this is needed by the employee concerned for health, social or other welfare reasons, and can be arranged without major inconvenience to the enterprise. In such case, the employee is entitled to exemption from the working-hour arrangements, which applies to the group of employees, of which he is a part.

C. Entitlement to Flexible Working Hours

845. The right to flexible working hours (cf. WEA section 10-2(3)) is a practically important provision. Flexible working hours may be all working-hour arrangements, which make working hours more adaptable to the individual employee's needs. The condition is that flexible working hours may be implemented 'without major inconvenience' for the enterprise.

D. Entitlement to Reduced Working Hours on the Basis of Health, Social or Welfare Grounds

846. The right to reduce working hours on the basis of health, social or other weighty welfare reasons (cf. WEA section 10-2(4)), is dependent on the reduction of working hours being arranged without major inconvenience to the enterprise.

847. When the agreed period of reduced working hours has expired, the employee has the right to resume previous working hours. Other conditions being equal, an employee working reduced hours shall have a preferential right to increase his or her working hours in the event of a vacancy in the enterprise, provided that the post wholly or essentially is assigned the same tasks.

§3. Ordinary Working Hours

848. Provisions concerning ordinary working hours are stated in the WEA section 10-4(1). The provisions must be seen in connection with the provisions concerning average calculation of working hours (cf. section 10-5). The main point concerning the calculation and limitations of ordinary working hours, regards the coherency with the regulations on overtime and overtime payment. As long as it is a question of work performed within ordinary working hours, in accordance with how these are calculated subject to the Act, it is not, pursuant to legislation, a matter of overtime work. If, on the contrary, it is a question of work performed beyond ordinary working hours, it is a matter of overtime work, which pursuant to the provisions of the Act implies a claim for an overtime surplus of 40% (cf. the WEA section 10-6(11)) and the use of overtime world is also subject to legal limitation.

849. Normal working hours must not exceed nine hours per twenty-four hours and forty hours per seven days (cf. the WEA section 10-4(1)) and pursuant to section 10-11(1) such hours shall normally be scheduled between 6 a.m. and 9 p.m. Work lasting more than five and half hours a day shall be interrupted by at least one break. The break shall be at least half an hour if the working hours are at least eight hours per day (cf. WEA section 10-9(1)).

850. In labour life it is however very common for the parties to agree – either by collective agreements or individual employment contracts – that the normal working hours shall be thirty-seven and half hours per week.

851. Furthermore, working hours must be arranged so that the employee has at least eleven hours continuous off-duty time per twenty-four hours (daily off-duty time), which shall be placed between two main work periods. Furthermore, the employee is entitled to a continuous off-duty period of at least thirty-five hours per seven days (weekly off-duty time) (cf. WEA section 10-8(1) and (2)). Night work and work on Sundays and public holidays may only be imposed as far as prescribed by law (cf. WEA sections 10-10 and 10-11).

852. For certain types of work, the WEA prescribes that the normal working hours may not exceed thirty-eight hours per week and nine hours per twenty-four hours.

853. Collective agreements generally have set ordinary working hours at 36.5 hours per week for double-shift work and 35.5 hours per week for triple-shift work. For non-interrupted triple-shift work, the collective agreements usually stipulate 33.6 hours a week.

854. For some work, the normal working hours may be extended/prolonged. This applies to work that is wholly or mainly of a passive nature, but the employee is obliged to stay at the workplace, for in case of need to perform work. In these situations, working hours may be extended for up to one-half of the passive periods, but not by more than two hours per twenty-four hour day and ten hours per seven days (cf. WEA section 10-4(2)). Normal working hours must not exceed forty-eight hours per seven days. Similarly, working hours may be extended for standby duty outside the workplace. In the latter situation, at least one-seventh of such standby duty shall, as a general rule be included in the ordinary working hours (cf. WEA section 10-4(3) – By the Act of 24 April 2015, which entered into force on 1 July 2015, the conversion factor was set at one-seventh. Before this amendment the conversion factor was stipulated at one-fifth of the standby duty). If the enterprise is bound by a collective agreement, the employer and the employee's elected representatives may by written agreement stipulate a different method for calculation. If the one-seventh conversion factor appears clearly unreasonable, the Labour Inspectorate may stipulate another method of calculation if so requested by the employer or the employees' elected representatives.

855. Preparatory and finishing work is part of the normal working hours.

I. Calculating Average Normal Working Hours

856. In many employment relationships, the workload may vary, so that some periods are very busy while others are quieter. In these situations, there is a need for a more flexible working hour system than the general rules stipulates concerning fixed working hour per day or week. This is the framework for WEA section 10-5 regarding calculation of average working hours.

857. The employer may not implement calculation of average working hours unilaterally. Such an arrangement is dependent on a written agreement between the employer and the individual employee, an agreement between the employer and the employees' representative in enterprises bound by a collective agreement, or with approval by the Labour Inspectorate.

II. Subject to Written Agreement Between the Employer and the Employee

858. Subject to written agreement between the employer and the employee, the normal working hours may be arranged in such a way that the total number of working hours in a period not exceeding fifty-two weeks, on average is no longer than the normal working hours prescribed in section 10-4 (nine hours per day and forty hours per week), and so that the total working hours does not exceed ten hours per twenty-four hours and forty-eight hours per seven days. This is stipulated in WEA section 10-5(1), which was amended by the Act of 24 April 2015 No. 20, and entered into force on 1 July 2015. Before this amendment, the total working hours per twenty-four hours could not exceed nine hours, and not exceed forty-eight hours per seven days. This amendment gives the employer a somewhat wider margin in order to arrange the working hours, if so needed. However, the amended provision now also stipulates a prohibition for the employer, who has engaged the employee on a temporary employment contract based on WEA section 14-9(1) letter f) (temporary employment on a general basis not exceeding twelve consecutive months) against entering into an agreement on average calculation of the working hours.

III. Subject to Written Agreement Between the Employer and the Employees' Representatives – Approval Given by the Labour Inspectorate

859. If the enterprise is bound by a collective agreement, the employer and the employees' representatives may similarly enter into a written agreement to the effect that normal working hours shall be arranged in such a way that the total number of working hours in a period not exceeding fifty-two weeks, on average is no longer than the normal working hours prescribed in section 10-4, but that the normal working hours do not exceed twelve, five hours per twenty-twenty-four hours and forty-eight hours per seven days. The limit of forty-eight hours per seven days may be calculated according to a fixed average over a period of eight weeks, provided that normal working hours do not exceed fifty-four hours in any one week. This is stipulated in WEA section 10-5(2), which were amended by the Act of 24 April 2015 No. 20, and entered into force on 1 July 2015. Before this amendment, the total working hours per twenty-four hours could not exceed ten hours, and not exceed forty-eight hours per seven days.

860. Subject to approval given by the Labour Inspectorate, the average calculation may be made correspondingly for a period not exceeding twenty-six weeks, so that the total working hours do not exceed thirteen hours per twenty-four hours, or forty-eight hours per seven days (cf. WEA section 10-5(3)). The limit if forty-eight hours per seven days may be calculated according to a fixed average over a period of eight weeks.

861. Before the Labour Inspectorate makes its decision, the working-hour arrangements shall be discussed with the employees' elected representatives. Records from these discussions and a drafted work schedule shall be enclosed with the application. When making the decision, the Labour Inspectorate shall attach particular importance to the health and welfare of the employees (cf. WEA section 10-5(3)).

862. If the employees work at different times of the day, a work schedule shall be prepared showing which weeks, days and at what hour each employee is supposed to work (cf. WEA section 10-3). When preparing or amending the schedule, particular emphasis shall be placed on the regard for the health and welfare of the employees.

863. The work schedule shall be prepared in cooperation with the employees' elected representatives, and it shall be easily accessible to the employees.

864. In this connection can also be mentioned that an account shall be kept of the hours worked by each employee (cf. WEA section 10-7). This account shall be accessible to the Labour Inspectorate and the employees' elected representatives.

§4. Overtime Work

865. Work in excess of what the WEA prescribes as normal working hours, are regarded as overtime work (cf. WEA section 10-6(2)). Overtime work must not take place except in cases when there is a specific and time-limited need for it. Overtime work must therefore not be instituted as a permanent arrangement.

866. Before imposing overtime work, the employer shall, as far as possible, discuss the necessity of such work with the employees' elected representatives (cf. WEA section 10-6(3)).

867. Attempts shall be made to distribute overtime in such a way that the individual employee is not put under undue pressure. Overtime work must not exceed ten hours per seven days, twenty-five hours per four consecutive weeks or 200 hours during a period of fifty-two weeks, (cf. WEA section 10-6(4)). However, the total working hours (overtime and regular hours together) must not exceed thirteen hours per twenty-four hours or forty-eight hours per seven days for any employee. The limit of forty-eight hours per seven days may be calculated according to a fixed average over a period of eight weeks; however, the total working hours in accordance with WEA section 10-5(2) and section 10-6(5) shall not exceed sixty-nine hours in any single week.

868. If the enterprise is bound by a collective agreement, the employer and the employees' representatives may enter into a written agreement to the effect that overtime work does not exceed twenty hours per seven days, and not exceed fifty hours over a period of four consecutive weeks. According to such an agreement, the total amount of overtime work may not exceed 300 hours during a period of fifty-two weeks.

869. The Labour Inspectorate may on application in special cases permit total overtime work not exceeding twenty-five hours per seven days or 200 hours during a period of twenty-six weeks (cf. WEA section 10-6(6)).

870. It should be emphasized that the WEA distinguishes between work in excess of normal working hours (overtime work) and work in excess of agreed working hours (extra work). If a collective agreement or an individual employment contract stipulate regular working hours that are shorter than those prescribed as normal working hours in the WEA (cf. section 10-4), work beyond such hours will not be subject to the statutory conditions and restrictions. If, for example, the regular working day is set at seven hours in a full-time position, the statutory restrictions will not apply if the employee is asked to work two hours in addition to the agreed seven hours. In everyday language, the two hours of extra work is often referred to as overtime, but in terms of the WEA only work in excess of nine hours per day is regarded as overtime work. However, also work in excess of agreed working hours is subject to a specific and time-limited need in WEA section 10-6(1).

871. Whether the employer may require the employee to work the mentioned additional hours, and whether the employee is entitled to extra pay for such work, depends on the agreement between the parties.

I. Compensation

872. For overtime work, a supplement of at least 40% shall be paid, in addition to the pay received by the employee for corresponding work during normal working hours (cf. WEA section 10-6(11)).

873. The employer and the employee may agree in writing that overtime hours shall wholly or partly be taken out as off-duty time on agreed dates (cf. WEA section 10-6(12)). However, the overtime surplus may not be taken out as off-duty time. Such an arrangement might imply an increase of the use of overtime work.

II. Obligation to Perform Overtime Work

874. Whether the employees are obliged to work beyond ordinary working hours – perform overtime work – will in principle depend on how this matter is regulated in their employment contracts. If the employment contract does not provide a basis for something else, a duty to perform overtime work within the limits of WEA section 10-6(4) is common. This is also the presumption of the Act (cf. WEA section 10-6(10)), as long as the total working hours per day does not exceed thirteen hours. However, the answer to the question will nevertheless depend upon a concrete assessment. If an employee has agreed upon working hours from 10 a.m. until 2 p.m. and the employee has expressed that the employer cannot rely on him or her performing work in excess of this time frame – the employee is, for example, dependent on child minding and has made arrangements for this time frame – the employee will not be obliged to work more than the stated time. The question of whether the employee is obliged to work beyond ordinary working hours will in principle be the same, regardless of whether it is a question of overtime work pursuant to the statutory regulations, or the working hours specifically agreed in the employment contract. If it is a question of overtime beyond the limits of section 10-6(4), overtime will be dependent on the employee's consent in each individual case (cf. section 10-6(7)).

875. With regard to claims for overtime payment pursuant to the WEA section 10-6(11), the employee is entitled to a surplus of at least 40% based on the salary, which is paid for corresponding work during ordinary working hours. Pursuant to the Act, the employee may only claim for such compensation if the ordinary working hours pursuant to the Act, are exceeded. Work beyond the agreed working hours in the above-mentioned example, is not regarded as overtime work pursuant to the WEA. Thus, the Act does not warrant a claim for special compensation in such situations, but a claim for compensation may be agreed or warranted by a collective agreement.

876. If an employee is obliged to perform overtime work, the employer is nevertheless obliged to exempt the employee from such work when the employee requests exemption for health reasons or for weighty social reasons (cf. section 10-6(10)). Health reasons are in principle an absolute basis for exemption, but it may be practical to have the cause documented by a doctor's certificate, at least if it is a question of exemption from overtime work over a long period of time. Weighty social reasons may be, for example care of small children, participation at major family events, etc. Also when the employee, on the basis of other personal reasons, requests to be exempted from overtime work, the employer is obliged to exempt the employee. However, this is subject to the condition that the work can be postponed or performed by others without harm. It is presupposed that the employer consults with the employees' representatives, if there is doubt whether the work can be postponed or performed by others.

877. The reasons for exemption stated in section 10-6(10) includes the right to be exempted from work beyond agreed working hours, even if it does not concern overtime work in relation to the regulations of the Act. Overtime work beyond the limits in section 10-6(4) are, as mentioned, voluntary (cf. section 10-6(7)).

878. The work shall be interrupted by at least one break if the daily working hours exceed five hours and thirty minutes. If the daily working hours total at least eight hours, the breaks shall collectively amount to at least thirty minutes (cf. WEA section 10-9(1)).

879. During the break, the employee shall not perform work, and he or she shall be free to leave the workplace. Under these circumstances, the break is not regarded as part of the working hours pursuant to the Act. However, if the employee is not free to leave the workplace during the break or if there is no satisfactory rest room, the break is regarded as part of the working hours (cf. also Rt. 1995 p. 1).

880. The break is also counted as part of the working hours in another situation. This applies when an employee works more than two hours after normal working hours (cf. the WEA section 10-9(2)). In these situations, the employee shall be allowed a break of at least thirty minutes, and the break shall be regarded as part of the working hours. However, when conditions so necessitate, the break may be reduced or postponed. Breaks which are placed after the end of ordinary working hours shall be subject to remuneration as overtime, but shall not be included in the number of hours it is permitted to work overtime pursuant to section 10-6.

§5. Daily and Weekly Off-Duty Time

881. An employee shall have at least eleven hours continuous off-duty time per twenty-four hours (cf. WEA section 10-8(1)). Furthermore, an employee is entitled to a continuous off-duty period of thirty-five hours per seven days (cf. WEA section 10-8(2)).

882. In enterprises bound by a collective agreement, the employer and the employees' elected representatives may agree in writing upon exceptions from the provisions regarding daily and weekly off-duty time (cf. WEA section 10-8(3)). Such an agreement may, however, only be entered into if the employee is ensured corresponding compensatory rest period or, where this is not possible, other appropriate protection. Off-duty periods shorter than eight hours per twenty-four hours or twenty-eight hours per seven days may not be agreed upon.

§6. Night Work and Work on Sundays and Public Holidays

883. For night work and work on Sundays and public holidays, the WEA contains special provisions in sections 10-11 and 10-10. The purpose of these provisions is to limit the use of such work. Hence, the Act stipulates that such work is only permitted when necessitated by the nature of the work (cf. sections 10-11(2) and 10-10(2)).

884. Work between the hours of 9 p.m. and 6 a.m. is regarded as night work. However, work in two shifts that fall between the hours of 6 a.m. and 12 midnight is not regarded as night work (cf. WEA section 10-11(1)).

885. The public holidays are not defined in the WEA, but in the Act related to public holidays section 2, it is stated that 1 and 17 May are regarded as public holidays. As a general rule, no work shall be performed from 6 p.m. on the day preceding a Sunday or public holiday until 10 p.m. on the day preceding the next working day. On Christmas Eve, and on the Saturdays preceding Easter Sunday and Whit Sunday, no work shall be performed from 3 p.m. until 10 p.m. on the day preceding the next working day.

886. For night work or work on Sundays and public holidays, the employer shall discuss the need for such work with the employees' elected representatives before imposing the work (cf. sections 10-11(3) and 10-10(3)).

§7. Special Regulations Concerning Night Work

887. For an employee who regularly works more than three hours at night, normal working hours shall on average not exceed eight hours per twenty-four hours. The average shall be calculated over four weeks (cf. WEA section 10-11(5)). The provision regards normal working hours, so that overtime work comes in addition to the stipulated normal working hours.

888. In enterprises bound by a collective agreement, the employer and the employees' representatives may agree in writing that the above-mentioned provision shall be departed from. In such case, the employees shall be ensured corresponding compensatory rest periods or, where this is not possible, other appropriate protection.

889. It must also be noticed that an employee who mainly works at night shall be offered a medical examination before commencing employment and subsequently at regular intervals.

890. An employee who regularly works at night will be entitled to exemption from the working-hour arrangement that applies to the employee group if such exemption is needed by the employee concerned for health, social or other weighty welfare reasons and can be arranged without major inconvenience to the enterprise (cf. WEA section 10-2(2)).

891. If there are other days that, subject to the employee's religion, are equivalent to Sundays and public holidays, the employer and the employee may by means of a written agreement concerning work on Sundays and public holidays other than those referred to in this provision. If so, the employee is entitled to corresponding time off on the days that are corresponding to Sundays and public holidays subject to the employee's religion (cf. WEA section 10-10(5)), and paragraph 1000 below.

§8. Employment Relationships That Are Exempted from the Working Hours Provisions

892. The general working hour provisions of the WEA provide a relatively inflexible system. To meet the requirement for more flexible working-hour arrangements, the Act contains several exclusionary provisions.

I. Employees Holding Managerial or Particularly Independent Posts

893. For certain types of positions, working hours are only regulated to a small degree (cf. the WEA section 10-12(1) and (2)). This applies to employees in leading positions, and employees who hold a particularly independent position within the enterprise. For these employees, the nature of the work requires great flexibility and the regulations of the WEA regarding working hours do not provide adequate regulations regarding their work time.

894. However, the requirements are stringent as to what types of employees will be included in these categories, and this must be considered in relation to each individual employee.

895. An employee who holds a leading position must necessarily have clear managerial functions. The *travaux préparatoires* of the Act mention some positions, where the central question seems to be whether the employee himself or herself must consider and determine the requirements of his or her own work efforts, and therefore also to a major degree his or her own working hours. Title and salary can provide some indication, but will in itself not be decisive. If an employee's working hours are subject to regular control, it is not likely that the employer may be regarded as working in a leading position. It should however be noted that the term 'leading position' is more wide-ranging than the term 'chief executive' and 'the one who, in the employer's absence, manages the business' (cf. the WEA section 15-16 and section 1-8(2)).

896. As regards employees in particularly independent posts, it is not regarded as sufficient that the individual himself or herself is able to control the working hours, or has flexible working hours. The employee must prioritize the work tasks, and thus 'decide himself what is to be done, what shall be delegated to others, when and how the work shall be performed. Just to be working on a project is not sufficient'. It is also stated in the preparatory works that supervisors and others in corresponding positions who during work hours follow those they are set to manage will usually not be comprised by the exclusionary provisions, and comprised by the otherwise applicable working hour regulations.

897. Also in respect of employees in 'leading' and 'particularly independent' positions, the working hours shall be arranged in such a way that employees are not exposed to adverse physical or mental strain, and so that they are able to observe safety considerations (cf. WEA section 10-2(1)).

II. Trade Unions with More Than 10,000 Members

898. With a few exceptions, trade unions with more than 10,000 members may enter into a collective agreement concerning working hours which departs from the statutory regulations concerning the length and placing of the normal working hours (cf. WEA section 10-12(4)). Thus, such trade unions may, *inter alia*, enter into a collective agreement to the effect that night work and work on Sundays and public holidays can be performed to a wider extent. To a certain extent, this also applies for overtime work. In practice, the major trade unions may therefore agree upon a working-hour arrangement, which is regarded as most adequate for the particular field of activities in question.

899. Furthermore, the employer and the employees' elected representatives may enter into written agreements concerning temporary performance of night work (section 10-11(4)), work on Sundays and public holidays (section 10-10(4)), average calculation of working hours (section 10-5(2)), extended overtime (section 10-6(5) and (9)) and shorter daily/weekly off-duty time (section 10-8(3)), if the enterprise is bound by a collective agreement. However, the Act stipulates definite limits for such agreements.

III. Divergent Employment Contracts Between the Employer and the Individual Employee

900. Such employment contract may be entered into regarding religious holidays according to the employee's religion, regarding average off-duty every other Sunday and public holiday, average calculation of working hours.

901. Thus, the employer and the individual employee may agree in writing that the employee shall perform work on Sundays and public holidays, allowing the employee corresponding off-duty time on the days that are corresponding to Sundays and public holidays according to the employee's religion (cf. WEA section 10-10(5)).

902. In addition, the employer and the individual employee may agree in writing to a working-hour arrangement that ensures that the employee will be off-duty on average every other Sunday and public holiday over a period of twenty-six weeks, provided however that the weekly twenty-four-hour off-duty period falls on a Sunday or public holiday at least every fourth week (cf. section 10-8(4)).

903. Furthermore, the employer and the individual employee may in writing agree upon average calculation of normal working hours (cf. WEA section 10-5(1)). The requirement for a written agreement is based on the consideration for public control, and the parties need for clearness. An oral agreement concerning average calculation may, however, be valid between the parties.

904. As mentioned, the agreement must imply that the working hours on average are as long as the normal working hours subject to the general regulations. In addition, the working hours within a single week must not exceed ten hours per twenty-four hours and forty-eight hours per seven days.

905. The Labour Inspectorate may provide special permission for extended use of overtime work and average calculation of the working hours, in excess of the limits, which follow from the general regulations. Further, the Labour Inspectorate may consent to working-hour arrangements that derogate from the provisions regarding weekly off-duty time. All of the mentioned provisions emphasize that, when making a decision, the Authority shall attach particular importance to the health and welfare of the employees. Furthermore, that the working-hour arrangement shall be discussed with the employees' elected representatives, before permission is given. Records of the discussions shall be enclosed with the application.

906. There are also other situations where the Labour Inspectorate may grant permission that differs from the general working hour regulations.

907. To the extent that divergent working-hour arrangements are established, this implies that the general provisions on maximum hours and scheduling, etc. may be deviated from. This means that the divergent working-hour arrangement is legitimate in relation to the public interests. However, this does not automatically mean that a divergent arrangement is binding upon the individual employee. That is an issue that must be considered separately.

908. If an individual employee has entered into an agreement regarding a divergent working-hour arrangement, this implies that he is also bound to perform work within the framework of the agreement. Presumably, the same applies when an individual employee has consented to a divergent working-hour arrangement.

909. Divergent working-hour arrangements established on the basis of an agreement between the employer and the employees' elected representative, will generally only comprise the employees whom the employee representative may represent – in practice, employees who are union members. However, if a majority of the employees are bound by the agreement, the employer may make the provisions of the agreement concerning working hours applicable to all employees who perform work of the kind covered by the agreement.

910. For non-union member employees, their employment contracts may be interpreted so that they shall follow a specially stated working-hour arrangement, and in such case the employer's agreement with employee representatives concerning deviating working hours will not be binding for them. However, it is often expressly stated in the employment contract – or presumed – that also non-union member employees shall follow ordinary working hours of the company. If so, also these employees will be bound by agreements concerning deviating working hours, which the employees' representatives enter into with the employer (cf. Rt. 1985 p. 78).

911. A deviating working-hour arrangement established through dispensation from the Labour Inspectorate will cover all employees in the enterprise who perform work of the kind which the dispensation concerns. Whether the individual employee is obliged to perform work according to such working-hour arrangements, must be decided in the same manner as described above regarding agreements between the employer and the employees' elected representatives concerning deviating working-hour arrangements.

912. Diverging working-hour arrangements established by collective agreement between an employer and a trade union with more than 10,000 members may also be made applicable to all employees who perform work of the kind covered by the agreement, if a majority of the employees are bound by the agreement.

913. Within the framework of statutory regulations, collective agreements and employment contracts the employer may, by virtue of the managerial prerogative, determine how the working hours shall be arranged, and whether overtime work shall be used. Also as regards working hours, the managerial prerogative must however be practised in a just and reasonable way.

914. The statutory framework for working hours, and the abnormal working-hour arrangements that may be established, set only maximum limits for working hours. However, working hours may be subject to additional restrictions on a different basis. In practice, it is significant that many collective agreements state that, in a great number of areas, the regular working week is stipulated to be totally 37½ hours. For many professions, it is also normal to schedule working hours according to custom or as agreed with the individual employee, e.g., from 8.30 a.m. to 3.30 p.m. In such cases, the employment contract must, in the absence of other indications, be interpreted to the effect that the working hours shall be what is customary in that particular trade.

915. Hours can also be arranged so that the employee has some latitude as to when the working day shall start and end, as is practised in government service with regard to the central administration. There, specific rules on flexible working hours ('flexi time') are drawn up in a framework agreement, so that all employees must be present during the 'core time' (9.00 a.m. to 2.30 p.m.), while 'peripheral working hours' are from 8.00 to 9.00 a.m. and from 2.30 p.m. to 6 p.m. The peripheral hours are those in which the time at which the employee starts and finishes work may vary from day to day.

§9. Entitlement to Reduced Working Hours

916. Under certain circumstances, an employee may be entitled to have his or her normal working hours reduced. The conditions for such reduction are that it is necessary due to health, social or other weighty welfare reasons. Furthermore, it is a requirement that the reduction of working hours can be arranged without major inconvenience to the enterprise (cf. WEA section 10-2(4)):

- It must be assumed that an employee, who is working part-time subject to the above-mentioned provision, is obliged to notify the employer if the reasons which were the basis for the working hour reduction, have lapsed. If so, the employee will be obliged to resume previous working hours. When the agreed period of reduced working hours has expired, the employee has the right to resume previous working hours.
- Other conditions being equal, an employee working reduced hours shall have a preferential right to increase the working hours in the event of a vacancy in the enterprise, provided that the post wholly or essentially is assigned the same tasks (cf. WEA section 10-2(4)).

917. Disputes between the employer and the employee concerning application of the provisions regarding entitlement for reduced working hours or off-duty periods, shall be resolved by the Dispute Resolution Board (cf. WEA section 10-13, and section 17-2).

§10. Work Performed by Children and Young Persons

I. Survey

918. For work performed by children and young persons, the regard for protection has particular emphasis. On this basis, the general rule is that children under 13 years of age may not perform work, while children between 13 and 15 years of age may perform light work, and young persons between 15 and 18 years of age may perform work to a wider extent. The WEA also stipulates specific requirements with regard to the length of the working hours, off-duty periods, and overtime and night work may usually not be performed. By ‘children’ are meant persons under 13 years of age, and persons between 13 and 15 years of age. By ‘young persons’ are meant persons between 15 and 18 years of age.

919. Internationally, child labour is prohibited and specifically regulated through different conventions.

II. Type of Work

920. According to the WEA section 11-1, there is a general prohibition of children who are under 15 years of age or attending compulsory education performing work in accordance with the Act. The prohibition does not prevent children from performing common duties as a part of a family, such as cleaning their own room and doing laundry, dishwashing etc., as long as the extent of the work is reasonable within family relations (cf. also paragraphs 181–182 above); within these limitations, the WEA does not comprise such work.

921. Subject to the WEA section 11-1(1), children over 13 years of age are entitled to perform light work, which may not be detrimental to their safety, health, development or schooling. In addition, children over 14 years of age, who attend compulsory education, may perform work that forms part of their schooling or practical vocational guidance, provided the work may not be detrimental to their health or development. The school authorities shall approve the practical guidance. Furthermore, children who are under 15 years of age or attending compulsory education may perform cultural or similar work.

922. In general, persons under 18 years of age must not perform work that may be detrimental to their safety, health, development or schooling.

III. Working Hours

923. Working hours for persons under 18 years of age shall be arranged so that they do not interfere with their schooling or prevent them from benefiting from their lessons (cf. WEA section 11-2(1)).

924. For children who are under 15 years of age or attending compulsory education, working hours must not exceed two hours a day and twelve hours a week. On days without teaching, the child may work for seven hours a day and thirty-five hours a week. If the child is working as part of an arrangement involving alternating theoretical and practical education, the total of working hours and school hours must not exceed eight hours a day and forty hours a week (cf. WEA section 11-2(2)). These children may not perform work between 8 p.m. and 6 a.m. (night work).

925. For young persons between 15 and 18 years of age, and who are not attending compulsory education, the working hours must not exceed eight hours per day and forty hours per week (cf. WEA section 11-3(2)). These persons may not perform work between 11 p.m. and 6 a.m. Work between 9 p.m. and 11 p.m. is regarded as night work, and may not be performed by young employees unless necessitated by the nature of the work, or unless there is an exceptional and time-limited need for it.

926. If natural disasters, accident or other unforeseen events render it necessary that work is carried out in order to avert danger or damage to life or property, and where it is strictly necessary to employ the young persons concerned in the work, young persons between 15 and 18 years of age may perform such work. If so, the young persons shall have a subsequent compensatory rest period (cf. WEA section 11-3(3)).

927. When children work for two or more employers, working hours shall be calculated as a total of the hours worked for all employers. The employer is obliged to obtain information concerning hours worked for other employers (cf. WEA section 11-2(4)).

IV. Breaks and Time-Off

928. Persons under 18 years of age shall have a rest break of at least thirty minutes, if possible continuous, if daily working hours exceed four hours and thirty minutes (cf. section 11-5(1)).

929. Children under 15 years of age, or who are attending compulsory education, are entitled to a continuous off-duty period of at least fourteen hours within each period of twenty-four hours. Young persons between 15 and 18 years of age who are not attending compulsory education, are entitled to a continuous off-duty period of at least twelve hours per twenty-four-hour period (cf. section 11-5(2)).

930. Persons under 18 years of age shall have a continuous off-duty period of at least forty-eight hours per seven days. The off-duty period shall as far as possible be on a Sunday or public holiday (cf. WEA section 11-5(3)).

931. Persons under 18 years of age who attend school, shall have at least four weeks holiday per year, of which at least two weeks shall be taken during the summer holiday (cf. section 11-5(4)).

932. In special cases, the Ministry may by Regulation provide exceptions from the above-mentioned provisions (cf. WEA section 11-5(5)).

§11. Holidays

I. Annual Holidays

933. With some exceptions, employees have a right to holidays and holiday pay regulated in the Holiday Act: Act No. 21 of 29 April 1988. According to section 5(1), employees have a right to twenty-five work days of holiday time each holiday year. This includes Saturdays and will therefore normally constitute four weeks plus one day. However, it is very common that employees, subject to individual or collective agreement, or subject to practice within the enterprise, to be entitled to five weeks of holiday.

934. The holiday year follows the calendar year (cf. section 4). Employees, whose sixtieth birthday falls before 1 September in the holiday year, shall be given an additional six days of holiday time (cf. section 5(2)). The employee may demand that eighteen work days be allocated to holiday time during the period June 1 to September 30, and that the remaining time-off be taken as an uninterrupted holiday during the holiday year. The employer and employee may agree in writing that the employee shall take a holiday in advance or that up to twelve workdays of holiday time shall be rescheduled to the following holiday year. However, rescheduling more days than that is prohibited (cf. section 7). If the employee has not been able to take holiday leave due to illness or statutory parental leave, the remaining holiday time shall be transferred to the following year (cf. section 7 No. 3 second paragraph). Within the above framework, the employer shall schedule the holiday after discussing it with the employees and in ample time before the holiday. If unforeseen events force the employer to reschedule the holiday, the employees have a right to compensation for documented expenses incurred because of the rescheduling (cf. section 6). An employee who is completely incapacitated before the holiday commences may require the holiday to be postponed until later in the holiday year. The requirement must be supported by a medical certificate and be submitted no later than the last working day before the holiday should have commenced (cf. section 9 No. 1 first paragraph). Employees who have been completely incapacitated during the holidays may require a corresponding number of holidays postponed and given as a new holiday later in the holiday year. This requirement must be supported by a medical certificate and be submitted without undue delay after the work has been resumed (section 9 No. 1 second paragraph).

II. Holiday Pay

935. Holiday pay comprises 10.2% of wages, etc., paid during the previous calendar year (accrual year). For employees who are entitled to five weeks of holiday, holiday pay comprises 12% of wages, etc.

936. For employees over 60 years of age with a right to additional holiday time, the percentage shall be increased by 2.3% points (cf. section 10). Holiday pay shall be issued on the last regular payday before the holiday, but the employee may demand payment at least a week before holiday commencement. On termination of employment, all accrued holiday pay shall be paid on the last regular payday prior to leaving (cf. section 11). The employer is liable for damages if he fails to comply with the provisions of the Holiday Act relating to holiday time and holiday pay, such damages including those for financial loss and a fair compensation for loss of welfare (cf. section 14).

Chapter 4. Remuneration and Benefits

§1. Wages and Wage Systems

I. Wages

937. The employer is of course obliged to pay the employee wages. Wages may consist of payment in money, in kind or a combination of both, as is the usual case for domestic help and seamen. Calculation of wages and amount thereof may be agreed between the parties, but it will frequently be stipulated in collective agreements or established in some other way. It may be agreed that the employee shall be paid per time unit (by the hour, day, week, etc.) or per unit of output (piece-work). In the latter case, a minimum wage shall usually be paid regardless of output. Furthermore, various salary increases shall be paid, including service increments and for work under unfavourable conditions such as dirty work or working in the tropics, for example.

938. However, the employee bears the risk if he is unable to come to work at the appointed time, although this principle is modified by particular rules for special situations such as e.g., illness. If the worker is unable to come to work on time because of unforeseen events such as bad weather and transport strikes, he or she has no right to wages during such absence. The same applies to absence due to prison detainment (cf. Rt. 1992 p. 1482), even if later proven that the employee was not guilty of the charges for which he or she was held in custody.

II. Wage Systems

939. Wages as recompense for work provides only a basis. In a number of cases, an employee may have a right to wages even if he or she is not working, for example during sick leave. But this basis also says nothing about wages depending on whether work is being done, or whether the employees have a right to wages if they place their labour at the employer's disposal at the appointed time and place.

940. This question depends on the interpretation of the employment contract between the parties, and hence the wage system on which the employments contract is based: a time-wage system or an incentive-wage system. If it is a time-wage system, the wage is set according to time unit (wage per hour, day, week, month, year), in which case it will suffice that the employees have placed their labour at the employer's disposal for the agreed time. If it is an incentive-wage system, wages will depend on output volume, number of units sold, etc. In such cases, wages will basically depend on the work yielding results. Incentive-wage systems include various piecework systems (used in parts of industry and the building and construction trade) and commission systems (in the sales and service industries).

941. However, the two different wage systems are not totally separate. Most incentive-wage systems entitle workers to a minimum wage per time unit, and in many cases, time-wage systems will be based on a certain amount of work being performed over a certain period of time. Basically, we can say that in incentive-wage systems, workers bear a greater risk as to the yield of their labour than they do in time-wage systems.

942. Incentive-wage systems are based on the tenet that the individual employee will exert greater effort when the wage is linked to the work carried out rather than the time spent on the job. However, these wage systems have weaknesses: workers can be pressured, increased production or sales might affect quality and safety might be ignored. Thus, the WEA section 4-1(2) stipulates that the organization, arrangement and management of wage systems shall be arranged in such a way that the employees are not exposed to adverse physical or mental strain and that due regard is paid to safety considerations.

943. Incentive-wage systems cannot be used where work output cannot be measured directly in terms of produced or sold volume, etc. This includes e.g., work of a supervisory or controlling nature and administrative work. Hence, 'clerical' work is traditionally based on time-wage systems.

944. Some bonus systems aim at combining time-wage systems with incentive-wages systems. In such a system, the time-wage portion and the alterable bonus portion may be larger, smaller or equal – depending on what may be agreed upon – and the alterable portion will more or less depend on the production of the enterprise or a department etc. It may be recommended that productivity agreements are established at enterprises where a bonus system is used (cf. e.g., the IA (2012) section 4.3).

945. In practice, the wage system may be established partly by nationally based collective agreements, and partly by locally based special agreements in addition to the individual contract of employment.

946. It may further be agreed, e.g., by collective agreement, how a wage system may be changed, and the rights and duties of enterprise and employees in that regard. Thus, the IA (2012) section 4.1.5 stipulate that if notice of termination of the agreement on the rates in a pay system has been given, usually with one month's notice, and new agreement on the pay rates has not been reached, 'the individual employees shall be paid 45% of their average hourly earnings, exclusive of all supplements, in the last known quarter. Corresponding performance of work is presupposed'. Because such reduction of the work to be performed is permitted by the collective agreement, it is not to be considered a 'go slow' action contrary to the peace obligation following a collective agreement (cf. also paragraphs 1557 and 1581 below), nor contrary to the regulations on leave of absence in the Basic Agreement (2014) sections 8-1 et seq., nor a 'conflict' in that regard (cf. ARD 1986 p. 124; also ARD 2005 p. 318 concluding that specific offshore remuneration should be paid in such a situation, nor a duty to inform the State Mediator according to the LDA section 16). Similar reduction of the work to be performed, in other situations than regulated by the collective agreement, is a breach of the peace obligation (cf. ARD 1987 p. 27).

§2. Minimum Wage

947. Norway has no legislation regulating minimum remuneration, but collective agreements containing such provisions are common.

948. Some collective agreements are made generally applicable by law within certain sectors and/or geographical areas (*see* paragraphs 1499–1505). If so, all employees within the given sector/area will be entitled to receive the minimum wage under the agreement.

949. Subject to compliance with collective agreements affecting the employee's employment, an employer and employee may agree upon the level of salary to be paid and upon any arrangements for future salary increase.

§3. Equal Wages for Work of Equal Value for Both Women and Men Within the Same Enterprise

950. According to the Gender Equality Act (of 21 June 2013 No. 59) section 21, women and men in the same enterprise shall have equal pay for the same work or work of equal value. The pay shall be stipulated in the same way for women and men regardless of gender. The term 'pay' means ordinary remuneration for work as well as other supplements, advantages or other benefits provided by the employer.

951. In connection with the above, the right to equal pay for the same work or work of equal value shall apply regardless of whether such work is connected with different trades or professions or whether the pay is regulated by different collective wage agreements. Whether the work is of equal value shall be determined after an overall assessment in which importance is attached to the expertise that is necessary to perform the work and other relevant factors, such as effort, responsibility and working conditions.

952. If there are circumstances that give reason to believe that there has been direct or indirect differential treatment in contravention of section 21, among other provisions of the General Equality Act (GEA), such differential treatment shall be assumed to have taken place unless the person responsible proves on a balance of probabilities that such differential treatment nonetheless did not take place. Thus, the employer has the burden of proof in such circumstances (cf. GEA section 27).

953. An example in this regard is the judgment recorded in ARD 1990 p. 148. In this case, the male engineers in charge of a department and the female bioengineers in the same hospital laboratory were paid in accordance with the main collective agreement in the municipal sector, which resulted in partly differential wages. The Labour Court found the lower wages not to be in accordance with the GEA section 5, which also implied that the provisions stipulated in the collective agreement had to be invalid. There were no significant difference regarding the working or responsibility conditions, neither were there any significant differences regarding qualifications or skills. The decisive factor had to be whether the standards for stipulating the wages were the same for both women and men.

954. An employee who is of the opinion that discrimination has occurred regarding the stipulation of payment, shall be entitled to demand that the employer provide a written confirmation of the pay level and the criteria for the stipulation of the wage payment of the persons with whom the employee in question is making a comparison. An employee who suspects discrimination must sign a confidentiality declaration, before he or she is informed about the pay level and the stipulation of the pay in relation to a certain other employee or group of employees. The employer also has an obligation to inform the person in question who the employee compares himself or herself with, of what information has been released and to whom. This follows from the GEA section 22.

955. Further, the employer has the burden of proof in cases where differential treatment regarding payments are based on other circumstances than gender (cf. WEA section 13-1(1) and 13-2(1), and the ADA (of 3 June 2005 No. 33) section 4; cf. also the Act on Equal Treatment of Disabled Persons (of 20 June 2008) section 13).

§4. Particulars of Time-Wage Systems

956. In time-wage systems, wages are calculated according to time units. Very often, the wage system is stipulated in the collective agreement, in which case it must be differentiated between minimum wage rates, standard wage rates and maximum wage rates.

957. If the collective agreement stipulates minimum wage rates and the parties are bound by the agreement, there is no allowance for agreeing to lower wages. On the other hand, higher wages may be agreed, and minimum wage rates are often based on the assumption that the employee will receive certain raises according to further assessment or under specified conditions. In such cases, it may be breach of agreement if the employer consistently pays all employees according to the minimum wage rates in the collective agreement (*see* e.g., ARD 1952 p. 52).

958. With normal wage rates, employees are salaried according to the rates, and there is no allowance to arrange higher or lower wages for the individual employee. The assumption, of course, is that the collective agreement does not authorize special wage increases, either explicitly or by premise.

959. Maximum wage rates signify that one may not arrange higher wages than stipulated in the collective agreement, unless the agreement allows it. On the other hand, lower wage rates may be agreed upon with the individual employee.

960. Combinations of these three wage systems are conceivable, for example where the collective agreement stipulates that the wage shall not be lower than a specified amount and not higher than a certain maximum amount. In practice, the minimum wage and standard wage systems are the ones of particular importance.

961. As already stated, it would be contrary to collective agreement if an enterprise were to pay all employees in a particular employee group the fixed minimum wage. Nor may the enterprise give all employees the same addition to the minimum wage rates. The collective agreement states that there must be an assessment, and that the increases must be determined according to said assessment. With regard to minimum wage rates, it is assumed that the individual increases must not be so slight as to be without any practical significance. But it is also assumed that an enterprise may set a maximum wage limit, and that such a practice will not be contrary to the collective agreement. Furthermore, we must note that the increases in question are established after conferring with shop stewards. But if the negotiations with shop stewards do not result in an agreement, the wage increases shall be based on the assessment of the enterprise, unless otherwise stated in the collective agreement (cf. e.g., ARD 1983 p. 252).

962. The time-wage system discussed here may be characterized as a flexible system, where the wage may be adapted considerably to the qualifications, skill, etc., of the individual employee. However, the system has the weakness that the employer's assessments may tend to be the deciding factor, and that personal sympathies and antipathies might be reflected in wage setting and wage adjustment. Such tendencies may be counteracted by the participating of employees' representatives in the evaluation of the work and the employee in question, e.g., through committees (cf. the description below of systematic job evaluation and of the piece-work system).

§5. Particulars of Differentiated Wages, Systematic Job Evaluation and Piece-Work

I. Differentiated Wages and Systematic Job Evaluation

963. In order to contribute to wages reflecting the qualifications required for the work, and the conditions under which the work is performed, guidelines for systematic job evaluation in the individual enterprises are stipulated in BA (2014), Supplementary agreement VII. Before such systems are introduced at the enterprise, an agreement must have been reached between the parties, and the guidelines do not apply to systems that do not give a mathematical link between the result of the assessments and wages (cf. section I of the Supplementary agreement).

964. It is emphasized that systematic assessment has to be irrespective of sex, and may be a useful tool in promoting equal pay for men and women at the enterprise. It is further emphasized 'that it is highly important to promote methods for systematic job evaluations that are capable of improving working conditions for the individual employees and give a pleasant working environment', and that the agreement must be applied in an expedient manner, that is in keeping with the organizational conditions and development strategies at the enterprise (cf. sections II and III of the Supplementary agreement).

965. A wage system based on job evaluation is based on descriptions of the jobs to be placed in the system, and an agreement on the factors to be taken into account in the evaluation, and if a points system is to be applied, the weighting in points of each factor. A committee shall determine where each job should be placed in the system, and the results of the evaluation are to be converted to wage groups. The management and the employee or group of employees concerned shall cooperate in drawing up the job description, and the description shall include enough details to convey a general impression of what the job consists in, and the conditions under which the job is done. The factors shall be sex-neutral and as relevant as possible, such as competence, how demanding the work is, responsibility, working conditions, etc. The committee shall consist of an equal number of members from the management and the employees, and shall assess the individual job on the basis of the job descriptions, on-site observation and interviews with employees and supervisors. The individual employee is entitled to see the assessment of his or her own job. When job evaluation results are known, the ordinary local negotiating parties at the enterprise shall determine the wage groups based on the evaluations (cf. section III of the Supplementary agreement).

966. Assessment of proficiency and qualifications on a systematic basis, and the use of the results in the local wage system, follow the same pattern (cf. section IV of the Supplementary agreement).

II. Piece-Work Systems

967. The use of piece-work may be regulated in detail by collective agreements, but it may also simply be stipulated that piece-work is allowed (cf. e.g., the IA (2012) section 4.5).

968. Piece-work may be defined as work in which the wages, in whole or in part, vary according to performance, produced volume, etc. Usually, the piece-rate must be agreed before the work commences.

969. It should be distinguished between piece-work based on one-time rates, and piece-work based on stipulated rates.

970. One-time piecework rates are usually agreed on the basis of negotiations between the company representative and the worker(s) engaged to do the work, and the employees are usually guaranteed individual hourly wages. In practice, one-time rates are used in special contracts and jobs that do not fit in with the general piece-work systems.

971. Stipulated piece-work rates can be either work-studied rates or free contract rates. Free contract rates may e.g., be used for work operations that are repeated in production. Such rates are then established through free negotiation between the company representative and the worker(s) engaged to do the work. While the free contract rates may be established simply by agreement, the work-study rates (also frequently called work-assessed rates) are a result of quite thorough proceedings.

III. Work Studies

972. Guidelines for work studies – time and motion studies – are stipulated in BA (2014), Supplementary agreement VI. Use of work studies in an enterprise shall be based on that agreement, unless the use of work studies does not give a mathematical link between the result of the studies and the wages. It is a condition that the parties at the enterprise have agreed to the use of work studies, before the studies are initiated (cf. section I of the Supplementary agreement).

973. Section II of the Supplementary agreement stipulates that work studies may not be used to reduce the employees' earning possibilities during the term of the collective agreement, unless a right of revision ensues from that agreement, or a special agreement. It is furthermore stipulated 'that it is highly important to promote methods that are capable of improving working conditions for the individual employees and give a pleasant working environment', and that the agreement must be applied in an expedient manner, that is in keeping with the organizational conditions and development strategies at the enterprise.

974. Section IX of the Supplementary agreement stipulates that payment during work studies shall be in accordance with the wage system at the enterprise. Employees earning piecework rates, who through additional time studies or method studies, are prevented from maintaining their normal earnings, shall be guaranteed their average hourly earnings.

975. Section III of the Supplementary agreement stipulates that the employees shall elect one or more work-study representatives to be the employees' experts on work-study matters, for a period of usually two years. Those elected should not at the same time hold positions of trust as regular negotiators. They should have technical insight and an interest in work study. The enterprise shall ensure that work-study representatives receive the necessary theoretical and practical training in such studies, and ensure that these representatives maintain the level of theoretical and practical needed to be able to understand and evaluate submitted study material and carry out spot checks. The representatives shall be paid regular average earnings while employed as such, and during training periods.

976. Section IV of the Supplementary agreement stipulates that work studies comprise studies of methods, as well as of extra time, and of basic time. It is further stipulated that studies of methods and extra time are normally performed before any basic-time studies.

977. Method studies aim at organizing work and the method of performing it, so that the work can be done in the best possible manner. The employees that normally perform work should be consulted during the studies.

978. Extra-time studies are performed to record all extra time used at a workplace or in a department, both with a view to making improvements and for determining necessary additions to the adopted basic-time studies. Additions of time for personal needs are usually not included under extra-time studies. Time for personal needs is the time the employee requires irrespective of the nature of the work, such as going to the toilet, getting a drink of water, etc. Time for rest is the extra time rest necessary for extremely tiring work. Should personal additions and possible necessary rest time not have been determined during the time and motion studies, they shall be determined by negotiations between the parties at the enterprise (cf. section V of the Supplementary agreement).

979. Basic-time studies are conducted to find out how much time an employee of average skill and standard performance takes on one operation. Standard performance is the work performed by an experienced employee who is familiar with the working method, tools and machinery used. If necessary, studies shall be carried out on several workers with experience of the operation concerned.

IV. Calculating and Negotiating Piece-Work Rates

980. Piecework rates are calculated on the basis of the time for the task with pay for standard performance. Before basic-time studies are initiated, the basis for the calculation shall be agreed upon between the parties to a collective agreement or to a special agreement at the enterprise (cf. section VI of the Supplementary agreement). When piecework rates have been calculated, they shall be submitted for approval to the employee or group of employees by whom the work is to be done. They shall be allowed to see the time studies and calculations, including the assessment of performance. If an agreement not reached, the work-study representatives of the employees and the enterprise respectively shall go through the study material together. Should an agreement still not be reached, the parties of the Basic Agreement (LO and NHO) recommend that the enterprise's proposals be adopted provisionally, and that the final result – after the question has been settled through further negotiations or decisions – be applied retroactively with effect from the date the provisional piecework rates were adopted (cf. section VII of the Supplementary agreement).

V. Revision of Piece-Work Rate Agreements

981. Section VIII of the Supplementary agreement stipulates that revision of piecework rate agreements is allowed when changes in wage levels follows revisal of collective wage agreements, or when changes in methods, machines, workplaces or materials take place, or the production system of the enterprise changes, or some piecework rates are much older than the other rates at the enterprise, or when piecework rates are 'evidently wrong', for instance as a result of calculating errors.

VI. Surveying

982. In some trades, survey arrangements are established in connection with a piecework wage system in order to ascertain the magnitude of the job that has been done. This is especially prevalent in the building and construction trades (*see* ARD 1989 p. 58 on the employer's obligation to draw or pay survey fees).

VII. Piece-Work Deprivation

983. It is usually assumed that piece-work yields a higher hourly pay than regular hourly wages. Workers who do not get to do piece-work are therefore in a more unfavourable position. Hence collective agreements frequently contain rules stipulating that additional wages shall be paid, on specified conditions, in lieu of piecework. Basically, however, this type of payment is not based on an incentive-wage system, but on a time-wage system where the compensation for piecework deprivation is included as a part of the hourly wage.

§6. Special Remuneration

984. Not infrequently, collective agreements will make provision for special remuneration in addition to the regular wage, for example, for particularly dirty work, work in remote geographical locations, exceptionally demanding work, etc. In practice, e.g., oil-drilling companies have had rules on payment of remuneration for work with oil-based drilling mud, building and construction workers have been entitled to high-mountain bonuses and bus drivers have received bonuses for driving articulated buses. Such wage provisions can give rise to disputes of various kinds. The dispute may concern whether the conditions for the remuneration exist, i.e., whether the location can be considered remote, the mountain high, etc., or whether or not the drilling mud is oil-based. Another question might be whether the worker should be paid the remuneration only during the period he is working in the remote location, with oil-based mud, etc., or whether the remuneration shall be included if the worker is liable to be assigned to such work. Such questions must be decided on the basis of an interpretation of the individual wage provision. The Labour Court has thus found that remuneration for work with oil-based mud is payable for each shift involving work with oil-based mud, even if the individual was not working with the mud throughout the entire shift (ARD 1985 p. 120). A third question is whether remuneration such as that above shall be taken into account when calculating other remuneration. For example, should the remuneration for driving an articulated bus be included in the basis for calculating overtime pay, holiday pay, etc.? Such questions must be specifically regulated in the collective agreement. According to section 5.1.5 of the IA then, remuneration for public holidays, etc., shall be included in the calculation of holiday pay, but not in the calculation of overtime pay. In other cases, the question must be decided according to an interpretation of the wage provision. The Labour Court has thus found that the articulated-bus remuneration must be included in the basis for calculating overtime, as are mileage pay and remuneration for settling the purse and monthly tickets. On the other hand, remuneration for inconvenient hours was not considered a part of the calculation basis (ARD 1984 p. 22). In interpreting this question, emphasis will be placed on what the parties have practised. If the issue is vague, but the enterprise has over the years calculated remuneration based on a faithful interpretation of what is implied by the wage provision, without objection from the employees or their organization, the practice may be decisive in a subsequent dispute on the issue.

§7. Compensation for Public Holidays and the National Holidays of 1 and 17 May and for Work on These Days

985. The legislation does not stipulate anything regarding compensation for the public holidays New Year's Day, Maundy Thursday, Good Friday, 2nd Easter Monday, Ascension, 2nd Pentecost and 1st and 2nd Christmas Day. However, to a large extent collective agreements, e.g., Workshop Agreement section 5.1.1, stipulate that compensation for such holidays shall be paid as regular working days, unless the movable holiday is on a Sunday. However, there is usually a requirement that the employment has lasted or will last for at least thirty days continuously.

986. According to the Act relating to 1 May and 17 May as national holidays, employees who must work on these days are entitled to the same bonuses as for working on Sundays according to agreement or regulations. In lieu of such an agreement or regulation, the employee is entitled to his or her basic rate plus at least 50%.

§8. Sick Pay, Etc.

987. Employees' entitlement to wages during their own sickness, sickness of their children and of those minding their children, etc., is regulated in the SSA.

988. The Act entitles the employee to sick pay based on 100% of the normal wage or other remuneration (cf. SSA section 8-16), for a period up to fifty-two weeks. However, the annual income must in total be at least half of the Social Security Services' Basic Amount (*Grunnbeløp*) (cf. SSA section 8-3(2)), and social security benefits are limited to six times the Basic Amount (cf. SSA section 8-10(2)). Consequently, social security benefits will not always be equal to full wages. Hence, entitlements for sick pay may also be stipulated in the collective agreement or an individual employment contract, so that the employee is guaranteed sick pay beyond the statutory limits. The same applies to absence during pregnancy and immediately after childbirth. Section 4-4 of the Ship Labour Act has special rules concerning seamen's rights to wages, etc., during sickness and injury.

§9. Due Date and Mode of Payment

989. Basically, payment of wages falls due in arrears, but other arrangements can be made (cf. e.g., the main collective agreement in the public sector, which stipulates that wages shall be paid on the 12th of the month unless decided otherwise). According to WEA section 14-15, employees shall be paid at least twice a month, unless decided otherwise. Other pay intervals may of course be agreed. In practice, monthly payments are largely used also for employees salaried by the hour, day or week, and for employees salaried according to piece-rates (cf. e.g., BA LO-NHO (2014) section 11-1).

I. Payment

990. In practice, wage payment through a bank is quite common (cf. e.g., BA LO-NHO (2014) section 11-2), which establishes that wages may be paid through a bank if preferred by the enterprise.

II. Wage Deductions

991. It is self-evident that an employer may not deduct wages and holiday allowance freely. Exhaustive, detailed rules on this matter are set forth in WEA section 14-15(2) and (3). Deductions may be made when agreed in advance in writing or when authorized by law, and with regard to statutory instalments in pension funds or sickness insurance funds. When authorized by collective agreement (cf. for example BA LO-NHO (2014) section 11-3), union dues and dues to information and development funds or low-wage funds may be deducted from wages. Finally, wage deductions may be made to compensate for injury or loss to the enterprise caused by the employee either intentionally or negligently in connection with his or her work. However, the employer may deduct only from the portion of the wages that exceeds what the employee reasonably needs to support himself or herself and his or her household (cf. Rt. 1988 p. 1031). Unfair wage deductions are punishable (cf. WEA section 19-1 and Rt. 1981 p. 1112).

992. There is reason to stress that wages not paid because of absence, etc., is colloquially known as a wage deduction, e.g., when an employee has come one hour late to work, or the employees have participated in an one-hour political strike. In both cases, work is not being done during the hour in question, and it follows from the general tenet of 'no work, no pay', that the employer has no obligation to pay wages in such cases (cf. ARD 1983 p. 30). As regards the regulations restricting the right to deduct wages, such cases do not represent wage deductions, as wages are not earned and, consequently, should not be included in any calculation as far as wages are concerned.

III. Statement of Wage Calculation, Etc.

993. An employee shall have an opportunity to check the deductions that were made and that the wages are calculated correctly, thus WEA section 14-15(5) stipulates that the employee shall on payday or immediately thereafter receive a written statement of wage payment, method of calculation and possible deductions.

IV. Errors in Calculating Wages

994. Sometimes errors in wage calculation occur, in which case the question arises of whether the employer can demand repayment if the employee has received more than the wages due, and whether the employee has a right to payment in case he or she has been paid less than the wages due. These questions are very similar, but on closer inspection, they are nevertheless different, thus each will be treated separately.

995. It should, however, first be mentioned that the question regarding the employer's right to demand repayment, will have to be considered separately from the question regarding the employer's right to deduct wages for the amount paid in excess. Thus, an employer was held not to have deducted wages correctly, although the wages had been paid, with reservations, while negotiations were going on regarding a new collective agreement. Later, the new collective agreement with wage increases came into force from a later time than the employer had expected and on which assumption the wages had been paid. However, a unilateral reservation was not sufficient, and per se no agreement (Rt. 1981 p. 1112). The correct procedure would have been that the employer obtained permission from the employees to deduct wages, or to obtain a decision of a court stating what amount the employees were obliged to pay back, and then obtain the amount due through the prescribed procedures.

996. Regarding either back pay or repayment, there are two opposing factors to consider. The settlement factor, that settlement for a wage period should be final, weighs against later adjustments. On the other side, there is the correctness factor – that the settlement should be correct. The settlement factor weighs more heavily over time because the parties will then have made arrangements accordingly. If the parties are faithful with regard to settlement, then that, too, weighs in favour of settlement being final. Also an important factor is who is to blame for the incorrect settlement. The employer is usually the one who calculates wage payments, etc., and hence will be the most logical person to blame for the incorrect settlement. However, if the wage calculation is made on the basis of a time sheet submitted by the employee, then the latter will be the most likely to blame if the error is found on the time sheet.

V. Repayment of Excess Wages

997. Error in wage calculation was deemed to give the employer the right to demand repayment of the surplus wage payment, etc., in a case where the employees were notified immediately that the wage calculation was incorrect. The matter involved holiday pay, and due to a computer error, the holiday pay was calculated for a month more than was the employees' due. As soon as the error was discovered, and before payment was made, the employees were informed about the error in a circular. All employees thereby had the opportunity to be appraised of the situation within reasonable time (NAD 1981-83 p. 569 *Gulating*). Similarly, the demand for repayment was deemed justified where, prior to the wage review, wages were paid according to the ostensibly ratified rates. Wages were paid with this reservation posted on the pay slip of each employee, and being that the new wage rates entered into effect at a later date than originally assumed; it was judged that, by virtue of this reservation, the employees had been adequately appraised that the payments were not final. Failure to open and check one's pay slip was not considered a significant factor, as it constituted an omission on the part of the employee at his or her own risk (NAD 1981-83 p. 803 *Frostating*). The latter factor illustrates the requirement that an employee must be able to substantiate his or her good faith that repayment could not be claimed. On this basis, repayment was also condoned in a case involving an employee who was employed full-time, but whose employment has been reduced by one-fourth, and was paid full-time wages due to an error. In this case, it was stressed that the employee very easily could have checked that his scale wage, which was specified on the pay slip, was the same as previously. Consequently, the employer's claim for repayment was sanctioned, even though the error was discovered six months after the payment had taken place (RG 1983.902 *Alstahaug*).

VI. Back Payment of Omitted Wages

998. An employee can claim back payment of omitted wages due to an error by the employer. If such errors are reported within reasonable time, back payment may be claimed in most cases. However, the short wages may also have come about because the employer has based the calculations on a particular interpretation of the rules, e.g., a provision in the collective agreement, while the employees might have a different interpretation. For example, there are cases of disagreement as to whether special bonuses are to be included in the basis for overtime pay, holiday pay, etc. Such questions frequently arise after a period of time during which the employer has based the wage calculations on his or her own interpretation. In such cases, the Labour Court has consistently ruled that back payment cannot be claimed for any part of the period that has elapsed, but only from such a time the employees advance the claim through their trade organization, *see* e.g., ARD 1986 p. 136, ARD 1986 p. 149, ARD 1985 p. 109 (in the two latter judgments the back-payment claim was judged in part to be statute-barred; cf. also Rt. 1995 p. 1, and earlier judgments (ARD 1955 p. 126, ARD 1955 p. 144, ARD 1956-57 p. 242, ARD 1956-57 p. 264 and ARD 1959 p. 222)). In ARD 1963 p. 141, back payment was condoned as of the time the employee had joined his union, because it seemed reasonable in view of the special circumstances of the case.

VII. Securing Wage Claims

999. Unpaid wages may not be subject to distraint or lien (*see* section 2-5, cf. section 2-7, of the Satisfaction of Claims Act), nor may undue wage claims be transferred or pledged (section 12 of Act No. 4 of 14 August 1918 relating to the entry into force of the system(s) of legal procedure). According to section 51(1) of the Shipping Act, seamen's claims for wages and other remuneration for service aboard ships are secured by maritime lien in the ship. Other groups of employees have no statutory lien for their claims.

VIII. Priority over the Employer's Bankrupt Estate, Etc.

1000. According to section 9-3 of the Satisfaction of Claims Act, employees have priority over their employer's bankrupt estate for unpaid wages, holiday pay, etc. However, this priority does not apply to remuneration to an employee who has been general manager or who alone, or together with persons close to him, has had at least a 20% share in the enterprise, or remuneration to an employee who is close to the general manager or to persons who alone or jointly have had at least a 20% share in the enterprise (cf. e.g., Rt. 1995 p. 1317). These exceptions concern remuneration earned while the employee held such a position and earned during the last six months prior to the probate courts received the petition (closing date) for debt settlement proceedings or bankruptcy/liquidation.

1001. Generally, the priority is limited to claims with a deadline no further back than three months from the closing date, and limited to six months wages. The priority does not include wages and holiday pay for the period of notice beyond the general rules of the WEA relating to periods of notice (WEA section 15-3), unless a longer period of notice follows from a collective agreement entered into earlier than six months prior to the closing date. If an employee has had income after the closing date, his priority will generally be reduced correspondingly. Claims for holiday pay are usually limited to thirty months. The priority includes not only wages and other remuneration based on the employment, which includes holiday pay, but also claims for pension and for loss of income.

IX. Government Guarantee for Wage Claims

1002. Other creditor groups' extensive use of security, however, has resulted in inadequate coverage for the employees, in spite of their priority. Consequently, the government guarantees for payment of wage claims that cannot be covered due to the employer's bankruptcy/liquidation, etc. (cf. Act relating to the state guarantee for wage claims in the event of bankruptcy/liquidation, etc.). According to the Act, the government may advance claims against the employer or the bankrupt/ liquidated estate in order to recover some of the amount, if possible. The guarantee arrangement includes only claims that have priority pursuant to the Satisfaction of Claims Act, and amount paid to the individual employee may not exceed three times the social security basic amount. For seamen, claims for leisure pay and free passage home, etc., are also covered (cf. section 2 of Regulation No. 999 of 28 October 1998).

1003. The government guarantee no longer applies if the employee transfers his or her claim before bankruptcy/liquidation proceedings are instituted and, similarly, if a third party has redeemed or covered the employee's claim prior to institution of bankruptcy/liquidation proceedings (section 1(5) of the Act). A person who takes a job for an employer in spite of the fact that he or she knew, or should have known, that the employer was incapable of fulfilling the wage obligations, may be denied coverage (cf. section 7(1)). The Norwegian Labour Inspectorate handles applications on government guarantee (cf. section 4-11 of Regulation No. 999 of 28 October 1998).

X. Limitation Period for Wage Claims, Etc.

1004. According to section 2 of the Limitation Period for Claims Act, the general limitation period for wage claims are set to be three years. The limitation period runs from the date on which the creditor first has the right to demand performance. For claims arising from breach of contract, the limitation period runs from the date when the said breach commences.

Chapter 5. Incapacity to Work

§1. Absence of an Employee Due to Illness

1005. According to WEA section 15-8, it is prohibited to dismiss an employee because of absence due to illness or an accident. This prohibition is legitimate during the first twelve months of illness. As a result, one could say that illness is a legitimate form of absence.

1006. If the employee is dismissed during this period, it will be assumed that it has to do with the illness, unless the employer can prove that something else was the reason for dismissing the employee (WEA section 15-7).

1007. The employee has to let the employer know what the reason for absence is, for example by handing over a medical statement.

§2. Payment During Illness

1008. The employee's right to receive payment during illness can be particularly specified in the employment contract or in the collective agreement. If not specified, the rules of Chapter 8 of the SSA are applicable. Benefits from social security will nowadays not always give the employee 100% payment during illness. It is therefore important that the right to receive payment during illness is also stated in the employment contract or in a collective agreement.

1009. By virtue of section 8-19 of the SSA, most ill employees will receive 100% payment during the first sixteen days of illness (this is called the employer's period, provided that the employee has worked for the employer at least two weeks before the illness commences. This is the so-called waiting period. Illegal absence is not calculated as part of the waiting period.

1010. When an employee is unable to work because of a work-related accident, a waiting period is not required. The employer only has to pay wages for period equal to the days, for which the employee normally should have been paid (cf. SSA section 8-18(4)). If the inability establishes during the employee's vacation, the employer's period will start on the day the employee was supposed to start working again.

§3. Self-Certified Sick Leave Form or Doctor's Confirmation

1011. In order to be entitled to receive wages from the employer when absent because of illness, the employee has to report to the employer on the first day of absence that the cause of absence is illness. This is required both when the employee uses a so-called self-certified form for leave because of illness, and when a doctor confirms the inability.

1012. A self-certified sick leave form means that the employee can inform the employer that illness is the cause of his absence. A self-certified sick leave form can be used up to three calendar days per time of use, counting from the first day the employee is absent as a result of illness.

1013. The employee has to have been employed at least two months before he or she is taken ill, in order to be allowed to use a self-certified form for leave because of illness.

1014. The employer may demand a written statement from the employee stating that the absence is a result of illness (cf. SSA section 8-27). If the employee has been absent more than four times during a twelve-month period, without presenting a doctor's statement stating that the absence is a result of illness, the employer may decide that from that time on the employee will have to present a doctor's statement within the first three days of illness in order to be entitled to wages when absent because of illness.

1015. Should the employee not report that the absence is due to illness, the right to receive wages when absent because of illness will not be established until he or she makes that report, unless the employee should have had a good reason for not reporting the illness earlier.

1016. After the employer's period has ended, the social security system will take over the payment compensation during absence because of illness. The main rule is that such compensation will not be granted when the annual income is less than 50% of the social security basic amount, or when the income is six times higher than this basic amount.

1017. When it is obvious that the employee is ill and the illness is contagious or may influence the work, for example when it results in an extra safety risk or when the illness influences the work environment in one way or another, the employer may order the employee to leave the workplace, even when the employee has not reported that he or she is ill using a self-certified form for leave because of illness, or a doctor's statement (cf. also Act of 5 August 1994 No. 55 on measures to counteract contagious illnesses section 4-12); and paragraph 1113 below.

§4. Child's or Child-Minder's Sickness

1018. When the employee has a child under the age of 12 and has to take care of this child because of illness, the employee has the right to take a leave of absence by virtue of WEA section 12-9(1).

1019. This is also the case when the child has to be taken to a medical examination of any kind and the person responsible for the daily childcare is ill, or is absent because of another child's illness.

1020. The employee has the right to take this leave of absence up to and including the calendar year in which the child turns 12. However, the employee can only use it for ten days each calendar year, or a maximum of fifteen days if the employee has two or more children in his or her care. An employee is regardless entitled to leave of absence when the Social Security System provides with care allowance, attendance allowance or training allowance.

1021. By virtue of WEA section 12-9(5), the employee has the right to use a double amount of days when he or she has sole responsibility for the care of a child. The employee who has sole responsibility for the care for a child may transfer up to half of the days of such leave each calendar year to the mother or father with rights to access. The employee can also transfer these rights to the person he or she is living with, when this person does not have the care for his or her own children.

1022. The employee that needs to take a leave of absence because of necessary care for a child can receive a so-called care allowance from the employer up to ten days per calendar year. When the employee has the care for more than two children, he or she can receive care allowance up to fifteen days. The amount of days is up to twenty or thirty days when the employee is a single carer.

1023. The employer will provide care allowance when the employee has been employed at least four weeks. However, it will need a reimbursement from the Social Security System when the amount of days exceeds ten.

§5. Chronically Ill or Handicapped Child

1024. When the child is chronically ill or is handicapped, there is an extended right to a leave of absence (WEA section 12-9(3)). The right to take a leave of absence in this case consists of twenty days per calendar year until the year the child turns 18. This right to take a leave of absence can be exercised up to and including the calendar year in which the child turns 18.

1025. It is possible that the employee who is the caretaker for a chronically ill or handicapped child has to take part in a course or other training to be able to take care of and treat the child. By virtue of WEA section 12-9(3), the employee has the right to take a leave of absence when a well-known health institution or public competence centre offers the course or training.

§6. Care of Close Relatives

1026. According to WEA section 12-10, the employee who is taking care of close relatives in the terminal stage in the home shall be entitled to twenty days of absence to take care of the individual patient. Considered as 'close relatives' are children, grandchildren, parents, grandparents, brothers and sisters and common law spouses.

1027. When taking this leave of absence, the Social Security System will provide so-called nursing allowance (cf. SSA section 9-12).

§7. Pregnancy, Childbirth and Adoption

I. Pregnancy

1028. Pregnant employees have the right to leave of absence with full payment when they have to undergo a pregnancy check and this cannot reasonably take place outside working hours (WEA section 12-1).

1029. The pregnant employee has the right to take up to twelve weeks' pregnancy leave of absence (WEA section 12-2). According to WEA sections 12-2 to 12-6, the employer has to be notified of the pregnancy leave as soon as possible and not later than a week in advance in the case of absence in excess of two weeks, not later than four weeks in advance in the case of absence in excess of twelve weeks and not later than twelve weeks in advance in the case of absence in excess of one year. Disregard of such notice periods shall not entail that an employee must postpone the leave of absence if it is necessary owing to circumstances unknown to the employee before expiry of the notice period (cf. WEA section 12-7). In this case, the employer has to be notified as soon as possible.

1030. By virtue of section 14-3 of the SSA, women who work in a high-risk work environment have an extended right to pregnancy allowance. Entitlement to this extended right to pregnancy allowance is established when she has to quit her job due to the pregnancy and there is no possibility of transferring her to another post within the company. The right to receive pregnancy allowance starts the day the employee has to stop working and lasts until three weeks before the birth. From that time, she will receive birth allowance from the Social Security System.

II. Childbirth

1031. After giving birth, the mother shall have leave of absence (maternity leave) for the first six weeks unless she produces a medical certificate stating that it is better for her to resume work. This would be the case when the woman cannot take care of the child herself, for example when the child will be given up for adoption, is not viable or is in an incubator and for psychological reasons it is better for the mother to go to work.

1032. The father of the child is entitled to two weeks' leave of absence in order to assist the mother. If the parents are not living together, the right to leave of absence may be exercised by another person who supports the mother (WEA section 12-3(1)).

1033. In addition, the parents shall be entitled to leave of absence (parental leave) pursuant to the provisions of WEA section 12-5 and of sections 12-2 and 12-4 for a total of twelve months.

1034. In the case that only one of the parents have the care for the child, the right to take parenting leave can be exercised by another person supporting the mother as well.

1035. In addition, each of the parents is entitled to leave of absence for up to twelve months for each child. This leave must be taken immediately after the parents' leave of absence pursuant to WEA section 12-5(1). An employee who has partial leave of absence pursuant to section 12-6 is nevertheless not entitled to leave of absence pursuant to WEA section 12-5(2).

1036. When the employee has sole responsibility for the care of a child, he or she has the right to take up to two years of parental leave (WEA section 12-5(3)).

A. Maternity Allowance

1037. By virtue of the SSA section 14-9, maternity allowance is granted over a period of forty-nine weeks (245 days) with full daily rates or fifty-nine weeks (295 days) with reduced daily rates. Full daily rates indicate that the maternity allowance is paid with 100% of the basis of calculation. Reduced daily rates indicate that the maternity allowance is paid with 80% of the basis of calculation. The SSA section 14-7 stipulates how the basis of calculation is estimated. It is stated that the maternity allowance provided to each of the parents is calculated on the basis of their income, to the same extent as regards the rules stipulating the entitlement to contribution because of illness from the Social Security System.

1038. In the case of a multiple birth, the benefit period is extended with seven weeks (thirty-five days) with reduced daily rates for each child. It is extended to five weeks (twenty-five days) when receiving full daily rates.

1039. The basic rule is that the benefit periods for both parents are consecutive and they can divide this benefit period when they both meet the requirements for the right to receive maternity allowance. However, exempted from this division are ten weeks which are reserved for the father and ten weeks which are reserved for the mother of the child.

1040. However, the last three weeks before the birth and the first six weeks after the birth may only be used by the mother (SSA section 14-9(5)). Maternity allowance will not be received after three years from the child's birth or the care takeover (in relation to adoption). In the event of the child's death during the benefit period, maternity allowance will be granted up to six weeks (thirty days) of the normal benefit period (SSA section 14-9(6)).

1041. For the mother to be granted maternity allowance, she needs to have had an active working life for at least six of the last ten months before the birth. The same goes for the father's right to receive maternity allowance (SSA section 14-6).

1042. The right to receive these allowances is conditional upon the fact that the employee is not working.

1043. As mentioned birth contributions may be granted with full or reduced daily rates. The mother can choose which type of daily rates she wants to receive, but she has to make this choice before the benefit period commences. The choice she makes cannot be changed during the benefit period. Her choice of daily rates also applies to the father of the child who will receive maternity allowance (cf. SSA section 14-9(3)).

1044. The benefit period commences when the woman ceases her work, at the latest three weeks (fifteen days) before the birth, regardless of whether she has chosen maternity allowance with full or reduced daily rate (section 14-10). If the employee should not make use of the right to receive maternity allowance in the last three weeks before the birth, the benefit period will be shortened accordingly.

1045. The mother may start the benefit period up to twelve weeks (sixteen days) before the birth, but has to receive maternity allowance the first six weeks after the birth.

1046. The father's benefit period is regulated in SSA section 14-13. He has the right to receive maternity allowance during the benefit period after the first six weeks after the birth, provided that the mother either goes back to work, starts or returns to a fulltime education or is unable to look after the child because she is admitted to a hospital or is so ill that she is completely dependent on the father looking after the child.

1047. If the mother goes back to work part-time, the father can receive graded maternity allowance.

1048. Pursuant to SSA section 14-12, fourteen weeks (seventy days) of the benefit period are reserved for the father.

B. Breastfeeding: Time-Off for Nursing Mothers

1049. Pursuant to WEA section 12-8, women who breastfeed have the right to take the time off to do so. They can take at least half an hour twice a day. They can also demand that their working day is reduced by an hour a day.

1050. According to the WEA section 12-8(2), the employee has the right to receive wages for time off for breastfeeding her child during the first year of the child's life, but only for time off that does not exceed one hour per day. This right only arises if the agreed working hours are seven hours or more.

III. Adoption

1051. Adoptive parents have the right to take two weeks of care leave when they take over the care of the child. This is not the case when adopting stepchildren or when the adopted child is older than 15 (cf. WEA section 12-3).

1052. The adoptive parents, when taking over responsibility for care of the child, have the same right to take parenting leave of absence as other parents, at least as long as they receive allowance from social security system (cf. WEA section 12-5). This is applicable from the time the adoptive parents take over the responsibility for care of the child, even when this happens before the adoption licence has been issued. Also in this case, there is no right to take parenting leave when adopting stepchildren or when adopting a child who is older than 15 years of age.

1053. The above is also applicable when foster parents take over the responsibility for care of the child.

1054. It is a similar situation for the employee who has or receives parental responsibility when the other parent dies and has had less than usual access to the child (cf. WEA section 12-5(4)).

1055. In all the above-mentioned situations, the employer has to be notified of the employee taking a leave as early as possible (cf. WEA section 12-7).

1056. Pursuant to SSA section 14-5, the employee will receive adoption contributions etc. when adopting a child under 15, following the same system as for the maternity allowance. Adoption of spouse's children does, however, not give the right to receive adoption money.

1057. Adoption money will be received for a period counting up to fifty-six weeks (280 days) with reduced daily rates, or up to forty-six weeks (230 days) with full daily rates (cf. SSA section 14-9).

1058. The benefit period commences at the time as to when the adoptive parents take over the responsibility for care of the child. Couples who adopt together can divide the benefit period between the two of them. The adoptive father has to use at least ten weeks of the benefit period (this is the statutory paternity leave).

§8. Military Service or Other National Service

1059. According to WEA section 12-12(1), the employee has the right to take a leave of absence when voluntarily or compulsorily joining the military service or other national service, or similar forces.

1060. To the same extent, the employee has the right to leave of absence due to voluntary service up to twenty-four months in forces participating in international peacekeeping operations.

1061. The employee must notify the employer as soon as possible after a binding agreement of such service has been concluded.

1062. An employee who wishes to continue his or her employment after completion of such service shall notify the employer before commencing the service. The employer is not obliged to allow the employee to resume his or her duties until one month after receipt of notification of the date on which the employee can resume work (cf. WEA section 12-12(2)).

1063. Pursuant to WEA section 15-10, the employer is not allowed to dismiss the employee owing to leave of absence pursuant to section 12-12. This special prohibition includes male employees as well as female employees.

1064. It has to be expected that this prohibition also include those subject to military or national service who request to commence their service before the age of 19.

1065. The prohibition disables the employer to dismiss the employee during the probationary period. However, a leave of absence because of military service can prolong the probationary period (cf. WEA section 15-6(4)).

1066. One must assume that time for 'exercises etc.' is included in the time limitation of twenty-four months. Any extensions to, or renewals of, the engagement exceeding twenty-four months does not fall within the said section. One has to further assume that this protection applies not only during the actual service, but will also apply to any termination caused by the employee volunteering, and it is explicit in section 15-10(1) that the protection also includes periods where the employee is not absent from work. The employee will for example continue working for the employer for some time before the voluntary service begins.

1067. The rule generally applies to voluntary service in official forces participating in international peacekeeping operations. The rule is hence not restricted to UN operations (or OSCE, NATO or EU) but any international operation. The requirement is that the forces are official, that is, organized by the Norwegian government for participation in international operations. If service in such forces becomes mandatory, the protection against dismissal according to section WEA 15-10(1) will apply.

1068. The legal protection against dismissal is deemed to be applicable during the time of period with the current employer. Presumably then, an employee who has served up to twenty-four months is entitled to further leave (of the same length) with a new employer.

1069. Unless other grounds are shown to be highly probable, such service shall be deemed to be the reason for dismissal immediately prior to or during the period during which the employee is absent from work owing to leave pursuant to section 12-12 (cf. WEA section 15-10(2)). The employer always has the burden of proof in these matters. The termination of such a contract can be based on curtailed operations or rationalization and, in that case, has to be judged by the rules of WEA section 15-7.

1070. The employee who wishes to continue in the national service after his or her service has ended has the duty to notify the employer about this before the service commences (cf. WEA section 12-12(2)).

1071. Staying away from work before travelling to carry out military or national service, without finishing the working relationship with the employer, will be seen as if the employee does not want to be bound by the employment contract any longer.

§9. Laying-off (Absence Without Payment)

1072. When a company temporarily has to downsize its activities, it will in many instances be in the employer's and employee's interest that the employment relation does not end by termination of contract, but is maintained in a way that the employer's duty to pay salary ends as well as the employee's duty to fulfil his or her working duty. When there is a need to expand again, the employee can resume the work.

1073. For the employer, this is a quite attractive arrangement, because the employee can resume work more or less right away. Further, should the employer have to hire someone new, that person would have to be trained accordingly. For the employees, this arrangement is also – generally – advantageous, as it usually is more convenient to continue work at the previous workplace instead of finding another place to work; which also might have as a consequence that the employee would have to move to another place in the country or elsewhere.

I. The Right to Lay off Employees

1074. The employer's opportunity to lay off employees is not directly founded on the law, but such an opportunity is implied, *inter alia* in the Act regarding salaries in connection to temporary redundancies, in the Act relating to the labour market, section 8, as well as WEA section 15-3(9) and the SSA, section 4-7. In any case, the employer's opportunity to lay off employees has developed through practice in the working life, collective agreements and legal precedent (cf. also below sections 1096–1098).

1075. When the opportunity to lay off employees is regulated in collective agreements, agreements with an employee concerning an extended opportunity to lay off may be in conflict with the principle of invariability and therefore invalid. That will also be the case, should there be an agreement with the individual employee that laying-off shall not take place, or that wages shall be paid to a larger extent than the collective agreement stipulate.

II. Executing the Right to Lay off

1076. Laying-off is basically an offer from the employer to the employee, offering that the employee is temporarily freed from the duty to perform work, while at the same time the employer is freed from the duty to pay salary.

1077. Lay-offs have in court practice been accepted on conditions equivalent to those stipulated in BA (2014), even in lieu of any specific agreement thereupon (cf. below paragraphs 1096 et seq.).

BA section 8-3 stipulate that a lay-off notice has to be given at least fourteen days in advance. When dealing with unforeseen incidents like major accidents, natural incidents etc., the notice required is only two days.

1078. If the enterprise lays off employees without observing the period of notice stipulated, the employees are entitled to their usual wages until the period of notice expires (cf. BA section 8-3(6)).

1079. Notification about laying-off has to be given in writing to the employee, unless the employer and the representative of the trade union agree on a different procedure. The notice shall state the probable length of the lay-off. When this is not possible, continued lay-off shall be discussed with the shop stewards within one month and each following month, unless otherwise agreed between the parties. At these discussions, the parties shall consider the question of whether conditions warrant continued lay-off, or whether dismissals must be effected (cf. BA section 8-4(3)).

1080. Laying-off must have an objective reason and cannot last longer than six months unless the parties agree that valid reasons still exists for a longer period of time (cf. BA section 8-1(2)).

III. The Employment Relationship During the Lay-Off Period

1081. Employees who are laid off are still connected to the company and have the right and duty to start in the company again as long as the work relation has not formally been terminated. When an employee, whose contract has not been terminated during the lay-off period, is not reinstated after the lay-off period, the company has to pay salary for the period of notice (cf. BA section 8-6).

1082. When employees' work contracts are terminated during lay-off periods, they still have to perform their work duties during the notice period, unless the employees have agreed to a new labour contract, which prevents them from doing that. In that case, the employer does not have to pay the salaries during the notice period (cf. BA section 8–6).

1083. An employee who is laid off for more than three months and wants to resign in order to take other work may end the working relationship without giving notice (cf. BA section 8–6).

IV. Laying-off and Termination of Contract

1084. The employee is not obliged to give notice with the special short period of notice pursuant to WEA section 15-3(9), which stipulates the notice period to fourteen days counting from the day the employee received the lay-off notice from the employer. The employee can choose to give notice using the period established in the labour contract or in the legislation. Should the employee have been offered work at a new employer, and should that work commence, in e.g., two months, the employee may choose to apply the time of notice stipulated in WEA section 15-3(1), i.e., one month calculated from the beginning of the next month.

V. Laying-off and Termination of Contract: Employer

1085. The employer does not have the short notification period the employee has when he or she wants to terminate the contract during lay-off. In this case, the notification period set out in the labour contract or in the legislation applies.

1086. During the notification period, the employee has the right to receive salary, given that the employee is still available to work for the employer during this period. When the employee does not want to or is not able to perform the work for the employer, the employee is not entitled to receive salary. The right to receive salary does not cover the period for which the employee starts working for another employer. Further, an employee is supposed to carry out work elsewhere during the lay-off period, and is not entitled to unemployment benefits if suitable work is refused. Thus, work for another employer is usually not in conflict with the obligation of loyalty (cf. also decision of 16 February 2012 Borgarting (LB-2012-28693)).

VI. Laying-off and Termination of Contract: The Employee's Right to Continue in His or Her Position During a Termination of Contract Procedure

1087. Pursuant to WEA section 15-11 an employee, whose contract is terminated, has the right to continue in his or her position after the notification period has ended. The employer cannot avoid this right for the employee to continue in his or her position by laying off the employee.

VII. Laying-Off and the Duty to Pay Salary: Unemployment Benefits

1088. In the Act regarding salaries in connection to temporary redundancies (TRWA 1988), there are rules about the employer's duty to pay salary during lay-off. The purpose of this Act is to avoid unlawful use of all kinds of laying-off. The Act is applicable to all employees except fish processing plants.

1089. Lay-off is defined as a temporary leave of absence for the employee related to a reduction or halt within an employer's enterprise, regardless of whether the employer makes the decision himself or not.

1090. During the first period after laying-off (the employer's period), the employee has the right to receive salary and other work compensation from the employer. This employer's period lasts for up to ten working days.

1091. If the employee during the last eighteen months has been laid off full-time or part-time without salary for thirty weeks in total, he or she has the right to receive salary and other work compensation from the employer for the excess period he or she has been laid off.

1092. This quite long lay-off period is supposed to give the employer sufficient time to consider whether there seems to be economic basis to maintain the number of employees, or whether the employment relationship for some of the employees will have to be terminated.

1093. Full payment per workday during the employer's period shall be equivalent to the average salary for a normal workday, no matter how many hours the employee would have worked on any particular day (cf. TRWA section 4(2)).

1094. When the duty to pay salary comes into effect again after the end of the thirty weeks lay-off period, the lay-off salary shall be equivalent to the average week salary, no matter how many working days the employee would have had in any particular week.

1095. An employee who is laid off, due to lack of work or other circumstances which the employer cannot influence, may be granted unemployment benefits as a member of the Norwegian National Insurance Scheme (cf. the National Insurance Act section 4-7). It may in this connection be made reference to Rt. 2014 p. 336. Two employees in a print shop were partially laid off due to adverse negative market trends within the industry. Their claims for unemployment benefits under the National Insurance Act section 4-7 had been denied by the Social Security Court. The Supreme Court stated that there was no requirement that a work shortage should be the result of unpredictable or unexpected events in order to award unemployment benefits. That understanding of section 4-7 did not follow directly from the wording of the Act, and would involve a too restrictive interpretation of the provision. Neither the legal history, preparatory works nor social security case law implied any requirement that market developments needed to be regarded as unexpected. The Social Security Court's decision was found invalid. In lieu of this Supreme Court case, there was implemented a new section 6-1 in the Regulations regarding amendments in the regulation on unemployment benefits due to lay-off, of 30 January 2014 No. 82. This section now states that it will generally be assumed that the conditions following from the National Insurance Act section 4-7 are met if the documented agreement between the employer and the employee supports that the basis for lay-offs exists, which demonstrates that the employer has done what could reasonably be expected in order to prevent lay-offs and that the employer did not have the power to influence the cause of the lay-offs.

§10. Other Forms of Legitimate Absence

I. Educational Leave

1096. The right to education is an important part of the modern knowledge-based society, and sufficient education is a necessary condition, for companies as well as employees, to be able to meet the challenges on the markets and the working life.

1097. The employee's right to take 'educational leave' was established in 2000 (WEA section 12-11). The section is based on the view that education takes time and often will demand that the employee will have to take a full-time or part-time absence from work. If the right to education would be on the condition that the employee either has to stop working, and look for a new job later, or is dependent on the company's manager finding an adequate reason to give the employee a leave of absence, the possibilities for the employee to obtain an education would be weaker than when the right to take a leave of absence is established by law.

1098. The right to educational leave in WEA section 12-11 does not give the employee the right to receive salary, but salary can be determined specifically or may follow according to a collective agreement. The employees have to finance their education themselves, either by using their own money or by loan or scholarship possibilities.

1099. The right to educational leave includes part-time educational leave as well as full-time leave (cf. WEA section 12-11); stipulated in order to establish the best possibilities for combining work and education.

1100. The legislation includes both permanently and temporarily employed as well as full-time and part-time employed employees. To have the right to take an educational leave, the employee has to have a job history of at least three years. In addition, the employee has to have been employed with the same employer for the last two years, legal leave of absence included.

1101. An employee who wishes to take an educational leave has to notify the employer in advance. The WEA section 12-11 provides more detailed rules about this notification: it has to be in writing and containing information about the course's contents, length of the course and so on. The employer has to notify the employee in a written statement as soon as possible, at the latest within six months if it is expected that the employee will not be able to take an educational leave.

1102. As well as when taking another form of leave of absence, an educational leave implies a temporary stop of the parties' rights and duties within the working relation. After the leave of absence has ended, the employee has the right and the duty to resume work on the conditions as agreed upon in the employment contract.

1103. The employee taking an educational leave cannot keep the employer from dismissing e.g., because of down-signing of the company. On the other hand, the employee has the right to resume work after the agreed absence period has ended, when this can be achieved without substantial disadvantages for the employer.

1104. Since WEA section 12-11 gives the employee the right to take an educational leave, and provides certain rules for such a leave of absence, the employer is not entitled to set different rules. Therefore, the employer cannot expect the employee to keep working for some period of time after having completed the education.

1105. An employee may have the right to take educational leave more than one time (cf. WEA section 12-11(3)), provided that the company will not be too much affected by repeated study leaves. It is therefore required that the employee has to wait twice the amount of time of the last educational leave, and at least one year, since the last leave of educational absence commenced.

II. Public Office

1106. Pursuant to WEA section 12-13, the employee has the right to take a leave of absence when this is necessary to fulfil public duties. For example, when the employee is a witness or lay judge in a legal case, or is a party in such a case.

1107. Even though it is not explicitly mentioned within the section, the employee has to notify the employer of the absence in advance and as early as possible. The provision does not require permission from the employer.

III. Labour Representatives

1108. By virtue of many collective agreements, the employee that is a union representative has the right to take time off to attend meetings of his or her organization or to take part in courses or attending other learning possibilities (cf. the Basic Agreement LO–NHO (2014) section 10-6).

IV. Welfare Reasons

1109. Collective agreements also contain rules on short leaves, like for example a death in the close family, dental inspections or treatment, immediate sickness at home, moving to a new house and a special request to give blood during working hours. Pursuant to the collective agreements, there is an entitlement to salary when taking one of these short leaves usually limited to one day.

V. Religious Holidays

1110. Employees who are not a member of the Norwegian church have the right to take two days off from work on religious holidays. The employer has to be notified in advance (cf. the Act on Religious Communities of 13 June 1969 No. 25 section 27a and paragraph 790 above).

§11. ACCIDENTS AT WORK: INDUSTRIAL INJURIES OR DISEASES

I. The Welfare System According to the SSA in Relation to Industrial Injuries: An Introduction

1111. By industrial injury, it is often meant a personal injury, disease or death, which rises from an industrial accident, or other accidents at work. A disease may also be approved as an industrial injury, if it is reckoned to have arisen as a result of work-related influences, and in addition is one of the diseases mentioned in the Regulation of 28 July 1997 No. 902.

1112. The industrial injury needs to have arisen, or the malicious influence needs to have taken place, while the employee was covered for industrial diseases. This point of departure implies that the employee need to be among the groups mentioned in the SSA sections 13-6 to 13-13, that is to say employees, fishermen, military personnel, students or self-employed, among others. Most employees are covered through their employment relationship (mandatory cover for industrial injury); hence, the SSA section 13-6 which states explicitly that employees that are members of the social security insurance system are covered. Persons who work as self-employed or as freelancers, on the other hand, need to subscribe for a voluntary insurance in order to be covered for industrial injuries.

II. Individual Rights Related to Industrial Injuries and Other Work-Related Diseases

1113. When an industrial injury or a work-related disease has arisen, there are possibilities for obtaining economic compensation from, in principle, a total of four different arrangements, but in the practical life only three: the general social security system, the special rules concerning industrial injuries pursuant to the SSA Chapter 13, the general rules regarding torts but only to a most limited extent, e.g., the Act relating to industrial injury insurance. In this section, all of these arrangements are dealt with.

1114. The same kinds of benefits may be made regarding industrial injuries and work-related diseases as other injuries or illnesses, e.g., expenditures regarding medicine, sick pay and disability pensions. In addition, regarding industrial injuries or other work-related diseases, the employees may also apply for permanent injury compensation. This is a benefit which other injured and disabled are not entitled to.

A. Terms of Entitlement for Being Covered for Industrial Injury According to the SSA

1115. In order for a person to be covered for industrial injuries and other work-related diseases, the person needs to be a member of the Social Security System (cf. SSA section 13-6 first subsection). Members are all that have their residents in Norway, or works within the country. In addition, the person needs to be employed, if the person is not a student or fisherman or one of the other mentioned groups in sections 13-6 to 13-13.

1116. An employee is covered only whilst working in his or her workplace within his or her working time (cf. SSA section 13-6 second subsection). That is to say that injury that arises in the spare time does not qualify for cover. An employee is not covered for industrial injuries according to the SSA while travelling to or from his/ her workplace, unless this transportation is included as a part of the employment situation.

1117. In this relation, the Supreme Court judgments, Rt. 2000 p. 220 and Rt. 2000 p. 1028, may be mentioned. Both related to situations where the employees were travelling from their residences to their respective workplaces in the morning. Both of the cases regarded employees whose workplace primarily was ambulatory. Both of them were artisans who used service cars, and were salaried from the moment they left their residences. Both died in car accidents on their way to the first work assignments of the day. The deaths were not considered to be regarded as industrial injuries/ deaths. In the first case, two judges dissented against the majority of three judges, but in the second judgment the ruling was unanimous.

1118. In order to get cover for industrial injury, it is a basic condition that there actually exists an industrial injury, work-related disease or death related to a work accident. Injuries that develop gradually, and/or over time, is not covered for, e.g., are employees that slowly worm out after many years with heavy work.

1119. The injured employee's participation to the injury, will not lead to loss of entitlement to benefits from the social security system. On the other hand, cover for industrial injuries may be declined when the accident is found not to have any connection to the employee's work situation at all.

1120. Another judgment worth mentioning is Rt. 2006 p. 1129. In this case, a doctor was injured while getting arrested by the police in his own medical practice. He injured his knee during a mild struggle. The police suspected that he had driven his car under the influence of alcohol. The injury was considered and approved as an industrial injury, despite the fact that the doctor partly resisted the arrest, and had acted in such a manner that gave the police reason to believe he was under the influence of alcohol.

1121. Equal to industrial injury are certain diseases. The basic condition is that the disease needs to have arisen in relation to the conditions within the working place or working situation in large. There are few diseases that are recognized as industrial injuries, according to SSA Chapter 13, considering the large number of diseases that can be somewhat related to injuries, damages or deaths resulting from the working situation.

1. The Different Benefits

1122. Recognition of an injury as an industrial injury gives entitlement to a number of benefits that employees otherwise do not enjoy.

1123. Based on the construction of the SSA, there can be made a distinction between four phases of receiving benefits:

- the sick pay phase, which entitles the injured person with the right of receiving sick pay and other benefits for health care;
- the work clarification phase, which entitles the injured person with the right of receiving rehabilitation allowance, for a period when the injured person needs to be economically secured during a transition period due to work-related measures, medical treatment or other follow-up from the Labour and Welfare Administration. The rules regarding the work clarification allowance was introduced on 1 March 2010;
- the disability phase, which entitles the injured person with the right to disability allowance, basic benefit and attendance;
- disability pension, which entitles the injured person with the right to retirement benefits.

1124. In every phase, there are made two main types of benefits. That is the benefits that are supposed to cover for the work-related income that has lapsed, and benefits that are supposed to cover for the extra expenditures.

1125. In addition, and as mentioned above, the recognition of an injury as an industrial injury the injured person may be entitled to compensation for permanent injuries. Compensation for permanent injuries is supposed to cover a non-economic loss. This compensation responds to the permanent injury compensation pursuant to section 3-2 according to the Act relating to compensation in certain circumstances (TCA) of 13 June 1969 No. 26.

2. Subsistence

1126. During the sick pay phase, there are no certain indifferences between the industrial injuries situations and other situations with entitlement to sick pay. The level of benefits is the same, but sick pay related to industrial injuries is also made during the first fourteen days of an employment relationship.

1127. There are some special rules that apply during the disability period. The injured person will be entitled to disability pension with a disability degree of only 30%.

3. Extra Expenditure

1128. During the sick pay phase, the social security system give full cover for expenses due to expenditures for medical care, dental care, physical treatment, medical supplies etc. Employees covered for industrial injuries or other work-related diseases do not have to pay a deduction.

1129. The most important situation when established permanent disability related to industrial injury is that the injured person may receive both a basic benefit and attendance, without still having to be a member of the social security system.

4. Special Advantages

1130. Special advantages concerned industrial injuries or other work-related diseases is explicitly recited at the end of the single chapters pursuant to the SSA. For a detailed list of these advantages, *see* section 13-2 second subsection of the SSA.

B. Compensation for Permanent Injury

1131. This is a special compensation according to the SSA for persons with industrial injuries or other work-related diseases, and provides compensation for reduced possibilities for life development, as a result of the damage. The damaged person needs to have been afflicted with a permanent and substantial damage of a medical nature, in order to get compensation.

1132. The damage is considered substantial when the medical invalidity is rated to approximately 15% or more. The annual compensation for permanent injury constitutes 75% of the Basic Amount according to the social security standards, in maximum compensation situations, and runs for as long as the injured person is alive.

III. Industrial Injury Insurance

1133. According to the Industrial Injuries Insurance Act (IIIA) of 16 June 1989 No. 65, the industrial injury insurance comes in addition to the rules pursuant to the SSA regarding benefits due to industrial injuries.

1134. According to the IIIA section 3, the employer is obliged to take out insurances to cover industrial injuries and work-related diseases (industrial diseases) as specified in Chapter 3 of the Act. Such industrial injury insurance shall entitle employees to full compensation regardless of whether any person is to blame for the injury.

1135. The state is exempt from the obligation to insure. Employees in the state or in a municipality or county municipality which is exempt from the obligation to insure may claim compensation for injuries as specified in Chapter 3 directly from their employer. For the employer, the insurance is to be regarded as liability insurance. The employer is not personally liable for those damage cases that are covered by the Act.

1136. The Act contains provisions stating that an injury or disease is to be considered as to be caused during work, on the work place and within the working time, unless the insurer can prove that this is evidently not the case (cf. section 11). This reversed burden of proof serves as a measure in order to strengthen the employee's position in relation to the insurance company.

1137. According to section 11 in fine, in considering whether an injury or disease entitles one to coverage, any special tendency on the part of the employee to contract such injury or disease shall be disregarded unless such special tendency must be regarded as the completely dominant cause.

1138. According to the Act, the injury or disease needs to have been caused by a work accident. That is to say a sudden or unexpected outside event, or a concrete time-limited outside event that leads to a strain that is to be regarded as unusual considered what would normally be the case in the individual work situation.

1139. The Supreme Court has assumed a rather wide understanding of the concept of industrial injury (cf. Rt. 2005, p. 1757). In this case, a plumber was moving under scaffoldings in order to pick up some bolts that were lying around. When he was about to stand up again after collecting the bolts, he interpreted the situation in a way that made him think that a rather large beam was falling from the scaffoldings down to the place where he was located. As a natural reflex, he tried to bend the upper body away from the direction of the (imaginary) falling beam. While doing this, he accidentally incurred a knee injury. The Supreme Court considered the injury to be an industrial injury. The judges emphasized the fact that the employee at the time was in a rather difficult position, together with the extraordinary load of the impact of the deflection manoeuvre.

1140. Cases regarding industrial injuries are supposed to be handled by the insurance company that the employer is insured by. The compensation is estimated on the basis of standardized rules. The reason for this standardization is to make sure that the result, in the large number of cases, are supposed to wind up to be at the same level as according to the Act relating to compensation in certain circumstances of 13 June 1969 No. 26, but this is not always the case. The industrial injury insurance has to a large part made redundant the rules related to compensation on the basis of torts, within the area of entitlements for compensation for industrial injuries or diseases regarding employees.

1141. When practising the provisions pursuant to the Industrial Injury Insurance Act, the principles from the general rules of torts are relevant. Regarding the terms related to causation, the judgment in Rt. 1992 p. 64 is the most important. The condition that is considered the cause of the injury needs to be assumed to have been the necessary condition for the injury to arise (cf. also, *inter alia*, Rt. 2003 p. 338). On the other hand, minor or accidental causes are, as a general rule, ignored.

IV. Damages

1142. An employee who is afflicted from an injury or damage in the working place may, in addition, be entitled to compensation for damages from the employer himself. The employer may be liable for damages if the industrial injury or the work-related disease arose as a consequence of negligence (additionally the employer liability and the non-statutory strict liability may also be of relevance). To this post, the employee is referred to claim the employer for damages that are not covered or provided for by the social security system. But the employer is not liable for any claims that does follow from the Industrial Injury Insurance Act (cf. section 8). The insurer is liable in such circumstances, and not the employer himself.

1143. The insurer may only require recourse with an employer that has caused the damage or injury intentionally (cf. section 8(2)). The right to require recourse also includes reimbursement to the social security system.

Chapter 6. Job Security

§1. Termination of Employment

1144. Employment contracts that are not fixed term are usually terminated by giving notice. The period of notice is set forth in the various statutes by rules which may to a large extent be departed from by collective agreement. Some rules are nevertheless invariable, including WEA section 15-3(2 and 3), which stipulate minimum periods of notice for employees with long-term employment.

1145. A dismissal shall be in writing. Before making a decision regarding dismissal with notice, the employer shall, to the extent that it is practically possible, discuss the matter with the employee and the employee's elected representatives unless the employee himself does not desire this (cf. section 15-1). Regulations on consultations may also be stated in collective agreements, such as the BA (2014) section 10-2. Consultations are regarded as a rule of order. Therefore, neglect of consultations will not automatically lead to invalidity of the dismissal. However, for dismissals by the employer, it is given that consultations shall take place.

1146. The dismissal shall be handed personally to the employee or sent to him by registered letter. Furthermore, the dismissal shall contain information on the employee's right to remain in his or her post during legal proceedings on the fairness of the dismissal (section 15-11), the employee's right to negotiate the dismissal and to take legal action according to WEA section 15-11, section 17-1 and section 17-4 (*see* paragraphs 1071 et seq. for more), and on the appurtenant deadlines. If the dismissal is not in writing, or if it fails to include the above information, it is not thereby invalid, but there is on the other hand no deadline for taking legal action (according to WEA section 17-4(3)). However, non-fulfilment of the formal requirements could also invalidate the dismissal, Rt. 1992 p. 1175. The employee may demand that the employer state the grounds for the dismissal, and – if requested – that the grounds be stated in writing (WEA section 15-4(3)):

- An illustrative example as regards invalid termination of an employee, because of the employee's behaviour, is Rt. 2009 p. 685. In this case, the County Council wanted to terminate an employee who had been convicted of sexual offences (cf. WEA section 15-7). The employee was employed as a web editor in the county. He was arrested in October 2005 by police on suspicion of violating the PC by sexual behaviour in the form of chatting online with a mentally retarded girl aged 14. Her function level was that of a child at the age of 7 or 8 years, of which the employee should have been aware.
- The employee informed his superiors about his arrest and later on also that criminal proceedings would be instituted against him. The case was heard in City Court in 2006 and the case received wide coverage in local newspapers. The City Court found the web editor guilty of one violation and one attempted violation of PC

section 201 letter (c). The web editor also informed his superiors about the verdict and referred them to his lawyer for more information about the case.
- The employee applied on 7 March 2006 on leave from his position as web editor when he realized that the case was a burden for the organization. The application was granted on 13 March 2006. It was decided that he should continue in the county, but now as a consultant. In early September 2006, on the basis of requests from the 14-year-old girl's relatives, a personnel case of the former web editor was administratively created and it was assessed whether there was just cause for dismissal as a result of the criminal case. There was again a lot of media focus on the case, which resulted in the employee leaving his workplace on 18 September 2006. Subsequent meetings were held between him and the employer's side in order to reach a solution to the personnel case. Leave was extended. The employee wanted to return to work, but the employer stated on 1 December 2006 that they did not have confidence in him in relation to external operations, and that they would either negotiate a voluntary agreement or give him notice.
- The employee received a notice of termination on 15 December 2006 from the County Council. It was agreed that he should not resume his work, but continue with paid leave. Consultations were again held on the 19 January 2007. The employee was finally terminated by letter dated 20 March 2007. The former web editor filed a suit against the county claiming the dismissal be declared invalid.
- The county was acquitted by the City court in January 2008, and the employee was required to leave his position no later than 1 March 2008. The Court of Appeal, however, declared the termination invalid. The dismissal was essentially justified by the offences which had taken place nearly a year and a half ago, and found that it would be manifestly unreasonable if the employment should continue (cf. WEA section 15-12), and issued an order for the employee's to leave his position while the court proceedings were still ongoing.
- The Supreme Court found that the employee had adequately informed his superiors about the criminal case and that the county had waited too long before the employee was dismissed. The notice of termination was therefore held invalid. Neither the long leave of absence nor the lack of trust among colleagues made it 'clearly unreasonable that employment be continued' (cf. section 15-12, first subsection).

1147. When dismissed, the employee is entitled to a written job reference, the contents of which are stipulated in WEA section 15-15 (Rt. 1990 p. 560).

§2. Protection Against Dismissal

1148. Since 1936, there have been rules limiting the employer's prerogative to dismiss employees. The dismissal must be 'objectively justified on the basis of circumstances relating to the enterprise, the employer or the employee' (WEA section 15-7(1)). Somewhat similar provisions are found in section 5-6 of the Ship Labour Act. The object of these rules is to protect employees against the personal misfortune of a dismissal when the enterprise has insufficient grounds for it. For example, a dismissal because the employee is getting married (Rt. 1939 p. 65), because he is affiliated with a particular political party (ARD 1978 p. 65) or because he has been afflicted with a non-contagious disease (Rt. 1988 p. 959) is unfair.

1149. Unless otherwise agreed between the parties, fixed-term contracts may normally not be terminated during the agreed period of service (cf. Rt. 2012 p. 168). If the parties have agreed that the employment shall be subject to termination, WEA section 15-7 will apply, and just cause is then required (cf. also paragraphs 627–628 above).

I. The Employer's Termination of Employment for Reasons Related to the Employer

1150. Operational measures such as rationalization and work reduction are regarded as justifiable grounds for dismissal, but only if the employer has no other suitable work to offer the employee (WEA section 15-7(2)). If a rationalization process leads to reduction or termination of certain positions, it is not given that the employees who hold the affected positions will be terminated. It must be considered whether other employees in job categories that are basically not affected by the rationalization, are to be included in the rationalization process. This must be based on an overall assessment where considerations of the redundant employee must be weighed against other employees who are in danger of being terminated. In addition, qualifications (including suitability and experience), length of service, age and family situation be regarded as objective and justifiable selection criteria. Furthermore, when contemplating dismissals because of rationalization, reductions, etc., the needs of the enterprise must be weighed against the inconvenience to the individual employee.

1151. The entire employer's business represents the selection circuit, unless there are reasonable grounds to refine the selection circuit to specific business sections or departments. If the enterprise is in financial difficulties requiring a shutdown of some of its autonomous sections, dismissals might be justified by evaluating the individual sections separately, cf. Rt. 1992 p. 776. In this case, there was a significant geographic distance between the individual sections, and each section appointed its own employees. Thus, the Supreme Court found it reasonable to consider the individual section separately. Even dismissal of one single business section manager, who also was the only employee in this section, due to shutdown of the business section (one single department within a larger business group), was considered as made on justifiable grounds (cf. Rt. 2015 p. 1332). The employer had not considered the dismissal of one of the other employees in another business section within the region, instead of the dismissed employee. The Supreme Court concluded that it was objectively justified to limit the circle of selection for dismissal to the individual business section, although this only had one employee, cf. WEA section 15-7(1) and (2). Emphasis was put on the enterprise's previous practice in regard to workforce reductions.

1152. The selection of those to be dismissed must be made fairly. There must be no preferential treatment, and especially long employment periods must be taken into account (cf. Rt. 1966 p. 393, Rt. 1972 p. 1330, Rt. 1986 p. 879). Some emphasis should also be placed on discussing the dismissals with the employees' trade organization

(Rt. 1987 p. 117 and Rt. 1992 p. 776), and on social factors such as family responsibilities, etc. (Rt. 1986 p. 879).

1153. Transferring the enterprise from one owner to another is in itself insufficient grounds for dismissal (WEA section 16-4(1)). It could be that a bankrupt enterprise is started up again by new owners, but that does not constitute a transfer according to section 16-1(2), nor does starting up with fewer employees than previously constitute an operational reduction according to section 16-1(1). However, the employees have priority with regard to new employment according to section 14-2(1) (cf. Rt. 1986 p. 320 and Rt. 1992 p. 1039).

1154. The fairness of a dismissal coerced by a third party, e.g., the general public or a principal contractor, must be judged in the same way as a dismissal coerced by the other employees of the enterprise or by an organization.

1155. In the case of mass dismissals, i.e., notice of dismissal given to at least ten employees within a period of thirty days without being warranted by reasons related to the individual employees, special rules apply (cf. section 15-2). An employer contemplating collective redundancies shall at the earliest opportunity enter into consultations with the employees' elected representatives with a view to reaching an agreement to avoid collective redundancies or to reduce the number of persons made redundant (cf. section 15-2(2)). If redundancies cannot be avoided, efforts shall be made to mitigate their adverse effects.

1156. When rendering a legal judgment on the fairness of a dismissal, an evaluation must be made, and the courts are not bound by the employer's assessments. In part, case law has particularly stressed the employer's prudence in handling the dismissal. In part, the courts may examine whether there are proper and sufficient grounds for the dismissal. The courts may also question the scope of the employer's assessment, whether it has included the fairness factors pertaining to the employee. The employer's own appraisal of dismissal as warranted by operations, the employee's qualifications, etc., may indeed be stressed in the legal assessment, but the emphasis to be placed on the employer's appraisal is more a question of practicality than of legal consideration and evaluation (cf. Rt. 1984 p. 1058).

1157. When a decision regarding operating restrictions, operational changes or shutting down the business is made by the employer, a particular question is whether the employees may bring the decision before the courts, demanding the decision invalid, before any notice has been given. The provisions pursuant to the WEA are written with a view to the situation where the notice is actually given to one or more employees. This applies both to the substantive fairness requirements and the procedural provisions (cf. Rt. 1989 p. 508 (*Norsk Jern*), where the Supreme Court clarifies this). In principle, it is not excluded that a decision will be invalidated by the courts, even in situations where no employees have yet been given a notice of dismissal. Such an action would have to be instituted on the basis of the general provisions pursuant to the Dispute Act (cf. Rt. 1989 p. 508), and not by the special procedural provisions pursuant to the WEA. It would, however, be doubtful whether a single employee will have sufficient legal connection to the claim in order to institute such a claim (cf. the Dispute Act section 1-3(2)). It would therefore be more convenient if the claim is instituted by several employees together, e.g., as a so-called class action (cf. the Dispute

Act Chapter 35), or by the employees' trade union (cf. the Disputes Act sections 1-3 and 1-4).

1158. Should such a decision be made on the basis of incomplete proceedings by the employer, or by proceedings on the basis of an incorrect or incomplete factual basis, which may be regarded to have had a significant impact on the decision that was made, the decision could presumably be declared invalid. The reality will then be that the employer will have to reconsider the decision. Otherwise, however, the employer's decision regarding operating restrictions, operational changes or shutting down the business will necessarily have to be made on the basis of a total assessment of all circumstances in the present situation. Thus, the role of the courts will in such cases be limited (cf. paragraph 257 above).

1159. It could be that it is promised – by the employer or by political bodies – that employment relationships will not be terminated. In principle, such promises may well be regarded as legally binding and could make the employer liable for the financial loss on the part of the employees. Such promises, however, have to be interpreted on the basis of the present situation, when the promise was given. It will therefore be a presumption that the promise was made on the basis of the situation, as it seemed at the time when the promise was given. When the situation later has changed, it will often lead to the fact that the promise cannot be maintained. Promises made by political bodies will also – in many cases – depend on the follow-up resolution of parent bodies, e.g., on public funding. It may also be the case that such promises must be regarded more as a political statement of intent other than as a binding promise (cf. NAD 1981-83 p. 438 Eidsivating Court of Appeal).

II. Closing Down the Activities of an Enterprise

1160. In general, an employer is entitled to close down the activities of the enterprise, and may in that regard give the employees their notice of termination of the employment relationship. Should ten or more employees be given notice, the Norwegian Labour and Welfare Administration (NAV) has to be informed (cf. WEA section 15-2(3)).

1161. However, the closing down of a larger enterprise may affect the surrounding community to quite an extent. Therefore, the Act on notification of closure of activities of enterprises, of 6 June 2008, No. 38 aims at finding alternatives to such closure, and prescribes the procedure to be followed. Possible measures to reduce the negative consequences for the employees are also to be considered.

1162. The Act applies to enterprises employing thirty or more employees. Such enterprise may not decide finally to close its activities, before the county has been informed, and not until thirty days have passed after such information about a planned closure has reached the county. This period may be prolonged with further thirty days, should actual alternatives exist to the closing down of the enterprise (cf. section 3).

1163. The information to be submitted to the county is the number of employees, the activities of the enterprise, an evaluation of the consequences of a closure for the employees and for the local community, the background for the planned closure, considerations as regards alternative activities for the enterprise, as well as what seems necessary for a continuation of the present activities, and whether discussions have taken place with the employees (cf. section 3). The county may request further information.

1164. After submitting the notification of closure to the county and until the consultations has been finalized, the company is not entitled to make any legal or factual dispositions that may substantially impair the value of the company (cf. section 6).

1165. The county council shall, as soon as possible and within thirty days, convene for consultation meetings with representatives of the owner, the management and the employees, as well as representatives of the municipality, Innovation Norway and the Labour and Welfare Administration (cf. section 5). The purpose of such consultation meetings is to consider measures for continued operation or other alternatives to closure. Throughout the consultations, compensation and restructuring opportunities for the employees and possible measures for the local community should always be considered.

1166. Should consultations not be successful, the county shall as soon as possible notify the enterprise and the other participants that consultations are terminated.

1167. Should the enterprise not fulfil its obligations pursuant to the Act, the county may impose fines and fees according to sections 7 and 8.

III. The Employer's Termination of the Employment for Reasons Related to the Employee

1168. Dismissals for reasons related to the employee will in particular be dereliction. Still, it is not required that dereliction is so serious that it is regarded as a gross breach of duty and therefore can lead to a summary dismissal according to WEA section 15-14(1).

1169. The employee's circumstances must be evaluated in connection with circumstances related to the employer and the interests of the enterprise (Rt. 2001 p. 1362). The irregularities must not become insignificant when judging the employment situation as a whole (cf. e.g., Rt. 1963 p. 1013). Both new and old circumstances related to the employee may be relevant to the evaluation of the dismissal, including previous closed incidents. Provided that the circumstances are relevant and that there has not been a too long time since they took place, they may be taken into consideration. Prior dismissal warnings will also have a bearing on the judgment (Rt. 1956 p. 578). Prior warning of the consequences of a particular breach of duty is also emphasized (Rt. 1992 p. 1023).

1170. Subjective reasonableness factors such as dismissal being an overwhelming burden on the employee must be taken into account. Such factors become less important, however, when the dismissal is precipitated by the employee himself, than by reductions, rationalization measures, etc. (Rt. 1992 p. 1039).

1171. If the employee must be absent from work in order to serve time in prison, a long-term absence will be fair grounds for dismissal (cf. Rt. 1992 p. 1482 on being absent from work in order to serve more than two months in prison). In brief, absences due to prison time, the convict's re-socialization must be stressed, among other things.

If an employee is absent because he is being held in custody, restraint should be shown in giving notice prior to a verdict, as it is not yet known whether the employee alone should carry the risk for the absence (cf. Rt. 2011 p. 74 concerning an employee who was absent from work for four weeks due to custody, and was found not to be guilty in the following criminal case).

1172. In addition, an employee's extracurricular activities may warrant dismissal. This is particularly true where the job requires that the employee has a good reputation, and is especially applicable to employees in public service. For example, the employee may make improper statements on social issues (Rt. 1982 p. 1729).

IV. Termination of the Employment Because of the Age of the Employee

1173. According to section 15-13a (1), the employer may by the point of time the employee turns 72 years (by the Act of 24 April 2015 No. 20, which entered into force on 1 July 2015), terminate the employment without giving a notice of dismissal. It is not required that the termination is based on an objectively justifiable reason. A lower age limit may be stipulated in the employment contract or in the collective agreement when necessary for reasons of health (e.g., for nurses or other employees who are exposed to heavy work/extensive risk of wear and tear) or safety (e.g., for police officers or firemen or other employees who perform work within public or general protection/security), cf. WEA section 15-13a(2). A lower age limit, but never below 70 years, may be imposed by the employer if the age limit is made well known to the employees, it is practised consistently by the employer and the employees are entitled to an adequate pension scheme, cf. WEA section 15-13a(3). It is a requirement that lower age limits according to both WEA section 15-13 a (2) and (3) has a justifiable basis, and will not have a disproportionate effect, cf. WEA section 13-3(2). This also means that the termination of the contract must not be in violation of the rules and principles regarding discrimination in WEA Chapter 13.

1174. Before terminating the employment, notice shall be given by the employer six months prior to the termination. The notice must be in writing, but no further formal requirements are stipulated. The statutory provision also stipulates that a conversation between employer and employee shall take place before notice is given, unless the employee does not desire to do so. Should the employee wish to resign, a notice of at least one month must be given, but not necessarily in writing.

1175. The Ship Labour Act section 5-12 stipulates that dismissing a seaman so that he or she must leave the job at the age of 70 years old will be deemed justified. However, resignation before the age of 70 may be agreed upon in the employment contract, in a collective agreement or the pension scheme if the age limit has a justifiable basis, and will not have a disproportionate effect.

1176. It was previously stated that the age limit of 62 years was not contrary to the Council Directive 2000/78/EC (of 27 November 2000) on establishing a general framework for equal treatment in employment and occupation (cf. Rt. 2010 p. 202 (*Nye Kystlink*), where the Supreme Court also referred to some judgments of the EU-Court: Grand Chamber of 22 November 2005, *Werner Mangold v. Rüdiger Helm*

(C-144/04) (item 63), Grand Chamber of 16 October 2007, *Félix Palacios de la Villa v. Cortefiel Servicios SA* (C-411/05) (item 68), and Third Chamber of 5 March 2009, *Age Concern* (C-388/07) (item 51)). It had to be vested with the legislator to consider whether the interests of the employees' safety and health were sufficiently weighty to justify this exception.

1177. There was previously no exception for seamen employed after reaching 62 years of age, at least not unless otherwise is agreed upon (cf. Rt. 2010 p. 202 (*Nye Kystlink*)).

1178. According to the WEA, an age limit set by a company may be legally introduced if the age limit is objectively justified and does not involve disproportionate intervention in relation to the person or persons who are discriminated on the basis of age (cf. WEA section 15-13 a, section 13-2(2)). As a consequence of the EU Directive 2000/78/EC, the attitude of the Norwegian Supreme Court seems now to be more restrictive than previously, especially since the ECJ decision C-447/09 *Prigge* (cf. paragraph 1066 below).

1179. Company-internal age limits of 67 years have, however, traditionally been deemed as valid in Norwegian law (cf. Rt. 2011 p. 964 (*Gjensidige*) section 43). The case concerned to what extent a company-internal age limit of 67 years of age was in breach of the prohibition against age discrimination.

1180. The Supreme Court emphasized that the age limit came into force upon pensionable age, and that there existed a company pension scheme in the undertaking that provided entitlement to a 'very favourable pension'. Furthermore, the age limit was based on paramount socio-political considerations where, *inter alia*, regard for work distribution amongst the generations has been emphasized. These considerations were viewed by the Supreme Court as objective and reasonably based on legitimate purposes, and therefore in accordance with the directive.

1181. The employee argued that the employer's internal age limit was based on considerations which exclusively applied to the company's needs, and claimed that the EC Court requires that any discrimination has to be based on broader socio-political requirements. The Supreme Court found this to be a 'too narrow approach' and found, following a thorough review of the *travaux préparatoires* that the decisive aspect would have to be that company-internal age limits of 67 years have traditionally been considered valid in Norwegian law. The assumption has been that the age limit has been practised consistently, that it has been known among the employees and that the employee in question upon retirement will receive a satisfactory occupational pension. Since these assumptions were considered met, the age limit was in accordance with the exclusionary provision in the EC directive and therefore also with the WEA section 13-3(2).

1182. In Rt. 2012 p. 219 (*Helicopter Pilot*) which concerned the issue of whether the employer on the basis of a collective agreement, could demand that helicopter pilots retire upon reaching the age of 60, the Supreme Court seems to express a more restrictive view on which purposes that can justify the introduction of special age limits. In spite of the fact that the employees had very favourable pension schemes, that the arrangement was known among the employees and had been practised consistently, the Supreme Court found that the special age limit was not in compliance with the WEA section 15-13 a (cf. 13-3(2)). It must be noted, however, that the age limit of 60 years deviates significantly from the one of 67 years in the *Gjensidige* case. Furthermore, that an age limit of 60 years is not to the same extent viewed as a common and traditionally accepted age limit as the one in the *Gjensidige* case. The stated differences nevertheless do not reduce the impression that the Supreme Court's *Helicopter Pilot* decision seems to restrict the area of application for the exclusionary provision in the WEA section 13-3(2).

1183. First, the Supreme Court stated that the clauses of the WEA shall be interpreted such that they are in accordance with the EU Directive 2000/78/EC on equal opportunities in working life and case law of the EC court. Hence, the European Court of Justice Case C-447/09, *Prigge* (25 September 2011) was given special emphasis upon the decision. In C-447/09, the EU court found that a separate age limit for aviators could not be based on safety considerations or health, and all the while the national certificate regulations allows aviation until the pilot reaches 65 years of age. As the Supreme Court viewed the matter, it then followed directly from the *Prigge* decision that safety considerations or health issues could not justify the age limit of 60 years for the helicopter pilots.

1184. Neither the other stated considerations, such as regard for a dignified retirement, consideration for swifter advancement for younger pilots or the consideration for safeguarding a good pension scheme, made the age limit legitimate. To what extent the considerations in themselves were justifiable, was not considered by the Supreme Court as the 60 years age limit was nevertheless not deemed as an adequate and necessary means to achieve the stated purposes.

1185. It should further be observed (cf. Rt. 2011 p. 609 (*SAS Pilots*)), that the airline SAS had to reduce the number of pilots, and pilots who had reached the pension age (60 years) according to the collective agreement, were given notice of termination, although the age limit for such work was 65 years. The Supreme Court did not consider these notices of termination invalid. It was necessary to reduce the number of pilots, and the purpose of this arrangement was to minimize the negative effects for the individual pilots. Further, the arrangement was not disproportionate, as the most elderly of the pilots were entitled to a considerable pension.

1186. The Act of 24 April 2015 No. 20, which entered into force on 1 July 2015, made amendments in WEA section 15-13a. WEA section 15-13 a (3) now entails the criteria that are to be met in order for lower age limits to be lawfully imposed on employees, stated by the Supreme Court in Rt. 2011 p. 946 (*Gjensidige*), but the age limit may never be lower than 70 years. In addition, it is a requirement that such lower age limits are objectively justified and do not involve a disproportionate intervention in relation to the person or persons that are discriminated on the basis of age, cf. WEA section 13-3(2).

1187. Lower age limits that are applicable within local (municipalities/*kommuner*) or regional (counties/*fylker*) authorities, which are reasoned similarly as is stated by the Act on age limits for public officials and other employees with employment contracts that are incorporated into the State Pension Fund, section 2, shall apply until otherwise decided. Section 2 in the (so-called) Public Age Limit Act stipulates that the general age limit is 70 years. However, there may be stipulated lower limit age for positions in which:

- The service involves unusual physical or mental strain on the officials so that they normally are not able to carry out the work properly up to the age of 70.
- The service demands special physical or mental abilities, which are normally weakened in a more rapid manner before the age of 70, and this may impose a threat to the officials' ability to carry out the work in a proper manner.

1188. The lower age limits may be 68, 65, 63 and 60 years of age, and are stipulated in a number of different regulations.

§3. Procedural Method for Disputes over Wrongful Dismissal

1189. WEA section 15-11, section 17-1, section 17-3 and section 17-4 provide detailed procedural rules for disputes over wrongful dismissal. Consequently, one cannot prearrange to have such a dispute heard by a court of arbitration (Rt. 1992 p. 534). The employee has a right to demand negotiations with the employer (cf. section 17-3). The demand must be submitted two weeks after receiving notice. The employer is responsible for making sure that negotiations are held no later than two weeks after receiving the demand. If, instead of negotiating, the employee takes legal action, the employer may demand a negotiation meeting, and legal proceedings will then be postponed until the meeting is held. The employee has a right to be assisted during the negotiations by a shop steward or other adviser. Minutes shall be kept of the negotiations.

1190. Within eight weeks of the end of negotiations, the employee may bring action before the District Court stipulated by WEA section 17-4 to hear dismissal disputes, etc. Furthermore, the general rules of procedure pursuant to the Act relating to the Resolution of Disputes (the Disputes Act), will apply (cf. WEA section 17-1). If the employee is only claiming for damages, the deadline for taking action is six months (cf. section 17-4). However, the parties may agree to a longer deadline for taking action (section 17-4(1)). Proceedings before the Conciliation Council shall not take place (WEA section 17-1(3)). The court shall proceed with the case as quickly as possible and, if necessary, schedule the case out of turn. In the main hearing, court shall be convened by the district court with lay judges from a special committee familiar with working employment relations, unless the parties agree that lay judges are unnecessary (section 17-7). Rulings by the district court judge may be appealed to the CA and, further, to the Supreme Court. Also in the main hearing before the Court of Appeal, the court is convened with lay judges unless the parties agree that lay judges are unnecessary.

§4. Appeals Deadline

1191. The appeals deadline is one month (cf. the Dispute Act section 29-5(1) and section 30-3).

§5. Right to Remain in Post During Dismissal Case Proceedings

1192. Of practical importance is the provision in WEA section 15-11 which stipulates that, in general, the employee may continue his or her employment not only while the dispute is subject to negotiations, but until the case is settled legally. However, the right to continue working requires that action is taken before the end of the period of notice, unless the employee has notified the employer in writing that action will be taken within the eight-week deadline. In addition, the employee must indeed be able to continue working unless there are legal grounds for being absent (cf. Rt. 1992 p. 1482 (absence for more than two months while serving a prison sentence)).

1193. If the court finds it unreasonable to sustain the employment during the hearing, it may issue a ruling that the employee leaves the job. A deadline shall also be set for leaving the job (Rt. 1985 p. 412 and Rt. 1982 p. 1704), but the deadline may not be set for a date prior to the end of the period of notice. If the employee has left the job because the enterprise has ceased to exist, and the court finds it unreasonable to deem the employment to be existent after the cessation of the enterprise, the court may nevertheless stipulate that the date of the de facto departure shall be deemed the legal departure date pursuant to WEA section 15-11 (Rt. 1992 p. 776). The court may not stipulate that the employee shall leave, but uphold the right to wages or other benefits from the employment (Rt. 1983 p. 1558). In determining whether the employment shall continue, the nature of the job, among other things, must be taken into account (*see* NAD 1981-83 p. 376. Cf. also Rt. 1982 p. 1794, where considerable emphasis was placed on the fact that it was an executive post, where the necessary relationship of trust between the parties no longer existed.)

1194. According to the legislative history, if the dismissal is due to offences committed by the employee, then the dismissal shall usually be allowed (cf. Rt. 1986 p. 722 and Rt. 1992 p. 1547).

1195. In dismissals due to reductions in production, the principal rule is that the court shall decide against letting the employee go, and that a relatively strong argument is required to warrant dismissal (Rt. 1984 p. 400, 1987 p. 117, 1987 p. 1151). Another requirement is that the interest of the enterprise must weigh heavily in favour of dismissal (Rt. 1987 p. 692, Rt. 2000 s. 525, Rt. 2000 s. 739 and Rt. 2000 s. 1958), and the financial burden on the parties is relevant (Rt. 1991 p. 330, Rt. 1992 p. 1680 and p. 1688). The fact that other dismissed employees have not exercised their right to continue in their jobs is of no consequence (Rt. 1987 p. 117), but it may seem unreasonable if some of the employees who were made redundant remain at their posts (cf. Rt. 2000 p. 1958). The court evaluates the dismissal issue on the basis of the situation at the time of the decision to dismiss was made (Rt. 1990 p. 908, compare Rt. 1988 p. 1418, Rt. 1989 p. 225 and Rt. 1987 p. 1151). Emphasis may be placed on the probable outcome of the dismissal case (Rt. 1991 p. 330, Rt. 1992 p. 1680), on the fact that there are no other tasks to offer the dismissed (Rt. 1990 p. 908), or special complications in that the dismissed must work in another department (Rt. 1989 p. 1041), or that retaining the employment would threaten the existence of the enterprise (Rt. 1989 p. 1041). Any temporary injunctions requested by the dismissed shall also be treated in the same way (Rt. 1989 p. 792). The employer may not render illusory the employee's right to continue in the work by laying him or her off during the period of notice (Rt. 1984 p. 400 and ARD 1980 p. 25).

1196. An employee who believes he or she has been unlawfully locked out of the place of work after the period of notice or term of the contract of employment has expired shall be entitled to resume the post if the employee so requests within four weeks of such a lock-out (cf. section 15-11(5)).

1197. Though the question of resignation has been decided by the superior court in connection with the case preparation, the subordinate court may by the decision of the lawful dismissal, once again make a decision on the question if the employer so desires (cf. Rt. 1999 p. 1158).

1198. The right to continue in one's post does not apply to all employments. According to section 4-5 of Act No. 61 of 17 July 1998 relating to vocational training, dismissal protection pursuant to WEA section 15-7 and the procedural rules in WEA section 15-11 and following sections (cf. Rt. 1984 p. 1451), does not apply to apprentices. The same applies to participants in labour market schemes under the auspices of or in cooperation with the Labour and Welfare Service who are dismissed because they are offered ordinary employment or transferred to another scheme or because the scheme is terminated (WEA section 15-11(4)). Nor do seamen have a right to continue their employment while the case is being tried (cf. section 5-10 (2) of the Ship Labour Act). Nevertheless, seamen have the right to continue in their post during negotiations with the employer after having received a dismissal from the employer, according to the Ship Labour Act section 5-10 (1).

§6. Effects of Unfair Dismissals

1199. If the court finds the dismissal unfair, it shall render it invalid if so requested by the employee (WEA section 15-12).

1200. In special cases, the court may nevertheless rule in favour of terminating the employment if, after weighing the parties' interests, it finds that continuing the employment would be clearly unreasonable. Potential decline in business because of customers' fear of being infected by an HIV-positive employee, who later developed AIDS, was not considered a decisive factor by the Supreme Court, because the employee was fully capable of working, and there was no genuine risk of infecting others (Rt. 1988 p. 959).

1201. In cases of unfair dismissals, an employee may claim compensation (WEA section (2)), which is a common remedy if the courts find the dismissal unfair. There is no statutorily fixed amount to be paid. Compensation is estimated at the amount the court deems reasonable, and may include financial and non-financial losses (cf. Rt. 1991 p. 236). The same applies to section 5-11 (2) of the Ship Labour Act.

1202. Apportionment shall be based on an overall discretional assessment. The statutory provision does not contain an upper limit or, for that matter, a lower limit either. Nevertheless, it follows from the preparatory works of the Working Environment Act of 1977 that 'the compensation must, in all events, not be less than the economic loss he has suffered', assuming that 'the employee is not especially to blame' (cf.

Ot.prp.no. 41 (1975–1976) p. 75), that is to say that under such conditions the employee shall at least have his or her economic loss covered.

It is normally fairly easy to determine the employee's economic loss with regard to actual loss. This will normally be loss of salary based on the employee's income with the employer up until the point in time of the decision, with any deductions for salary that the employee may have earned elsewhere during proceeding of the case. The economic loss also includes any other documented losses that the employee may have suffered as a result of the dismissal.

1203. It is considerably more difficult to determine future economic loss in cases where there is a decision for cessation of the employment. Under such circumstances, an approximate evaluation must be made as to how long time it is reasonable to expect it will take before the employee is in employment at a corresponding income level – and which it is reasonable that the employer shall compensate. Among other things, the employee's age, length of employment and expectations on the relevant labour market will be relevant factors under the assessment. *See* amongst others Rt. 1997 p. 1506 (below paragraph 1087).

1204. In principle, the dismissed employee will, pursuant to general contract law principles, be obliged to attempt to limit the loss – by seeking other employment – and income from such work will be deducted upon apportionment of compensation. However, according to the preparatory works, this principle however only applies when the employee has been out of the position for a relatively long period of time, and it is therefore not correct to make deductions for any income the employee has received. This question also arises when the employee has been dismissed without notice and the dismissal is found unjustified and held void, and this question should be considered according to the same principles as when a dismissal with notice is held void (cf. Rt. 2012 p. 168 (*football players*) paragraphs 84–85, where the Supreme Court *inter alia* referred to the necessity of strengthening the effectiveness of the law and regulations regarding job security. Thus, no reduction were made for the income that the two football players had received during the remaining part of the first year, after they had left the club – i.e., nine months – while full reductions were made for the remaining year of the contract). This question has also been dealt with previously by the Supreme Court (cf. Rt. 2005 p. 518 and Rt. 2001 p. 1253). Further, Rt. 1999 p. 184 should be noted, where a dismissed cleaner was awarded salary during the thirty-five months she had been out of work. The Supreme Court did not find it proven that she would have found employment if she had looked for work. *See also* paragraph 684 above, and paragraph 1092 below.

1205. A relevant question in this regard is whether an employee will be entitled to compensation for loss of income if the employee has not made use of the right to remain in position while the case is pending, which would have prevented such economic loss. In this regard, it must be noted that the right to remain in post is a right and not a duty for the employee. In the event that the employee has 'reasonable cause' for not making use of this right, for example because the employer's conduct towards the employee indicates that it will be difficult for the employee to continue in the position while the case is pending, it would seem unreasonable to make deductions in compensation. On the other hand, it may be unreasonable to award the employee compensation if he chooses not to continue in the position solely because he for example feels offended by the dismissal.

1206. Factors which may be of significance for apportionment of compensation for economic and non-economic loss are, for example, that the employer's case processing has been blameworthy (even if this has been unintentional on the employer's side), that the employer has made groundless accusations towards the employee, that the case has been given unnecessary 'publicity', or that the employee was dismissed without, instead of with, notice.

1207. Such blameworthy conduct on the employer's side may in itself impose further loss on the employee in the form of problems on the labour market, with subsequent 'higher' loss of future income. In addition, such conduct may also justify compensation for non-economic loss. *See* among others Rt. 2001 p. 1253. In this case, a dismissal without notice was invalid, but the court found the employer had just cause for termination with notice. The employee was awarded compensation for future loss of income, and compensation for non-economic loss due to the employer's procedural errors (consultation meeting had not been held), that the employee had wrongfully been dismissed without notice, and because the notice letter contained incorrect and incriminating criticism. Reference is also made to Rt. 1991 p. 236, where a dismissed employee in addition to having their entire assumable economic loss compensated by the Supreme Court was also awarded compensation for non-economic loss as a consequence of the employer's blameworthy handling of the matter, even if the employee had a significant responsibility for those circumstances which resulted in the dismissal.

1208. In the overall assessment which takes place upon apportionment of compensation, the employer's economic situation and the employee's 'guilt' (contributory negligence) are also relevant factors.

§7. Agreed Benefits on Termination of Employment

1209. Upon termination of employment, the employee may be entitled to benefits stipulated in the employment contract or collective agreement.

I. Severance Pay

1210. Severance pay has practical importance (appendix 1 to the IA). According to this agreement, employees between the ages of 50 and 67, with long-term employment in enterprises covered by the arrangement, are entitled to a lump sum from the main organizations' fund when their services are brought to an end through no fault on their part or as a result of illness or poor health. The arrangement also includes non-union employees. The severance pay increases as of the employee's 50th birthday (NOK 18,000), reaching a maximum (NOK 57,000) for employees who are 62 years of age and thereafter decreasing to NOK 11,400 for those 66 years of age, based on the notion that the disadvantages would be greatest for employees who are well into their years, but with quite some time remaining before reaching pensionable age.

II. Golden Parachutes

1211. It may be practical for both the employer and employee to enter into an agreement that the employee shall receive a stipulated compensation when the employment is brought to an end. Such an agreement may be arranged in advance as part of the employment contract, but it may also be entered into later, possibly in connection with leaving the employment. Such an arrangement may be agreeable to the employer because he will then know the employee's demands, and the employer may want to avoid an assessment by the courts where the enterprise's negative aspects might be brought up. Such an agreement may also be agreeable to the employee because the employee, too, would want to know what claim he can bring against the employer, and the deadline for the claim would be stipulated in the agreement. Similarly, the employee may wish to avoid legal action with possible negative references to him or her. Court actions will always entail elements of uncertainty, both regarding the admissibility assessment, which includes judging factors pertaining to the employee, and perhaps not least regarding the amount of damages the court will decide on. A contractual regulation may entail that the employee has a right to the agreed compensation, regardless of whether or not the dismissal is unfair or wrongful. But that, in turn, will depend on the agreement and its interpretation. In practice, such agreements are made with employees in executive posts.

1212. An employee who has entered into such an agreement in advance may nevertheless bring legal action according to the general rules of the WEA, in that an employee cannot disclaim dismissal protection in advance (cf. section 1-9). On the other hand, if the agreement is entered into in connection with the employee's leaving his employment, the agreement will also be binding for the employee (cf. Rt. 2004 p. 297 and ARD 1981 p. 160).

1213. When using agreement constituting compensation on termination of the employment for the chief executive of the enterprise, the parties may agree that the chief executive relinquish the rights of WEA Chapter 15 which normally are due to employees (cf. section 15-16(2)). The reason for the rule was that the right to remain in one's post was used to achieve further compensation in additional to the agreed compensation of termination. The employer and the chief executive may by writing agree to arbitration of disputes over employment termination when it concerns executive managers in an enterprise (cf. section 15-16(1)).

III. Insurance Arrangements

1214. Related to such agreements are insurance schemes established within certain professions contingent on the employee's good health and entitling the employee to compensation if he or she cannot continue practising the profession for health reasons (loss of licence insurance) (cf. NAD 1984-85 p. 418 Gulating and NAD 1984-85 p. 731 (*Pilots*) and NAD 1988 p. 449 Oslo (*Diver*)).

§8. Summary Dismissal/Resignation

1215. While dismissal/resignation as described above is the termination of employment after a period of notice, summary dismissal/resignation means immediate termination (the same day). The contract is terminated. Summary dismissal or resignation generally requires that the opposite party has committed a serious violation. For example, the employee is guilty of serious misconduct, or the employer's production equipment is in such poor condition as to place the employees' lives or health at undue risk.

1216. In this regard, Rt. 1997 p. 1506 (Stryn apotek) may be mentioned; the Supreme Court held that three employees at a chemist's shop had been entitled to leave their work immediately (i.e., without giving notice of termination), because of an 'unusually poor' psycho-socially working environment; that they were entitled to compensation for the economic loss thus suffered, based on general contractual principles, as the WEA section 15-12 did not apply, and for a period of time of about two years, but not to compensation for their non-economic loss and inconvenience.

1217. The right to summarily dismiss an employee is regulated in WEA section 15-14(1). An employee may be summarily dismissed if guilty of gross breach of duty or other major violation of the employment contract, for example refusing to work overtime (Rt. 1965 p. 1075), or to work at the indicated place (Rt. 1971 p. 310). The employer shall confer with the employee's shop steward before dismissal is decided, unless the employee himself or herself does not wish it.

1218. If the court finds that the dismissal was unfair, it shall be rendered invalid, unless the court nevertheless finds that continuing the employment would obviously be unreasonable. Similarly, the court may decide that the employment shall come to an end if the court finds that the conditions for fair dismissal exist (WEA section 15-14(3)). The employer must, however, so demand. For example, a pilot's attempt to smuggle goods for personal use was not considered a serious breach of duty, among other things because it was a first offence in an employment that had lasted more than fifteen years, although it was deemed to constitute just grounds for dismissal in accordance with WEA section 15-7 (cf. Rt. 1992 p. 1023).

1219. Similar rules apply pursuant to the Ship Labour Act, section 5-14. Repeated violation of provisions on mandatory temperance, etc., is considered a serious breach of duty (Rt. 1992 p. 1573). Before ordering a dismissal, the employer shall discuss the matter with the seaman and the seaman's elected representatives, in accordance with the rules in section 5-1.

1220. Disputes concerning the fairness of summary dismissal are treated in the same way as disputes over dismissal with notice, but the employee does not have a right to continue his or her employment during the proceedings unless otherwise decided by the court (WEA section 15-11(3)).

1221. For unfair summary dismissal, an employee may claim for damages for financial and non-financial tort (WEA section 15-14(4)). *See also* paragraph 1080 above. Needless publicity of the employee's dismissal may in itself entitle the employee to damages, even if the dismissal is admissible. Cf. Rt. 1937 p. 62, where the employee was awarded considerable economic compensation on this basis, although the dismissal as such was lawful; similarly Rt. 1997 p. 58.

§9. Termination Due to Accidents, Fire and Similar

1222. Where fulfilling an employment contract is rendered impossible due to unforeseen extraordinary events, the traditional basis has been that the employment contract is waived. Typical examples are a shipwreck, factory fire, etc. This basis was used until 1956 as regards worker protection legislation and until 1985 for the previous SA.

1223. Where there were events and conditions beyond the control of both parties, making it impossible to continue work and attributable neither to changes in the employee's personal circumstances nor to the enterprise, the Supreme Court nevertheless found that the employee could not carry the risk for such a work impediment alone. The employee was a German citizen employed in an orchestra, and following the liberation in 1945, it was impossible to hold a concert with Germans in the orchestra. Hence, the employee's wage claim was not categorically waived (Rt. 1953 p. 607). In reality, the decision implies that the termination of employment must be considered on the basis of the general rules on dismissal and dismissal protection, so that the general periods of notice shall apply, and not the shorter periods of notice as currently stipulated in WEA section 15-3.

1224. According to the WEA, the rule is that the employment contract is not invalidated when operations must be stopped in whole or in part because of fire, accidents, forces of nature, etc., but the period of notice may be reduced to fourteen days (cf. section 15-3(10)). According to the Ship Labour Act, seamen have a right to a one-month period of notice (section 5-2(1)) if the ship is lost in connection with a maritime accident, or if after such accident is beyond repair, and this maritime accident necessitates a termination of the employment. For the termination of the ship master's employment, a period of notice of three months shall nevertheless apply.

§10. Lay-Offs (Temporary Redundancy)

1225. Frequently, however, it may be more suitable to lay off employees than to give them notice (cf. also paragraphs 965–985 above). Because of its suitability, the practice of lay-offs has grown and become regulated through the collective agreements (cf. *BA* sections 8-1 et seq.). The courts have also allowed temporary redundancy, on similar conditions as stipulated in the Basic Agreement, even in lieu of any specific agreement thereupon (from recent years may be mentioned RG 2007 p. 1176 *Gulating*, *Borgarting* 17 June 2011, and 13. January 2011, *Haalogaland* 25 June 2010 and RG 2010 p. 797 *Borgarting*). However, the right to lay off workers may be barred by (special) agreement or collective agreement (ARD 1982 p. 249). Nor may lay-offs be used in permanent production cutbacks; dismissals shall then be used (*see* RG 1986 p. 98 *Eidsivating*). According to BA section 8-1, all things being equal, lay-offs shall be based on seniority (cf. ARD 1990 p. 169, where differences in seniority were minor).

1226. Employees who are laid off without pay in connection with cutbacks or stoppage, have a right to resign with a shorter period of notice than otherwise. The period of notice is fourteen days, regardless of what period has been agreed or stipulated by law (WEA section 15-3(9)).

1227. According to Act No. 22 of 6 May 1988 (TRWA) relating to wage obligation during lay-off, the employer must pay wages for twenty days; the so-called employer-period (cf. section 3(1)). According to section 3(2), if the employee has been laid off – in whole or in part – for a total of twenty-six weeks during the last eighteen months, the employer's wage obligation reapplies. These rules nevertheless do not apply to lay-offs due to labour disputes (cf. section 3(3)).

§11. Basic Principles

1228. In accordance with WEA section 15-3(10), the death of the employer or bankruptcy does not entitle the enterprise to give employees a shorter period of notice. According to WEA section 14-2(7), former employees who were dismissed in connection with a bankruptcy/winding up have priority to new employment if the enterprise continues or resumes after the bankruptcy. The same applies if the enterprise is insolvent and bankruptcy proceedings have not been instituted because there are no funds for bankruptcy proceedings (Rt. 1986 p. 320). In such a situation, continuation or resumption of the enterprise is not considered a transfer of the enterprise, hence that WEA section 16-1(1) does not apply.

§12. Transfer of Enterprises from a Bankrupt Estate

1229. When an enterprise is transferred as a going concern from a bankrupt estate to a purchaser, the basic question is whether a somewhat modified continuity principle should apply, or whether a closing-down principle should be used as a consequence of the bankruptcy.

1230. In the case of a normal transfer of an enterprise, it follows from Directive 2001/23/EC Article 3 that rights and obligations, arising from a contract of employment or from an employment relationship, as a main rule are transferred to the purchaser. This provision is, as mentioned above, not applicable in the case of bankruptcy (cf. the Directive Article 5). Nevertheless, Member States have a margin of appreciation to decide otherwise through national legislation. Member States may thus decide that the transferor's financial obligations are transferred.

1231. According to Norwegian law, the transfer of an enterprise from a debtor to a bankrupt estate entails that the bankrupt estate as a main rule accedes to the employment contract (cf. The Creditors Security Act section 7). From the opening of the bankruptcy proceedings, the bankrupt estate as such is responsible for wages and other remuneration. The bankrupt estate has three weeks within which to decide whether to accede to the employment contract or not. If the employment contracts are not continued, the employees can be terminated with the usual notice period. Their claim for wages and other remuneration during this period will be paid as a liquidation dividend. Additionally, wages of employees in a liquidation phase are protected by the Wage Guarantee Act, by which the state guarantees payment of up to three months of wage claims against bankrupt employers. Termination of employees with regard to a reduction in workforce will have to be objectively justified. In summary, the transfer of an enterprise from the debtor to a bankrupt estate is basically built on a principle of modified continuity.

1232. With regard to transfer from a bankrupt estate to purchaser, Norwegian national law follows the rules in the Directive relating to transfer of enterprises, and makes an exception for transfer from a bankrupt estate (cf. WEA section 16-1(2)). The *travaux préparatoires* of the Act assumes that the purchaser shall not be responsible for claims such as accrued wages, holiday pay, etc. However, it is not clear whether other rights and obligations arising from the employment relationship will apply in the relationship between the purchaser and the employees who continue their work in the enterprise.

1233. It should probably be assumed that neither the bankrupt estate nor the purchaser can terminate all employees en bloc, if it is clear that the enterprise will continue its activities with at least some of the employees. As regards the evaluation of how extensive a reduction in workforce should be, the bankrupt estate as well as the purchaser will have a wide margin of appreciation. Termination of all employees, however, will be a disproportionate measure, and thereby contrary to the requirement for objectivity. A Supreme Court judgment (Rt. 1995 p. 849 (*Keiserinnen*)), provides support for this view. The selection of the employees who shall be terminated must be fair and objective (cf. WEA section 15-7).

1234. In relation to the employees who continue their work in the enterprise, it should probably be assumed that the original employment contracts continue, unless, of course, the purchaser and employee should agree to revise their agreement. Thus, the relationship cannot be construed such that a new employment relationship has been established. As a general rule, a new probationary period cannot be agreed upon. Rights which are connected to and derived from the employment period – perhaps a consecutive employment period – will therefore follow the employee, and accrue so that the employment period with the original employer, with the bankrupt estate and with the purchaser are added together and viewed as one. The equivalent must be the case regarding any special obligations that the individual employee has undertaken according to contract, such as working during an agreed stipulated time.

1235. In relation to the purchaser, an employee who is of the opinion that he or she has been wrongfully terminated by the original employer (debtor) or by the bankrupt estate, will have the right to bring or continue a legal action against the purchaser to have the termination declared invalid, and thereby get the position back. Equally, the employee must have the right to remain in his or her post until the case is finally decided, unless the court should decide otherwise (WEA section 15-11). Compensation for economic and non-economic loss for an invalid termination (WEA section 15-12), can, however, hardly be asserted against the purchaser. Regarding the economic claims, the *travaux préparatoires* the Act build on a closing-down viewpoint. Such claims must therefore be asserted against the bankrupt estate.

1236. An employee who is terminated in connection with bankruptcy is given priority for new employment in the enterprise (WEA section 14-2). If several of the previous employees are entitled to priority, the purchaser's discretion in the event of bankruptcy is decisive to a wider degree than in the case of priority due to termination because of reduction in production not related to bankruptcy. Probably the right to wider discretion must also apply in the event the employee was terminated because of reduction in production, but before bankruptcy proceedings were opened.

1237. If in reality there is a transfer of an enterprise formed as bankruptcy proceedings in order to be free from the employer's obligations towards the employees, the employees' legal position must be evaluated as if bankruptcy proceedings had not taken place (cf. the Directive's Article 5 No. 4).

1238. In summary, the transfer of an enterprise from a bankrupt estate to the purchaser should most suitably be characterized by the continuity principle rather than by the closing-down principle. The continuity principle is nevertheless modified as regards economic claims asserted at the opening of bankruptcy proceedings.

§13. Death, Illness, Etc., of an Employee

1239. If an employee dies, the employment contract naturally dissolves, but there may be certain repercussions such as a claim for death benefit according to agreement or statute. Death can also precipitate a claim for pension.

1240. If the employee stays home because of accident or illness, the employer cannot claim any damages based on non-fulfilment of the employment contract. WEA section 15-8 prohibits the dismissal of an employee during a stipulated period because of absence due to an accident or illness. In this connection, may also be mentioned that an employee's being HIV positive alone is no just reason for dismissal. On the other hand, the general public's fear of infection may constitute a just reason, but that fear must have a solid manifestation (Rt. 1988 p. 959). Furthermore, WEA section 15-9 prohibits dismissing an employee because of pregnancy, and there is a general ban on dismissing an employee who exercises his or her legal right to take a leave of absence in connection with pregnancy, childbirth or adoption (cf. WEA section 15-9(2); *see also* section 5-8 of the Ship Labour Act).

1241. In this connection should also be mentioned WEA section 15–10, which prohibits dismissal because the employee has been summoned to military service, etc., or has volunteered to serve in the UN contingency force (cf. paragraphs 950 et seq. above).

1242. The Act of 8 May 1900, section 10, sixth subsection, related to measures against tuberculosis, stipulated that a teacher with infectious tuberculosis being immediately relieved of his or her duties may be seen as a casuistic manifestation of this viewpoint. Today this provision is to be found, somewhat reformed, in the Act related to control of communicable diseases, of 5 August 1994 No. 55 (cf. also paragraph 908 above).

§14. The Employee's Own Termination of the Employment Contract

1243. In general a dismissal which is based on circumstances related to the employee can be a very stressful experience. In such a situation, it can sometimes be appropriate to give the employee the option to terminate his or her employment contract himself or herself.

1244. Especially after a summary dismissal, it will be much harder to acquire a new employment. The possibilities, however, will be better if one actually has chosen to resign. The employee can obtain a reference from the employer stating that he or she has resigned from the position himself or herself. However, such a reference does not indicate that the employer has waived his or hers right to comment on the reasons for the termination.

1245. Correspondingly, there are also advantages for the employer in allowing the employee to resign from his or her position. Upon termination from the employee, the employee subsequently cannot, at least usually, claim that the dismissal was unfair. It is therefore worthwhile allowing the employee resign even though it might be desirable for employers to show the organization's attitude through a dismissal/summary dismissal.

1246. The validity of the termination of the employment contract by the employee must be considered in the light of, and according to, the act related to conclusion of agreements, etc., section 36 and not according to the WEA section 15-7. The latter provision applies only to the employer's dismissals of employees. However, there is a clear connection between the dismissal provision in WEA section 15-7 and the provision in the act related to conclusion of agreements, etc. (section 36). According to case law, it is not seldom assumed that the employees' own termination of the employment contract can be set aside pursuant to the provisions of the act related to conclusion of agreements, etc. Section 36 if the employer is regarded to have forced the employee to terminate the employment contract, if the conditions for a dismissal according to the former WEA section 60 (now section 15-7) or a summary dismissal according to the former WEA section 66 (now section 15-14) were not fulfilled.

1247. The reason for these disputes is that the employee often is given the opportunity to either terminate the employment contract himself or herself or to be given a dismissal by the employer. Especially, in situation where the employee is given little time to consider the situation or is not given sufficient time in order to seek advice from external advisors, the employee often chooses to terminate the employment contract. The employee often regrets that he or she terminated the contract and files a claim before the courts, stating that the termination is invalid, and that the termination, in reality, was the result of an unfair dismissal from the employer. The cases are somewhat difficult because, in general, there is nothing wrong that an employee terminates the employment contract. Although the employee's decision is occasioned by the employer's request it does, however, not indicate that such 'pressure' from the employer in all situations leads to invalidation of the termination. Often there may be good reasons for this choice. It is therefore only in situations where the employer cannot legally achieve the same result by termination of the employment contract, through a dismissal, pursuant to the provisions of WEA section 15-7, that it is possible to set aside the employee's own termination pursuant to the rules of the act related to conclusion of agreements, etc. (section 36). The basis for this thesis is that the employee's own termination of the employment contract can under no circumstances be unreasonable in the legal sense of section 36 if the employer could have achieved the same result based on WEA section 15-7.

1248. It is, however, not given that the employee's own termination without further shall be set aside as invalid in situations where it is doubtful whether the employer had the right to make use of WEA section 15-7. In such cases, all circumstances need to be considered. The employee's job record, the nature of the business, the amount of time the employee was given in order to consider what he or she should do, whether an external advisor has been used, and finally it must be placed emphasis on the amount of time from when the employee's own termination was a fact and until it later as retracted. It is also important that employees are made aware of the prolonged waiting period for unemployment benefits, due to their own termination of the contract. It is stipulated in the SSA section 4-10(1) (cf. (2)), that the waiting period in situations where the employee resigns is eight weeks.

1249. Employees who claim that the resignation in reality was a result of an involuntary termination by the employee must act according to the provisions in WEA section 15-11. It is also important to note that the notice deadlines in WEA section 15-13 also are applicable when the employee terminates the employment contract, and that there is no requirement for a written termination declaration when it comes to the employee's own termination, as does the dismissal given by the employer (cf. section 15-5). Evidence considerations imply that communication in writing is preferable also for the employee's own termination.

1250. It may also be appropriate to mention Rt. 2009 p. 723 in this context. The case concerned claims on damages against a former employer, from an employee who had resigned with immediate effect. The case raised questions concerning the scope of the special procedural provision in the WEA Chapter 17, and the interpretation of section 17-4 on time limits for instituting legal proceedings.

1251. In the Court of First Instance in 2005, the employee (A) was sentenced to a suspended prison sentence for ninety days, with a probationary period of two years and a fine of NOK 15,000 for various violations of the Alcohol Act for several years. At Christmas that year, the employer was contacted by an employee of rehabilitation services in the municipality, stated that A during work time had sold liquor to clients of the rehabilitation services. This resulted in that the general manager on 30 December 2005 made a phone call to A, who was on holiday in Tenerife. The general manager announced that A had the choice between two options – either 'to be suspended with immediate effect in order to be summarily dismissed and that he would call the police', or to terminate the employment contract himself with immediate effect.

1252. A representative of rehabilitation services also made phone calls to A. The CA held that the representative expressed the view that A should resign in order to avoid the risk of getting the police involved and that he would try to make sure that A could get a job in a new enterprise. The representative could, however, not promise that A would be given a new job there. In January 2006, A resigned with immediate effect. He was not offered a new position in the new enterprise.

1253. In a letter dated 18 January 2006, A's lawyer claimed that the resignation had occurred under questionable circumstances, and requested a meeting with the employer to negotiate pursuant to the former WEA section 61 (now section 17-3). The meeting never took place. On 18 May 2007, the employee (A) instituted legal proceedings against the former employer, demanding compensation and redress.

1254. The Supreme Court found that:

the disputed issue has always been whether A's employer has been guilty of liability breaches in connection with the conditions that A resigned on, based on the provisions in the WEA and not in contractual obligations. The case is therefore of a nature which, according to the travaux préparatoires falls within the core of the WEA Chapter 17, and I find it clear that the special procedural provisions will apply.

1255. The Supreme Court also found that 'there is nothing in the provisions that indicates that they should be interpreted so that they do not apply if the employee resigns, either generally or in those situations as to which the Appellant refers to. On the contrary, the purpose of the WEA Chapter 17 implies that such an exemption does not apply'. The provisions relating to litigation deadlines thus were applicable in this case. This indicates that the procedural provisions in WEA Chapter 17 are applicable to the same extent either it is the employer or the employee that terminates the employment contract. Since A only demanded compensation, the litigation deadline was six months from the time of when the resignation was given to the employer (cf. WEA section 17-4).

Chapter 7. Transfer of Enterprises

§1. Background

1256. When an enterprise is transferred from one employer to another, one of the questions that arises is what effects such a transfer will lead to when it comes to employment relationships, especially considering the employees that are attached to the enterprise. Correspondingly, this also applies in situations where the transfer only regards a part of an enterprise.

1257. In legal terms, the point of departure will be that the employer, as a consequence of his or her managerial rights, will have the power to determine whether the enterprise is about to be transferred to another employer. As far as this goes the situation is not, principally, in a different position from when the employer decides to change the operation of the enterprise, restrict the activities of the enterprise or possibly deciding to shut down the operations completely. Nor is there any doubt about the fact that the legislation is based on this view, but the point of departure does not set forth what effects such a transfer should have, with regard to employees' employment relationships. Therefore, there may be good reasons for pointing out the different considerations that prevail in such situations.

1258. A transfer of an enterprise will often be based on an understanding that the activity of the enterprise will continue after the transfer is completed, but with another employer in charge of the activity. It will most certainly be an advantage for the receiving employer to be able to take over an enterprise that is still running, and that not only consists of physical assets, but also of operational assets that take place within the organizational framework. In addition, equally important is the position, which the enterprise has acquired in relation to the outside world, concerning among others the clientele and suppliers etc. It will be considered as a considerable asset, in itself, if the receiving employer has the opportunity to take over an enterprise with an incorporated workforce. It will also be in the receiving employers interests to receive an enterprise together with the employees.

1259. From the employees' point of view, it will be considered as an advantage that the employment relationships can be continued with the new employer, instead of the employment relationship being terminated. Especially where the transfer is only of a part of the enterprise, it could, on the other hand, be questioned whether the individual employee should have the opportunity to stay with the original employer, so that the employee may continue working within the part of the enterprise which is not to be transferred. It may be argued that the employment contract originally was entered into with the original employer, and it may be asked whether the employer, by deciding the transfer, unilaterally can bring an end to his or hers commitments according to the employment contract. This applies especially in employment relationships that imply an extraordinary personal attachment to the employer, and also where the receiving employers' economic position is significantly weaker than that of the original employer.

1260. The above-mentioned questions lead to another question. This regards whether the original employer should be able to be released from his or her responsibilities in relation to the employees from the time the transfer takes place. In addition, the question also regards whether the original employer still will be responsible for the transferred employees, after the transfer of the enterprise, and for how long his or her responsibility will last. Another question regards what kind of responsibilities will exist between the original employer and the receiving employer on the one hand, with regard to employees on the other hand. In this situation, the question will often concern either joint and several liability or alternative liability. In addition, there could also be a question on recourse requirements with regard to the relationship between the original employer and the receiving employer.

1261. The WEA does not provide with any provisions with regard to the legal relationship between the original and the receiving employer. It may be noted that the EU Directive Article 3 No. 2 opens for the possibility to provide for such legal rules, when it comes to the duty of disclosure between the two parties. Norway, has, on the other hand, chosen not to make use of this possibility (cf. Ot.prp.no. 79 (2000-2001) item 8.1).

§2. Survey

1262. Pursuant to the WEA Chapter 16, there are provisions regarding transfer of enterprises which aims to clarify the different effects such a transfer will lead to within the employment relationship, and provisions regarding how the employer shall proceed in relation to the employees. The rights and duties, according to the individual employment contract, are stated in WEA section 16-2. The rights and duties according to pension benefits are stated in WEA section 16-2(3). Collective agreements and the employees' rights according to the collective agreement, are stated in WEA section 16-2(2). Protection against unfair dismissal, as a consequence of the transfer, is stipulated in WEA section 16-4, and section 16-7 aims to clarify the protection of the employees' elected representatives. In addition, the WEA section 16-5 provides with rules concerning information and consultation with the employees' elected representatives, while WEA section 16-6 contains rules that regards the employer's responsibility to provide information to the employees, who are inflicted by the transfer of the enterprise.

1263. These provisions are based on the Council Directive 2001/23/EC of 12 March 2001 on the approximation of the laws of the Member States relating to the safeguarding of employees' rights in the event of transfers of enterprises, businesses or parts of enterprises or businesses. This directive is to be regarded as a coordination directive, which involves a fusion of the two prior directives, without material changes. The purpose of the directive is partly to protect the employees, in order to make sure that their rights are being safeguarded, and partly to prevent any national inequalities to have a direct impact on the common marketing function.

1264. With some minor modifications, one may say that the rules provided by the WEA are conducting the minimum rights according to the directive. The case law that is provided by the European Court of Justice will therefore be of significance in order for understanding the rules according to the WEA Chapter 16:

- It should be mentioned that the Supreme Court – latest – has expressed the view that the provisions of the WEA Chapter 16 accomplish the EU Directive 2000/23/EU, 'and are thus to be applied according to the directive, as this has been interpreted by the European Court of Justice' (cf. Rt. 2012 p. 983 (*Drill Rig*) paragraph 60).
- Further, Rt. 1997 p. 1954 and Rt. 1997 p. 1965 should be mentioned. In both cases, the Supreme Court held that there was no clue indicating that the Norwegian rules of the WEA went beyond the rules stipulated in the directive. The Supreme Court stated this again in Rt. 2001 p. 248.
- According to Article 8 of the directive, it does not intervene with the Member States' right to use or fix their own legislation or regulations, which are more convenient to the employees. The Norwegian Supreme Court assumed, as stated above, that the Norwegian legislator had not yet availed this possibility. With this as a point of departure, one must assume that in order for assuming that the Norwegian provisions differ from the directive, it requires specific evidence.

1265. In addition to the WEA, the Holidays Act section 12 needs to be noticed. This section states that if there is a change of ownership (owner or lessee) of an enterprise, the new owner assumes the previous owner's obligation to give annual leave in connection with holidays and pay holiday pay pursuant to the present Act. Holiday pay to which entitlements were acquired under the previous owner may still be claimed from him.

1266. In order for the provisions in WEA Chapter 16 to be applicable, the transfer needs to be a transfer of an enterprise or a part of an enterprise, in such a manner that it is this which has been the object of the transfer. In addition, for the purposes of the WEA, transfer shall mean transfer of an autonomous unit that retains its identity after the transfer. This term is also known as the requirement of continuity. Moreover, it needs to be a transfer of such a nature, as to which it is applicable to this set of rules. All of these three terms need to be fulfilled.

§3. The Object of the Transfer: An Entire Enterprise or a Part of an Enterprise

1267. Pursuant to the WEA section 16-1, the provisions regarding transfer of enterprises are applicable in situations, which involve 'transfer of an enterprise or a part of an enterprise'. According to the *travaux préparatoires* to the WEA, it is assumed that this expression includes 'transfers of all kinds of enterprises, which are covered by the scope of the WEA, whether it regards production, purchases or services etc.', and that the object of the transfer 'as a point of departure also includes the public sector'. Further, it is also assumed that the enterprise does not need to be engaged in commercial operations only. The provisions will therefore also be applicable to enterprises, of which the operations are based on ideal purposes. Whether an enterprise is organized as a company with limited liability, an unlimited liability partnership, a foundation, a single person firm or in any other way, is without any significance in this relation.

1268. The *travaux préparatoires* assumes that the provisions will be applicable to transfer of an entire enterprise, and to transfers of local unities, and parts of local unities of an enterprise. The term 'enterprise' is chosen because the WEA is supposed to be applicable to all kinds of enterprises, no matter if they are to be regarded as manufacturers, service companies, companies that engages in intellectual activities or public administration. In order for an activity to be regarded as a transfer of an enterprise, the European Court of Justice has established that as a basic demand, there need to be an acquisition of an independent economic entity: 'the term entity includes an organized entity of persons and assets as a whole, which makes it possible to exercise an economic activity with an independent purpose' (cf. the European Court of Justice case C-172/99, *Liikenne* (25 January 2001) and case C-13/95, *Süzen* (11 March 1997)). Pursuant to WEA section 16-1(1), it is now explicitly stated: 'transfer shall mean transfer of an autonomous unit that retains its identity after the transfer'. The same assumption has been made by the Supreme Court in Rt. 2001 p. 248 (*Olderdalen Ambulanse AS*) and Rt. 2006 p. 71 (*SAS Braathens*). *See also* Rt. 2010 p. 330 (*Bardufoss Airport*) and Rt. 2012 p. 983. (*Drill Rig*), where the drill rig was considered an autonomous unit, cf. also Rt. 2001 p. 71 as regards a movable platform. Transferring of a single ship from a shipping company will usually not be considered a transfer of a part of an enterprise, cf. the Ship Labour Act of 21 June 2013 No. 102 section 5-6 (4).

The judgment by the European Court of Justice in the case C-392/92 (*Schmidt*), may be mentioned. Schmidt was employed as a sanitarian with a bank branch, as the only sanitarian. After expanding the premises, the bank entered into an agreement with a cleaning company (Spiegelbank) stating that this company was to do the sanitary work, resulting in Schmidt being given a notice of dismissal. The cleaning company offered Schmidt continued employment with the same bank branch, but with a lower salary. The European Court of Justice assumed that the directive could be applied even though the transfer only included a single activity, such as sanitary work. It was not considered critical that the activity was of a complementary nature, which not necessarily was connected to the enterprise's financial purpose. Nor was it considered critical that the transfer did not include a transfer of a physical asset, or that the transfer only included a single employee.

In addition may be mentioned the EFTA Court of Justice case E-2/95 (25 September 1996, *Stavanger Catering AS*). After the expiration of a catering agreement, the catering assignment was put out to tender, resulting with another company getting the assignment. Also a situation like this had to be considered as applicable to the provisions regarding transfer of enterprises.

1269. Even though the expression 'part of an enterprise' is regarded as a far-reaching term, it needs to be mentioned that the above-mentioned cases regarded situations where the transferred activities were of permanent character. It therefore seems to be made an appraisal to the activities that are of a short-term nature and are considered to be of a limited scope.

1270. In this context, one may notice the European Court of Justice case C-48/94 (*Stroe-Moelle Akustik AS*), where a builder had transferred, from one entrepreneur to another one, a concrete and temporarily limited part of an assignment. The court said that the case law at that time presupposed that 'the transfer regards an economic entity, which is organized in a stable manner, and that its' activities are not limited to the exercise of a specific construction'. This situation does not exist where an enterprise transfers one of their contracts to another enterprise, with the purpose of completion of the work. Such a transfer may be applicable to the directive if, and simultaneously, there is transferred an organized whole of entities, which enables the receiving party to continue the transferred enterprises activities, or some of these. This is, on the other hand, not the case when the transferred enterprise only makes available some of the employees and some materials, to the new entrepreneur, in order to complete the ongoing contract.

§4. The Requirement of Continuity

1271. The essential question regarding whether the rules concerning transfer of enterprises are applicable, seems to be whether the receiving employer drifts the activities of the enterprise in such a way that the requirement of continuity is being fulfilled. In order of making this assumption, one has to consider a number of different factors, and the assessment needs to be made on the basis of a holistic assessment of the relevant factors, which also includes consideration of the purpose of the provisions. The individual circumstances may not be assessed on an isolated basis. *See* in this regard the European Court of Justice case C-24/85 (*Spijkers*). From more recent years, may also be mentioned C-101/87 (*Bork*), C-209/91 (*Rask*), C-48/95 (*Stroe-Moelle*) and C-340/01 (*Sodexho*).

1272. A transfer which only includes a transfer of less significant assets gives no reason to make appreciable consideration to (cf. Rt. 1997 p. 1954). Further, it is not decisive whether the activity of an enterprise or the part of the enterprise, which is the object of the transfer, was running at the time of the transfer. The decisive factor is assumed to be whether the activity has finally ceased to exist, or whether there is only a temporary stop in the activities (cf. Ot.prp.no. 71 (1991-92) p. 32).

1273. The European Court of Justice has not yet clarified how long the activities may be stopped before the transfer takes place, in order for the transfer not to be fulfilling the requirement of continuity. In some cases, the directive have been applied if the activities have been temporarily stopped for about two or three weeks. In the cases C-287/86 (*Ny Mølle Kro*), and C-29/91 (*Redmond Stichting*), it was assumed that a temporarily stop in the enterprise's activity did not in itself result in exclusion of the applicability of the directive. The same assumption is made in Rt. 1997 p. 1954. The Supreme Court noted among other things that it should not be emphasized – to the disadvantage of the employee – the fact that before the start up, by municipal auspices, there was a stop in the activities for about a month. Further may be noted the judgment in Rt. 1995 p. 849.

1274. Further, questions regarding how to draw the outline, and how the different factors shall be emphasized in relation to one another, are some of today's most debated question within modern labour law. This is a legal area which is subject to intensive development and where the final word not yet has been said. Therefore, there is a good reason to look more closely at this question.

1275. Part of the problem lies within the combination between the employees and the assets, and that the assets may vary in an endless number of ways. The same goes for the employees' coordinated activities, including their competence and cooperative relationship, efficiency, etc. In addition, we need to include different kinds of assets, such as the different kinds of stock rooms, and different kinds of legal rights connected to the activities: such as for instance rental rights concerning location and equipment, the right to make use of trademarks, logos, inventions, operating methods, etc.

1276. When dealing with capital-intensive activities, where there are rather large economic investments that have been made behind every individual workplace/employee – such as for instance the situation within shipping and offshore – the traditional business structure will imply that the significance of assets will have to dominate the total picture in a totally different way when regarding the question on the continuity of the activity under a transfer, than would be the case when dealing with labour intensive activities. In the last situation, the economic investments behind every individual workplace/employee will be of rather minor significance, for instance the situation concerning telemarketing.

1277. When dealing with forms of operations other than the traditional ones, the picture drawn above changes significantly. For instance, a shipping company, which has hired a ship, will not have invested substantial amounts of capital behind every employee on board. The same situation applies where the activities of an enterprise take place in leased premises and perhaps also with leased equipment. If the activities of an enterprise are run solely by hired or leased assets, the significance of the employees' coordinated activities necessarily need to dominate the picture, together with the right to make use of the hired or leased assets. In operational matters, the significance of the different assets shifts from the traditional investments in assets to the right of using other people's assets. Transfer of an enterprise will in this situation be characterized by the fact that there takes place a transfer of the right connected to the use of the assets, and not a transfer of the assets themselves. Thus, it is the interaction between the assets and the employee, and the organization of this interaction that need to be the decisive factors when making assessments as to whether the activities are considered to have been keeping their continuity after being transferred to the receiving employer.

1278. The relationship to the operational rights is, however, further complicated by the fact that it may concern both the right to run the activities itself, and the right to use the implicated assets. Such a pairing of two completely different rights may occur when dealing with tender, but may also occur in other situations.

1279. In such situations, when the transfer of the enterprise especially refers to the transfer of rights and not assets, one may also assume that the transfer of the enterprise especially relates to the transfer of the right to run the activities – the rights in connection to exercise the activities – or possibly combined with the right to make use of the necessary assets.

1280. Such transfers give rise to certain questions regarding the employees' legal position during the transfer. The aim of the directive is to safeguard the employees' legal position, regardless of what a transferor or an acquirer may wish to do, and if there are based too strict requirements on the enterprises' identity, this may result in a narrowing of the scope of the directive. The acquirer's commitments to enter into the employee's contracts are thus narrowed to the same extent. The question is, however, whether the enterprise is to be characterized by the activities concerned, or whether there are other requirements, and whether too much emphasis is given to the assets – including rights off different kinds – and to little emphasis to the significance of the employees.

1281. Against this background, there are good reasons to look more closely at the case law that exists, concerning these questions.

1282. The fact that the activity is the same, or similar, both prior to the transfer and after is a necessary, but not in itself sufficient condition. The transfer of the activities in itself is, thus, not sufficient in order for there to be an actual transfer of an enterprise, making the rules pursuant to the directive and the WEA applicable (cf. the judgment by the European Court of Justice in C-13/95 (*Süzen*), premises 21).

1283. This stance was unequivocally assumed by the *travaux préparatoires* pursuant to the amendment of 15 June 2001.

1284. If there is no transfer of assets or employees, and there exists plans that indicate a significant restructuring of the prior assets, there will not be possible to state that the enterprises' identity has been retained. But even though it does not exist plans that indicate a significant restructuring, the enterprise's identity will hardly be retained if neither the assets nor the employees are transferred. Illustrative is Rt. 2002 p. 248 (*Olderdalen Ambulanse AS*), where the Supreme Court found that the enterprises' identity was not retained.

1285. In Rt. 2002 p. 248, an ambulance company terminated the operating agreement with the county because the subsidiary was insufficient, according to the company. This company had three employees, who were offered employments with the company that got the new operating agreement with the county, Olderdalen Ambulanse AS. A condition was that the 'employees' would not join a trade union. The three 'employees' accepted the offer, but did not accept the conditions, and three other candidates were hired instead. During the following lawsuit, there had to be decided whether there had taken place a transfer of the enterprise, and whether the enterprise had retained its identity.

1286. The Supreme Court considered it undoubtedly that the ambulance operation within the original company was an independent economic entity, but did not find that the necessary identity was retained after the completion of the transfer. Admittedly, the operation was 'run in the same way as previously', and the citizens hardly noticed any difference on the services. But, while:

> the identity of a production company to a large extent may be attached to the location of the company, to assets in the form of real estate and to operational equipment and goodwill as a consequence of the clientele, brands etc., a company that provides services will to a larger extent be characterized by the service itself, and thereby the personnel that provide the service. Both sanitary work and security operations will be provided for without the employer, not to an extent worth mentioning, has his or her own assets involved in the activities.

1287. The service that was provided for was assumed to exist between these two kinds of activities. The services, which concern the providing of ambulance services, involve personnel, who have a significant function in the assignments that are executed. But at the same time, an ambulance car is included, with appropriate equipment, as a totally necessary and capital-intensive part of the activities. When neither the employees nor the car was included in the activities, which Olderdalen Ambulanse AS (the receiving employer) continued after the transfer, it actually has not taken place a transfer of an enterprise, which provides protection in relation to the employees, according to the directive, and consequently no protection from the WEA Chapter 16 are provided either. Reference is also made to Rt. 2011 p. 1755.

1288. However, based on later legal developments within the EU, it is doubtful whether this judgment could be maintained (cf. also Rt. 2006 p. 71 (*SAS – Braathens*), and the European Court of Justice case C-340/01 (*Abler*)).

1289. In the *Abler* case Sodexho had, after a tender, been given the opportunity to enter into an agreement with the hospital Wien Speising concerning the operation of the hospitals' main kitchen. The food was to be prepared within the hospital premises, and both water and energy as well as the necessary machinery was placed at Sodexho's disposal. Earlier the company Sanrest had had the contract with the hospital, but they could not match Sodexho in the tender. Sodexho did not take over, from Sanrest, cost calculations, menus, diet schedules, recipes or experience reports. The European Court of Justice found that there had been a transfer of an enterprise. During the holistic assessment, the court stressed that considerations had to be taken in respect of what kind of activities the transfer included, and consequently also which activities that are exercised, and what operations that are used. Operations which include running a main kitchen may not be seen as an activity, in which the labour is to be considered as the most significant part of the activity, because the operation demanded a lot of inventory and equipment. In addition, the production should, according to the contract, take place in the hospital kitchen, and the transfer also included a take-over of Sanrest's clientele – there was actually a permanent clientele. Therefore, the transfer was to be considered as a transfer of an economic entity.

1290. The different results in the cases mentioned above may be based on a much larger extent of continuity as a consequence of the terms related to the principal's production equipment, and then also considering the localization, which were imposed in the *Abler* case – in comparison: the same term was not imposed in the case of *Olderdalen Ambulanse AS*.

1291. Further, the cases of C-232/04 and 233/04 (*Güney-Görres*) need to be noted, which in all material respects continue the views of the *Abler* case.

1292. As a conclusion may be noticed that the question concerning whether an enterprise's activities have kept their identity after a transfer, naturally is to be considered as a question of whether the requirement of continuity is fulfilled. Speaking in terms of labour law, the view on continuity is not a new innovation, but has been assumed, among other things when regarding the provisions concerning protection against unfair dismissal (cf. Rt. 1978 p. 160, Rt. 1995 p. 849, and ARD 1970 p. 16).

1293. Illustrative for the view on continuity, when dealing with restructuring within a group of companies is Rt. 2006 p. 71 (*SAS – Braathens*). The different transactions between the groups' different companies, entities and business fields with a view on coordination, rationalization and increased efficiency, were considered by the Supreme Court in its overall context. The assessment was consequently made on the basis of a holistic evaluation of the restructuring.

1294. When SAS (an airline company) had taken over the shares of Braathens (another airline company) in 2001, there was started a coordination project, which aimed to implement integration and coordination of the activities within the two companies, including also the ground handling. The ground handling was organized as independent entities in both of the companies. In May 2002, Braathens decided that the ground handling should be shut down, in order for the company to buy the same services from SAS. A framework agreement was established shortly after. A later framework agreement also included de-icing. The Supreme Court found that the de-icing agreement had to be seen in context with the other ground services, because they 'both objectively and timely were in close relations to one another'. Further the 'ground services that SAS undertook to provide for Braathens plains in essence was to be regarded as the same activities as the ones that Braathens had run'. The ground handling services on an airport could not be characterized by any simple factors. The question regarding the identity of the enterprise's activities then had to be determined on the basis of a holistic evaluation, considering all the factors that are relevant, according to European Court of Justice case law. The nature of the services was basically, and to the full extent, the same, and used the same infrastructure as previously. Additionally, a significant amount of economic values were transferred (i.e., to say approximately 25% of the total equipment that the earlier company (*Braathens*) had used), as was a substantial part of the employees, and the clientele was basically the same as earlier. In other words, the Supreme Court found that a transfer of an enterprise had taken place, on the basis of a nuanced and holistic evaluation of all the relevant factors.

§5. The Different Transfer Situations

1295. It is without any doubt that a transfer by a purchase contract is to be regarded as applicable to the rules pursuant to the WEA Chapter 16. The same goes for unilateral dispositions, such as transfers by gift, inheritance or settlements between spouses (cf. Rt. 1995 p. 1625).

1296. It is not a requirement that there has to be a contractual relationship directly between the earlier and the new employer, even though this is not stated explicitly in section 16-1. Rental agreements and leases etc. that terminate in such a manner that it results in changes on the employer's side, are also applicable to these provisions. Cf. Rt-2015-718 *(Kirkens bymisjon)*, where the contract between the municipality of Oslo and Kirkens Bymisjon was not prolonged, because the municipality itself took over the activities that Kirkens Bymisjon previously had carried out; therefore, a transfer of enterprise had taken place.

1297. Mergers, splits and other ways of association are also applicable to these provisions.

1298. Purchases and sales of company shares which do not result in any changes as regards the entity on the side of the employer do not constitute a transfer of an enterprise. A corporation is regarded as the same (legal) entity, even if the majority of shares change owners.

1299. Transfers that take place during debt negotiations with creditors are also applicable to the provisions. The same goes for a transfer that takes place during an insolvency situation (cf. Rt. 1995 p. 1624 and Rt. 1995 p. 1636), where this was established in accordance with the Holidays Act section 12. The same also goes for the situation when a mortgagee enforces the activities according to the act related to the enforcement of claims, of 26 June 1992 No. 86, section 11-55 and further (cf. Rt. 1995 p. 270).

1300. If the employer goes bankrupt/is liquidated, the question that often arises is whether the transfer of an enterprise's activities to the bankruptcy estate constitutes a transfer of enterprise, which is applicable by the rules pursuant to WEA Chapter 16. In situations where the bankruptcy estate chooses to carry on the activities and enters the employment contracts, there will also be asked whether the provisions pursuant to Chapter 16 are applicable (cf. Rt. 1995 1636). According to section 16-1(2) sections 16-2 (which regards pay and working conditions) and 16-4 (which concerns protection against unfair dismissal) shall not apply in connection with transfer from a bankruptcy estate.

1301. The principal problem in this relation is whether such a transfer to a bankruptcy estate and then a transfer from the bankruptcy estate to a new acquirer have to be regarded as constituting a termination of the employment contract, or whether the employment relationship is to be considered as being continued. According to Article 4 (1) of the directive, and as a rule of principle, such a transfer does not constitute a termination of an employment contract. This view does not, however, preclude that there may take place a termination based on economic, technical or organizational conditions, that involves employment-related changes. The situation regarding the bankruptcy/liquidation of an employer is stated in Article 5 of the directive.

§6. Rights and Obligations Pursuant to the Employment Contract, After the Transfer

1302. According to the WEA section 16-2(1) the rights and obligations of the former employer ensuing from the contract of employment or employment relationship in force on the date of transfer shall be transferred to the new employer. Claims pursuant to the first paragraph of section 16-2(1) may still be raised against the former employer.

1303. Whether the rights or the obligations was gained prior to or after the transfer is not significant. It is not significant that the new employer was aware of the employees' rights and obligations, and it is not significant whether the former employer or the new employer did not intend that the employees should be a part of the transfer. Such intensions cannot limit the employees' rights according to the WEA (cf. Rt. 1995 p. 849). The new employer is not only obliged to pay the employees their wages, but is also committed to fulfilling other requirements as well. This regards claims concerning earned, but not yet paid wages, claims concerning holiday pay, other allowances according to the employment contract.

1304. It may also be stressed that these provisions are mandatory, in the sense that they cannot be departed from by agreement to the detriment to the employee (cf. WEA section 1-9). Notice also the EFTA-judgment in E-3-95 (*Norske Fabricom AS*) which expressed that 'the employees may not renounce rights according to the directive, and that the rights not even with the consent of the employee may be limited'.

1305. It needs to be stressed that the rights in question are those ones that ensue from the employment contract or the employment relationship 'in force on the date of transfer' that is transferred. The deciding factor will therefore be whether the employment contract has been finally terminated at the time of transfer. The former employer and the new employer may not agree on another date of transfer, other than the actual one, to the detriment of the employees' rights to remain in their employment contracts (cf. the European Court of Justice case C-305/94 (*Rotsart*). If the employee has been dismissed by the former employer, but makes use of the right to remain in his or her post pursuant to WEA section 15-11, it follows from section 16-2(1) that the right to remain in position during the negotiations and legal proceedings needs to be respected by the new employer. The same goes for the situation where the employee has been ruled in favour of his or her dismissal being unjust, from the former employee, which also seems to be the view that has been established in the *travaux préparatoires*.

1306. The former employer is, however, not free from commitments according to the employment contract, based on the transfer (cf. WEA section 16-2(1) second subsection). This provision states that the employee may still raise claims that have their basis in the employment contract before the time of transfer with the former employer.

1307. Further, the new employer shall be bound by any collective agreement that was binding upon the former employer. This will, however, not apply if the new employer within three weeks after the date of transfer at the latest declares in writing to the trade union that the new employer does not wish to be bound. The transferred employers nevertheless have the right to retain the individual working conditions that follow from a collective agreement that was binding upon the former employer. This applies until the collective agreement expires or until a new collective agreement is concluded that is binding upon the new employer and the transferred employees.

1308. The employees' right to earn further entitlement to retirement pension, survivor's pension and disability pension in accordance with a collective service pension scheme shall be transferred to the new employer pursuant to the provisions of the first and second subsection of section 16-2 (cf. section 16-2(3)). The new employer may elect to make existing pension schemes applicable to the transferred employees. If the employees' previous pension schemes cannot be maintained after the transfer, the new employer shall ensure the transferred employees the right to further earnings of pension entitlement through another collective pension scheme.

1309. A significantly worse pension scheme than before, which implies that the employee chooses not to be transferred to the new employer and results in a termination of the employment relationship, may be considered to have been occasioned by the employer (cf. WEA section 16-4(2)).

§7. Protection Against Dismissal Due to Transfer of an Enterprise

1310. According to WEA section 16-4(1), a transfer of an enterprise to another employer is not in itself grounds for dismissal with notice or summary dismissal from a former or new employer. A dismissal will, however, be legitimate if it is due to other circumstances regarding the transfer, and the fairness of the dismissal will have to be determined according to section 15-7(1) of the WEA. That is to say that a dismissal that could have been executed, even though a transfer was not a topic at the time, will not be considered to be in violation of section 16-4(1). This may be the case when dealing with operational restrictions, rationalizations or dismissals due to conditions on the employee's side.

1311. If a contract of employment or employment relationship expires because a change of employers involves major changes in the working conditions to the detriment of the employee, the termination is deemed to be a consequence of circumstances relating to the employer (cf. section 16-4(2)). If such changes in working conditions happen as a result of the fact that an employee is given a dismissal followed up with an offer to continue in his or her position on altered conditions, the situation falls under the application of section 16-4(1). The point of WEA section 16-4(2) is that substantial changes in the working conditions to the detriment to the employee, without the employer providing the employee with a notice of dismissal, shall be deemed to be a consequence of circumstances relating to the employer (*see*, in relation to this, WEA section 15-7(1)).

1312. In the event of disputes pursuant to section 16-4, the provisions of sections 15-11 and 15-12 shall apply correspondingly with the exceptions of section 15-12, first subsection, final sentence. The provisions of Chapter 17 shall apply correspondingly insofar as they are appropriate.

§8. Right of Reservation, Etc.

1313. An employee may object to transfer of the employment relationship to the new employer (cf. section 16-3(1)). According to section 16-3(2), an employee who objects to transfer of the employment relationship to the new employer must notify the former employer of this in writing within the time limit specified by the employer. The time limit may not be shorter than fourteen days after information is provided pursuant to section 16-6.

1314. Equally important is the employees' preferential rights. According to section 16-3(3), an employee who has been employed by the enterprise for a total of at least twelve months during the two-year period prior to the date of transfer, and who asserts his or her right of reservation pursuant to section 16-3, has a preferential right to a new appointment at the former employer for one year from the date of transfer unless the vacant post is one for which the employee is not qualified. The preferential right lapses if the employee fails to accept an offer of employment in a suitable post not later than fourteen days after receiving the offer. Preferential rights pursuant to sections 14-2 and 14-3, however, take precedence over preferential rights pursuant to section 16-3(3).

1315. Another important right is the employee's opportunity to choose whether to be transferred to the new employer or not, which follows only from non-statutory rules, that is to say from case law. It need, however, to be stressed that the employees' right to choose is substantially much more limited than the situation is regarding the right of reservation. The right implies in short terms that the employee will have an opportunity to choose if the transfer results in a non-unsubstantial negative change in the employee's working conditions. The changes need to 'be of such a radical character, and have a manifest significance related to the employee's present as well as future situation' that the right to choose is trigged (cf. Rt. 2000 p. 2047 (*Lovisenberg*)).

1316. If the transfer includes the entire enterprise, as a whole, or an independent entity of the enterprise, the point of departure may be that the employee may not oppose to the fact that the employment relationship is being continued with the new employer (cf. Rt. 2000 p. 2058 (*Miljøtransport*) and Rt. 2000 p. 2047 (*Lovisenberg*)).

1317. In Rt. 2000 p. 2047 (*Lovisenberg*), the case was that the former municipal psychiatric care which was placed at the Lovisenberg/ Diakonhjemmet sector was distributed between the two private hospitals – Lovisenberg diaconal hospital and Diakonhjemmet hospital. Lovisenberg was a corporation and Diakonhjemmet was a foundation. The Supreme Court found unanimously that the employee could not oppose the transfer. The transferred institutions and entities 'continued their activities basically as they had been run before the transfer' in 'the same premises and with the same employees, the same assignments, the same patients, the same equipment and the same local board'. It was found that the employees had not made probable any future and negative changes within their collective employment conditions, and it had no significance that the transfer involved that the activities were transferred from the public sector to the private sector.

1318. If the transfer regards limited entities of an enterprise, the employment situation and the employment relationship may easily alter the content of reality, meaning that the employee may maintain and relate to the original employment contract (cf. Rt. 1999 p. 977 and Rt. 1999 p. 989).

1319. The employee, of course, needs to give the employer notice that he does not wish to be transferred to the new employer. Whether a time limit similar to the fourteen-day limit pursuant to section 16-3(2), is reasonable to assume, taken into consideration that the provision needs to be looked at on a holistic basis.

§9. Representation

1320. According to WEA section 16-7, it follows that if the enterprise retains its autonomy, the elected representatives of the employees affected by the transfer as referred to in section 16-1 shall retain their legal position and function. If the enterprise does not retain its autonomy, the transferred employees who were represented prior to the transfer shall still be adequately represented until a new election can be held (cf. section 16-7(2)).

§10. Information to Employees

1321. The former and new employer shall as early as possible inform the affected employees concerning the transfer as referred to in section 16-1. Information shall particularly be given concerning matters referred to in section 16-5, second subsection (a) to (f), which concerns the reason for the transfer, the agreed or proposed date for the transfer, the legal, economic and social implications of the transfer for the employees, changes in circumstances relating to collective agreements, measures planned in relation to the employees, rights of reservation or preference and the time limit for exercising such rights.

1322. It is regarded as important that the information is provided even though the employees are not represented by elected representatives. According to WEA section 16-6, the employees shall be given the same information, which also shall be provided when the employees are represented by elected representatives.

Chapter 8. Pensions

§1. Retirement Pension from the Norwegian Social Security System

1323. Everyone who has lived in Norway for at least 40 years after the age of 16 will be entitled to a minimum retirement pension from the age of 67, paid by the national security system. All employees automatically become members of the Norwegian social security system, and membership is mandatory.

1324. The Norwegian pension system has recently been revised. The revised system was gradually introduced from 1 January 2010 and is fully implemented since 1 January 2011. According to the new pension system, all the years the member is working will count when determining the size of the pension. The accumulated pension for each member will be expressed in a pension fund for the member, which is adjusted on an annual basis.

1325. The accumulation of pension rights and the calculation of the total state pension will depend on when the member is born. Members who are born between 1943 and 1953 will continue to earn a state pension according to the old regulations. Members who are born between 1954 and 1962 will earn a state pension according to a combination of the previous rules and the new rules. Members who are born in 1963 or after will earn a state pension according to the new rules.

1326. The revised system generally provides members with a larger degree of freedom to decide when and how they desire to receive their retirement pension, and to what extent the member wants to receive pension benefits in combination with working. It is possible to start drawing retirement pension from the age of 62 if sufficient pension rights are earned. It is possible to work and draw a retirement pension at the same time without reduction in the pension. How much retirement pension the member choose to draw and from what age will affect the size of the pension received later on.

§2. Occupational Pensions

I. General Background

1327. Entitlement to a pension in addition to the pension paid by the social security system may be based on employment. In many cases, entitlement to such an additional pension follow from the Occupational Pensions Act of 21 December 2005 No. 124. For public servants, etc. such an entitlement will follow from the Act regarding the State's Pension Fund of 28 July 1949 No. 26. Entitlement for additional pension may also follow from a collective agreement, which is the case for municipal employees.

1328. It must, however, be emphasized that entitlement to such additional pension is not given. In employments that are not covered by the above-mentioned or corresponding regulations, entitlement to such an additional pension – and the extent of such an entitlement – will depend on what has been or what must be deemed to have been agreed in the employment contract. It may, for example, have been agreed that the employer shall pay a specified amount to the employee each month through a stated period of time, until a stated age, or for as long as the employee lives. Most often further terms will have been agreed, for example that the employee must have resigned or have reached a certain age, and have been in employment with the employer during a specifically stated period. Correspondingly, it may have been agreed that a certain percentage of the employee's salary shall be paid by the employer upon retirement.

1329. For such forms of additional pension, it may have been agreed that payments shall be paid into, and later out of, a pension fund. In other cases, payments are made directly from the employer. In the latter case, the pension can best be said to be paid through operations.

1330. The occupational pension schemes in the private sector have been subject to changes due to the extensive reform of the state pension system. This change amounted to a third pension scheme alternative, in addition to the defined contribution scheme and the defined benefit scheme, the so-called occupational pension scheme.

II. Mandatory Occupational Pension: The Occupational Pensions Act

1331. The Occupational Pensions Act entered into force on 1 January 2006. The Act implies that most employers must have an occupational pension scheme for their employees.

1332. The Act applies to enterprises that have employees in their service, and where at least two individuals are employed who both have work hours and salary which constitutes 75% or more of a full-time position. In addition, companies with only one employee in a position of such extent are also comprised by the Act if the employee in question does not have ownership interests (cf. the Occupational Pensions Act section 1). Employees under the age of 20 and employees in part-time employment of less than 20% of a full-time position may be excluded from the pension scheme.

1333. For all practical purposes, the Act's term 'enterprise' corresponds to the WEA's concept of employer.

1334. Employers who are comprised by the Occupational Pensions Act are obliged to establish a pension scheme 'in accordance with the Company Pensions Act, the Defined Contribution Pensions Act or the Occupational Pension Scheme Act (of 13 December 2013 No. 106)' which safeguards employees' pensions in accordance with the provisions of the Occupational Pensions Act (cf. section 2 of the Occupational Pensions Act).

1335. According to the Defined Benefit Pensions Act, the Defined Contribution Pensions Act and the Occupational Pension Scheme Act, all three types of pension scheme must include an insurance element that ensures that the employees continue to earn pension entitlements in the event of disability. In these situations, the life insurance company will continue to pay the contribution on behalf of the disabled employee, and the employee will receive ordinary occupational pension at the time of retirement. When establishing a pension scheme for the employees, the employer is free to decide whether or not to include additional insurance elements, such as for example group life insurance, disability pension and dependent pension.

1336. Employees may also be required to contribute to their own pensions, but such contributions will not reduce the minimum requirement for employers' contributions. Administrative costs connected to the scheme shall be covered by the employer (cf. the Occupational Pensions Act section 4).

1337. Employees can demand that a pension scheme is established. If an employer omits to fulfil the obligations in this regard, the employee is entitled to a contribution being paid in accordance with the minimum requirement of the law at the point in time when the obligation to establish a pension scheme arose.

1338. The minimum requirements of a pension scheme depend on whether the scheme is a defined contribution scheme, occupational pension scheme or a defined benefit scheme.

III. Defined Contribution Schemes

1339. According to a defined contribution scheme, the employers pay a predefined annual contribution, often set as a percentage of the employees' salary.

1340. The size of the employees' future pension will depend on the size of the contributions and the investment return, and the employee will bear the risk of poor investment. Defined contribution pension schemes can be established in a bank, life insurance company, pension fund or an investment firm. Some larger companies establish their own pension funds.

1341. For pension schemes established according to the Defined Contribution Pensions Act, the statutory minimum contribution from the employer is 2% of the employees' salary between 1 and 12 G. 'G' is an abbreviation for the social security basic amount, which is a standardized value adjusted by the legislator on an annual basis (cf. section 162 above). The contributions from the employer cannot exceed 5% of the employee's salary between 1 G and 6 G, and 8% between 6 G and 12 G. Contributions are not paid for a salary below 1 G and above 12 G.

IV. Occupational Pension Schemes

1342. The Ministry of Finance's proposal for a new Occupational Pension Scheme Act were finalized and adopted in Parliament before Christmas in 2013. This means that companies from the 1 January 2014 may enter into a pension scheme according to this new pension legislation.

1343. The new occupational pension scheme is a 'hybrid' of the defined contribution schemes and the defined benefit schemes. The employer may provide annual pension contributions for their employees for up to 7% of wages between 0 and 12 G, with the possibility of an additional contribution of up to 18.1% for income between 7.1 and 12 G. The statutory minimum contribution from the employer, according to this occupational pension scheme, is 2% of the employees' salary between 1 and 12 G.

1344. The new occupational pension scheme opens up for an annual pension contribution of a much higher percentage, than what follows from the defined contribution scheme.

V. Defined Benefit Schemes

1345. In a defined benefit scheme, the pension will normally be stipulated as a certain percentage of the employee's salary on retirement. Subject to full qualifying time, which is often thirty years, the share which is paid by the employer is the difference between the set percentage of the employee's salary and the employees calculated retirement benefits from the social security system.

1346. Under a defined benefit scheme, it is the employer who will bear the risk of poor investment return or increased costs. Defined benefit pension schemes can only be established in a life insurance company or in a pension fund.

1347. For defined benefit schemes, there are minimum requirements for old age pension. If the payment period is ten years, the old age pension for the predominant group of the employees shall at least correspond to the contributions pursuant to a defined contribution scheme. If the period of payment is longer than ten years, the added value shall be taken into consideration when assessing whether the predominant group of employees are ensured an old age pension that at least corresponds to the contributions pursuant to a defined contribution scheme (cf. the Occupational Pensions Act section 5).

1348. For pension schemes established according to the Defined Benefit Pensions Act, the employees total pension at the time of retirement shall not exceed 100% of the employee's salary up to 6 G, 70% of the salary between 6 G and 12 G and 0% above 12 G.

1349. There is a trend for many companies to convert their defined benefit pension schemes to defined contribution pension schemes, among other things because a defined benefit scheme is often more expensive for the employer to operate and also have volatile costs for the employer.

§3. Early Retirement Pension

1350. The AFP scheme (joint pension under collective agreement) arranges for employees to resign upon reaching 62 years of age. The scheme is based on collective agreements, and consequently it will not apply to all employment relationships, only to the ones where a collective agreement establishing AFP is applicable. The scheme is financed by the enterprises participating in the scheme and the state.

1351. The more specific terms follow from the collective agreement, but generally the employee is entitled to resign but upon having reached 62 years of age. At the time when the employee resigns, he or she must 'be employed and be a genuine employee', and the company must have participated in the scheme for at least two years. Furthermore, the employee must have been employed in the company during the past three years, or have been a member of the scheme for the past five years. The employee must neither receive any pension nor corresponding payment from the employer that does not correspond to an obligation to perform work.

1352. In order to be entitled to pension from the AFP scheme, the employee's pensionable income must exceed the national insurance basis amount on an annual basis, and the employee must in addition have had a corresponding income during the year prior to resignation. Besides that, the employee must have at least 10 years of earned points in the national insurance fund from that year in which the employee reached 50 years of age up to and including the year prior to resignation, and during the ten best years as of 1967 up to and including the year of resignation the average pensionable income must have been at least twice the national insurance fund's base amount.

1353. It must be noted that employees who have agreed with the employer to resign with AFP at a specified point in time will not be entitled to payments from the scheme if such an agreement has been entered into less than six months prior to the desired withdrawal date for AFP. Employees who are obliged to resign before reaching 67 years of age cannot be members of the scheme.

1354. Employees receiving AFP pension will as a main rule receive a pension corresponding to the old age pension which the employee would have received from the national insurance fund upon reaching 67 years of age, if the individual in question had not taken out AFP – but nevertheless not more than 70% of the work income. In addition, there is a tax-free AFP supplement of NOK 950 per month, and a further supplement may be granted for a spouse who is supported by the pensioner.

1355. The employee and the employer can agree that the work effort gradually be reduced with corresponding withdrawal of graduated pension. This only applies for employees in a full-time position and the work effort must be reduced with at least one day a week in order to qualify for pension. Such an agreement must be entered into in writing.

1356. The AFP scheme guarantees pension payments to employees who make use of the scheme up to the age of 67, regardless of the payment capability of the company.

Chapter 9. Discrimination

§1. Equal Opportunities and Anti-discrimination

I. Legal Basis

1357. Equal opportunities is a basic human right, and equal treatment of employees has, during recent years, come more strongly into focus on a national as well as an international basis. It is a question of an equal treatment requirement which applies through the entire employment. At the same time, there is reason to emphasize that this law development is also of a fundamental and principal nature with regard to the actual right to be employed and therefore obtain work. It is therefore natural that – already in the introduction – a general overview of these equal treatment requirements is provided.

1358. In legislation as well as in the following is mentioned partly a prohibition against unequal treatment, and partly a prohibition against discrimination. There is no actual substantive difference in the differing terminology.

1359. The employee's protection against various grounds for discrimination and prohibition against unequal treatment is regulated by the WEA, the Gender Equality Act, the Sexual Orientation Anti-Discrimination Act, the Anti-Discrimination and Accessibility Act and the Ethnicity Anti-Discrimination Act.

1360. The WEA handles protection against discrimination on the basis of political views, membership in trade unions or age (WEA Chapter 13). Of practical importance is also the direction in the Working Environment Act section 4-1(3) that a business shall be made suitable for employees of both sexes. The Gender Equality Act concerns protection against discrimination on the basis of gender, and is mainly aimed at improving women's position (cf. the Gender Equality Act section 1 and also the WEA section 13-1(4)). The Sexual Orientation Anti-Discrimination Act concerns protection against discrimination on the basis of sexual orientation, gender identity and gender expression (section 1). The Anti-Discrimination and Accessibility Act concerns protection against discrimination on the basis of actual, assumed, former or future disabilities (sections 1 and 5). The Ethnicity Anti-Discrimination Act prohibits discrimination on the basis of ethnicity, religion, belief, national origin, citizenship, skin colour and language (cf. sections 1 and 5).

II. The Requirement of Equal Treatment and Protection Against Discrimination in an International Perspective

1361. As mentioned above, protection against discrimination and the subsequent requirement for equal treatment is one of the basic human rights – of major significance to the individual – but perhaps not least as an expression of society's basic and equality-based view of humanity. This view of equal worth may be seen expressed through a number of international conventions, declarations etc., and has done so for a long time.

1362. Of the general international conventions which would be natural to mention are EHRC, ICCPR, ICESC, CERD, CEDAW and the ILO Convention No. 111.

1363. On the European level are mentioned regulations in connection to the EU, including Article 28 of the EEA Agreement with ordinance (EØF) 1612/68, and Articles 69 and 70 of the EEA Agreement (cf. below), and the European Social Pact (1961).

1364. Human rights shall, pursuant to section 92 of the Constitution, be of fundamental significance in Norwegian law. Central human rights conventions have also then been incorporated through legislation into Norwegian law, but also otherwise these conventions are of significance for the interpretation of the Norwegian regulations.

1365. Pursuant to the Act of 21 May 1999 No. 30 concerning the strengthening of the position of human rights in Norwegian law, the Human Rights Act (HRA) has been adopted, which in section 2 refers to the European Human Rights Convention, the Convention on Civil and Political Rights and the Convention on Economic, Social and Cultural Rights; it follows from section 3 of the Act that clauses in these conventions take precedence over clauses in *inter alia* the WEA.

1366. The Women's Convention is incorporated through the HRA (cf. section 2). The Anti-Race Discrimination Convention is incorporated through the Ethnicity Anti-Discrimination Act (cf. section 5).

1367. The EU Court has played a central role in the development of protection against discrimination and has had direct significance for how national legislation on the area of discrimination has been shaped.

1368. The EU's directive on ethnicity and framework directive on equal treatment in working life is not seen as part of the EEA Agreement. Norway, however, has politically arranged to introduce legal standards which are in line with the anti-discrimination protection in EU.

1369. The various bases for discrimination are closely related, something which comes into view *inter alia* in the structure and use of terminology in the three ADAs, the Gender Equality Act and the WEA, and in the underlying principal line of thought. It must therefore be assumed that decisions and principles which are expressed in one of these sets of regulations will be of significance also with regard to the remaining sets of rules. For example principles which are developed in relation to protection against discrimination on the basis of gender will also have a linkage value to the other discrimination bases.

1370. To illustrate this there is Stavanger City Court's decision of 12 May 2006 (105-075777TVI-SBYR) concerning age discrimination, where the court brought in practice from the EU court concerning gender discrimination (the *Bilka* decision) when the matter concerned the principal understanding of the prohibition against discrimination on the basis of age. On this occasion, the court noted *inter alia* that 'the same considerations and requirements to objective basis will apply in cases concerning age discrimination'.

1371. It should be noted that clauses that protect against unequal treatment on the basis of gender have been statutory since the former Equal Opportunities Act came into force in 1978. Thus, there exists a fairly long practice from the Ombudsman for Equal Status and the Complaints Commission for Equal Status.

III. The Ombudsman for Equal Status, the Complaints Commission for Equal Status and the Courts

1372. The Equality and Anti-Discrimination Ombud (the Ombudsman), the Equality and Anti-Discrimination Tribunal (the Tribunal (a Commission)) shall supervise, enforce and contribute to the implementation of *inter alia* the Gender Equality Act, the Ethnicity Anti-Discrimination Act, the Anti-Discrimination and Accessibility Act and the Sexual Orientation Anti-Discrimination Act. The Ombudsman makes statements, while the Tribunal reaches decisions that work towards the discontinuance of discrimination.

1373. The Ombudsman and the Tribunal are free of charge and functions as an alternative and a supplement to the ordinary courts. The Ombudsman undertakes an objective evaluation of cases, which are processed and thereafter make a declaration as to what extent discrimination has taken place. The Ombudsman shall attempt to achieve that the parties voluntarily comply with this statement (cf. the Anti-Discrimination Ombudsman Act section 3(3)). If voluntary compliance is not achieved, the Ombudsman's declaration can be brought before the Tribunal.

1374. The Tribunal can adopt a resolution that a breach is present of a discriminatory legislation (cf. section 7 of the Anti-Discrimination Ombudsman Act). The Tribunal can instruct cessation, correction and other measures, which are necessary in order to ensure that discrimination ceases. The Tribunal can set a time limit for the fulfilment of the instruction. If the time limit is breached, the Tribunal can pass a decision for a coercive fine in order to ensure the implementation of the instruction (cf. the Anti-Discrimination Ombudsman Act section 8(1)).

1375. The Tribunal's decision can be brought before the ordinary courts of law 'for full review of the case'. The time limit to bring an action is three months, counting from the day of the receipt of notification of the decision from the Tribunal (cf. the Anti-Discrimination Ombudsman Act section 12). An action may also be brought to the courts without it first having been processed by the Ombudsman or the Tribunal.

1376. Neither the Ombudsman nor the Tribunal can award compensation for economic or non-economic loss upon breach of the anti-discrimination legislation or equal opportunities legislation. This belongs to the area of the ordinary courts of law.

1377. In accordance with the WEA section 13-9(2), economic loss can be claimed covered pursuant to standard rules governing damages (also applies upon notification). Corresponding applies according to the Ethnic Anti-Discrimination Act section 25, the Sexual Orientation Anti-Discrimination Act section 24, the Anti-Discrimination and Accessibility Act section 31 and the Gender Equality Act section 28. In an employment relationship, liability shall exist irrespective of whether the employer can be blamed for the discrimination. In other sectors of society, liability shall exist if the person who has committed the discriminatory act can be blamed for doing so. In accordance with the Working Environment Act section 13-9(1), non-economic loss can be claimed compensated without regard to the employer's guilt (also applies upon notification). The same applies pursuant to the above-mentioned ADAs and the Gender Equality Act.

1378. A person who intentionally commits a gross breach or participates in a gross breach of the Ethnicity Anti-Discrimination Act may be punished to fines or imprisonment for up to three years.

1379. Provisions stipulated by collective agreements, employment agreements, company regulations, by-laws, etc., which are in breach of the principle of equal treatment and protection against discrimination covered by the WEA Chapter 13, are invalid (cf. the WEA section 13-9(2)).

IV. Shared Burden of Proof

1380. In cases concerning discrimination, shared burden of proof applies (cf. the Gender Equality Act section 27, the Ethnicity Anti-Discrimination Act section 23, the Sexual Orientation Anti-Discrimination Act section 23, the Anti-Discrimination and Accessibility Act section 30 and the Working Environment Act section 13-8). The burden of proof thus passes to the employer if it can be relied on that there are reasons to believe that circumstances exist which indicate that discrimination has taken place, either directly or indirectly, in breach of one of the acts.

1381. Shared burden of proof aims of increasing the efficiency of enforcement of the prohibition against either direct or indirect discrimination. It will usually be the employer who, in the specific case, has both knowledge and documentation of decisions, which have been taken. If the burden of proof had rested on the claimant, in accordance with what is the usual procedural principle, the claimant would usually have major problems trying to demonstrate that discrimination has actually taken place.

1382. In order for the burden of proof to pass over to the employer, the one who feels he or she has been discriminated against must present information which gives reason to believe that illegal discrimination has taken place. A job applicant who, for example, has not been given the position he or she has applied for, must also establish a presumption for discrimination but demonstrating that there are indications present whereby unfair emphasis has been given to the applicant's disability, ethnic origin, etc.

1383. If there is a presumption that discrimination has taken place, it rests upon the employer to substantiate that there nevertheless has not taken place any illegal discrimination. The employer must also prove that there is a greater probability of discrimination not having taken place than that discrimination has taken place.

V. Direct and Indirect Discrimination

1384. The Gender Equality Act section 5, the Ethnicity Anti-Discrimination Act section 6, the Sexual Orientation Anti-Discrimination Act section 5, the Anti-Discrimination and Accessibility Act section 5 and the WEA section 13-1(1) all prohibit direct or indirect discrimination. The concepts are further specified the different provisions, but the following description shall be relied on with regard to the WEA Chapter 13.

1385. Access to discrimination is narrower when applied to direct discrimination than where it is a question of indirect discrimination.

1386. In employment situations, direct discrimination is to say that an employee, as a consequence of one of the protected bases for discrimination, is treated worse than another individual is, has been or would be in a corresponding situation. The purpose of the prohibition against direct discrimination is to ensure formal equality between individuals. In the event of indirect discrimination, focus is directed towards how neutral clauses, conditions and practice actually function. It is indirect discrimination if an apparently neutral clause, condition or practice actually places individuals who are included by one of the protected bases for discrimination – for example women or individuals from a minority background in a worse position than other individuals. A practice which leads to part-time workers being treated less advantageously than individuals working full-time would, for example, may often be considered as indirect discrimination against women because far more women than men work part-time.

1387. Three terms must be fulfilled in order for it to be either direct or indirect discrimination. There must be a causal connection between the basis for discrimination and the treatment an individual who feels he or she has been subject to discrimination has been exposed to. If the treatment does not have any connection with the basis for discrimination, for example gender or ethnic origin, no discrimination has taken place. Action is not necessary in order for the requirement of causal connection being fulfilled. Also omissions may imply direct or indirect discrimination. If a job applicant is not summoned to a job interview because the individual is from a minority background, the requirement for a causal connection will be fulfilled. There is no requirement for intent to discriminate. In order for a causal connection to be present, it is sufficient to note that the effect of an action, or omission, is that an individual has actually been discriminated against. This simplifies the situation with regard to evidence. In addition to causal connection, it is a condition that the employee as a result of the act or omission has been placed in a worse position than others. Thus a comparison must be made between the situation of the individual who feels himself discriminated against and the situation of other individuals. Finally, it must not be a question of permitted direct or indirect discrimination.

1388. Indirect discrimination is allowed if discrimination can be objectively justified. In the *Bilka* case from 1984, the EU Court formulated it in such a manner that a company pension scheme which placed more stringent conditions for membership on part-time workers than full-time workers, and which therefore affected more women than men, could be legal if 'the measures chosen by *Bilka* correspond to a real need on the part of the enterprise, are appropriate with a view to achieving the objectives pursued and are necessary to that end'. Through this, the justification for existing schemes with gender-distorted effects were focused on. In Norwegian law, this principle is expressed so that indirect discrimination is allowed '…if the differential treatment is suited to promote the purpose of the Act, the negative impact of the differential treatment on the person or persons whose position will worsen is reasonably proportionate in view of the intended result, and the differential treatment will cease when its purpose has been achieved.' (cf. the Gender Equality Act section 7). The exception is worded in the same way in the other anti-discrimination acts, but is somewhat differently in WEA section 13-3(2). However, the understanding of the different provisions on positive differential treatment must be assumed to be the same as in the Gender Equality Act.

VI. Especially Concerning Discrimination on the Basis of Pregnancy and Childbirth

1389. Discrimination on the basis of pregnancy and childbirth were, up until June 2002, counted as indirect discrimination. In June 2002, the former Equal Opportunities Act section 3 (now the Gender Equality Act section 5) was amended so that pregnancy discrimination was deemed to be direct discrimination. The main intent was to bring Norwegian legislation into line with practice in the EU Court, where there is a complete prohibition against pregnancy discrimination regardless of what consequences this could result in for the individual company.

1390. In the preparatory works to the former Equal Opportunities Act (which is still valid due to the fact that the new Gender Equality Act is regarded as a modernization of the former Act, which does not entail any additional rights and duties to the parties involved), it is stated that the prohibition against discrimination on the basis of pregnancy is a core area where protection against discrimination is absolute. The prohibition shall be more stringent the more closely discrimination is connected to the actual pregnancy and birth, and the briefer the absence connected hereto. Outside of this core area, different treatment on the basis of birth-related absences of longer duration and care responsibility or care tasks generally will be counted as indirect discrimination where cases may be imagined which will be deemed as lawful discrimination. The EU directive on equal opportunities specifies women's rights to reinstatement following completed maternity leave. Women are also entitled to benefit from each and all improvements in work terms, which she would have been entitled to during the absence. The corresponding must be relied on in Norwegian law.

VII. Especially Concerning Harassment

1391. Harassment constitutes a special kind of discrimination. It is characterized by a deeply offensive or insulting manner, which is felt to be an assault against the individual's integrity. In the Ethnicity Anti-Discrimination Act, harassment is defined as 'act, omissions or statements that have the effect or purpose of being offensive, frightening, hostile, degrading or humiliating' (cf. EADA section 9). Pursuant to WEA section 13-1(2), harassment on the basis of political views, membership in an employees' organization or age are to be deemed as discrimination and are therefore prohibited.

1392. According to the Sexual Orientation Anti-Discrimination Act section 8, harassment on the basis of sexual orientation, gender identity or gender expression shall be prohibited. By sexual harassment is meant acts, omissions or statements that have the effect or purpose of being offensive, frightening, hostile, degrading or humiliating. The same follow from the Anti-Discrimination and Accessibility Act section 8, as far as regards harassment on the basis of disability.

1393. In 2005, the former Equal Opportunities Act section 8a was extended to also include harassment on the basis of gender (now the Gender Equality Act section 8). An example of harassment on the basis of gender is that female employees are branded as useless because they are women, or harassed in other ways because they are women. Sexual harassment and harassment on the basis of gender can overlap each other.

Chapter 10. Working Environment, Internal Control and Work Inspection

§1. The General Requirement for a Fully Satisfactory Working Environment

1394. One of the main objectives of the WEA is to ensure for employees full safety against physical and psychological damaging effects. The general requirement for the working environment is stipulated in section 4-1(1), and states that the working environment should be fully satisfactory. The expression is milder than the concept used in section 1-1(a), which states full safety for employees in the working environment. Thus, it is enough that the working environment in an enterprise is fully responsible, even when there is not full protection for the employees.

1395. Most employments are associated with elements of risk. Pursuant to section 4-1(1), these risk factors are considered acceptable as long as the enterprise's working environment is fully responsible.

1396. This indicates that the requirement for a fully satisfactory working environment is preventative. Therefore, it is not required that the working environment factors result in or may result in physical or psychological damaging effects, or that the Labour Inspectorate has issued an order or made an individual decision.

1397. The requirement for a fully satisfactory working environment is based on a standard the content of which must be decided according to a wide, balanced and total assessment of all relevant conditions, *inter alia* the ordinary social development of society and in the working life. Thus, this implies that the requirement for a fully satisfactory working environment may change over time. This interpretation is in accordance with the objective of the act set forth in section 1-1(a), which states a standard of welfare 'at all times consistent with the level of technological and social development of society'. On this basis, the requirement for a fully satisfactory working environment is dynamic.

1398. There are several different factors that influence the work environment in an enterprise and it is evident from WEA section 4-1(1) that all the factors in the working environment that may influence, shall be attached meaning to. This applies regardless of whether the influence is on the physical or psychological health of the employee.

1399. The requirement to the different working environmental factors in section 4-1(1) shall according to both an individual and a joint consideration provide a fully satisfactory working environment.

1400. The connection between section 4-1(1) and section 1-1 shows that the demand for a fully satisfactory working environment includes the protection of employees against physical and psychological damage. Therefore, the influence on the employees' heredity, which may affect the employees' children, is included in the requirement for a fully satisfactory working environment.

I. The Employer's Responsibility

1401. Pursuant to WEA section 2-1, the employer is obliged to ensure that the Working Environment Regulation's requirements for a fully satisfactory working environment are complied with at all times.

II. The Employee's Obligation to Cooperate for a Fully Satisfactory Working Environment

1402. Employees have a responsibility to ensure the requirements for a fully satisfactory working environment are complied with and the obligation to active cooperation. Thus, pursuant to section 2-3(1), the employee is not only obliged to cooperate on the design, implementation and follow-up of the enterprise's systematic work on health, environment and safety, but also to participate in the organized safety and environmental work in the enterprise.

1403. In addition, there are more specified obligations for the employees. For example, the employees are obliged to use offered safety equipment, end dangerous work when necessary, comply with orders from the Labour Inspectorate and cooperate when developing and carrying out plans to follow up.

1404. Employees who are assigned to lead or control other employees are obliged to make sure that safety and health are taken into consideration during the planning and the execution of the work duties belonging to their area of responsibility (section 2-3(3)).

III. The Employer's Responsibility for Other Employers

1405. Pursuant to WEA section 2-2(1), an employer has duties not only to his or her own employees, but also duties – more limited – as regards employees of other employers, working at the site etc. of the employer. The general principle is that the employer is under the obligation to ensure that the enterprise of the employer is organized, and that the employees carry out their work under conditions ensuring even other employees a fully satisfactory working environment. Further, it is also a duty for the employer to cooperate with other employers, in order to ensure that a fully satisfactory working environment is achieved.

1406. In situations where there is more than one company that needs to be coordinated, it is the main company that is responsible for coordinating the separate company's health, environment, and security work (section 2-2(2)). When there are in total more than ten employees and none of the companies can be appointed as the main company, a written agreement regarding which company that is responsible for the above shall be made. When such an agreement cannot be reached, the Labour Inspectorate needs to be notified and will decide who is responsible for the coordination.

§2. Organized Safety Work

1407. The Working Environment Committee (section 7-1) is a committee partly consisting of members representing the employer, and partly members representing the employees. Members of the committee will advise the employer on every matter concerning the working environment in the enterprise and has in addition a certain authority to make binding resolutions.

1408. The arrangement concerning safety representatives may be mentioned in this context. A safety representative shall be elected by and among the employees of the enterprises (cf. WEA section 6-1). Regarding the larger enterprises, several safety representatives may be elected. Enterprises with more than one safety representative shall have at least one senior safety representative, who shall be responsible for coordinating the activities of the safety representatives (cf. WEA section 6-1(3)). The safety representatives shall safeguard the interests of employees in matters relating to the working environment. They shall ensure that the enterprise is arranged and maintained, and that the work is performed in such a manner that the safety, health and welfare of the employees are safeguarded in accordance with the provisions pursuant to the WEA (cf. WEA section 6-3). As soon as a safety representative learns of circumstances that may result in accident and health hazards he shall, among other things, bring the matter to the attention of the employer and may even notify the Labour Inspectorate. Additionally, when the Labour Inspectorate are inspecting an enterprise, a safety representative shall be contacted (cf. WEA section 18-4(1)).

1409. According to section 6-3, safety representatives have the right to stop dangerous work. When the representative finds that the employee's life or health is in immediate danger, and this danger cannot be averted in any other way, the work can be stopped until the Labour Inspectorate decides whether it is safe or not to continue working. The employer or his or her representative shall be notified of the stop and the reason for this, without delay.

§3. The Objective of Systematic Health, Environment and Safety Work: Internal Control

1410. An important instrument to carry out the requirements regarding fully satisfactory working environment is systematic health, environment and safety work – the internal control (section 3-1)). The provision impose the employer to make sure that the systematic health, environment and safety work are carried out on every level of the company, often referred to as HSE work. The objective of the work is to ensure that the employees' health, environment and safety are taken care of. The systematic health, environment and safety work shall be done together with the employees and the employees' representatives.

1411. Internal control is a form of control in addition to the traditional form of control based on the public authorities' control. The traditional form of control is based on the public authorities ensuring that the enterprise complies with the statutory law's requirements, while in a system based on internal control, the enterprise shall have its own organizational wiring which shall ensure compliance with the fixed requirements for the working environment. Thus, the public authorities' control shall make demands to the enterprise's system and routines, and keep control of this. The general principle of internal control is not only regarding the enterprise's safety and working environmental (the internal environmental), but also includes environmental measures (the outer environment).

1412. In practice, the traditional system of supervision has not been fully satisfactory, mostly due to the fact that public and detailed supervision need access to a lot of resources. Thus, satisfactory supervisions may only be made within a small number of enterprises, and certain work-operations may only be supervised by letting the supervisory authority stay at the enterprise over a longer amount of time. In addition, detailed supervision needs special knowledge as regards preparedness measures, technical arrangements etc. In order to develop such know-hows, the authority need access to a lot of resources, and it is recognized that it is neither possible nor desirable in all areas within a public supervisory authority. Further, a number of enterprises have very complex and complicated operations. When the enterprise itself has developed know-hows and established internal systems for managing their own operations, it would be most appropriate that public supervisory authorities make use of this expertise in the supervisory work. Systems regarding internal controls are based on collaboration between the enterprises and the public supervisory authorities, which to a large extent is a part of a larger trend.

1413. The requirement for an organizational wiring to comply with the fixed demands for the working environment implies that the person in charge of the enterprise shall establish clearing firm courses for tasks and responsibility in the enterprise. The management – the managing board or the managing director in a limited company – has the superior responsibility.

1414. The requirement subject to the person responsible for ensuring compliance with these requirements includes both a responsibility to follow up, and an access to delegate parts of the responsibility to subordinated employees. Therefore, the system of internal control can be described as a system based on responsibility in lines.

1415. The system of internal control is based on the premise of active co-determination from the employees throughout working environmental committees and safety representatives. Therefore, the working environmental committees must as soon as possible be a part of the process concerning working out, carrying out, practising and revision of the enterprise's system of internal control. The principle of co-determination is identical to safety representatives.

1416. Non-compliance with the internal control regulation will regularly consist in waivers, and therefore, the obligation to act actively will consist in an obligation for the employee to notify his or her superior of the matter, unless the employee himself or herself is able to take necessary action.

I. Systematic Health, Environment and Safety Work

1417. Health, environment and safety work is systematic work which ensures that the activities in the enterprise is planned, organized, carried out and maintained to make sure that the employees' health, environment and safety are being taken care of. In section 3-1(2), the work is more closely described:

1418. Systematic health, environment and safety work entails that the employer shall:

(1) establish goals for health, environment and safety;
(2) have an overall view of the enterprise's organization, including how responsibility, tasks and authority for work on health, environment and safety is distributed;
(3) make a survey of hazards and problems and, on this basis, assess risk factors in the enterprise, prepare plans and implement measures in order to reduce the risks;
(4) during planning and implementation of changes in the enterprise, assess whether the working environment will be in compliance with the requirements of this Act, and implement the necessary measures;
(5) implement routines in order to detect, rectify and prevent contraventions of requirements laid down in or pursuant to this Act;
(6) ensure systematic prevention and follow-up of absence due to sickness;
(7) ensure continuous control of the working environment and the employees' health when necessitated by risk factors in the enterprise (cf. (c));
(8) conduct systematic supervision and review of the systematic work on health, environment and safety in order to ensure that it functions as intended.

1419. Additionally, the enterprise shall make a survey of its activities according to risks and problems, and on this basis assess factors that might be a risk to health, environment and safety in the enterprise. Risks can be described as the possibility that something unwanted may happen and the consequences they may result in. This does not only concern big accidents, but also includes *inter alia* problems with cooperation, strain injuries, illness, etc.

1420. On the basis of the survey covering the risks in the enterprise, a plan regarding how to reduce the risks shall be made. The plan shall describe what shall be done, by who and when to do it.

1421. A list of priority according to the rank of gravity shall also be made. The plan shall ensure that the measures are carried out at the time agreed, and therefore, it is in practice important that one person have the responsibility to follow up compliance of the time limits.

II. The Responsibility for Running Systematic Health, Environment and Safety Work in the Enterprise

1422. The employer is responsible for running the systematic health, environment and safety work (section 3-1(1)). Even though systematic health, environment and safety work must be run on every level of the enterprise, the management of the enterprise still has the main responsibility. The objective is to implement the health, environment and safety work in the superior management and the planning of the enterprise, and thus, the work will be prioritized.

1423. The statutory provision explicit determines that the systematic health, environment and safety work 'shall be carried out in cooperation with the employees and their elected representatives'. The employees are on the other hand obliged to cooperate to this work (cf. section 2-3(1)). To achieve a good result, it is necessary that the employees take part in the planning, the daily running, making the survey and finding good solutions. After all, it is the employees who generally know where the shoe pinches.

§4. Occupational Health Service

I. The Requirement for an Occupational Health Service

1424. According to section 3-3(1), the employer is obliged to provide occupational health services if so necessitated by risk factors in the enterprise, and the consideration whether the enterprise have such an obligation shall be made as a part of carrying out the systematic health, environment and safety work.

II. What is an Occupational Health Service?

1425. The term 'occupational health service' is not defined in section 3-3. However, the *travaux préparatoires* to the WEA has stated that an occupational health service means interdisciplinary plans of safety and health personnel who work together, and do not include individual safety and health personnel who is employed by the enterprise, or individual consultants or personnel doctors.

III. Voluntary Occupational Health Service

1426. Though, if it is not necessary according to the risk factors at the enterprise to provide occupational health service, the enterprise may still establish a voluntary occupational health service. This kind of occupational health service will, from the point of departure, not be included in WEA section 3-3. To the extent that voluntary occupational health service becomes a part of the systematic health, environment and safety work, or in any other way being connected to supervision or the assessment of whether the enterprise has a fully satisfactory working environment, the point of departure is easily missed. In these situations, clear lines must be kept in such a way that the voluntary occupational health service's statements and activity are built on a real 'free and independent position in questions regarding working environment', as the WEA states. It is important that such information is given to the management of the enterprise as well as the employees and other people involved.

IV. The Occupational Health Service's Tasks

1427. According to section 3-3(2), the occupational health service shall assist the employer, the employees, the Working Environment Committee and safety representatives in creating safe and sound working conditions. Thus, the occupational health service shall have in mind matters in the enterprise that needs to be supervised out of consideration for the employees' safety and health, control of the employees' health and promote work concerning health, environment and safety measurements. Also, the occupational health service has a major part in connection with adaptation for employees with reduced capacity for work (section 4-6).

V. The Occupational Health Service: Free and Independent Position

1428. According to section 3-3(3), the occupational health service shall have a free and independent position as regards working environment matters. Accordingly, the occupational health service shall only take academic considerations into account. Still, in practice this may be problematic, *inter alia* because the employer is the occupational health service's principal. However, it will be in conflict with the requirements regarding independence if the employer had the opportunity to force the occupational health service to make assessments and decisions contrary to what academic considerations and understandings require. Likewise, if the occupational health service should submit to such demands, it will be in conflict with its free and independent position.

§5. The Psychosocial Working Environment

I. Starting Points

1429. The working environment in an enterprise is not only dependent on a number of different physical working environment factors, but also much on the purely human relationships within the business. To the individual employee's satisfaction in the working place, these interpersonal relationships, often referred to as the psychosocial factors, could be just as important as the physical working environment.

1430. While legislation and statutory regulations regarding workers' protection and working environment were quite thorough and detailed when it comes to the physical working environment, the regulation of the psychosocial factors are significantly more limited. This is due partly to the fact that the interpersonal relationships are far less suited to regulate by law. The interpersonal relationships are rather based on unwritten social norms for how people should relate to each other, as well as in society in general and in the workplace in particular. Therefore, interpersonal relationships are also dependent on the individual's personality, temper and nature, and sociability with other people.

II. The Psychosocial Working Environment and Adaptation for Employees with Reduced Capacity for Work

1431. Already when it comes to planning and the detailed formulation of the work, the psychosocial working environment shall be in focus (section 4-1(2)). The provision states that the 'organization, arrangement and management of work, working hours, technology, pay systems, etc. shall be arranged in such a way that the employees are not exposed to adverse physical or mental strain and that due regard is paid to safety considerations'. A similar provision is given in section 10-2(1) as regards working hours' arrangements.

1432. It appears from reading the two provisions that they are formed in a way that the protection from physical strains has the same focus as the protection from psychological strains.

1433. An important provision of the psychosocial working environment is section 4-2(2), where concern for the individual employee's matters are in focus. The provision states that the design of each employee's working situation shall be made to enable the employee's professional and personal development through his or her work, and that the work shall be organized and arranged with regard for the individual employee's capacity for work, proficiency, age and other conditions.

1434. Also, section 4-2(1) is important, which may be considered as a part of the employees' right to codetermination. The provision states that the employees and their elected representatives shall be kept continuously informed of systems used in planning and performing the work. Additionally, they shall be given the training necessary to enable them to familiarize themselves with these systems, and they shall take part in designing them.

III. Harassment or other Improper Conduct

1435. According to section 4-3, the work shall be arranged in order to preserve the employees' integrity and dignity and efforts shall be made to arrange the work so as to enable contact and communication with other employees of the enterprise. Moreover, the provision forbids that the employees are subjected to harassment or other improper conduct, and employees shall, as far as possible, be protected against violence, threats and undesirable strain as a result of contact with other persons.

1436. The general requirement for a fully satisfactory working environment, and the specific requirement for the union, also includes the employer's obligation to ensure that the employees are not subject to harassment in the working situation. The decree to prevent harassment or other improper conduct is a specification of the general requirement for a fully satisfactory working environment. Also, the employer is obliged to investigate if the circumstances indicate such action.

1437. In practice, it may be hard to find the real cause of the harassment because it happens as an interaction between the way the person who is subject to the harassments acts, and the other's behaviour. The dynamism that arises implies that the possibilities to solve difficult cooperation issues are better the earlier these difficulties are notified and tried solved, while its more difficult the longer time the difficulties have the opportunity to develop and fasten. Therefore, it is essential that the employer have a system to ensure a running and open dialogue as regards cooperation. The Labour Inspectorate may prohibit the employer from introducing such a system in the enterprise. Such lacks regarding the working environment may also be considered as a breach of the law towards the employee in question, and therefore, result in liability for the employer, and may similarly be relevant in connection to the rules regarding unfair dismissal.

IV. Sexual Harassment

1438. As stated in paragraphs 1293–1295, sexual harassment etc. must be assessed in the same manner. This kind of circumstances may be considered as a special variant of harassment, and are in conflict with the provision mention above regarding a fully satisfactory working environment, and of the Gender Equality Act or the Sexual Orientation Anti-Discrimination Act etc. For the employee who is guilty of this kind of conduct, dismissal or summary dismissal may be considered as justified.

§6. Special Precautions to Ensure Safety

1439. Preventing injuries and diseases is of course an important objective included in the requirement for a fully satisfactory working environment. Section 4-1(2) explicitly states that when planning and arranging the work, emphasis shall be placed on preventing injuries and diseases.

1440. In connection to this, section 3-2(1) states specific requirements in order to ensure safety at the working place. The employer shall ensure that employees are informed of accident risks and health hazards that may be connected with the work, and provide the necessary training, practice and instruction. The employees charged with directing or supervising other employees shall have the necessary competence to ensure that the work is performed in a proper manner with regard to health and safety, and ask for expert assistance, when this is necessary.

1441. When employees become aware of faults or defects that may involve danger to life or health and they themselves are unable to remedy the fault or defect, they must immediately notify the employer. If an employee suffers injury at work or contracts diseases, which the employee believes result from work or conditions at the working premises, the employee shall notify the employer. And an employee who considers that he cannot continue without involving danger to life or health shall interrupt work. For work, which may involve particular hazards to life or health, written instructions shall be prepared prescribing how the work is to be done and what safety measures are to be implemented (cf. section 3-2(3)). The provision aims to include work that involves higher risks than what is considered as normal, or working places with abnormal risks.

I. Specific Requirements in Relation to the Physical Working Environment

1442. Section 4-4(3) explicitly states that machines and other work equipment shall be designed and provided with safety devices so that employees are protected against injuries, and if the employer make available living quarters to employees they shall be properly constructed, equipped and maintained (cf. section 4-4(4)).

1443. Section 4-4(2) especially mentions the occupational conditions at the working place. The reason for this is *inter alia* the large number of employees who are off sick because of musculoskeletal disorders. Therefore, the provision states that the working place:

> shall be equipped and arranged in such a manner as to avoid adverse physical strain on the employees. Necessary aids shall be made available to the employees. Arrangements shall be made for variation in the work and to avoid heavy lifting and monotonous repetitive work. When machines and other work equipment are being installed and used, care shall be taken to ensure that employees are not subjected to undesirable strain as a result of vibration, uncomfortable working positions and the like.

II. The Chemical and Biological Working Environment

1444. According to section 4-5(1), the working environment shall when handling chemicals or biological substances, be so arranged that employees are protected against accidents, injuries to health and excessive discomfort. Chemicals and biological substances shall be manufactured, packed, used and stored in such a manner that employees are not subjected to health hazards.

1445. According to section 4-5(3), the enterprise shall have the necessary routines and equipment to prevent or counteract injuries to health due to chemicals or biological substances.

1446. However, in particular section 4-5(2) is worth noting, which states the so-called substitution obligation. The point is that chemicals and biological substances, which may involve health hazards shall not be used if they can be replaced by other substances or by another process which is less hazardous for the employees. This substitution obligation involves an obligation to activity to the employer.

1447. Moreover, please note the obligation to note and keep a record in section 4-5(4). The obligation to keep a record imposes an obligation to keep record of hazardous chemicals and biological substances. The record shall include information on physical, chemical and hazardous properties, preventive safety measures and first aid treatment. The obligation to note imposes that containers and packaging for chemicals and biological substances shall be clearly labelled with the name and composition and a warning in Norwegian.

III. Requirements for Manufacturers, Suppliers and Importers, Etc.

1448. Regarding the working environment at the enterprises, the provisions of the WEA are mainly addressed to the employer. The employer shall comply with the requirements, in such a manner these requirements are designed at any time.

1449. However, when it comes to complex working environmental issues, the employer in question will often have limited opportunities to ensure that the WEA's requirements are fully met.

1450. This applies especially to machines and other work equipment, and chemicals and biological substances. In these situations manufacturers, suppliers and importers will often have significantly better knowledge about the product's features and composition. In many cases, the manufacturers, suppliers and importers will easily ensure that the legislative requirements for the working environment are met because they are those who bring the products into the market.

IV. Requirements for Manufacturers, Suppliers and Importers of Chemicals or Biological Substances

1451. According to section 5-4(1), any person who manufactures or imports chemicals or biological substances that will be used or expected to be used in the enterprise shall:

(1) obtain information concerning the chemical's or substance's composition and properties;
(2) adopt the necessary measures to prevent accidents and injuries to health or excessive discomfort or inconvenience to the employees;
(3) notify the agency specified by the Ministry of the chemical's or substance's name, composition, physical and chemical properties, and whatever supplementary information is required in order to determine how hazardous the substance is;
(4) ensure proper packaging so as to prevent accidents and injury to health;
(5) label the packaging with the name of the chemical or substance, the name of the manufacturer or importer and a clear warning in Norwegian; the label shall be submitted with the notification required pursuant to (3).

V. Requirements for Manufacturers, Suppliers and Importers of Machines and Other Work Equipment

1452. According to section 5-5(1), (3) and (4) any person who produces, imports, sells, hires out or lends machines and other work equipment shall ensure that it is designed and provided with safety devices in accordance with the requirements of the WEA. This shall be done before the working equipment is delivered for use. When designing, care shall be taken to ensure that devices and equipments can be used for their intended purposes without involving excessive inconvenience or discomfort.

§7. Employees with Reduced Capacity for Work

1453. According to section 4-1(4), it is a general requirement for passageways, sanitary facilities, work equipment, etc. which shall 'to the extent possible and reasonable' be designed and arranged so that employees with disabilities can work at the enterprise. This requirement applies regardless of whether the enterprise already have employees with limited mobility and work capacity, and the aim is to prevent employers from acting reluctant for employing occupationally disabled because of difficult conditions at the working place. In this connection, the Letter of Intent regarding a more inclusive working life must be mentioned. The goal is a reduction of sick leave by 20%, and to employ more employees with reduced capacity for work, and to increase the real pensionable age.

§8. The Labour Inspectorate

1454. The Labour Inspectorate is a public administrative body under the Ministry of Labour. The Labour Inspectorate shall supervise compliance with the provisions of and pursuant to the WEA (cf. section 18-1(1)). The Labour Inspectorate may issue orders, coercive fines and halt the activities of the enterprise.

I. The Labour Inspectorate's Responsibilities

1455. Traditionally, the supervision of enterprises complying with the rules, and especially the requirements for a systematic HSE work, is a central part of the work of the Labour Inspectorate and is still part of the most important activities. However, the Labour Inspectorate's effort shall at a greater extent concentrate on the chosen area of commitment connected to the including working life:

- psychosocial working environment;
- arrangements/ergonomics;
- chemical and biological influence;
- serious risk of accidents.

II. Legal Authority for Labour Control and Labour Reactions

1456. The Labour Inspectorate's tasks according to WEA sections 18-1 to 18-9 can be divided into two categories; legal authority to control and legal authority to react. The division is the reason for the systematic placing of the provisions.

1457. The legal authority to control entitles the Labour Inspectorate to investigate and control the compliance of the requirements of the WEA. The legal authority to demand free access to the enterprise, the inspection authority (section 18-4) and to demand information can be placed within this category. The objective of these rules is to give the Labour Inspectorate sufficient basis to assess if the enterprise's activities comply with the requirements pursuant to the WEA.

1458. The legal authority to react entitles the Labour Inspectorate to issue administrative sanctions, provided that the enterprise does not comply with the requirements of the WEA. The legal authority to issue orders and other individual decisions (section 18-6) and to halt the work (section 18-8) are within this category. The objective of these rules is to provide the Labour Inspectorate with an effective instrument towards illegal activities.

III. Inspections

1459. Inspections are an important part of the Labour Inspectorate's supervision activity and the Labour Inspectorate's access to the enterprise is stated in section 18-4.

1460. According to section 18-4(1), the Labour Inspectorate shall have free access at all times to any premises subject to the WEA. As a general rule, the employer or his or her representative is entitled to be present during the inspection (section 18-4(2)), and the provision also entitles to prohibit the employer to be present, if necessary by his or her representative. An important limitation to the employer's right to be present is stated in the provision – the supervision staff may decide that the right shall not apply in two different situations. Partly, when interviewing the employees and partly when the presence of the employer would entail a major inconvenience or endanger the purpose of the inspection.

IV. The Obligation to Provide the Labour Inspectorate with Information

1461. Section 18-5 states an extensive obligation for the employer as well as employees and others to give information to the Labour Inspectorate, and this obligation is not limited by the obligation of secrecy.

V. Protection of Sources of Information

1462. According to section 18-2, the Labour Inspectorate shall, when it is informed of circumstances that are in contravention of the WEA, keep the name of the informant secret. Without the informant's consent, the Labour Inspectorate is not entitled to disclose the name of the source, and the same applies to circumstances that may disclose the informant's identity.

VI. Appointing Specialists

1463. Special expertise may be necessary to carry out the supervision. Therefore, section 18-1(1) states that the Labour Inspectorate may appoint specialists to conduct controls, inspections, etc., on behalf of the Labour Inspectorate. The specialists are in the same way as the Labour Inspectorate's staff, entitled to free access to the enterprise's working place and to buildings, means of transport, stores, areas, etc. where machines, technological devices and equipment or toxic and other substances that may involve health hazards, are present.

VII. The Right to Appoint a Special Board of Inquiry in Case of Disasters

1464. Even though it is not directly stated in the WEA, the *travaux préparatoires* to the WEA state that the king, without a special legal authority, is entitled to appoint a special board of inquiry when catastrophic disasters occur or when the investigation is presumed to be especially extensive or complicated.

VIII. Individual Decisions Regarding Products, Etc., Which Entail Danger to Life or Health

1465. Section 18-6(3), (4) and (5) provide the Labour Inspectorate with the legal authority to make individual decisions regarding products that entail danger to life or health. The Labour Inspectorate may partly forbid such substances, partly require inspections and partly order that the enterprise takes the necessary measures to avert such danger.

IX. Coercive Fines and Halt of the Enterprise

1466. The Labour Inspectorate may according to section 18-7 impose a continuous coercive fine if the time limit set for implementation of the order has expired and the order has not been implemented. The coercive fine runs 'for each day, week or month that passes', until the implementation is fulfilled. Still, coercive fines may be imposed as a single payment fine, therefore an amount fixed once and for all. Also, the provision states that the Labour Inspectorate may waive accrued coercive fines.

1467. According to the WEA section 18-10, the Labour Inspectorate may issue a violation fine if a business entity or a person acting on the behalf of the entity has neglected to comply with an order or decision made by the Labour Inspectorate, (cf. WEA section 18-6). The violation fine may be issued even though not a single person can be blamed for the negligence. The violation fine may not exceed fifteen times the basic amount, as stipulated in the SSA.

1468. Halting of the enterprise may also be issued according to section 18-8 in the event of immediate danger, even if no order has been issued. In these situations, the Labour Inspectorate may halt those activities that are associated with the dangerous situation. Additionally, section 18-6(2) contains a legal authority for the Labour Inspectorate to demand that necessary measures shall be implemented immediately in the event of immediate danger.

X. Legal Authority to Demand Fees

1469. According to section 18-3, enterprises subject to the WEA, may be ordered to pay an annual inspection fee or fees to cover expenses relating to control, approval and certification or to required examinations or tests.

§9. Penalties

1470. Violations of labour legislation are punishable (cf. Chapter 19 of the WEA). Penalties may be imposed directly on the enterprises. The penalty is partly dependant on the company's finances, but cases have shown that the fines can reach up to several millions. In this relation shall only be mentioned that WEA section 19-1(1) states that 'any proprietor of an enterprise, employer or person managing an enterprise in the employer's stead who wilfully or negligently breaches the provisions or orders contained in or issued pursuant to this Act shall be liable to a fine or imprisonment for up to one year, or both'. WEA section 19-1(2) states that 'by case of particularly aggravating circumstances, imprisonment up to three years may be imposed'. In deciding whether such circumstances exist, particular attention shall be paid to whether the infringement partly has or could have led to serious danger to life or health– among other relevant circumstances. Criminal liability for enterprises is stated in section 27 (in effect from 10 October 2015) of the PC (of 2005) (cf. WEA section 19-3). The previous provisions on criminal liability for enterprises were stated in the PC (1902) section 48a and 48b.

1471. In this relation the case in Rt. 2012 p. 770 may be mentioned. The judgment deals with a case of enterprise penalties under the PC section 48b. An operator fell 9 meters down from an unsecured platform. As a result of his injuries, he was 100% disabled. The Supreme Court found that the company should be imposed a penalty according to the PC section 48b. The company's safety systems were not improper in itself, but the system should have taken into account that because of the design of the platform the employee was tempted to climb over the security fence and use the unsecured part of the platform in order to perform their work tasks. On these grounds, the Supreme Court found that there existed system failures which represented objectively breaches of the WEA. The enterprise's penalty was set at NOK 500,000.

Chapter 11. Covenants of Non-competition, Non-solicitation and Non-recruitment

§1. Non-competition Clauses

1472. Covenants of non-competition may be defined as conditions preventing or hampering the employee, at the end of the contract period, from taking a job with a competitor of the previous employer or from starting or taking part in a competing enterprise.

1473. By the Act of 18 December 2015 No. 104 (in force from 1 January 2016) there are now given restrictions on the access to enter into non-competition clauses or agreements, the maximum duration of such clauses, the employee's right to receive compensation if the non-competition clause is invoked by the employer etc. The new provisions are to be found in WEA Chapter 14 A. Non-competition clauses often stipulate that the employee is not entitled to start up, take employment with, or have any other interests in a competing business for a certain period after the employment has ceased, cf. WEA section 14 A-1(1).

1474. Non-competition clauses shall only be deemed valid to the extent that the employer has a special need for protection against competition when the clause is invoked by the employer, cf. WEA section 14 A-1. Whether the basic requirement of 'special need' is met, is to be assessed on a discretionary basis. Trade secrets and know-how developed in the enterprise will normally fill the requirement. If an employee has acquired such knowledge, the employer should normally have a 'special need' for protection against competition.

1475. A non-competition clause/agreement must be entered into in writing between the employer and the employee, in order to be valid. The clause/agreement must entitle the employee compensation equivalent to the employee's full salary amounting up to eight times the basic amount (*G*) – stipulated in the Act on Social Security and Welfare, and 1 G is pr. 1 May 2016 NOK 91 740 – based on remunerations the employee has received in the last twelve months prior to the termination of the employment. For salaries between 8 and 12 times the basic amount (*G*), the compensation may be limited to 70%. The compensation may be reduced by up to 50% of other salaries/incomes the employee receives during the duration period of the non-competition clause/agreement.

1476. A non-competition clause/agreement may not be made valid, or invoked by the employer, for more than one year, counting from the termination of the employment contract. In connection with the termination of the employment contract, the employer has to provide the employee with a written statement describing whether, and to what extent, the agreed non-competition clause/agreement will be invoked by the employer. This statement shall be presented by the employer no later than four weeks counted from the time the employee made a written requirement for such a statement. The employer's statement shall also entail a description of why the employer is of the opinion that he or she has a special need for protection against competition.

1477. If the employee terminates the employment, and a written statement has not already been provided by the employer, the employee's notice of termination will serve as a written requirement for a statement from the employer, providing the employer with a deadline of four weeks. If the employee is given a notice of termination from the employer, and a written statement has not already been provided by the employer, the employer has to give the statement at the same time as the notice of termination of the employment is handed over to the employee. If the employee is summary dismissed (cf. WEA section 15-14) by the employer, and a written statement has not already been provided by the employer, the employer has to provide the statement within one week, counted from the time the notice of dismissal was handed over to the employee. The written statement is binding for the employer for three months after being handed over to the employee. If the statement is given in connection with a notice of termination, the statement is nevertheless binding upon the employer the entire period of notice (cf. WEA section 15-3 if the employee is entitled to a longer notice period than what is agreed between the parties).

1478. A non-competition clause/agreement will no longer apply if the employee is dismissed without due cause based on the employee's individual circumstances (e.g., if the employee neglects to perform his or her work in a sufficiently proper manner, etc.). This means, for example, that a non-competition clause cannot be maintained if the employer dismisses the employee as a result of the company's circumstances, such as workforce reductions. Further, the clause will lapse if the employee resigns because the employer has provided valid grounds for it by neglecting to fulfil his or her obligations.

§2 Non-solicitation Clauses

1479. A non-solicitation clause may be defined as an agreement between the employer and the employee which limits or prohibits the employee from contacting the employer's customers when the employment contract has been terminated, cf. WEA section 14-A-4(1). A non-solicitation clause has to be made in writing in order to be valid and can only be made applicable to customers who the employee has had contact with or responsibility for the past year from the date in which the employer provides a written statement on whether the non-solicitation clause will be invoked. Nevertheless, the clause cannot in any case be invoked for a longer time than one year counting from the date of termination of the employment contract.

1480. Upon written request from the employee, the employer shall within four weeks provide a written statement of whether and to what extent the clause will be invoked. The statement shall specify which clients are to be covered by the clause.

1481. The provisions regarding non-competition clauses and non-solicitation clauses do not apply to the chief executive if he or she in a written agreement has wavered such rights in return of severance pay before the employment contract is terminated.

§3 Non-recruitment Clauses

1482. A non-recruitment clause may be defined as an agreement between the employer and other enterprises that prevent or restrict employee's opportunities to take employment in other enterprises, cf. WEA section 14-A-6(1). According to WEA section 14-A-6(2), an employer may not enter into a non-recruitment clause. However, a non-recruitment clause may be agreed during negotiations of transfer of enterprises (cf. WEA Chapter 16), and may be applied during the negotiations and until six months after the termination of negotiations, if these prove unsuccessful. Further, a non-recruitment clause can also be concluded from the time of the transfer of enterprises and can apply for up to six months, provided that the employer has informed all affected employees, in writing.

Chapter 12. Inventions by Employees: Entitlements to the Result of the Work

1483. In general, it may be relied on that the result of an employee's work devolves on the employer. Where material goods are produced, this is in no doubt, and is *inter alia* based on the fact that it is the employer who own, or have at his or her disposal the materials and is going to sell what has been produced. But also when the work results in an intellectual product, such as an invention, intellectual work or a registered design, the employer will most often have some form of entitlement to this, when it has been produced as part of the employment relationship. It is a part of this entitlement that the employee must respect and safeguard the employer's operational and business secrets, even if it is the employee himself who has obtained knowledge of this for the employer.

1484. For intellectual products, the basic principle applies that it is the individual who has created the intellectual work who owns the copyright, for example a journalist who has prepared an article for a newspaper (cf. the Copyright Act of 12 May 1961 No. 2).

1485. Copyright may be transferred to others, for example the employer, which presupposes an agreement to this effect. In this connection, section 39a of the Act must be noted. The clause states that transfer, which entails an entitlement to use the work in a specific way or by specific means does not give the acquirer the right to do this in other ways or by other means.

1486. If an employee makes a patentable invention, the situation is regulated by the Act of 17 April 1970 No. 21 regarding the right to employees' inventions (the Employee Invention Act (EinA)). According to section 3 of the Act, the main rule is that employees have the same right to their inventions as other inventors have, but the employer may – depending on how close the connection is between the contractual employment relationship and the invention – either claim to have the rights to the invention transferred to him in whole or in part, or to exploit the invention in his or her business.

1487. If the invention has been made without connection to the contractual service, the employer has priority to enter into an agreement with the employee to the effect that the employer takes over the rights to the invention, either in whole or in part. Under all circumstances, the assumption is that exploitation of the invention falls within the company's area of activity (cf. section 4 of the Act). If such an agreement is entered into, the employee is entitled to reasonable compensation even if an agreement to the contrary had been concluded before the invention was made, except where the value of the right acquired by the employer does not exceed the value of the services the employee may reasonably be expected to perform in return for his or her remuneration or other benefits that may be associated with the employment. In determining the amount of the compensation, special consideration shall be given to the value of the invention, the extent of the right that the employer has acquired, the employee's conditions of employment and the degree to which the employment may in other respects have contributed to the invention (cf. section 7 of the Act).

1488. The employee can only to a limited extent waive the rights according to the Act (cf. section 7 first subsection and section 9).

1489. In connection with software programmes, the Act of 12 May 1961 No. 2 regarding copyright in literary, scientific and artistic works etc. (The Copyright Act) section 39g must be noted. The provision regulates copyright to software programmes, which have been created by an employee during the performance of tasks which are included by the employment relationship or in accordance with instructions by the employer. Such copyright will as a main rule be transferred to the employer, unless otherwise agreed between the parties.

1490. Correspondingly must be noted the Act of 15 June 1990 No. 27 relating to the protection of layout designs for integrated circuits section 4 second subsection, which states that exclusive rights to integrated circuit design which are produced during employment, will be transferred to the employer unless otherwise agreed.

Chapter 13. Employee Co-determination

§1. The General Rule

1491. With regard to the statutory rules, the collective agreements and the individual employment contract constitute an outer limit of the managerial rights, while the rules regarding the employees' co-determination imply that the workers have the right to influence the decisions made on the basis of the managerial rights. Therefore, according to the rules regarding co-determination, the workers are able to influence the inner content of managerial rights.

§2. The Objectives of the Rules Regarding Employees' Co-determination

1492. The rules are built on the basis of both ideal and efficient objectives. According to an ideal objective, it is considered as best in accordance with the democratic principles in the society, and therefore, it has also been a part of the working life, to leave more room for democracy. The 'inner democracy' is considered as an objective itself, built on the basis of the workers' rights as employees to influence the decisions made by the employer. The efficient objectives are founded on the recognition of the fact that the employees' right to exercise influence may have a positive effect by increasing the workers initiative, knowledge and willingness to contribute, for the benefit of the enterprise. Accordingly, the objective is that both the employees in the private and public sector have the same principle forms of codetermination.

§3. The Constitutional Provision Regarding Employees' Co-determination

1493. The principle of the employees' right to co-determination on their place of work is stated in the Constitution section 110 second subsection. According to the statutory provision, legislation may state detailed rules. In the meaning of 'law', collectively agreed rights of the workers' influence are also accepted. Even some business sectors may state the co-determination by ordinary agreements between the employer and employees. By using the term 'the place of work', this includes the enterprise the employees are hired by and not only the place where each employee is performing his or her working tasks. This seems to be the best interpretation according to the purpose of the statutory rule.

1494. The constitutional right does not estimate any limits regarding which decisions the employees by the codetermination may be given the right to influence. Therefore by law, it is up to the *Storting* (the Parliament of Norway) to decide the limits of co-determination.

§4. The Link between Statutory Representation and the Statutorily or Collectively Agreed Cooperation Bodies

1495. The statutory law gives the employees the right to be represented in the enterprises managing bodies and in working environment committees. In addition, the WEA and collective agreements stipulate rules regarding how employees can influence the decisions made by the enterprise through information and discussions with the shop stewards when the employer is planning changes, which include employees' working conditions.

1496. Employees' possibility of exercising influence on the decisions is best when they can present their views as early as possible. The sooner the representatives can be a part of the process, the better their chance of influencing the result. WEA section 15-2(2) is based on the idea of information and discussion as early as possible when the employer is considering mass dismissals.

§5. Co-determination and the Size of the Enterprise

1497. On the general level, the organizing of employees' co-determination is first and foremost relevant to enterprises of a certain size. In enterprises with only a few employees, there is in practice a better possibility to exercise influence in a less formal way than in enterprises with a much larger number of employees. The rules reflect this by stipulating stricter rules for larger enterprises.

§6. Private Limited Companies and Other Company Forms

1498. The rules of co-determination are in some ways different between the private and the public sector, and the rules may also differ between the different company forms in the private working life. Some industries have their own system for co-determination.

I. The Corporate Assembly

1499. According to the Act relating to Private Limited Companies section 6-35(1) and the Act relating to Public Limited Companies (section 6-35(1)), the general rule is that larger limited companies – companies which the last three fiscal years on average had more than 200 employees – shall elect a corporate assembly with twelve or more members if the general meeting and the shareholders have so decided. The number of members must be divisible by three. The general meeting elects two-thirds of the members, and the employees elect the last third. Unions, who represent two-thirds of the employees or a majority of the employees, may even elect observers and deputy board members.

1500. The corporate assembly elects the board and controls the board and the managing director's administration of the company. If agreed by the parties that the company shall not have a corporate assembly, the board will take over the corporate assembly's most important functions.

1501. The observers shall increase the employees' contact with the employer. They have the right to speak and suggest, but not the right to vote. The observers may also demand that a question is being debated and that voting should make the decision.

II. The Board

1502. The workers' representation in the board depends on the number of employees in the company. In private limited companies, which in the last three fiscal years on average had more than thirty employees, and do not have a corporate assembly, two-thirds of the employees may demand that one of the members of the board, one observer and one deputy board member, shall be elected by and among the employees (cf. section 6-4).

1503. If the company in the last three fiscal years on average had more than fifty employees, and does not have a corporate assembly, the majority of the employees may demand that up to one-third, but at least two, of the members of the board shall be elected by and among the employees.

1504. Consequently, the employees' representation is depending on the employees' claim of representation in companies, which does not have a corporate assembly. This means that the right to representation is voluntary for employees, contrary to the rules regarding representation in the corporate assembly.

III. Corporations

1505. The Act relating to Private Limited Companies and the Act relating to Public Limited Companies also provides access for corporations to establish joint representation for the employees in corporations – if the company owns one or more other companies, or where two or more independent companies by ownership interest or by having a mutual management are connected in a group (cf. section 6-5). This system of representation safeguards the employees' possibility to exercise influence on decisions regarding the whole corporation and not only the managing entities in the single company. The Council for Corporate Democratization may decide that this system of representation shall be instituted.

IV. Election Rules

1506. According to the Regulation of 18 December 1998 No. 1205, the main rule is that the employees' representatives are elected by and among all employees in the limited company. Workers who have been employed in a position that on average make 50% of the working hours per week for full-time who perform the same tasks, and have been employed by the company for the last three months has the right to vote (cf. section 8 and section 9). The election is secret, in writing, and is being held as majority election, unless two-thirds of the workers entitled to vote claim that the election shall be conducted as proportional representation. The election period is two years.

V. European Works Councils: Co-determination in SE Companies

1507. If a corporation consists of companies in different countries, decisions made by the management may inflect each individual company in the individual country. Co-determination in individual enterprises will in such cases be based on the decision the corporate management has made, but will not be able to influence corporate management's plans and decisions with regard to international corporations. On this basis, it is necessary to develop employees' co-determination in corporations and to give them a possibility to exercise influence where the real decisions are made, and where the financial interests are. This is the reason why Directive 94/95 EEC regarding European works councils was implemented in the EEA agreement. The purpose of the directive is to increase the employees' right to information and discussion in companies, which are represented in different countries, and in corporations, which include companies in different Member States. The directive only concerns international corporations and state corporations which employ more than a thousand employees in Member States and at least 150 employees in at least two of the countries. According to the directive, a European works councils shall only be established if the employees' so require.

1508. By the legislative Decree No. 2157/2001, the EU permitted the creation of European companies (hereinafter referred to as 'SE'). SE companies are characterized by the fact that there must exist at least two companies, which fall under the various EU/EEA countries' legislation before an SE company can be created. The SE directive followed this. The objective of the directive is to ensure the employees' right of involvement because the employee by the establishment of an SE company will no longer be governed by the national provisions applicable.

§7. Co-determination When the Employer Goes into Bankruptcy/ Liquidation

1509. A majority of the employees or a local union, to which belong a majority of the employees of the enterprise, may petition the bankruptcy court to nominate a representative to the employees as a member of the creditor's committee. Still, the bankruptcy court may decide because of the economic position of the bankrupt estate, to ignore such a request.

§8. Council for Corporate Democratization

1510. To maintain a suitable and flexible organizing of the statutory system of representation, the Council for Corporate Democratization was established. The council shall consider application concerning exceptions and disputes regarding the employees' right to representation in the companies' decisive organs.

§9. Working Environmental Committee, Safety Representatives, Etc.

1511. Enterprises which regularly employ at least fifty employees, shall have a working environment committee in which the employer, the employees and the safety and health personnel are represented. Working environment committees shall also be formed in enterprises, which regularly employ between twenty and fifty employees when so required by any of the parties at the enterprise. Where working conditions so indicate, the Labour Inspectorate may decide that enterprises with fewer than fifty employees shall establish a working environment committee.

1512. The working environment committee shall contribute to establish a fully satisfactory working environment in the enterprise, and participate in planning safety and environmental work and shall follow up developments closely in questions relating to the safety, health and welfare of the employees.

1513. The statutory rules in WEA section 6-1 relating to safety representative are also a part of the employees' co-determination at the place of work. The safety representative shall be consulted during the planning and implementation of measures of significance for the working environment within the representative's safety area, including establishment, exercise and maintenance of the enterprise's systematic health, environment and safety work.

1514. The safety representatives shall be elected at all enterprises with more than ten employees. The Labour Inspectorate may, following a concrete assessment of the circumstances at an enterprise with fewer than the employees, decide that it shall nevertheless have a safety representative.

§10. The Rules Regarding Information and Discussion in the WEA

1515. Under the provisions of WEA, Chapter eight employees' are, through their shop stewards, given the right to information and discussion. The objective is to ensure that the shop stewards are provided relevant information regarding the employees, and to safeguard that the employees, through their shop stewards, are given a possibility to exercise influence on the decisions made by the company management. The rules do not provide employees with a right of veto or a right to make decisions, but there is a possibility of presenting their statement in certain situations before the management are making their decisions.

1516. The statutory rules are implementing EU Directive 2002/14/EC. As mentioned, the statutory rules only concern enterprises that regularly employ at least fifty employees. The reason is the importance of not imposing administrative, financial or judicial burdens, which will restrain the establishment and development of small and medium-sized companies. On the other hand, the rules are designed to include both public and private enterprises.

I. Matters Subject to Information and Consultation

1517. The obligation to inform and consult is incumbent to the employer. The statutory rules in WEA section 8-2 are meant to be minimum rights, and it is given that also other matters than those, which are lined-up, can be subject to information and consultation. Moreover, it is relevant to observe the rules in connection with the corresponding rules in the BA (2014) sections 9-3 et seq. when it comes to carrying out the information and consultation process.

II. Information and Consultation with 'the Shop Stewards'

1518. Information and consultation shall take place together with 'the shop stewards', but this definition is not further specified in the WEA. There is no doubt that the unionized employees' election of representatives is included. But if the employees are unionized in different unions and with different shop stewards, the WEA does not directly answer the question. The same applies to enterprises where the number of unionized employees is low or none of the employees are unionized.

III. When the Information and Consultation Shall Take Place

1519. When the information shall be provided depends on the character of the information. Generally, the main rule is that the information shall be provided before the information is given to the other employees. The information concerning the current and expected development of the enterprise's activities and economic situation shall be provided at 'an appropriate time'. The point of time is depending on the character of the enterprise, and in which way the information will affect the employees. As regards the market, stock-exchange usages may require caution of giving the information at a too early stage.

1520. Information and consultation concerning the current and expected workforce situation in the enterprise, and decisions that may result in considerable changes in the organization of work or conditions of employment, shall take place as early as possible. This implies that information shall be provided and discussion must be done already at the planning stage, which means the point of time the employer is still considering different measures. The objective of the rules is among other factors that shop stewards, who can have another perspective on the matter of subject, may provide additional facts or other point of view, which may influence or change the basis of the decision. The employees shall, through their shop stewards, be given the possibility to put forward their point of view before the management is making their decisions on the current subject.

IV. Carrying Out the Obligation to Inform and Consult

1521. According to section 8-2(3), the information shall be provided in such a way that it is possible for the elected representatives of the employees to familiarize themselves with the matter, make appropriate investigations, consider the matter and prepare any discussions. The discussions shall be based on information provided by the employer and take place at the level of management and representation appropriate for the matter concerned, in an appropriate manner and with appropriate content. The discussions shall be conducted in such a way that it is possible for the elected representatives of the employees to meet the employer and receive a reasoned response to any statements they make. In this connection, it will be reasonable to keep the minutes of the discussion meeting.

V. Sensitive Information

1522. As a general rule, the information provided to the shop stewards are not subject to confidentiality. According to section 8-3, the employer may impose a duty of secrecy on employees' representatives and any other advisers if the needs of the enterprise dictate that specific information should not be disclosed. Therefore, the employer must impose secrecy.

1523. The employer may in special cases omit to provide information or participate in discussions if this would clearly be damaging to the enterprise at the current time.

1524. A dispute regarding secrecy may be brought before the Council of Corporate Democratization by the shop stewards or one-fifth of the employees.

VI. Sanctions in Case of Breach of the Rules Regarding Information and Consultation

1525. If the employer has made a decision without fulfilling the obligation to inform and consult, the decision will as a main rule be considered as valid. However, the Labour Inspectorate may issue orders and make such individual decisions to ensure that the enterprise is fulfilling their obligations. The breach may also be subject to criminal prosecution according to WEA section 19-1.

1526. Breach of the obligation to inform and consult may also be subject to disputes regarding unlawful dismissals and redundancies. A breach may inflect the working relationships and therefore also the working environment which may lead to other negative effects such as sickness absence, reduced effectiveness and efficiency.

VII. Other Rules Regarding Information and Consultation

1527. For the sake of the context, the WEA also has other rules regarding information and discussion, such as in connection with mass dismissals and transfer of an enterprise, establishing control measures, etc.

§11. Collectively Agreed Liaison Committees

1528. Collective agreements often stipulate further regulation, which concretes and precisely defines the statutory provisions regarding codetermination. The Basic Agreement of 2014–2017 between LO–NHO in particular, has designed a model for other collective agreements. Therefore, the rules in the agreement will be presented below. Please note that as the general rule, the rules do not only apply to enterprises which employ a larger number of employees.

I. The Principle of Real Influence

1529. The necessity and mutual consensus on the need of good and trusty relations between the enterprise and the employees is explicitly recognized in the Basic Agreement, section 9-1. On this basis, the provision states that the employees by codetermination and cooperation, with their experience and knowledge shall contribute to create the economic assumptions of the further development of the enterprise, and to and for secure and satisfying working conditions for the benefit of both the employer and the employees. According to section 9-2, the conditions must be arranged so that the individual employees, through their shop stewards or otherwise, are able to exercise genuine influence on the general efforts of the enterprise to improve efficiency, reduce production costs, improve competitiveness, exploit new technology, facilitate necessary restructuring, etc. To achieve this objective, the provision suggests that this should be done through decentralization and delegation of decision-making authorities within the organization of the enterprise.

II. Information and Consultation

1530. According to the Basic Agreement section 9-3, the management of the enterprise shall discuss with the shop stewards the ordinary operations of the enterprise concerning matters relating to the financial position of the enterprise, its production and its development, matters immediately related to the workplace and everyday operations and general wage and working conditions at the enterprise. The discussions shall be held as early as possible and at least once a month, and otherwise whenever requested by shop stewards.

1531. When it comes to discussions concerning reorganization of operations, the management of the enterprise shall as early as possible discuss with the shop stewards reorganizing of importance for the employees, and their working conditions, including important changes in production systems and methods employment matters, including plans for expansion or reduction (cf. sections 9-4 and 9-6(2)).

1532. Before making any decision on matters that concern the employees' jobs and working conditions, the enterprise shall allow shop stewards to present their views. In cases where the management of the enterprise finds that the shop stewards' comments cannot be taken into consideration, the reasons for this must be given (cf. section 9-6(1)).

1533. Furthermore, the management shall discuss company matters such as mergers, demergers, selling or closing down all or part of the business, or reorganization of the legal form of the business with the shop stewards as early as possible (cf. section 9-5).

1534. The shop stewards shall be informed about the reasons, and the legal, economical and working consequences. The management of the enterprise shall provide for a meeting to be held between shop stewards and the new owners. If the enterprise is considering whether to close down, the possibility of continued operation, including whether the employees desire to take over the business, shall be discussed with the shop stewards (cf. sections 9-5 and 9-6(2)).

1535. The parties' right and obligation to discussions are presupposing the parties' mutual will to discuss the matter, which is subject to discussion. This means that the parties have to be willing to closely discuss in full measures the further consequences of the different alternatives in such a way that all the alternatives are being illuminated as well as possible.

1536. In this connection, notice the provisions in sections 9-7 and 9-8. The provision in section 9-7 stipulates a right for the shop stewards to see the accounts of the enterprise when they so request. Moreover, the shop stewards shall be allowed to study matters, which concern the financial position of the enterprise, to such extent as the shop stewards need this information in order to safeguard the interests of the members. According to section 9-8, the employer shall provide external advisors to the shop stewards when they so request.

III. Company Committees

1537. In order to make the cooperation between the management and the employee more efficient, the provision in section 12-1 stipulates that each enterprise with at least a hundred employees, a work council shall be established consisting of representatives from the management and the employees.

1538. Works councils shall also be established in enterprises with fewer than hundred employees whenever so requested by one of the parties and the parties' central organizations (cf. section 12-1). To prevent double work and unnecessary meetings, a joint works and working environment council may be established. The main tasks of the council are, through cooperation, to work for the most efficient production possible and for the maximum well-being of all who work at the enterprise. In this connection, the tasks of the company committees are to make informative and confidential reports from the management on the financial status of the enterprise and of its standing in the industry, as well as questions that are important to the employees and their working conditions, and reports of the enterprise's activities and plans regarding the enterprise.

IV. Departmental Committees

1539. According to section 13-1, departmental councils should be established in enterprises which employ more than 200 employees and independent departments under their own management with authority to make decisions on matters concerning the department. Departmental councils may deal with the same matters as the work council, but limited to the department of the company (cf. section 13-3).

V. Information Meetings and Corporate Conferences

1540. The Basic Agreement Chapter XV states that information meetings shall be held at least once a year for the employees of an enterprise or its separate departments, at which the management gives a general briefing on the position and future prospects of the enterprise (cf. section 15-1).

1541. Company conferences may also be held where members of the works council and the departmental committees attend, in which the management presents information concerning the status of the enterprise and the tasks ahead, and the further work of the committees is discussed (cf. section 15-2).

VI. Corporation Committees

1542. The Basic Agreement Chapter XIV stipulates the provisions regarding corporation committees. In this connection, corporation means an amalgamation of legally and/or administratively independent units, which financially and in part also administratively and commercially form one unit. This may be limited companies and/or divisions forming an amalgamation (cf. section 14-1, the agreed comment).

1543. In corporations, the management makes the decisions. These decisions may affect all the enterprises included in the corporation. Therefore, it is important that the employees are able to exercise influence on the decisions, which are being made by the group of management, because a codetermination limited to the subordinated enterprises will be of limited significance. This is why the Basic Agreement stipulates rules regarding corporation committees (cf. section 14-1). The corporation shall establish a coordinating shop steward committee in groups having enterprises that use a joint collective agreement. This committee shall discuss matters with representatives for the management of the group and the enterprise.

VII. Development of the Company, New Technology and Working Studies and Control Measures

1544. Besides the provisions of the Basic Agreement, the provisions of the supplementary agreements are also important to the employees' codetermination. Supplementary Agreement I is stipulating that questions regarding the enterprise's development include the participation by the employees at the enterprise shall be central in the projects. In connection with the development measures, the organizations have established a financial support scheme. Supplementary Agreement IV concerning technological development and computerized systems, provides more precisely rules about information and training, and states how the employees' participation shall be put into practice and stipulates the shop steward's position when it comes to questions regarding the use of new technology and computerized systems. In particular, the agreement states the importance of the new technology shall not only be considered from a technical or financial point of view, but also on the basis of social considerations. The consideration shall be based on such an overall view, for instance in consequence analyses, when designing, introducing and using these systems. The agreement also contains rules regarding storage and use of personal data concerning the employees at the individual enterprise. Instructions governing the storage and use of personal data shall be prepared at each enterprise in collaboration with the shop stewards. Supplementary Agreement VI states guidelines for the use of time and motion studies, and Supplementary Agreement VII states a framework agreement on systematic job evaluation as a basis for determining differentiated wages, and how job studies and the job evaluation shall take place, and that the employees' participate in these questions. The same applies to Supplementary Agreement V regarding control measures in the enterprise.

§12. Collectively Agreed Sanctions in the Case of a Breach of the Rules Regarding Information and Discussions

1545. In the case of an occurrence of a material breach of the rules concerning information and discussions, and the parties have followed the rules of procedure, the sanctions commission may impose a fine up to NOK 300,000. Any fine imposed pertains to HF-B (the central organizations' joint measures for development of enterprises).

1546. Similar applies to shop stewards who violate the provisions regarding confidential information. In this way, the central organizations underline the importance of the Basic Agreement's rules regarding information and discussions being complied with.

§13. Co-determination in the Public Sector

1547. In government enterprises, which are organized as state corporations, the employees have a right to representations in the enterprises' decision-making bodies, which practically correspond to the provisions of the Act of Limited Companies (cf. the Act of State Corporations of 30 August 1991 No. 71 sections 20 and 33). Public enterprises established by special law, the rules regarding codetermination are depending on the provisions of this law. Agreements regarding the employees' codetermination may also be made between the employer and the employees in the public administration.

1548. To avoid conflicts between the employees' co-determination and the political elected bodies' exercise of authority, these agreements diverge on several points from the agreements in the private sector. In this manner, there is a dividing line between the decisions of political matter and other decisions.

§14. Co-determination as Employee or as a Member of a Union?

1549. The collectively agreed cooperation system is built on the employees' codetermination through their shop stewards. Thus, this system gives the organized employees the right of codetermination. Therefore, the system can better be characterized as a democracy of organizations, rather than a democracy of employees. On the other hand, the collective agreements also stipulate that the employment itself shall institute a right to influence. The collective agreements also set a proportional representation of different groups of employees, such as the composition of company committee on certain conditions in the Basic Agreement (2014) section 12-2. Other collective agreements set a minimum requirement in order to give co-determination to the organization and the union's shop stewards.

1550. The system of the right to representation in the company legislation, is based on each employees right to vote, regardless of whether the employee is unionized or not, on the condition that the terms for the right to vote are fulfilled. This is also equivalent to election of safety representative and members of the working environmental committee.

§15. The Effects of the Rules Regarding Co-determination When Not Complied With

1551. The most important guarantee in order to make sure that the rules regarding the employees' co-determination are being followed, is the thought of cooperation, which the rules are based on.

1552. If the rules are not being followed, it will result in a poor climate of cooperation, which may lead to a lower operating result. Decisions made without following the collectively agreed rules regarding codetermination, may be considered as violating the collective agreement, but do not give the employees a right to refuse to comply with the decision.

1553. Decisions regarding rationalizations and following dismissals may, if the collectively agreed regulations regarding co-determination are not being followed, become important to the evaluation whether the dismissals shall be considered as unlawful. In these situations, the vital question is whether the deficient procedures may have influenced the decision made by the company management.

Part II. Collective Labour Relations

Chapter 1. General Principles

1554. The legislation regarding collective agreements and use of industrial action includes first and foremost the LDA of 27 January 2012 No. 9 (LDA) which states the rules for collective agreements and the legal consequences of them, and regulates the entitlement to industrial action, meditation and the Labour Court. The conditions for employees in government service are regulated in the LDPS of 18 July 1958 No. 2. Central laws are also the Boycott Act of 5 December 1947 No. 1, and the WBA of 72 January 2012 No. 10 (WBA), which entitle the parties together to bring an unsolved dispute before the National Wage Board. The LDA as well as the WBA are recently revised, and the new acts of 2012 replaces the previous LDA of 5 May 1927 No. 1, as well as the WBA of 19 December 1952 No. 7. The Act of General Application of Collective Agreements (GACAA) of 4 June 1993 No. 58 is also relevant. This legislation may be described as the labour disputes legislation.

1555. Mainly the rules concerning employment disputes are built on four main principles. The right to establish and join organizations, the labour peace obligation, the principle of mandates and the access to make use of industrial action on certain terms.

1556. A collective agreement is an agreement 'between a trade union and an employer or an employer's association concerning the terms of working and wage or other working conditions' (LDA section 1 e and LDPS section 11). A collective agreement may be characterized as a framework agreement stipulating the norms for what an employment contract can contain for those conditions the collective agreement regulates, or regulates the relationship between the parties of the collective agreement. Main agreements, national collective agreements and special collective agreements are considered as collective agreements. The employee is always represented through a union while, on the employer side, the party may be either an employer or an employers association.

1557. Collective bargaining right is the right of employees, through their organizations, to demand discussions with their employers or the employers' organizations on wage and working conditions, etc. In practice, collective bargaining right is universally recognized in working life. Legally, it applies only to government service disputes, such as section 2 of the LDPS, which obliges both the state and civil servants' organizations with bargaining rights to take up negotiations on entering into a collective agreement.

1558. There is no statutory obligation beyond that of the LDPS for an employer to negotiate and possibly enter into a collective agreement with the employees' organization. On the other hand, the employees can resign from their jobs in sympathy with their organization in order to force the employer to the negotiating table, and leave their job at the end of their period of notice, which in such cases is usually fourteen days. In connection with such a labour dispute, the organization can also use blockades and boycotts against the employer's enterprise.

Chapter 2. Trade Union Freedom

§1. Freedom to Establish and to Join Trade Unions and to Perform Trade Union Activities

I. Main Principle

1559. The right to establish, to join and to perform trade union activities is fully recognized in Norwegian legislation, in (a) public as well as in (b) private law. That is also the case as regards employers' associations.

II. International, Constitutional and Legal Basis

1560. The right to establish, to join and to perform activities of a trade union or of an association of employers is, since 2014, expressed in the written constitution, cf. above paragraph 366.

1561. Norway has also ratified a number of international conventions and other international instruments recognizing the right to establish, to join and to perform trade union activities etc., i.e., the European Convention on Human Rights (ECHR) (1950) section 11 (which should be seen in connection with the Universal Declaration of Human Rights (1948) (UDHR) section 23(4)), the European Social Charter (ESC) (1961–1996) section 5, the ICESCR (1966) section 8(1), the ICCPR (1966) section 22, the Freedom of Association and Protection of the Right to Organize Convention (ILO-87) [1948], the Right to Organize and Collective Bargaining Convention (ILO-98) (1949), and the Labour Relations (Public Service) Convention (ILO-151) (1978). In this connection may also be mentioned the Collective Bargaining Convention (ILO-154) (1981), cf. also paragraphs 1558 et seq. below.

1562. Further, it is in the Norwegian Constitution stipulated since 1994, cf. paragraph 366 above, that human rights shall be respected and secured by the authorities of the state; supplementary rules on the implementation of international treaties to be stipulated by law. By the HRA (1999) section 2, it is stipulated that the ECHR (1950), the ICESCR (1966), the ICCPR (1966) – as well as the International Convention on the Rights of the Child (1989) (UNCRC) – shall have effect as Norwegian law, to the extent that the conventions are binding for Norway. Should provisions of Norwegian law not be in accordance with provisions of these international conventions, it is stipulated in the HRA section 3, that the latter shall apply (cf. also paragraph 428 above).

1563. In addition may be mentioned that Norway is party to the European Economic Agreement (EEA) (1992). In that connection is stipulated in the EEA Act (1992) section 2, in case provisions of Norwegian law should not be in accordance with provisions of the EEA agreement, that the latter shall apply.

1564. Furthermore, the WEA section 13-1(1) prohibits direct as well as indirect discrimination on the basis of membership of a trade union, as well as discrimination on the basis of enrolment or participation in a trade union (cf. section 13-2(3)). This prohibition applies to all aspects of the employment relationship, with the exception of discrimination deriving from membership of a trade union as regards wages and working conditions stipulated by collective agreements, (cf. section 13-2(4)). Discrimination that has a just cause, does not involve disproportionate intervention in relation to the persons in question, and is necessary for the performance of work or profession is, however, not to be regarded as discrimination pursuant to the Act (cf. section 13-3(1)).

1565. Thus, an employer may not set, as condition for employment, that the applicant shall be or remain unorganized. A 'yellow clause' will not be valid. However, it may be that an applicant accepts such an offer of employment, but at the same time makes it clear that the applicant will organize. In such a case, the Supreme Court held that such a condition was contrary to the WEA [1977] section 55 A, and therefore unjustified. However, as the applicant's acceptance was not in accordance with the employer's offer, no agreement had been concluded. Thus, the applicant did not recover damages for the employers breaking of an agreement. A certain compensation was, however, granted for the employers break of the provision of the Act (cf. Rt. 2001 p. 248 (*Olderdalen ambulanse*)). Today, it follows directly from the WEA (2005) section 13-9(3) that such a condition is invalid. Therefore, it may now be assumed that the reasoning of the Supreme Court can no longer be upheld.

1566. It should be observed that the prohibition against discrimination applies also to enrolment and participation in an employers' association, as well as to professional associations (cf. WEA section 13-2(3)). Further, the prohibition applies also to the employer's selection and treatment of independent contractors as well as employees hired in by the user company (cf. WEA section 13-2(2)).

1567. Provisions against discrimination for seamen are stipulated in the Ship Labour Act sections 10-1–10-9.

III. Trade Union: Term and Independence

1568. The term 'trade union' is not defined in the rules of the WEA on non-discrimination, but the *travaux préparatoires* to the Act are based on the view that the term 'collective agreement' – as defined in the LDA – should apply to the rules of the WEA. There is a close connection between the right to organize and the rules of the LDA on collective agreements, the peace obligation, labour conflicts, etc., and it follows of the definition in this Act of a collective agreement that the employees' party must be a trade union. Therefore, it may well be assumed that the concept trade union in the rules of the WEA should be understood in the same way as the term is defined in the LDA.

1569. The LDA has a very wide definition of the term 'trade union': 'any federation of employees or of employees' associations, the object of which is to promote the interests of the workers in relation to their employers' (cf. LDA section 1 c). The Act does not require that the association shall last for any particular time; the Act also covers temporary associations aiming to deal with a single matter as well as associations with a minimum of members and with no formal or stable administration. At least, that is the case as regards violations of the peace obligation according to law and collective agreements (cf. Rt. 1924 p. 525 and Rt. 1935 p. 316, and further ARD 1945-48 p. 129, ARD 1953 p. 81, and ARD 1962 p. 58). However, the term 'trade union' is probably, at least to a certain degree, modified in other relations, because the reasons to be considered will have to be differently evaluated. It is, of course, most important to counteract violations of the peace obligation. For that reason, a wide definition of the term 'trade union' should apply. As regards the conclusion of a collective agreement, the current contact with the counterpart of such agreements, perhaps also with the management of the enterprise, throughout the whole time of a collective agreement, as well as regards the termination of the collective agreement, possible renewed negotiations, prolongation etc. of such agreements, the situation to be considered is more complex. In such regards, a more strict definition of the term 'trade union' should apply, as it is then a question related to the obligations connected with the position as a party to a collective agreement with mutual rights and obligations. It should, thus, be observed that the Labour Court has expressed the view, that 'there will be a limitation, as to how loosely an association may be organized, in order to be considered as a trade union in the meaning of the Labour Disputes Act' (cf. ARD 2011 p. 206 (section 55, agreement regarding bonus for the employees)). Similarly, the Labour Court has stated that a trade union must 'have a certain structure', cf. ARD 2010 p. 296 (section 47, conclusion of a collective agreement with a 'in-house' association). The Labour Court has also observed that 'the association at the enterprise was at least very loosely organized' (cf. ARD 1985 p. 50 (at p. 60, position as party to a collective agreement rejected)).

1570. Norwegian labour law is based on the principle of trade union independence. A trade union must have an independent position as regards public authorities as well as employers and employers' association (cf. ARD 2010 p. 296, and previously ARD 1978 p. 98).

1571. Should an arrangement be concluded where the 'trade union' does not have sufficient independence in this respect, it may well be that the arrangement is not at all an agreement, and it would certainly not be a collective agreement. It is not so clear that this may also be assumed, should an employers' association not have the same independent position in regard to public authorities, because public authorities – e.g., the state – may conclude collective agreements. In such cases, the public authority may appear with competence to regulate as well as with competence to bargain and conclude an agreement, possibly through an employers' association.

1572. As regards independence with regard to public authorities, the Freedom of Association and Protection of the Right to Organize Convention (ILO-87) (1948) section 3 stipulates that workers and employers' organizations shall have the right to draw up their constitutions and rules, to elect their representatives in full freedom, to organize their administration and activities and to formulate their programmes, and that public authorities shall refrain from any interference which would restrict this right or impede the lawful exercise thereof. It may be held that this principle is also reflected in the ECHR (1950) section 11(2), which stipulates that no restrictions shall be placed on the existing of the freedom of association, other than such as are prescribed by law and are necessary in a democratic society.

1573. In this regard should be mentioned, that the activities of the trade unions in Norwegian labour law have never been under governmental supervision. This applies to the constitution of the trade unions as well as to the relationship between the trade unions and their members.

1574. Norwegian labour law is also based on the principle of trade union independence with regard to employers and employers' associations. This principle is not expressly stated in any act, but is considered to follow from basic labour law principles, as expressed in the Right to Organize and Collective Bargaining Convention (ILO-98) (1949). Section 2(1) stipulates that workers organizations, as well as employers' associations, shall enjoy adequate protection against any acts of interference by each other or each other's agents or members in regard to their establishment, functioning and administration. Further, it follows of section 2(2) that acts designed to promote the establishment of workers' organizations under the domination of employers or employers' associations constitute such interference. That is also the case as regards acts to support workers' organizations by financial or other means, with the object of placing such organizations under the control of employers or employer's associations.

1575. In practice, the question of trade union independence has been dealt with especially as regards wages and working conditions for foreign seamen. It should, however, be underlined that the question of trade union independence does usually not raise any doubt in this connection, as far as the situation in Norway is concerned, probably because this principle seems to be deeply rooted in Norwegian labour life. Therefore, it has not been considered necessary to establish any national agency in order to secure the independence of the trade unions – nor as regards trade unions for seamen on board ships registered in NIS – which is a possibility according to the Right to Organize and Collective Bargaining Convention (ILO-98) (1949) section 3.

1576. As regards foreign seamen on board Norwegian-owned ships under foreign flag, an agreement on internationalization of 1975 gave a general possibility to make exceptions from the ordinary collective agreement for foreign trades, on the condition that the country in question did have a recognized public shipping administration as well as 'bona fide' associations for shipowners as well as for seamen. The expression 'bona fide' association must have been used in order to make it clear that only associations could be taken into consideration, that were independent from public authorities as well as the counterparty on the employer or employee side.

1577. It may also be observed, as regards the NIS Act (1999), that it was considered unnecessary to stipulate expressly that a trade union should be 'bona fide' (independent), because the legal definition of the LDA (1927) section 1(3) was to be understood so that a trade union would have to be 'bona fide' in order to be covered by this definition.

1578. In dealing with the question of the lawfulness of a boycotting action against a ship registered under a flag of convenience, the CA considered the Seamen's Recruiting Office of Hong Kong to be a bona fide seamen's union, referring, *inter alia*, to the circumstances that the office was responsible for the engagement of seamen, and was supervising authority as regards wages and working conditions on board, cf.

ND 1980 p. 282 at p. 290. That argumentation does in this connection seem to miss the point.

IV. Norwegian Legislation

1579. Previously, before amending the Constitution and adopting section 101 in 2014, cf. above paragraph 366, Norway had no law on the freedom to organize, neither in general nor in working life. Certain special legislation may nevertheless be mentioned, such as the previous Petroleum Act (No. 11 of 22 March 1985), section 48, stipulating that licensee should ensure that arrangements were made so that trade union activity among their own employees and among personnel in contracting and subcontracting firms could take place 'in accordance with Norwegian practice'. This provision was thus, conditionally, based on the principle of the freedom to organize.

1580. From 1951 to 1978, 'Lex Askim' (provisional Act No. 4 of 14 December 1951 relating to the right to organize, etc., for supervisors in private enterprises) stipulated that supervisors had full freedom to be a member of the trade union of their choice, or not to be a member of any trade union (cf. also Rt. 1955 p. 276). However, after this Act was repealed, the right to organize must be considered in respect of the general rules on illegal coercion and boycott (cf. section 2 of the Boycott Act), and this applies to supervisors as well as workers. For a period (from 1927 to 1947), we had special provisions against forcing any worker or employer to join an association of workers or employers. When the Boycott Act was passed, it was found that these special rules could be abolished, because they were covered by the general rules in section 2 of the Boycott Act. Consequently, work stoppage or a threat thereof for the purpose of forcing certain workers to join a trade union, or undue pressure on an employer to get said persons to resign or to dismiss non-union employees if they do not join a union, will constitute an illegal action according to section 2 of the Boycott Act. The same applies e.g., if an enterprise is blockaded for the sole purpose of forcing its employees to join a certain union (Rt. 1959 p. 1080). On the other hand, a blockade against an employer who is hostile towards the union may be deemed justified, and the same applies to a blockade aimed at obtaining a collective agreement with the employer (NDS 1980 p. 282), unless the workers are demanding a collective agreement containing unreasonable terms (NDS 1981 p. 177).

1581. Blockade measures may be implemented to a greater extent against an employer who refuses to comply with resolutions made by the Wage Settlement Board (cf. section 5 of Act No. 58 of 4 June 1993 relating to general application of collective agreements, etc.).

1582. If an employer gives in to pressure from the enterprise's employees or from an organization and dismisses an employee, the dismissal must be considered in respect of the general fairness requirement of WEA section 15-7. It is not enough for the employer to plead that the enterprise would otherwise have suffered loss or damage. The damage must be weighed against the financial, social and human loss incurred by the dismissed, if the person was pressured into resigning. Both the dismissed and the employer can bring a damages action against the workers or the organization that exerted the pressure, and, according to WEA section 17-1(2), second paragraph, such an action may be cumulated with an action regarding unfair dismissal or notice. Such claims shall be judged according to the rules of the Boycott Act, in the same way as when an employer is pressured into serving notice to an employee for non-union-related reasons (cf. ARD 1949 p. 61, ARD 1950 p. 78, Rt. 1967 p. 1073, Rt. 1979 p. 770 and Rt. 1988 p. 198); *see also* section 5.4.4).

1583. Also the provision in LDA section 29(1), second paragraph, is significant to the freedom of association. On certain conditions, the provision gives a trade union with more than ten thousand members the right to cancel individual employment contracts entered into for a limited period of time, in order to force a collective agreement for its members at an enterprise. Normally, the union's members must constitute at least 50% of the employees for which the collective agreement is being demanded.

V. Participation in Trade Union Activities

1584. Discrimination of employees based on their participation or nonparticipation in trade union activities is a violation of the non-discrimination rules of the WEA (cf. section 13-1(1)), and is as a consequence of the right to establish, to choose and to be a member of a trade union. An exception may, however, be taken, should a sufficiently important just cause be the case (cf. WEA section 13-3(1)).

1585. To arrange and participate in trade union meetings etc. would thus normally be a fair right of a member, and an employee considering membership, as well as the right to make proposals, participate in the discussion and to vote on trade union matters. This would also be the case as regards questions concerning the working environment and safety in general and at the enterprise, as well as wages and working conditions, how different claims should be given priority before collective bargaining takes place, participation in lawful strikes or other lawful industrial action, as blockade and boycotting.

VI. The Right to Choose a Trade Union

1586. Employees are probably entitled to choose which trade union they wish to be a member of. This right is expressly stated in the ICESCR (1966) section 8(1)(a) and in the Freedom of Association and Protection of the Right to Organize Convention (ILO-87) (1948) section 2, and it must be assumed that this right be covered by the WEA's prohibition on discrimination (WEA section 13-1(1)).

1587. A modification may, however, be made, and limit the right to choose between trade unions, should a sufficiently important just cause be the case (cf. WEA section 13-3(1)). It could be a just cause that employees with leading or controlling functions should not be members of the same trade union as their subordinate employees – e.g., ARD 1994 p. 139 (*Nycomed*), which accepted such a limitation stipulated by the employer – or as regards public servants with controlling functions towards ordinary citizens.

1588. As far as taxation is concerned, it may be noted that income deductions for union dues may be claimed only by members of a trade union which is associated with a confederation of trade unions (cf. the Taxation Act section 6-20(3)), and not by members of other trade unions. It appears, however, as rather doubtful whether this provision can be said to be completely in compliance with international conventions on freedom of association (cf. *inter alia* ECHR, Articles 11 and 14). The question should presumably be answered in the negative, as such different taxation treatment of members of different trade unions directly interfere with the right of the employees to choose which trade union she or he wishes to join; as the policy and the basic views on a number of social questions may differ to quite a degree between the different trade unions, and such an interference can hardly be said to be necessary in a democratic country. This rather complex question is dealt with in detail in paragraphs 1754–1784 below: Addendum – further on the right of employees to choose trade union. It should be mentioned, however, that Oslo City Court (case No. TOSLO-2011-34224 of 9 January 2012) came to the conclusion that this provision of the Taxation Act is not in variance with the international conventions. The case was appealed to the Borgarting Court of Appeal. In the meantime, the Ministry of Finance decided that the members of the trade union in question *(Fellesforbundet for Sjöfolk)* were entitled to tax reductions for their membership fees, as from 2013. A general exemption from the Taxation Act section 6-20 was, however, not made. Thus, the CA concluded that the union no longer had a legal interest as regards the legality of the previous decisions of the Ministry, and dismissed the case (case No. LB-2012-79354 of 1 November 2013), cf. also below paragraph 1784.

VII. Right to Membership

1589. To the present day for an employee to be a union member is often a practical necessity and, as a general rule, one would assume that anyone who applies for membership in a trade union has a right to be accepted. One condition, however, must be that the applicant meet the general requirements for membership, e.g., as they pertain to the job he or she will be doing, but there are otherwise no just grounds for denying membership (cf. Rt. 1934 p. 842). The applicant's being member of an extremist political party in itself is no just grounds for rejection. It would be a different matter if his or her points of view and conduct should place a considerable burden on the organization which he or she wanted to become a member of (compare Rt. 1979 p. 770 and Rt. 1988 p. 198) (cf. also the ECTHR decision *ASLEF v. UK* (2007)).

VIII. Prohibited to Ask Whether an Applicant Is a Member of a Labour Organization

1590. According to WEA section 13-4(1), it is illegal, as mentioned above, for an employer to demand that a job applicant provide information on whether he is a member of a labour organization. The provision is aimed for employers' unilateral anti-union measures, and hence it hardly applies if the employer is bound by a collective agreement to e.g., hire only union labour. However, in practice, the free right to organize is widely established by collective agreements. We can especially note the provision in BA section 2-1, where LO and NHO mutually acknowledge the freedom of association of employers and employees. Based on previous record entries, this must apply to both the negative and the positive right to organize. Where such provisions exist, it is in violation of the collective agreement to allow the obstruction of employment or engagement because the employee or the enterprise is organized or is not organized. Hence one may organize non-union workers only through fair persuasion. In addition, the rules of law pertaining to unfair dismissal will entail liability for the employer, should he serve dismissal notice to an employee simply because he is not a union member. Such grounds for dismissal would also be in violation of the collective agreement where the enterprise is bound by said agreement. According to WEA section 15-12, such an improper dismissal would be invalid.

IX. Limitations with Regard to What an Organization Can Determine: Ultra Vires

1591. According to ordinary rules, the majority in a union will bind the minority through resolutions passed in proper organizational manner. This also applies to trade unions and employers' unions. However, there is a limit to what the minority must put up with. The issue came to a head in an action brought by three workers regarding the validity of a union resolution to take out group home insurance for its members. The Supreme Court judged the resolution to be void in a four-to-one vote (Rt. 1967 p. 1373). The majority of the judges found that, although there was nothing in the union's regulations preventing it from arranging a home-insurance scheme for its members, the scheme could not be made obligatory for those wanting to make other insurance arrangements for themselves. The resolution lay outside the union's primary aim as a trade organization and denoted 'a considerable encroachment on the individual's right of self-determination in matters of a purely personal nature'.

§2. Freedom Not to Join a Trade Union

I. The Validity of Closed Shop Clauses

1592. Today, the freedom not to join a trade union – the negative right to organize – seems to be recognized in Norwegian labour law. In recent years, this recognition has found its way through court practice as well as through legislation, in particular the non-discrimination provisions of the WEA sections 13-1 et seq. Thus, the legal situation may now be characterized, that the negative right to organize is recognized – if not in full – at least to a very large extent. Consequently, a closed shop clause can hardly be considered valid.

1593. In particular should be mentioned Rt. 2001 p. 1413 (*Norsk Folkehjelp*), where the employment agreement stipulated that the employee had an obligation to be member of at trade union associated with the Norwegian Federation of Trade Unions (*Landsorganisasjonen i Norge*). The Supreme Court considered this obligation contrary to WEA (1977) section 55 A (now WEA section 13-1), referring *inter alia* to the European Social Charter (ESC) section 5, and to the view expressed on a number of occasions by the Committee of Independent Experts, that such clauses were not in accordance with this provision of the ESC. This opinion of the Expert Committee was to be taken into consideration, and supported the view, that WEA (1977) section 55 A should be understood accordingly. In the Norwegian Supreme Court decision of 24 November 2008, the Court expressed the view that the general principle of freedom to organize in Norwegian law was authoritatively established by the decision in Rt. 2001 p. 1413.

1594. Furthermore, it follows from the *travaux préparatoires* to WEA (2005) section 13-1, that discrimination on the basis of membership of a trade union includes discrimination on the basis of non-membership of trade unions. Today, the decision of EctHR, *Sörensen and Rasmussen v. Denmark* of 11 January 2006, must also be taken into consideration (cf. below).

1595. It should also be mentioned, that a boycotting action against a shipowner, with the purpose to enforce the seamen of the ship in question to organize in a particular trade union – the International Transport Workers' Federation (ITF) – was considered unlawful by the Supreme Court as contrary to the Boycott Act section 2 (cf. Rt. 1959 p. 1080 (*San Dimitris*)). An action by the workers at an enterprise with the purpose to enforce one worker to be a member of the trade union may also constitute a breach of the collective agreement and thereby be unlawful (cf. today e.g., BA (2014) section 2-1 (*see* ARD 1950 p. 78 (*Det norske Arbeiderparti*)).

1596. Previously, the validity of closed shop clauses was in principle accepted (cf. *inter alia* ARD 1936 p. 36 (*Brastad Skibsbyggeri*)), and an arbitration court decision 26 August 1952 (*Samvirkelag*), but the question was raised as regards possible modifications to that principle. In the legal theory, the following summing up was given in 1978: 'Although closed-shop clauses must be considered valid, it must also be underlined that the clause must not be applied in such a way that it very unreasonably affects established employment relationships.'

II. Payment of Union Dues, Wholly or Partly: The 'Free Rider' Problem

1597. Since non-union employees are, by law and in practice, to a large degree treated equal to the union members – while the latter must pay, through the union dues, the costs connected to the efforts of the trade union to negotiate, survey and enforce the provisions stipulated in the collective agreement as regards wages and working conditions – the question may be raised, whether the non-union employees may be imposed an obligation to pay their part of these costs to the trade union. In other words, it is a question whether the non-union employees do have a right – protected by law – to remain 'free riders'. Today, the legal position seems to be, that the trade union may impose on the non-union employees to pay – only – the costs that are directly linked to the trade unions efforts in taking care of their interests, and – probably – not a proportionate part of the trade union costs connected to other activities of the trade union, not even of the costs connected to negotiations and other activities to establish and conclude a collective agreement:

- The EctHR decided, on 13 February 2007 in *Evaldsson v. Sweden*, that the non-union workers in the building industry should have their wages paid without reduction for the fee that the trade union – according to the collective agreement – should have for efforts connected with its measuring and calculation of the work done by the workers. The decision is based on the additional protocol of 20 March 1952, section 1 on protection of property, to the ECHR (1950), and not on ECHR section 11 on the freedom to organize. Further, the decision is based on the view, that the trade union would have the burden of proof as regards what costs were connected to the service of measuring and calculation, and what costs referred to the other activities of the trade union. Thus, the underlying principle seems to be that the trade union would have the right to claim that the measuring and calculations costs be paid by the non-union workers, because those costs were directly linked to the efforts of the trade union to take care of the interests of the non-union workers – provided, however, that the trade union could substantiate what costs were directly linked to those efforts.
- Similarly, the Supreme Court (by a majority of three, and a minority of two dissenting judges in Rt. 2008 p. 1601) held that non-union seamen were not obliged to pay to the trade union a fee equivalent to the fee that members of the trade union would pay.

Chapter 3. Trade Unions and Employers' Associations

§1. Description, Role and Structure

I. The Norwegian Confederation of Trade Union and the NHO

1598. The LO is definitely the largest and most influential employees' organization in Norway, with more than 895,000 members. LO has a strong position in the society and has set its stamp on the society's development for more than hundred years. The NHO is on the other hand the main representative organization for Norwegian employers, with more than 23,000 enterprises as members. Both organizations mainly consist of affiliated organizations representing different forms of trades, such as the Norwegian United Federation of Trade Unions (FF) and the Norwegian Transport Workers' Union (NTF). The affiliated organizations may also be consisting of under-organizations, especially representing those employees.

A. The Basic Agreement (BA)

1599. The Basic Agreement (BA) is an agreement between the NHO, including all its national and local associations and individual enterprises, and the LO including all its unions and associations (divisions). Part A of the BA (of 2014) deals with rules concerning the freedom of organization, industrial disputes, rights and duties of employers and shop stewards, lay-offs and so on. Part B represents the cooperation agreement. The object of this agreement is to strengthen and further develop cooperation between the employees, their representatives and the management in the individual enterprises and groups of companies. In addition, part C of the BA consists of eight supplementary agreements. These supplementary agreements apply in addition to the provisions of the BA and are appended to it as annexes.

II. Other Trade Unions and Associations

1600. Besides these two large confederations, many other national-based organizations and associations exists, representing the employees on the one hand and the employers on the other hand. One association among those representing the employers' interests is the Norwegian Association of Local and Regional Authorities (KS). This is the only employers' association and interest organization for municipalities, counties and local public enterprises in Norway. Another association is the Enterprise Federation of Norway (Virke), which has approximately 17,000 business members with a total of approximately 220,000 employees. The Norwegian government also is a considerable employer, and has entered into collective agreements with associations representing the civil servants. The tendency in the last couple of years is for an increase in the total number of labour union members in Norway.

1601. The Confederation of Vocational Unions (YS) is on the other hand a politically independent umbrella organization for employees, with a total of more than 227,000 members. Another employees' association is the Confederation of Unions for Professionals (*Hovedorganisasjonen for universitets-og hφyskoleutdannede*, UNIO), with more than 320,000 members, and further there is the Federation of Norwegian Professional Associations (*Akademikerne*) with about 180,000 members.

1602. The collective agreements are generally based on similar principles as the BA between LO and NHO. The same goes, to a large extent, for the content of the collective agreements regarding specific questions.

Chapter 4. Institutionalized Relations Between Employers and Employees

§1. General Introduction

1603. The employer shall ensure that the provisions laid down in and pursuant to the WEA are complied with. Especially in relation to working environment measures, in accordance with WEA section 3-1, the employer shall ensure that systematic health, environment and safety work is performed at all levels of the enterprise, in order to safeguard the employees' health, environment and safety. The employer shall in this connection make sure that the regulations concerning the establishment and election of safety representatives and working environment committees are complied with.

§2. Safety Representatives

1604. In accordance with WEA section 6-1, there shall be elected safety representatives at all enterprises subject to the act. The parties may agree in writing upon a different arrangement when the enterprise consists of less than ten employees. Such enterprises may also agree on not having a safety representative. The number of safety representatives at the individual enterprise, shall be decided in accordance with the size, the nature of the work and working conditions in general. A senior safety representative shall be elected at enterprises with more than one safety representative.

1605. The purpose of the system of safety representatives is that they safeguard the interests of employees in matters relating to the working environment, and especially in relation to making sure that the employees are not exposed to hazards from machines, technical installations, chemical substances and work processes (cf. WEA section 6-2(1)). The safety representatives shall be consulted during the planning and implementation of measures of significance for the working environment within the representatives' safety area, including establishment, exercise and maintenance of the enterprise's systematic health, environment and safety work (cf. WEA section 6-2(4)). The safety representatives shall be informed of all occupational diseases, occupational accidents and near accidents in his or her area, of reports and measurements relating to occupational health and of any faults or defects detected (cf. WEA section 6-2(5)). The most influential power the safety representative has in relation to the enterprise is the power to halt the work, if he considers that the life or health of employees is in immediate danger and such danger cannot be averted by other means. The work will be halted until the Labour Inspectorate has decided whether work may be continued (cf. WEA section 6-3(1)).

§3. Working Environment Committees

1606. Enterprises which regularly employ at least fifty employees shall have a working environment committee on which the employer, the employees and the safety and health personnel are represented (cf. WEA section 7-1(1)). The employer and the employees shall have an equal number of representatives on the committee. Representatives of the employer and of the employees shall be elected alternately as chairman of the committee. The working environment committee shall make efforts to establish a fully satisfactory working environment in the enterprise. The committee shall participate in planning safety and environmental work and shall follow up developments closely in questions relating to the safety, health and welfare of the employees (cf. WEA section 7-7(1)). If the working environment committee considers it necessary in order to protect the life or health of employees, it may decide that the employer shall implement concrete measures to improve the working environment within the framework of the provisions laid down in or pursuant to the WEA (cf. WEA section 7-2(5)).

§4. Rules Concerning Information and Consultation

1607. According to the WEA Chapters 8, 15 and 16 there are certain obligations regarding the employer's duty to inform and consult with the employees' elected representatives in given situations.

I. Obligation Regarding Information and Consultation According to WEA Chapter 8

1608. According to WEA section 8-1(1), the employer shall provide information concerning issues of importance for the employees' working conditions and discuss such issues with the employees elected representative, when the enterprise is employing at least fifty employees.

II. Information and Consultation in Connection with Collective Redundancies

1609. According to WEA section 15-2, an employer who is contemplating collective redundancies shall at the earliest opportunity enter into consultations with the employees' elected representatives with a view to reaching an agreement to avoid collective redundancies or to reduce the number of persons redundant. If redundancies cannot be avoided, efforts shall be made to mitigate their adverse effects. The consultations shall cover possible social welfare measures aimed, *inter alia*, at providing support for redeploying or retraining workers made redundant.

1610. The employer is obliged to give the employees' elected representatives all relevant information, including written notice concerning the grounds for any redundancies, the number of employees who may be made redundant and so on (cf.

WEA section 15-2(3)). The purpose of these obligations is to make sure that the employer and the employees' elected representatives actually discuss the need of redundancies and the possibility to avoid such redundancies. This section also obliges the employer to inform the Norwegian Labour and Welfare Administration before redundancies are effected.

III. Information and Consultation in the Event of Transfer of Ownership of Enterprises

1611. The former and new employers are obliged, as early as possible, to provide information concerning the transfer and discuss it with the employees' elected representatives (cf. WEA section 16-5(1)). They shall also as early as possible inform the affected employees concerning the transfer (cf. WEA section 16-6).

IV. Information, Cooperation and Co-determination Based on Collective Agreements

1612. According to the BA between LO and NHO part A Chapter IX, the object of the rules related to information, cooperation and codetermination is based on the need for good and trusting relations between the employees, their shop stewards and the enterprise, both in individual enterprises and in groups of companies. Among the many obligations given in this regard can be mentioned the obligation of the enterprise to discuss with the shop stewards, before adopting any decision on matters that concern the employee's jobs and working conditions (cf. BA part A, Chapter IX section 9-6).

Chapter 5. Collective Agreements

§1. The Legal Character of Collective Agreements

1613. To be regarded as a collective agreement, the agreement must constitute the terms for working and wage or other working conditions. This is a wide definition, which relates to all that a union and an employer association can dispute about. Another requirement is that the agreement is regarding an indefinite group of employees and not only a definite group of employees. In that way, the agreement has got a normative character by stipulating fixed rules for the employment contracts. If the agreement is only limited to define or change the content of the specific employment contracts, it will not be considered as a collective agreement. However, it can still be a collective agreement even if the agreement is only regarding the relationship between the parties and not wage or other working conditions. This includes agreements, which refer to other collective agreements. On the other hand, it is not considered as a collective agreement if the employer after negotiations with the shop stewards determines wage or other working conditions. Neither company regulations, instructions etc. which are stated according to agreements between the shop stewards and the employer, are considered as collective agreements.

1614. An agreement that neither establishes rights or obligations between the parties will not be characterized as a collective agreement. In addition to the requirement of written form, the question whether the parties have agreed to a collective agreement must be judged according to general contractual law. A collective agreement might also be invalid according to these rules or mandatory legislation.

1615. To make a collective agreement, the representatives need to have the parties authority before entering the agreement or else the agreement will be considered as invalid.

§2. The Requirement of Written Form

1616. To be considered as a collective agreement, the agreement must be in written form. If it is not, the agreement would not have the effect as a collective agreement. An agreement which is entered by oral consent, is however, not invalid, if it can be proved that this agreement is agreed between the parties.

1617. By written form, it means that the agreement is written down and signed by the parties' representatives.

1618. The reason for the requirement of written form is the general requirement of clarity. Still, it is considered as a collective agreement if a union has entered it by passivity. As long as it can be proved what the parties have agreed on, the agreement must be assumed as valid. In this connection, a section in the collective agreement, which during a period of time is not followed by the parties, may be considered as it has lost its content.

§3. Duration and Notice of Termination

1619. According to the LDA section 5(1), a collective agreement will last for three years, counted from the day it was signed unless the parties have otherwise agreed. In practice, the duration is usually two years. If the parties have stipulated that the agreement shall remain in force 'until further notice', the general rule in section 5(1) will not apply.

1620. If none of the parties has given notice of termination before expiration of three-year period of time, the duration of the collective agreement is automatically extended for one year LDA 5(3).

1621. If the agreement does not stipulate the time of notice, the general rule is that three months' notice is required. The notice must be in writing (cf. LDA section 5(2)); an oral notice is not valid.

A collective agreement may not be concluded for a specific period only; thus, even in such cases, the collective agreement will have to be terminated by written notice of termination. However, a temporary collective agreement may be concluded for the time, until a final collective agreement is concluded.

A collective agreement stating that it will last until further notice does not state the time of notice required. In such cases, the general three months' time of notice will apply.

§4. The Parties

1622. On the employee's side, it is required that the party is a trade union. On the employer side, the party may be an individual employer or a union of employers (cf. paragraph 1413 above).

1623. As regards the term union, reference is made to paragraph 1424 above. An organization including employers, self-employed individuals as well as employees, may sometime conclude an agreement between these different categories of members. Such an agreement will be a collective agreement only when the organization is organized in such a way, that the different categories belong to sub-organizations, with sufficient independence as regards wages and working conditions, that the requirements of a trade union are met.

1624. An organization must have the right to act with binding effect on behalf of the members. Otherwise, no collective agreement is concluded.

1625. A collective agreement is binding from the time the employer has become a member of the association. If the employer is still bound by another collective agreement, this agreement will be binding until properly terminated. An employer or employee, who resigns from the organization, will still be bound by the agreement until the agreement expires (cf. LDA section 7).

1626. A judicial reorganization of the enterprise, which includes only a formal change, e.g., fission or change of the company form, will have no influence on the right and duties according to the collective agreement by which the employer is bound. Should the enterprise have been definitely closed and later be reopened with a new employer the required identity may not be intact, in which case the new employer will not be bound by the collective agreement.

1627. The main rule concerning transfer of an enterprise is that the new employer will be bound by the collective agreement, which the former employer was bound by. The new employer may, however, within three weeks after the time of transfer in written form declare that he or she does not want to be bound by agreement (cf. WEA section 16-2(2)). This position however, departs from the general principle of the parties' equal position as the trade union does not have the same right. Exceeding of the time limit will have the effect that the new employer is bound by the collective agreement.

§5. The Labour Peace Obligation

I. Legal Disputes

1628. The LDA section 8 and LDPS section 20 prohibit the parties from attempting to settle 'legal disputes' with industrial action. 'Legal disputes' means disputes concerning 'the validity, interpretation or essence of a collective agreement or demands based on a collective agreement'. Such disputes shall be solved by proceedings and not by use of force. Unless the parties have agreed to solve the dispute by arbitration, disputes shall be settled by the Labour Court.

1629. As a main rule, there are no exceptions from the peace obligation as regards legal disputes, probably not even as regards abuse (cf. Rt.1977.902), but an exception may be made as regards working tasks involving health risk (cf. ARD 1961 p. 90 and ARD 1972 p. 89).

1630. The fairness and legality of a dismissal is also a legal issue. Hence taking or threatening to take, industrial action in order to solve such a dispute is illegal. In ARD 1936 p. 49, a dismissal of a shop steward was judged unfair and the enterprise ordered to withdraw the dismissal. As a result of the dismissal, the employees went on strike. The strike was in violation of the labour peace obligation, and both the trade union and the striking employees were ordered to pay damages to the company.

II. Economic and Other Disputes

1631. The labour peace obligation is also regarding economical disputes, i.e., disputes relating to what should apply, e.g., the size of the wage. The parties must respect whatever they agreed to in the collective agreement, and they have no right to force changes with industrial action. Only when negotiating a new agreement, the parties have a right to resort to strikes and lock-outs.

1632. The statutory provision in LDA section 8(1) must be interpreted in connection with the definition of strike, lock-out and dismissal in section 1, f and g. The definition of strike is narrower than what follows from the common language.

Only strike with the purpose of forcing the parties to reach a solution to the dispute is included in section 8(1).

1633. Working stoppage exists when the employees shut down their work, whether it happens immediately or after expiration of the employment agreement's period of notice, whether the dismissal is collective or individual, and whether the dismissals is given at the same time or the employees at the same time stop working. Both full and partial stop are encompassed by the term.

1634. Conditions that are not regulated by the collective agreement are not encompassed by the labour peace obligation. Thus the labour peace obligation is – to this extent – relative.

III. Political Strike, Etc.

1635. Consequently, the labour peace obligation does not pose an obstacle to a political strike. Such strike, however, must be brief and notified in advance. The notification shall include both the reason for the action and its duration. Because long-lasting political strikes may imply larger negative consequences, the consequences must be considered regarding the duration. In addition, the aim of the action must be neither to change the terms of the collective agreement e.g., as regards wages and working conditions nor to intervene in an ongoing or imminent wage settlement.

IV. Sympathy Actions

1636. The labour peace obligation is no impediment to actions supporting another industrial action (sympathy strike), provided that the sympathy action does not aim to alter the collective agreement between the parties involved in the sympathy action. Further, it is not required that the sympathy action will have a possibility to influence on the ongoing main conflict, in favour of one of the parties in that dispute, nor that the sympathy action may be considered reasonable. The sympathy action may be larger – more extensive – than the main conflict, and it is not required that the sympathy strike must be of a short duration. Thus, the sympathy strike may last as long as the main conflict. It is, however, required that the main conflict is legal, i.e., according to the provisions of the LDA or the LDPA; as regards a main conflict in another country, it is probably required that the main conflict fulfil the requirements of international law *inter alia* as stipulated in ILO Conventions Nos 87 and 98.

§6. The Principle of Mandatory Collective Agreements

1637. The normative effect of the collective agreement is stated in LDA section 6 and LDPS section 13. If the employment contract contains a regulation, which is not in accordance with the collective agreement binding upon the employer as well as employee, the agreed regulation will be invalid. In these cases, the collective agreement will automatically replace the regulation in the employment contract.

1638. The use of terms and conditions different from what is stated in the collective agreement towards unorganized employees, might be assumed as a breach of the collective agreement because the collective agreement usually shall be interpreted to also include unorganized employees, unless otherwise can be proved. As a general rule, it must be assumed that the other party in the agreement (the union) by entering the collective agreement, wanted to secure that the employer is not giving the unorganized employees different conditions according to the collective agreement, than the organized employees conditions.

§7. The Labour Court

1639. To settle disputes regarding the validity of the collective agreement, interpretation and demands on the basis of the collective agreement, the Labour Court is instituted (LDA section 33(2); cf. also section 1(i)). The Labour Court shall also settle disputes on the subject of violation of the labour peace obligation and the liability for breaches of the collective agreement and illegal work stoppage (LDA section 33(2), cf. also section 8(2) and section 9). However, disputes arising from the individual employment contract, including dismissals, shall be settled by the ordinary courts.

1640. Judgments by the Labour Court are final (LDA section 58(5)). As a general rule, the right to legal action is given the parent union or employers association which entered the collective agreement (section 35(1)). According to section 45(4), negotiations must have been tried between the parties before the dispute is brought before the Labour Court.

§8. The 'Double Track' Rules of Procedure

1641. The rules of procedure is based on the main rule that the settlement of disputes concerning individual employment contracts belongs to the ordinary courts – the district courts – and may be appealed to the Courts of Appeal, and possibly to the Supreme Court. The WEA provides certain special procedure regulations for disputes 'concerning rights or obligations pursuant to this Act' (cf. section 17-1(1)), for instance with regard to disputes on whether an employment relationship exists of a collective agreement, and claims based on collective agreements, belong exclusively to a separate court of justice, the Labour Court of Norway (cf. section 33 of the LDA). The same applies to disputes concerning breaches of the peace obligation, and liability for compensation due to breach of collective agreements and illegal cessation of work. The ARD are final and cannot be appealed (cf. section 58(5) of the LDA), unless the Labour Court should have exceeded its jurisdiction (cf. Rt. 2012 p. 1702). The access to take legal action pursuant to the regulations of the Act is reserved for the organizations as parties to a collective agreement (cf. section 35(1) of the LDA).

1642. Even if an individual employment contract refers to a collective agreement or to collectively agreed regulations, lawsuits are to be handled by the ordinary courts if the lawsuit concerns the employee's individual claims or more over his or her legal position, and legal action is taken by the employee or the employer. In such cases, the basis for the legal action is the individual employment contract and the legal position pursuant to this agreement, and the regulations of the collective agreement supplement the content of the employment contract. The parties to the collective agreement, usually the organizations, may however commence legal proceedings before the Labour Court, in order to obtain a decision regarding how the provisions of the collective agreement are to be interpreted. In this connection, they may include claims on the basis of an individual employment contract, if such a claim can be immediately decided upon such a decision (cf. section 34(1) of the LDA).

§9. Arbitration

1643. The parties in the collective agreement may agree to settle disputes by private arbitration (cf. LDA section 33(4)).

§10. General Application of Collective Agreements

1644. According to the act concerning General Application of Collective Agreements of 4 June 1993 No. 58, the Collective Agreement Board may decide that the collective agreement shall apply to all employments within an area or a branch.

1645. After the establishment of the EEA, which allows Norway (as one of the EFTA states) to participate in the Internal Market and constitutes a free labour market, it has become even more important to ensure that both Norwegian employees and foreign employees are treated equally in respect of wage and working conditions. The Act of 4 June 1993 No. 58 relating to general application of wage agreements, etc., makes it no longer possible for the parties of labour life to, completely on their own, find the solution to the questions that may arise, which are subject to the scope of this act.

1646. According to section 1-1, the purpose of the Act is to ensure for foreign employees terms of wages and employment, which are equivalent to those of Norwegian employees. This is in order to prevent employees from performing work on terms which, viewed as a whole, are demonstrably inferior to what is stipulated in nationwide collective agreements that apply to the trade or industry concerned or what is otherwise normal for the place and occupation concerned.

1647. Section 2 of the Act stipulates that the King may appoint a Board on Extended Application of Collective Agreements. The Board shall have a chairperson and four other permanent members. The members, with personal deputies, are appointed for three years. One of the members shall represent the interests of the employees and one shall represent the interests of the employers. According to section 3, the Board may decide that a nationwide collective agreement shall apply in full or in part to all employees carrying out work of the kind specified in the agreement within an industry or part of an industry, with the limitations provided by or pursuant to section 1-7 of the WEA. A decision concerning general application pursuant to the first paragraph may only apply to those parts of the collective agreement that regulate the terms of wages and employment of the individual employees. In special cases, the Board may stipulate other terms of wages and employment than those following from the collective agreement (cf. section 3(2)). The terms of wages and employment laid down in a decision of the Board shall apply as invariable minimum terms of the employment relationship between an employee covered by the decision and his or her employer (cf. section 3(5)).

1648. According to section 5, an organization as referred to in section 3 may initiate boycott aimed at forcing an employer to fulfil his or her obligations according to decisions made pursuant to the same section, regardless of the limitations following from the second and third alternatives given in section 2(c) of the Boycott Act.

1649. The Norwegian Labour Inspectorate supervises compliance with terms of wages and employment following from decisions concerning general application pursuant to section 3. The Norwegian Labour Inspectorate also supervises compliance with the obligations of main contractors laid down pursuant to section 9 (cf. section 8). In addition, and according to section 10, an employer who will fully or negligently fails to comply with a decision made by the Board on Extended Application of Collective Agreements is liable to fines. The same applies to anyone managing the enterprise on behalf of the employer.

1650. Decisions made by the Board on Extended Application of Collective Agreements pursuant to this act mainly concern the construction sector. Relevant in this connection is the different regulations pursuant to the General Application Act. Here can be mentioned:

1651. -The regulation regarding general application of collective agreements concerning construction sites generally in Norway (of 27 November 2014 No. 1482, which replaces the former regulations of 24 April 2013 No. 426 and of 20 December 2010 No. 1763),

1652. - The regulation regarding partly general application of the collective agreement concerning the IA within the shipping and shipyard industry (of 27. November 2014 No. 1829, which replaces the regulation of 22 March 2013 No. 381, and of 20 December 2010 No. 1764),

1653. -The regulation regarding general application of the collective agreement concerning cleaning companies (of 27 November 2014 No. 1483, which replaces the former regulation of 23 May 2013 No. 530, and of 21 June 2011 No. 673),

1654. - The regulation regarding general application of the collective agreement concerning the agricultural and horticultural industry (of 27 November 2014 No. 1481, which replaces the former regulation of 27 November 2012 No. 1196, and of 20 September 2010 No. 1739),

1655. - The regulation regarding general application of the collective agreement concerning fishing industry companies (of 27 November 2014 No. 1805),

1656. - The regulation regarding partly general application of the National Agreement for electricians of 3 February 2015 No. 815,

1657. - The regulation regarding general application of collective agreements concerning freight transport by road of 11 May 2015 No. 554, and

1658. - The regulation regarding general application of collective agreements concerning carriage of passengers by road of 27 May 2015 No. 815.

1659. The EFTA Court has, on 23 January 2012 (E-2/11), in an advisory opinion regarding the Regulation on partly general application of the collective agreement concerning the Engineering IA within the shipping and shipyard industry (2008), held that to what extent a collective agreement would apply, before being given general application by the Board on Extended Application of Collective Agreements, was of no importance for the questions raised (sections 105–106), that the Regulation had to be considered on the basis of the EEA Agreement section 36 and the general principles of EEA law (sections 32 et seq.); that the EU Directive No. 96/71 EF section 3 No. 1 did allow an EEA state to stipulate the length of working hours, as well as the length of ordinary working hours, adjusted to the different industries and that remuneration for overtime work had to be limited to the minimum wages (sections 54–59); that additional remuneration for overnights outside the residence of the worker, stipulated per hour worked, had to be kept within the frames of minimum wages, but could also have as consequence extra expenses for foreign employers (sections 70–87); and that refunding of expenses for journeys on specific occasions could hardly be considered as a part of the wages, nor necessary because of public order, etc. (sections 97–101).

1660. In the following decision of 5 March 2013, Rt. 2013 p. 258 (*STX Norway Offshare*), the Supreme Court held that the Regulations were within the framework of the directive.

Chapter 6. Collective Bargaining, Strikes, Lock-Out and Other Legal Forms of Industrial Action

§1. Collective Bargaining: Introduction

1661. Employees, through their trade unions, have a right to demand collective bargaining on wage and working conditions etc. with their employers or the employers' associations, and vice versa (cf. LDA section 3). Should the other party not meet to such negotiations, or should the negotiations not be ended by the conclusion of a collective agreement, strike or lockout may be carried into effect, provided that the conditions of LDA section 18 and section 25 are fulfilled, *see also* 1508 below. In practice, the right to collective bargaining is usually fully recognized within Norwegian working life.

1662. The right to collective bargaining is statutory when it comes to public service disputes, and at the request of the other party, the State and the Public Service trade unions are mutually bound to engage in bargaining for concluding collective agreements (cf. section 2 of the LDPS). Inappropriate passivity with regard to initiating, pursuing or closing collective bargaining, will be in breach of the LDPS (cf. ARD 1986 p. 61). Furthermore, if the right to collective bargaining is stated in a collective agreement, such passivity may be in breach of the collective bargaining agreement (cf. ARD 1986 p. 61 and ARD 1988 p. 19).

1663. In practice, collective bargaining does not always lead to an agreement. In such case, industrial action may be initiated through the use of strike, lock-out, go-slow, a ban on certain work tasks, a ban on working overtime etc. As a starting point, strike and lockout are legal forms of industrial action. However, even smaller industrial conflicts can cause severe detriment to society, hence the reason why the right to strike, lockout and other forms of industrial action has been subject to considerable restrictions in particular that possible previous collective agreements have expired, that due notice of termination has been given as regards the employment agreements, that the State Mediator has been notified, and that mediation has taken place (cf. the LDA sections 18 and 25).

I. Collective Bargaining and the Collective Agreements System: A Survey

A. General Background

1664. Collective bargaining means – in Norwegian labour law as well as defined in ILO Convention No. 154 (1981) Article 2 – that employers and employees, on a collective basis, negotiate in order to determine wages, working conditions and terms of employment. The regulation of relations between employers and employees may also take place, as well as the regulation of relations between employers or their organizations and an employees' organization or employees organizations. The parties of such negotiations may on the employer side be a single employer, or an employers' association, or a confederation of employers' association. On the employee side, it is required that the party is a trade union or a confederation of trade unions (cf. LDA section 1 e).

B. Legislation Bears the Imprint of a Framework Legislation

1665. The LDA, and the rest of the legislation relating to labour disputes, are based on the basic point of departure which stipulates that the organizations within the labour life – the employers' and the employees' organizations – shall by themselves agree on the terms of wages and working conditions that shall apply, through negotiations and entering into agreements. This point of departure also applies to the period of time, for which the terms of wages and working conditions shall apply between the parties. It also applies to what questions the parties find most suitable to regulate in this way. Based on this outline, the legislation relating to labour disputes is limited, in the sense that it stipulates the outer legislative frame regarding the access to make use of legislative means such as strike, lockout and other legal forms of industrial action with the object of enforcing an agreement regarding terms of wages and other working conditions. In other words, the legislation bears an imprint of being framework legislation.

1666. On this background, the organizations within the working life are mainly responsible for making sure that this system works properly in practice.

1667. The fact that the legislation bears an imprint of being a framework legislation is especially apparent as the State Mediator only appears at a very late stage of the process – after establishing that the negotiations between the parties do not lead to a solution. The non-statutory arrangements concerning the Norwegian Technical Calculation Committee (TBU) and the Contact Committee on Incomes Policy give an impression of a more offensive attitude from the government side.

C. Legislation Related to Labour Disputes: A Survey

1668. The way the legislation relating to labour disputes is built up, one may say that the use of industrial strife is accepted, but only when the given terms of such use are complied with. Mainly, the former collective agreement has to be expired and the individual contracts of employment need to have been given notice. In addition, the parties need to have tried to negotiate, and public mediation must also have taken place before an industrial strife commences. The LDA and the LDPS therefore has a number of provisions regarding the public institution of mediation – the State Mediator.

1669. In addition, the LDA is based on the basic principle implying that industrial strife shall not be used to resolve legal disputes – e.g., how to interpret a collective agreement, questions concerning a notice of dismissal or whether another measure taken by the employer is legitimate – and has a number of provisions regarding the court of justice – the Labour Court – related to, among other things, procedural provisions and provisions regarding the competence of the court.

1670. In other words, the legislation is based – pre-supposedly – on the fact that it should be possible to enter into collective agreements, and on the fact that it should be possible to negotiate on the terms and conditions subject to such agreements. The legislation also is based on the fact that the organizations – especially on the employee side – may play a rather significant role. On the other hand, the legislation only to some extent regulates questions concerning when and how these negotiations shall take place. A more detailed regulation on these matters may therefore be done by the parties – which in practice implies the employer's and the employee's associations and organizations – which to a large extent regulate these matters through collective agreements. Additionally, the associations' and organizations' very own by-laws will be of great significance.

1671. It will therefore be appropriate to begin with a presentation on how the system of collective agreements is built up, before the system of negotiation is presented in detail.

1672. A collective agreement may very well be entered into with only one employer as a party on the employer side and such agreements exists to a certain extent, but the questions that especially arise in connection to these agreements are not dealt with in this context. A practical example of a collective agreement that is entered into with only one employer is an agreement which implies that the employer has committed himself to comply with a different and specified collective agreement. On the employee side, there always has to be a trade organization, as a party to the collective agreement.

II. The System of Collective Agreements: A Survey

A. Basic Agreements, Nationwide Agreements and Local Agreements

1673. The system of collective agreements is in practice and to a large extent dominated by a pattern based on collective agreements in three levels – basic agreements, nationwide agreements and local agreements concerning the individual enterprise.

1674. A basic agreement is normally entered into between the main associations and organizations representing the employers' and the employees' interests – e.g., the BA entered into between NHO and LO.

1675. Nationwide agreements are normally entered into within a trade, and normally between the employers' and employees' associations and organizations at that specific level of trade – e.g., the IA entered into between the Federation of Norwegian Industries and the Norwegian United Federation of trade Unions can be mentioned.

1676. Local agreements are normally entered into within the individual enterprise, with the employer and the local trade union as parties.

1677. In addition to these collective agreements, there may also – on all three levels – be established special agreements and supplementary agreements between the parties and such agreements are entered into, to quite a large extent. It will be up to the parties to consider whether a question is most suited for regulation in a special agreement or a supplementary agreement. This question is more a question of negotiation and appropriateness, and is not considered as a legal matter.

1678. It is not uncommon that there, in practice, arises questions whether such special agreements and supplementary agreements shall be interpreted in the way that they only define precisely the already existing agreement. Or whether they shall be considered to come in addition to the already existing agreement, and shall therefore not be understood as if it has to be held within the frame of the terms and conditions stipulated in the already existing agreement. This question of interpretation has to be solved with especially consideration regarding the intention of the parties with the special agreement or the supplementary agreement.

B. The Relation Between the Basic Agreements, Nationwide Agreements and Local Agreements

1679. This pattern of collective agreements reflects the hierarchical organizational system, and the point of departure is also that collective agreements on a lower level need to be held within the frame of what can be established within a collective agreement on a higher level.

1680. To the extent that the nationwide agreement does not give access to deviation, a local agreement within a local enterprise – or a local special agreement or supplementary agreement – which deviates from the nationwide agreement, will not be valid, and the nationwide agreement is the agreement which applies. The same thesis applies if there, on the local level, is practised an interpretation of the local agreement that exceeds the frames to which the nationwide agreement stipulates for what can be agreed on locally.

1681. Regarding the basic agreements, the answer to this question is not always equally obvious. To the extent that the basic agreement stipulates that it applies as a part of a nationwide agreement – e.g., as part I – it may be a point of departure that the negotiations regarding the nationwide agreement concerns this agreement as a whole. If this point of departure is used as a basis, it would imply that the nationwide agreement may stipulate that the provisions pursuant to the basic agreement will be applicable on any given specification and exception; no matter what is stated in the basic agreement, e.g., concerning the invariability.

1682. However, the parties to the basic agreement are the main organizations on both the employer side and on the employee side. Both of these main organizations may have members who are organized on trade level – on respectively the employer side and the employee side – who in turn will negotiate on a nationwide agreement. Regularly, the main organizations will presuppose that the basic agreement shall apply as a part of the nationwide agreement. This presupposition may have materialized in the basic agreement, and will otherwise regularly be known by both of the organizations, which shall participate in the negotiation regarding the nationwide agreement. On the basis of both the legal system of collective agreements and on an organizational basis, it seems that both the organizations, which shall participate in the negotiations regarding the nationwide agreement, will be under the obligation of using the basic agreement as a basis – as a whole, and without alterations – resulting in the basic agreement being included as a part of the nationwide agreement: in practice most commonly as part I.

1683. In practice, the questions regulated in the basic agreements are in most cases thematically different from the questions regulated in a nationwide agreement. This circumstance simplifies the negotiations regarding the nationwide agreement, because such questions are not particularly of current interest when it comes to the themes that shall be negotiated on regarding the nationwide agreement. The legal point of departure contributes to a simplification of the negotiations regarding the nationwide agreement.

1684. It may occur that between the employers' associations and the employees' organizations – which are not attached to the organizations that are parties to the basic agreement – there is obtained an agreement on applying provisions pursuant to the basic agreement within their own collective agreement relationship, but with some modifications. In such a situation, the negotiating organizations will not be legally or organizationally obliged to make use of the basic agreement. They are free to give the basic agreement application, to the extent that this is suitable for the purpose, and with the alterations that seems appropriate. However, it is not sure that all the provisions pursuant to the basic agreement can be applied at all, due to the fact that the provisions pursuant to the basic agreement may be presupposing a membership in a main organization – either directly or indirectly, through an organization attached to the main organization.

III. The Technical Calculation Committee and the Coordinating Committee

1685. There are major social interests involved in the major wage settlements. After all, these settlements effect not only the organizations in question and their members. Hence the state has more or less involved itself in the wage settlements. Furthermore, the state has major employer interests to safeguard. Experience has shown that wage developments in the private sector of working life have an impact on corresponding developments in the public sector. State involvement was particularly strong during the implementation of 'comprehensive wage settlements'. The state and the main organizations then agreed that the nominal wage increase should be held within certain limits in return for tax reliefs or reduced social security contributions. To facilitate the parties' economic calculations, the Technical Calculation Committee was established, while the coordinating efforts resulted in the establishment of the Coordinating Committee. These bodies have considerable significance also where the wage settlement takes place primarily through negotiations between the main organizations or between their affiliated organizations ('decentralized settlements'); also cf. paragraph 383 above.

1686. The Norwegian Technical Calculation Committee (TBU) shall in connection to wage settlements present the most suitable numerical background-material and present it in such a manner that disagreement between the parties, regarding economic conditions, may – if possible – be avoided. The Technical Calculation Committee may be instructed to elucidate the numerical background-material for special political questions that may arise, in connection to wages. The committee shall, in addition, present reports that summarize the wage settlements. These reports are submitted to the Ministry of Labour.

IV. Other Wage Arbitration Bodies: Pendulum Arbitration

1687. The settlement of disputes may also be ordered in other ways. As an example can be mentioned that the King by the Act of 21 June 1966 No. 55 was given the authority to decide that a dispute should either be solved by settlement by a special wage arbitration board appointed by the king or by settlement by the National Wages Board in accordance with the rules of the Wages Board Act (1952, now 2012).

1688. Further, the Basic Collective Agreement for the Municipal Sector (HTA) (2010–2012) opens the door to certain local bargaining issues being solved by pendulum arbitration, if the parties cannot reach an agreement (cf. HTA Part A section 4.A.2 and Chapter 5 section 5.2). According to Part A section 6-2 of the Basic Agreement for the Municipal Sector (2010–2012), the employer and the local bodies of the trade unions can settle agreements where pendulum arbitration is the local arbitration model. In such case, the Arbitration Board can only accept or reject in whole the claims submitted by the employer's or the employee's side.

1689. At local bargaining, sometimes a set-up is used where the employer's last offer shall apply if the parties cannot reach an agreement (e.g., cf. Chapter 4A section 4.A.3 of the HTA (2012–2014) and subsection 2.3.3(4) and 2.3.4 No. 2 of the Basic Collective Agreement for the Civil Service (2012–2014)).

V. Wage Freeze and Wage Adjustment

1690. Wage freeze or wage adjustment can also be ordered through legislation. Among such provisions can be mentioned the Provisional Ordinance on Wage Freeze of 15 September 1978 (cf. the subsequent Act No. 73 of 17 November 1978 relating to wage freezes, and the provisional Act No. 70 of 21 December 1979 relating to wage adjustment (expiring 1 April 1982). The same applies to the period 1988–1990 (cf. the provisional Act No. 10 of 7 March 1988 relating to income and profit freeze, replaced by the provisional Act No. 16 of 22 April 1988 relating to income and profit adjustment, succeeded by the provisional Act No. 12 of 31 March 1989 relating to adjustment of income and profits (expiring 1 April 1990)). Violating these provisions was punishable (e.g., cf. Rt. 1990 p. 1300, in which the employee was nevertheless acquitted of receiving a wage increase in accordance with a local agreement on seniority promotion because he had reason to believe that the company had applied the law correctly).

§2. Debarment from the Right to Strike

1691. In this context, it should be mentioned that certain groups of civil servants are debarred from the right to strike. This applies to senior civil servants who – even though covered by the LDPS – do not have the right to resort to stoppage of work. A senior civil servant, who wishes to resign, must apply to the King for resignation. Furthermore, it may be assumed that servants of the Norwegian armed forces are debarred from the right to strike. The same assumption applies to employees of the Norwegian Parliament, as far as regards work tasks, which – because of their nature – are essential to prevent the activities of the Norwegian government from being paralysed or gravely affected. For these groups of employees, the state cannot use lock-out (cf. section 22 No. 5 of the LDPS).

1692. According to the previous Police Act of 1936 section 20, police officers were not given the right to strike. This prohibition was however abolished in 1995 when the new Police Act came into force.

§3. Strike and Lock-Out Notice

1693. In order to implement the use of industrial action, the collective agreement must be validly terminated and the term of notice must be expired. In addition, the individual employment contracts must be terminated.

1694. Thus, the LDA implies that the use of strike or lock-out must be initiated by a termination of the employment contracts within the term of notice decided by the contracts or by law (cf. Rt. 1934 p. 209). A notice must be in writing (cf. LDA section 15(1)), and may be given by the individual employees or by the employer, by a trade union or an employer's association by authorization from the individual employees or employers (cf. LDA section 15(2)). Notice may also be given as a collective notice from a trade union or an employer's association on the basis of the collective agreement or upon other legal basis between the organizations (cf. LDA section 15(3)).

1695. If the notice is given either by the individual employees or by the employer, the term of notice is normally fourteen days (cf. LDA section 15(1)) on the premise that a trade union is either a party in the dispute or acts on behalf of the employees (cf. Rt. 1985 p. 507). A corresponding provision is not found in the previous SA of February 30 May 1975 No. 18, or the current Ship Labour Act of 21 June 2013 No. 102. In such case, the contracts must be terminated within the individual term of notice (cf. the *travaux préparatoires* to the LDA, Prop. 134 L (2010-2011) p. 76, and also ARD 1992 p. 90, and further ARD 2004 p. 181 and ARD 2005 p. 77). As regards notice on strike as well as notice on lock-out, the notice must be clear about the core of the matter. If not so, the use of industrial action will be illegal and in breach of the collective bargaining agreement (cf. ARD 1982 p. 135), but it is not absolutely necessary that the notice does contain the similar information as prescribed for the notice to be submitted to the State Mediator according to LDA section 16(2) (cf. ARD 2010 p. 270 (47) and ARD 2010 p. 296 (55)).

1696. It is a common assumption that a trade union is authorized to give a collective notice on behalf of its members (cf. Rt. 1934 p. 209 and ARD 1992 p. 90). Such notice must mention by name the members comprised by the notice. Unless the employer's association is authorized to receive the notice on behalf of the individual employers, such notice must be given to the individual employers (cf. ARD 1992 p. 90).

1697. The collective agreements often state an opportunity to the organizations to exchange collective notices (e.g., cf. section 3-1 of the BA (2014)). Such notice only comprises the members of the organizations, and the opposite party has the right to get a name list of which employees are comprised by the notice (cf. Rt. 1934 p. 209, ARD 1962 p. 65, ARD 1976 p. 127; *see also* ARD 1980 p. 207, ARD 1992 p. 90, and ARD 2006 p. 399). The same applies to an expansion of the strike through further collective notice (cf. ARD 1985 p. 81), which also concerns the employer's passivity with regard to obtaining a name list.

1698. An obligation to work while a gradual cessation of work may be collectively agreed (cf. ARD 1985 p. 68). The same applies to safety work (cf. ARD 1986 p. 85), in which case the collective agreement neither carried a preference to such work for employees in a conflict, nor carried that the safety deputy was given a unique position in such case.

1699. Between the parties, it may also be agreed special bargaining procedures that must be completed before the use of industrial action (cf. ARD 2006 p. 8, *see also* ARD 2005 p. 279).

1700. LDA section 17 is based on the principle that a notice on strike or lockout cannot be retracted – wholly or in part – without the approval of the opposite party (cf. ARD 1983 p. 176 and sections 7 and 39 of the Contract Act of 31 May 1918 No. 4; *see also* ARD 1984 p. 118).

1701. As a general rule, a notice on strike or lockout must be unconditional and be given as a notice of full stoppage of work, so that it cannot be limited with regard to neither which work tasks are comprised nor its duration, unless the relevant collective agreement gives a legal basis for it, or if such limitations or conditions must be regarded as accepted by the other party (cf. ARD 1985 p. 76, ARD 1994 p. 182, and ARD 1995 p. 214). By sympathy actions in support of a conflict that regards the right to be organized and the right to enter into collective agreements, a notice may nevertheless be conditional (cf. section 3-6 No. 5 of the BA (2014); *see also* ARD 1995 p. 98 and ARD 1995 p. 129).

§4. Blockade and Boycott

1702. To be effective, a strike or lock-out is usually followed up with a blockade: the enterprise is closed to labour, or the strikers or dismissed workers are prevented from getting work elsewhere. The LDA equates such blockades with a strike or lock-out (LDA section 1 f and g, thus, all sides of the dispute are regulated by the same rules (cf. also Rt. 2001 p. 501)). However, if the blockade has no connection with a strike or lockout, it must be judged according to the stricter rules of the Boycott Act of 5 December 1947 No. 1. If the blockade is declared illegal, e.g., because it is carried out by illegal means, or it is considered disproportionate, the party who initiated the action may not just be held liable for damages, but may also be held liable to a penalty (cf. the Boycott Act sections 4 and 5).

1703. A blockade that consists of a block or an exclusion of labour, but that has no connection to a strike or a lock-out, is judged by the stricter rules of the Boycott Act (1947). The same applies to other forms of blockade or boycott, e.g., measures that aim to prevent the enterprise from getting access to goods, or a call to the customers not to buy goods from the enterprise. Furthermore, a boycott takes place if the employers refuse to cooperate with a strike-breaker in order to force the strike-breaker into quitting his or her employment. Conditional sympathy actions are also comprised by the rules of the Boycott Act (1947).

1704. The Boycott Act (1947) states a general and comprehensive definition of boycott, which comprises far more than boycotts within labour relationships. The regulation of the admission to implement boycott in labour relationship has, nonetheless, long been an important and disputed question. The Boycott Act [1947] relies on that a boycott is legal if held within the frames of section 2. A boycott is illegal when it is not given a reasonable notice beforehand or if the notice insufficiently clears the grounds for the boycott (section 2(d)). If the use of boycott that has an illegal aim, or if its aim cannot be reached without breaching the law, is also illegal (section 2(a)), but a boycott that aims to achieve a collective agreement is legal (Rt. 1997 p. 334). On the contrary, according to section 2 b, a boycott is illegal if the boycott is enforced or maintained by illegal means, e.g., by a threat about closure of labour in breach of a collective agreement (Rt. 1967 p. 1073) or by use of such closure of labour (ARD 1925 p. 130, cf. Rt. 1930 p. 712). According to section 2 b, the use of boycott is also illegal if it is implemented or maintained in a way that is unnecessary provoking or offensive, or by false or misleading information. These restrictions to the use of boycott are, in principle, not unlike those restrictions applying to the use of industrial action by the LDA.

1705. The case is somewhat different when it comes to the restrictions to the implementation of boycott according to section 2(c), which states that a boycott is illegal if it 'is not a reasonable proportion between the proposed interest and the damage following the boycott'. Thus the Boycott Act (1947) relies on a principle of proportion (cf. e.g., Rt. 1967 p. 1073), which demands a general consideration of both the parties' contradictory interests and the possible consequences to others (Rt. 1997 p. 334). Moreover, the provision prohibits a boycott that will seem 'inappropriate' or that 'will damage essential interests of society'. To these last two alternatives, case law has given little predominance in favour of the principle of proportion (cf. e.g., Rt. 1997 p. 334).

1706. The use of boycott in order to force an employer to agree to a collective agreement on standard terms, have been regarded as illegal (cf. Rt. 1997 p. 334). The same applies to a boycott towards an employer that has underpaid and unorganized workers or contractors, and a boycott in order to enforce that contribution to welfare funds or other common collective fees shall be comprised by a collective agreement. Furthermore, a boycott can be implemented towards an employer that acts in a hostile way against the collective institute. However, a boycott with demands to get the workers organized in a certain trade union is regarded illegal. The same applies to e.g., a boycott in order to enforce a collective agreement with predominance to labour if not the interests of the already employed at the enterprise are sufficiently taken care of (Rt. 1997 p. 334), or a boycott in order to enforce collective terms to be implemented from before the point of submitting the demand ('back pay'), or a boycott against all earlier members of the Nasjonal Samling, (a political party – Nazi Party – before and during World War II, cooperating closely with the German occupying forces in Norway 1940-1945) (cf. ARD 1949 p. 61).

1707. The use of illegal boycott can constitute not only liability for damages (cf. section 4 of the Boycott Act (1947), *see also* Rt. 2001 p. 501), but can also constitute criminal liability (cf. section 5 of the Boycott Act (1947). Lawsuits fall under the ordinary courts of law and not the Labour Court.

1708. According to section 3 of the Boycott Act (1947), the court can temporarily ban a boycott until it is legally decided whether it is legal (Rt. 1995 p. 1079). In such case, it is the circumstances prevailing at the point of the court's decision that is decisive, and not the circumstances prevailing when the boycott was notified (Rt. 1997 p. 334). Whether a similar temporary ban against alleged illegal industrial action can be decided on the basis of section 15-1 and the following, is far more doubtful.

1709. The reason why the law has more severe rules for a trade union's right to, for example, to enforce a blockade on the enterprise when the trade union has not declared strike at the enterprise, as opposed to when it has declared a strike, is because a strike means a sacrifice on the part of the strikers. During a strike, the employees acquire no salary, and the use of strike therefore means an economic burden which curbs strike abuse. A blockade alone, on the other hand, represents no such sacrifice; the boycott action is only a call for others not to work in the blockaded enterprise. Besides that a blockade without connections to a strike or lockout can be in violation with the Boycott Act (1947), it may also be in violation with the labour peace obligation stipulated in the collective agreement (cf. e.g., ARD 1995 p. 98).

§5. The Obligation to Work During Legal Industrial Action

1710. As a starting point, the employees that are subject to a strike or lock-out notice shall not perform any work. In such case, the employees can demand neither pay, etc. from the employer nor, in principle, to stay at the enterprise. The remaining employees who are subject to the strike shall still, as a starting point, carry on their work, but – on the premise that the conflict is legal – their obligation to work does not change because of the strike. However, the case will often be – especially if the strike is long lasting – that the remaining employees cannot be employed rationally. In such case, the collective agreements usually give the employer authority to lay off the remaining employees.

1711. Yet, the employees must be obliged to perform work that is necessary to prevent immediate damage on life or health, even if it may represent unusual work tasks. However, the extent of such an obligation depends on the individual position and other qualifications of the employee. The same applies when it is necessary to prevent physical damage on goods. In this case, the obligation to work is more comprehensive for a supervisor than a normal employee. Normal maintenance work is not comprised by this category. If the employer wishes further work to be done, it will in principle depend on an agreement with the employees. In practice, such an agreement is usually agreed with the trade union, and often in the way that the union grants 'dispensation' during the strike.

§6. STRIKE-BREAKERS

1712. Industrial action also connotes the term 'strike-breaker'. During a strike, an employer may wish to hire new employees to perform the work tasks that are otherwise performed by the strikers. The LDA does not prohibit the use of strike-breakers during a strike or lock-out, but it is regarded as 'a disloyal and socially condemnable act' that can start countermeasures. An employee that agrees to such employment is comprised by the term 'strike-breaker', and the strikers may – e.g., by in public declare the positions blocked – seek to prevent such employment. This form of blockade is comprised by the rules of the LDA and is therefore judged by the same rules as the industrial action itself, and not by the stricter rules of the Boycott Act (1947). Moreover, the employees that has not been called out, may refuse to cooperate with strike-breakers (cf. the principle of section 10-1 of the BA (2014) and Rt. 1979 p. 770). The same applies during a lock-out and when the employers seek to prevent the strikers from getting other labour during the strike.

1713. The same applies if non-strikers at the enterprise take over the strikers' jobs. On the other hand, if they continue their regular work – which is their duty unless special circumstances – they are not strike-breakers. If some of the shop assistants in a shop go on strike, it is not strike-breaking if their non-striking colleagues continue to serve customers at the counters and departments where the strikers previously worked, even if their workload increases. Usually, they can also be ordered to work at a counter or department where everyone has gone on strike, as long as the work is within the framework of their employment contracts. It is also not considered strike-breaking if the proprietor himself or herself, through his or her own efforts, tries to alleviate the impact of the strike. Similarly, employees in supervisory positions have a right to carry out tasks ordinarily relegated to their subordinates under normal circumstances, as long as said tasks are a natural part of their work. In the same way, supervisors at an enterprise are not considered to be part of labour disputes that do not involve themselves or their colleagues. During work stoppages, they have an obligation to carry on their normal work and other work their employer deems necessary to prevent material losses.

1714. A similar issue arises in the event of go-slow actions pursuant to the collective agreement in connection with local wage settlements (cf. ARD 1992 p. 49) and also paragraph 842 above). The terms of the collective agreement must be observed during such actions, also as regards the enterprise, e.g., as regards non-organized workers (cf. ARD 1988 p. 19).

1715. The employees of other enterprises are not obliged to perform work that is transferred to the enterprise from another enterprise that is stricken by a strike, if the purpose of the transfer is to support the enterprise that is stricken. But, if the purpose is to put forward one's own interests, the employees can normally not refuse to perform work. An enterprise that has accepted an assignment, but transferred the assignment to a sub-contractor, can itself take over and carry out the assignment if the sub-contractor later is stricken by a strike (cf. ARD 1924-25 p. 110 and Rt. 2001 p. 501).

1716. The above relates to legal industrial action. The situation is quite different in the event of an illegal use of industrial action. Such is considered an extraordinary event, which expands the scope of the employees' duties (cf. e.g., ARD 1945-48 p.

247 and ARD 1951 p. 140). The workers cannot then refuse to carry out work, even if said work is not part of their regular job description. The extent of their duties depends on the gravity of the situation. Moreover, those performing such work are not guilty of strike-breaking.

1717. The term 'strike-breaker' carries a trenchant moral and social stigma. Being condemned a strike-breaker can have a greater effect than any legal sanction. Calling someone a strike-breaker constitutes libel and can result in punishment and nullity. If a worker has in good faith brought up with his or her trade union, the matter of his or her obligation to work during a legal strike, and therefore been in good faith, it cannot be deemed strike-breaking if the worker infringed on the strikers' job functions, strictly speaking (cf. Rt. 1963 p. 430).

§7. Sanctions

I. Putting an End to the Violation of the Collective Agreement

1718. There is no doubt that a violation of a collective agreement must be put to an end as far as possible, and in principle there is no doubt that the Labour Court may decide whether the violation should be stopped. In such case, the Labour Court usually sets a deadline.

1719. The *KLP* case in ARD 2002 p. 90 is illustrative (cf. especially the grounds on 774 and the following).

II. Liability

1720. A breach of a collective agreement or illegal work stoppage constitutes liability for damages for the employer or employee in question. If the enterprise has acted in violation of the collective agreement by preventing negotiations on employees' wages as stipulated in the collective agreement, the enterprise will be liable for the loss incurred by the employees (cf. ARD 1988 p. 19). A sympathy strike in violation of a collective agreement can also constitute liability for damages (cf. ARD 1995 p. 202), and by a political demonstration strike in violation of the labour peace obligation (cf. ARD 2001 p. 243).

1721. Previously, organizations had a very strict liability for the breach of a collective agreement or illegal sanctions on the part of their members, but according to the current rules (section 9 of the LDA and section 23 of the LDPS), the union is liable only when it is guilty of the breach of contract or of perpetuating the situation constituting a breach of contract or the illegal work stoppage. Even if the organization itself is not guilty of the illegal situation, it may be liable if it refrains from doing what it can to bring the situation to an end.

1722. The workers' liability concerns those who take part in the strike, regardless of whether or not they are members of the trade union. In addition, the Labour Court has found that said liability also includes workers who have declared that they will stop working even if they did not participate in the strike (ARD 1960 p. 1). The Labour Court referred to the fact that it, to a large extent, was only a matter of circumstance whether or not the individual worker eventually walked out. In this connection will also be noted ARD 1981 p. 282, where the Labour Court did not distinguish between the individual workers' liability, although some of the workers had not participated in the strike throughout its duration for circumstantial reasons such as 'illness, being exempt from striking, holidays, etc.'

1723. As explicitly stated in section 9 of the LDA, a trade organization will be liable if it implements an action in violation of the collective agreement. But the organization will also be liable if it neglects to do whatever is necessary to end the situation. In other words, the organization has an obligation to take action. Hence it will be liable if it supports an illegal action, also if said support includes 'approving a strike by its stance, with the involvement entailed therein' (cf. ARD 1970 p. 72). The extent to which an organization must go to avoid liability depends on the situation. In many cases, it is enough that the organization condemns the action, because the strikers follow the union's orders and resume work. If the strike does not end, the organization must take serious measures to convince the employees that they are acting in violation of the collective agreement, and that they must resume work. Thus, the Labour Court has stated (cf. ARD 1945-48 p. 261), that the chairman of the local trade union should have called a meeting of the executive committee, beseeching an all-out effort to bring the situation under control. If that did not work, he could have called a meeting of the union members, asking them to vote against the illegal strike. He should also have contacted the union federation, stating that he was unsuccessful in his endeavour. He should by all means have done everything in his power to prevent this futile and ruthless strike. It was not considered sufficient that the chairman had requested the striking workers to resume their work. The union federation had by telegram and letter requested the local trade union to try to bring the strike to an end, but that was also considered insufficient. The union federation should at least have sent one or more elected representatives to the place where the strike was going on. Consequently, the union federation as well as the local trade union, and the twenty-two workers, were all held responsible for the economic loss that the enterprise had suffered.

1724. See also ARD 1996 p. 43; as a consequence of the peace obligation of a collective agreement, it was an obligation for the union to take active steps against the members that participated in the action. Also, as far as there might be some uncertainty about which members were involved in the action, it was a duty for the union to clarify the question so that the individual members could be confronted directly. Expelling members is not always a sufficient ground for liability exemption (cf. ARD 1952 p. 1); where the Labour Court found it possible that the federation and union still could exert influence over the expelled members. Further, ARD 1956-57 p. 218, may be observed, where the union's representative did go to the site of the action, and did inform the striking workers that the action was illegal, but added that it was up to the members to decide. The Labour Court found that this was not sufficient. 'It is not enough simply to show up at the workplace and let the members decide such issues.' Furthermore, it is not decisive that the by-laws of a federation of trade unions may stipulate that the superior union is not authorized to instruct the associated trade unions.

Even in such cases, the superior union will have to do whatever possible to avoid or limit any breach of the peace obligation (cf. ARD 1994 p. 62).

1725. The obligation to take action also applies to the employer's associations, which ARD 1997 p. 109 illustrates.

1726. In sum, it will not without further ado be sufficient that a trade union has dissociated itself from the action. The trade union must take use of all possible organizational measures.

1727. According to section 10 of the LDA (cf. also section 23 of the LDPS), the extent of the economic liability is to be stipulated by taking into account the extent of damages, the fault and financial capacity of the party causing the loss, the injured party's situation, and other circumstances. Under especially mitigating circumstances, damages may be waived altogether. The organization's liability will rarely be reduced out of consideration for the financial capacity of the party causing the loss (cf. ARD 1982 p. 150; *see also* ARD 1986 p. 79). In actions for damages against employees, the court has in some cases set damages at purely a pro rata figure (cf. ARD 1981 p. 282), where each of the 492 workers was ordered to pay 1/492 of the damages. Workers who have been especially active in initiating an illegal action may be ordered to pay a higher amount of damages than the other workers participating in the action. The same applies to shop stewards who have participated in the action. Shop stewards cannot escape said liability by resigning as shop stewards etc. before the strike is put into action.

1728. Basically, the employer can only claim damages for the financial loss incurred. Illustrative is ARD 1995 p. 202 regarding break of production, where the income for one year is regained and gives income to the following years, and where the Labour Court granted damages for the difference. If no financial loss exists, there are no damages to pay. This also applies to the individual loss items. An illustration is ARD 1945-48 p. 63, where the company claimed damages for loss of goodwill within its customers because it was unable to supply them with goods over a long period of time. This loss item was not accepted. The Labour Court pointed out that 'we assume that, with its current scarcity of goods, the company will be able to sell all the goods it manufactures or markets'. Non-financial loss may not be claimed (cf. Rt. 2012 p. 1702 (paragraph 66)).

1729. Here must be noted that a strike will frequently affect several employers, some of whom will not suffer financial loss. In practice, however, the Labour Court has found that the striking workers are liable for the loss incurred by the employers, even if they are employed with one of the employers who actually suffered no loss. The Court pointed out that the action would have damaged not only the enterprise in which they themselves were employed, but also the other enterprises embraced by the action (cf. ARD 1981 p. 236 and ARD 1981 p. 282).

1730. The damages may be reduced if the employer's actions were inflammatory, tactless or offensive (cf. e.g., ARD 1960 p. 31 and ARD 1972 p. 52). If the employer has been categorically adamant without trying to settle the dispute through negotiations, damages may be reduced depending on the circumstances (cf. ARD 1972 p. 52). On the other hand, some factors will aggravate the measuring out of damages, such as an illegal action instituted while the dispute was being negotiated (ARD 1964 p. 75, ARD 1966 p. 90, ARD 1974 p. 71), workers acting in opposition to their organization (ARD

1964 p. 49, ARD 1967 p. 1), and if an action continuing after it has been judged illegal or in violation of the collective agreement (ARD 1954 p. 100), providing that, of course, for practical reasons, it may take some time for the workers to resume work. The potential social harm caused by the action was also stated as an aggravating element (ARD 1972 p. 52 and ARD 1974 p. 71). To mitigate the workers' liability, it was emphasized that their organization failed to adequately inform them that the action would be in violation of the collective agreement (ARD 1949 p. 31).

1731. The workers' stand in connection with an action is also important. Shop stewards must ensure that the collective agreement is followed. Therefore, prompting or contributing towards an illegal confrontation would be inconsistent with their office. In a number of cases, the Labour Court has ordered shop stewards who have neglected such duties to pay more damages than the rank-and-file worker. Depending on the circumstances in each case, shop stewards have been fined three to four times as much as their shop mates. Like the organizations, shop stewards must actively try to prevent an action. Simply remaining passive, e.g., not attending a union meeting or refraining from speaking at the meeting, will not exempt a shop steward from additional liability. However, if shop stewards do their best to prevent the conflict, but participate in the work stoppage once it becomes a fact, they cannot be held more liable than their shop mates. The shop steward's future position with his or her shop mates would become difficult or impossible if he or she were to go on working while the others went on strike.

1732. As mentioned above, shop stewards will not avoid liability by resigning from their post etc., regardless of whether it happens before or during the strike. Neither does their liability disappear if they are expelled from their union during the strike (cf. ARD 1958 p. 111).

1733. Also other workers who are particularly active in effectuating a strike, e.g., strike leaders and members of action committees, can be held liable for more damages than the other strikers. In the few such cases tried by the Labour Court, the persons in question have been ordered to pay relatively high damages. In 1949, the Labour Court held each of the action committee's nine members liable for NOK 1,500 (ARD 1949 p. 28). Correspondingly, in 1974, eight members were held liable for NOK 5,000 each (ARD 1974 p. 71). However, if they have done no more than the others, then there is no reason for them to be held more liable. (Cf. ARD 1981 p. 282: 'The illegal stoppage was effectuated spontaneously and by unanimous vote. Furthermore, there have been no reports of pronounced activity by the members of the action committee'.)

1734. Section 10 of the LDA explicitly states that the 'financial capacity' of the party causing the loss shall also be taken into account. This factor varies significantly, depending on whether it concerns the individual workers or the union. The organizations will usually have considerable financial capacity. At the same time, it is important to keep organizations' liability high in order to maintain the preventive effect of the law of damages. Consequently, the Labour Court will usually not reduce the organizations' extent of liability. One example is ARD 1982 p. 150: 'Because the claim for damages is addressed to the trade unions and not the individual workers, the court has found it cannot reduce the size of damages out of consideration of the financial capacity of the party causing the loss.' In comparison, *see also* ARD 1986 p. 79 and ARD 1995 p. 202.

1735. The situation is quite different as regards the individual workers. It would be quite unreasonable if each person participating in an unofficial strike were to be held totally liable for the entire financial loss incurred by the employer. In practice, therefore, the Labour Court will usually limit their amount of damages to a specified amount. In some cases, the Court has divided the amount equally between the liable workers, stipulating no liability beyond the total amount of damages. In such cases, damages are proportionately divided. *See* e.g., ARD 1981 p. 282, particularly pp. 291–292, where each of the 492 workers was ordered to pay NOK 1,200 in damages. The total amount of damages was NOK 590,400. In other cases, the individual worker has been ordered to pay more than his or her exact share of damages. In the latter case, joint and several liability was applied, but with maximization of damages for the individual joint and several debtor. For example, in ARD 1966 p. 90, damages were set at NOK 44,000. Damages for each of the hundred workers were maximized at NOK 470.

1736. If both the organization and workers are liable, the organization will be jointly and severally liable with the employees. If the organization is held liable for a greater amount than the individual employee, which is usually the case, the organization will be solely liable for the additional amount. An illustration is ARD 1981 p. 237. Here, the trade union and the 128 workers were judged liable for NOK 300,000 in damages. Liability for the individual worker was calculated at NOK 1,200. Thus the trade union became solely liable for NOK 146,000, but also responsible for each worker's share. If one of the workers did not pay, the trade union would then have to pay his or her share. The same applies if individual workers, e.g., shop stewards and strike leaders, are held liable for a greater amount than the others. ARD 1945-48 p. 63 is an example. Here, the federation, the union and seventeen workers were held liable for NOK 20,000 in damages. The federation, union and the two shop stewards were held jointly and severally liable, though maximized to NOK 5,000 for each of the shop stewards. The other fifteen workers were judged liable for one-fifth of that amount.

1737. As a result of the purely proportional liability, the risk of an individual worker's failure to pay must be carried by the employer. In joint and several liabilities, the creditor has more people to deal with. But then difficulties may arise in recovering the disbursement of damages, because the decisions by the Labour Court do not specify how the cost of damages is to be shared. The judgment in ARD 1945-48 p. 63 did not specify how the NOK 20,000 was to be divided – after e.g., the federation had paid the amount – within the union, shop stewards and other workers. Among other things, the judgment makes no stipulation as to whether the shop stewards should pay a greater amount than their shop mates in the recourse.

§8. Dismissal

1738. Anyone taking part in illegal or contract-violating work stoppage or similar action, e.g., a go-slow, is guilty of violating his or her obligations according to the collective agreement, cf. also paragraph 842 above. The employer then has a right to dismiss the worker, provided the violation is serious (cf. section 15-14(1) of the WEA). In Rt. 1977 p. 902, the Supreme Court found dismissal justified in a case where the strike had lasted approximately one week, and where both the union and local chapter had denounced the action, warning the strikers not to continue. Similarly, we can note Rt. 1965 p. 1075, where four workers who refused to carry out mandatory overtime work, were justly deemed dismissed. They had been clearly ordered to work the overtime and they understood the consequences of refusing the order. We will also note ARD 1960 p. 139.

1739. Having dismissed someone, the employer is quite free to decide whether or not to re-employ the worker, as long as he does not act illegally or with intent to harm. Precedence shows no inclination by the court to place any notable emphasis on whether the employer has reinstated more or fewer of the other strikers (cf. Rt. 1962 p. 766 and Rt. 1977 p. 902).

§9. Dismissal with Notice

1740. Because the employer may have a right to dismiss the strikers, giving them notice may also be justified. We can see this in ARD 1980 p. 157, where, during an illegal action, a crane operator on a drilling platform had moved the crane beam within the departure-arrival sector for helicopters in order to make the strike more effective. The manoeuvre took place in violation of expressed order not to use the crane. The Labour Court placed decisive emphasis on the fact that the crane operator had refused an order involving safety given by the person in charge of safety, and the court found them to be justified according to section 15-7 of the WEA.

§10. Resignation as Shop Steward

1741. Shop stewards prompting or contributing to an illegal action will have violated their duties following as consequence of the collective agreement, and which rest upon them in their capacity as shop stewards. Such violation is usually to be considered as a serious breach of duties. (Cf. e.g., ARD 1958 p. 111, where the shop steward had initially tried to avert the conflict, but at a later meeting chose to join his shop mates, fully supporting a strike. The Labour Court held that this behaviour constituted a serious breach of duty.) The provisions of the collective agreements are primarily levelled against active behaviour; thus, shop stewards who have merely been too passive will usually not be considered as having seriously broken their duties, unless their passivity should be considered qualified. The employer's association (NHO) may, according to BA (2014) section 6-10, require that the other party to this agreement (LO) remove the shop steward from his or her capacity as shop steward, in which case it is a duty for the employees to elect a new shop steward immediately. Should the parties fail to agree as regards the removal of the shop steward, the question is to be settled by the Labour Court (cf. e.g., ARD 1991 p. 81). Of course, it is a serious breach of duties in this regard, should a shop steward threaten – while negotiating –

with the use of illegal industrial strife, unless the claims presented are satisfactorily met. In such a case, threatening that overtime work would not be carried out, the shop steward may be removed from his or her position (cf. ARD 2012 p. 297 (*Air Traffic Controller*)).

§11. Liability to Punishment for Violation of Collective Agreements

1742. Liability to punishment, which previously could make industrial actions very spiteful, has been gradually alleviated, and since 1956, it is no longer punishable to violate a collective agreement or participate in illegal actions judged according to the rules of the LDA. Probably also excluded are the applicability of other penal rules making violation of an employment contract a punishable offence, where said violation is connected with such actions (such as sections 324, 409-412, 421, 422 and 426 of the PC (1902)). The same must apply to other sanctions of a punishable nature, e.g., for breach of the peace (section 14 of the LDPS). On the other hand, it is still punishable to put into action or participate in an illegal blockade not connected with a strike or lockout (cf. section 5 of the Boycott Act (1947)). It is also punishable not to comply with decisions of the Wage Committee (cf. section 8 of the Act No. 58 of 4 June 1993 relating to the standardization of collective agreements, etc.).

§12. The Employment Relationship After Closure of Industrial Action

1743. When industrial action has ceased, the basic rule is that the employment relationship resumes. It must also be set as a basic rule that both the employer and the employees are equally entitled and obliged to resume work. In most cases, where it is a condition that an employee has been employed continuously, the employment relationship is not to be considered interrupted because of the fact that the employee has taken part in a strike. However, the time where the employees has been out of work because of the strike, is not to be taken into account when the total length of the time of the employment is to be calculated.

1744. If the employer, because of industrial action, has had to reduce the enterprise and therefore cannot offer work to the employees, the question arises whether the employee still has a right and duty to resume the work.

1745. The question of such, leads to the question of whether a dismissal in connection to labour disputes leads to a definite termination of the employment relationship, or if said means just a temporary break. This question is regulated neither in the WEA nor in the LDA. In previous labour law literature, it is used as a basic principle that also such dismissal leads to a termination of the employment relationship. However, it is doubtful whether this point of view may still be maintained. In more recent literature, dismissal in connection to labour disputes is characterized as ‘a type of suspension’ of rights and obligations in an employment relationship. In support of this, ARD 1976 p. 116 and ARD 1976 p. 188 can be mentioned; in which the Labour

Court, as a premise, decided that dismissals given in connection to legal industrial action does not lead to a permanent cease of the employment contracts. The same applies to a decision of Jæren district court of 27 August 1991 (unprinted).

1746. Thus, the principle is probably that the employers as well as employees are equally entitled and obliged to resume work after the cease of a legal industrial action. However, this principle will have to be applied so, that the employer's obligation to reinstate the employees does not commence until the enterprise, upon operational circumstances, can resume. In practice, operational circumstances can cause a gradual increase of work and a reinstatement of the employees by groups. The consequence of this point of view is that dismissals in connection to labour disputes must be regarded as a temporary cease – not a permanent termination – of the employment relationship. If this is used as a basis, the employment relationship may be brought to a permanent termination also during a legal labour dispute, but the otherwise current rules must then be observed; amongst others the rules regarding formal procedures according to the WEA section 15-4 and the general requirement of just cause according to WEA section 15-7(1). If a labour dispute causes a decrease of labour on a more permanent basis and the employees therefore must be dismissed, the employer supposedly must – at the consideration of which employees to dismiss – consider strikers and the remaining employees equally, which might be the situation where just a part of the employees has gone on strike.

§13. Statistics on Labour Disputes in Recent Years

1747. In 2011, there were two stoppages in Norway, and 526 working days were lost. In 2009, there also were two stoppages, and 180 working days were lost. Both 2009 and 2011 was years with mid-term settlements where a revision of the agreements during the main settlement in 2008 and 2010 took place. During the previous mid-term settlement in 2007, there were four labour disputes and 4,000 working days lost.

1748. In years with main settlements, such as 2008, there were 10 labour disputes and 62,500 working days lost. In 2010, 500,009 working days were lost. (Source: *Arbeidskonfliktar*, Statistisk sentralbyrå (www.ssb.no/arbkonfl/)).

Chapter 7. Settlement of Industrial Disputes and Protection of Vital Needs

§1. Compulsory Mediation

1749. As previously mentioned, strike, lockout and other industrial action may to quite a degree have considerable consequences for the whole society. Therefore, it is of the greatest importance to make sure that industrial action is not implemented until all efforts and possibilities have been thoroughly considered, in order to reach an amicable agreement between the parties. Accordingly, since the first LDA of 1915, it is required that the State Mediator be informed, when notice is given in order to implement a strike, lockout or other industrial action, so that the State Mediator may decide that no such action is allowed until mediation has taken place, for the time stipulated by the LDA.

1750. Consequently, the LDA (2012) section 16 stipulate, that the State Mediator shall immediately be informed, when notice is given in order to implement a strike, lockout or other industrial action. If voluntary negotiations are still going on when notice is given, the State Mediator shall also be informed immediately, should the voluntary negotiations be ended without a voluntary solution. In order to ensure that compulsory mediation will be a reality, the State Mediator must necessarily have some time to consider the matter, before a strike, lockout or other industrial action may take place. Therefore, the LDA section 18 stipulate, that no such action may take place until four workdays have elapsed from the time the State Mediator received the notification that the LDA section 16 requires. Further, the time of notice must have expired. As regards labour disputes in the public sector, the State Mediator shall be informed immediately, should voluntary negotiations be ended without a voluntary solution, and mediation shall commence within fourteen days (cf. the LDPS section 14).

1751. The State Mediator shall ban work stoppage until compulsory mediation has ended, if strike or lockout would harm general interests (cf. the LDA section 19(1)). Such prohibition must be sent from the State Mediator within two working days (cf. the LDA section 19(4)). Mediation shall commence immediately (cf. the LDA section 20(1)). One of the parties may demand an end to the compulsory mediation, but only when ten days have elapsed since the work stoppage ban was issued (cf. the LDA section 25(1)). If such ending is demanded, the mediation shall be ended within four days after said demand is submitted (cf. the LDA section 25(2)). In this regard, Sundays and other holidays count as any other day. The State Mediator cannot prolong this deadline against the parties will (cf. ARD 1982 p. 200). If one of the parties demands that mediation be ended within a longer deadline than four days, the other party may demand that mediation shall end within the deadline prescribed by law. Industrial action can be implemented only by the expiration of these deadlines. As regards labour disputes in the public sector, a party may demand that mediation shall end fourteen days after its commencement. The mediation shall then be ended one week thereafter at the latest (cf. the LDPS section 17, also section 20). Here too, no industrial action may be implemented while mediation takes place.

1752. During the period in which industrial action is thus prohibited, the collective agreement and the wage and working conditions that applied at the outbreak of the dispute shall remain in effect, unless otherwise agreed by the parties (cf. the LDA section 8(3) and the LDPS section 20 No. 2).

1753. The mediator authorities' task is to help the parties to reach an agreement, if possible. It will often be easier for the parties to accept a compromise proposal from a neutral body, than a proposal from the opposite party. Whether a submitted proposal is accepted, depends upon the parties. The parties may meet by representatives (cf. LDA section 21). Whether the representatives are authorized to accept compromise proposals 'put on the table' depends on the relationship between the representatives and their parties. Compromise proposals are often brought before the other bodies of the organization, or brought to the members for a referendum, with or without a recommendation from the representatives of the organization. The State Mediator is not entitled to demand a referendum, even if the State Mediator should believe that the compromise proposal would then be carried (cf. ARD 1982 p. 200). On the other hand, if a proposal is put to a referendum amongst the members, industrial action cannot be put into effect until the results of the referendum have come in (cf. the presupposition of LDA section 28). It would serve little purpose to take a vote and to implement industrial action while the voting is still in progress.

1754. How the individual parties organize their own votes, is an internal matter for the different organizations (cf. ARD 1984 p. 124).

1755. If a compromise proposal is put to a referendum amongst the members, the State Mediator shall, in agreement with the parties, set a deadline for when the results of the vote shall be available (cf. LDA section 26). The parties shall, when the results are available, immediately inform the State Mediator in writing about whether the results are accepted or rejected (cf. LDA section 27(1)). However, it is important to note that if the result is not available within the set deadline, the compromise proposal is regarded accepted (cf. LDA section 27(2)).

1756. If the compromise proposal is rejected, industrial action can be implemented within a four days' notice between the parties, unless a shorter deadline is stipulated by a collective agreement (cf. LDA section 28).

1757. Several organizations, especially different trade unions, will often be involved in the same conflict. The main rule is then that each organization individually decides whether it will accept or reject a submitted compromise proposal. Unless otherwise agreed between the trade unions involved, this main rule applies, even if organizations that represent only smaller groups of employees might thus overturn an extensive and complicated collective settlement. This is also the case on the side of the employers. Consequently, the State Mediator is not entitled to demand that a compromise proposal be put to a referendum amongst the members of the organizations involved, so that the decision of whether to ratify the proposal will be made on the basis of the total numbers of votes and numbers of qualified to vote of those professions thus joined together. Further, a trade union is not obliged to put a compromise proposal to a referendum amongst its members, only because other trade unions – perhaps even the majority – so decides, unless otherwise agreed.

§2. Wage Arbitration Board

I. The National Wages Board

1758. A special court of arbitration is established for disputes on wages and working conditions. According to the WBA of 27 January 2012 No. 10 (WBA) (cf. previously the WBA of 19 December 1952 No. 7, the parties may, if the dispute is not settled through mediation, jointly bring the dispute before the National Wages Board (WBA section 2(1)), and, as far as the state and trade unions representing public servants are concerned, LDPS section 26).

1759. The National Wages Board has one chairman and eight other members, cf. WBA section 3(1). The chairman as well as four other members are appointed by the King-in-Council for a period of three years, while the parties of the individual dispute each appoint two members (cf. WBA section 3(2) and (4)). Decisions of the National Wages Board are made by majority of votes (cf. WBA section 4(1)).

1760. The decisions of the National Wages Board has the same effect as a collective agreement (cf. WBA section 2(2)). The parties thereby get, *inter alia*, a labour peace obligation for the stipulated time, and the terms stipulated by the decision are also binding for the individual employment contracts.

II. Stipulation of Collective Terms by Authority of Special Act

1761. The significance of the Wages Board Act, as well as regards the decisions of the National Wages Board is, however, mainly related to compulsory arbitration, because voluntary arbitration is relatively rare. As already mentioned, a dispute can only be brought before a wage arbitration board if agreed by both parties. It is not sufficient that just one of the parties demands so. Furthermore, the Wages Board Act does not entitle any public body the right to demand compulsory arbitration. Thus, such authority may be obtained, usually by a separate act, enacted for the solution of the individual conflict or conflicts in question by the Norwegian Parliament (or by the government by Provisional Ordinance if the Norwegian Parliament is not in session (cf. section 17 of the Constitution). As regards the state and trade unions representing public servants, it may be observed that conclusion or amendments of collective agreements on separate issues may, by each of the parties, be brought before a special board for decision (cf. LDPS section 27). Request for such decision does, however, require that a general collective agreement does exist. Similarly, certain defined questions on adjustment of wages etc. may, on request of one of the parties, be decided by a specific board (cf. LDPS section 29). During the first years following World War II, the legislation allowed the government to refer all disputes in industrial relations to a wage arbitration board, as a part of the comprehensive economic regulation prevailing at that time. Since 1953, however, it is in general required that a separate Act be passed to order individual disputes to be settled by compulsory arbitration. Such authority has been enacted several times. However, the frequent use of compulsory arbitration does give reason to concern as regards the framework of the international conventions ratified by Norway, *inter alia* the ILO Conventions No. 87, 98 and 154.

III. The Procedures for the National Wages Board

1762. The procedures before the National Wages Board are, as far as applicable, the same as the procedures for the Labour Court of Norway (cf. the WBA section 5).

Chapter 8. Addendum on the Right of Employees to Choose a Trade Union

1763. As regards taxation, income deductions for paid union dues may be claimed for an amount not exceeding (2015) NOK 3,850 per year, but only by members of a trade union which is countrywide, has a collective agreement, and is associated with a confederation of trade unions. These provisions were adopted by the Act of 27 May 1977 No. 37, amending the Taxation Act (1911), as a consequence of the general settlement during the 1976 negotiations on the main collective agreements (cf. now the Taxation Act (1999) section 6-20(3)).

1764. Thus, members of a trade union, which is not associated with a confederation of trade unions, are not entitled to such income deductions, unless their trade union was founded before 1977, or an exception for the trade union has been granted by the Ministry of Finance. The employee's choice of a trade union belonging to the first category here mentioned will therefore have a direct and negative consequence as regards taxation treatment.

1765. In a human rights context, it is therefore a question whether this different treatment – between members of trade unions which are, or are not, associated with a confederation of trade unions, or otherwise excepted – is completely in compliance with the international conventions on freedom of association and the employee's right to choose which organization he or she wishes to be a member of, if any.[9]

1766. At the national level, it is of course a question of how the Norwegian Taxation Act is per se to be interpreted, based on the *travaux préparatoires*, practice by the Ministry, etc. The main points of the *travaux préparatoires* are (cf. NOU 1977: 19 pp. 16–20 and Ot.prp.nr. 69 (1976-77) that the activities of the trade unions are of direct importance for employees' income and for conditions at the workplace, and that the individual members consider the union dues as necessary costs in regard to their work, that it should be decisive whether the trade union has concluded a collective agreement, that it should not be required that the trade union should have at least 10,000 members, as that would have as a consequence an unreasonable difference in treatment, and that the activities of a trade union should be countrywide, which seems to have been one of the conditions agreed upon under the 1976 negotiations on the general collective agreements). Further, trade unions with members within one specific enterprise only, or within a specific group of enterprises only, were supposed usually not to have considerable expenses and should therefore be excepted, but also because the union dues might then be used for purposes outside those connected to the core of trade unions activities; should, however, such smaller and local trade unions carry out activities equivalent to those performed by traditional trade unions, the exception should not apply, and the Ministry would thus be entitled to grant a right to deduct the trade union dues.

---

9. See also Jakhelln Henning, 'Arbeidstakeres organisasjonsfrihet og fradrag for fagforeningskontingent – overordnede perspektiver og det menneskerettslige aspekt', in *Høyt skattet: festskrift til Frederik Zimmer* (2014), pp. 320–347.

1767. Against this background, the question is not only how the Taxation Act is to be interpreted, but also how the Ministry should apply the administrative authority to grant a right to deduct the trade union dues, and whether legal limitations in that regard would apply. That question was dealt with by the Parliament (*Stortinget*) caused by an initiative of the opposition aiming that the Taxation Act be amended (cf. Dok. 8: 152 S (2009–2010)). The initiative was not approved (cf. Innst. 43 S (2010–2011)) with an enclosed statement from the Minister of Finance, expressing the view that the parties to labour life ought to be easily surveyed and also predictable, and followed by the employees to the greatest possible extent in a number of confederations of trade unions which could easily be surveyed, that the taxation advantage should be limited to organizations taking their social responsibility seriously, that new trade unions generally would have the opportunity to associate to one of the confederations of trade union, but also that the taxation advantage for members of competing trade unions would be far-fetched as regards the purposes of this taxation advantage and that competing trade unions in the long run might lead to a greater focus on the isolated short-term interests of their members, at the expense of a more long-term and socially oriented perspective. Thus, it had been the practice of the Ministry to grant a right to deduct the trade union dues only in cases where a new trade union had been established for groups of employees who previously had not been represented by a trade union, and which had not had the opportunity to be associated to a confederation of trade unions; consequently, the practice of the Ministry was not to grant such tax deduction rights to new competing trade unions.

1768. Summarized, the *travaux préparatoires* are built on the view that membership of a trade union is of importance the employees, and that the confederations of trade unions will take broader and more social based considerations into account, than would trade unions for a limited group of employees. Further, the practice of the Ministry is based on the principle that centralized collective negotiations with the main organizations are to be encouraged. Therefore, the taxation benefits are limited.

It should be observed, however, that human rights issues were not dealt with at all either when the Taxation Act was amended in 1977, or when these regulations and practice were discussed more than thirty years later, in 2010.

1769. From a human rights perspective, the question is whether the system established by the Taxation Act can be said to be completely in compliance with the international conventions on freedom of association, as regards the right 'to form and to join trade unions for the protection of his interests' (cf. ECHR Article 11(1), further ESC part I Nos 5 and Article 6, ICCPR Article 22 No l); a term which must be assumed to comprise also the right to 'join organizations of their own choosing' (cf. ILO Convention No. 87 Article 2 and ICESC Article 8 No l), *inter alia* as the ECtHR has held that ECHR Article 11 does comprise also the right not to join a trade union (the negative right to organize) (cf. e.g., *Sigurjónsson v. Iceland* (1993) paragraph 35) taking into account other international instruments as well as international developments – and later on *Sörensen and Rasmussen v. Denmark* (2006) paragraphs 72–75; it may also be observed that each of them were members of different trade unions (cf. paragraphs 11 and 16). Further, the ECtHR has repeatedly stated that the ECHR is a living document which must be interpreted in the light of present-day conditions (cf. also *Demir* and *Baykara v. Turkey* (2008) paragraphs 65–86).

1770. The question will, thus, be whether the exception stipulated in the Taxation Act, which is obviously prescribed by law, can be considered 'necessary in a democratic society' (cf. ECHR Article 11(2); cf. also ILO Convention No. 87 Article 8(2), where it is explicitly stipulated that the 'law of the land shall not be such as to impair, nor shall it be so applied as to impair, the guarantees provided for in the Convention').

1771. It seems appropriate to start the considerations on this question with the question of why employees should have the right to choose between different trade unions. In that regard, the observations of the ECtHR seem relevant (cf. *ASLEF v. UK* (2007) paragraph 50 (exclusion of member of a trade union)).

1772. Historically, trade unions in the United Kingdom, and elsewhere in Europe, were, and though perhaps to a lesser extent today are, commonly affiliated to political parties or movements, particularly those on the left. They are not bodies solely devoted to politically neutral aspects of the well-being of their members, but are often ideological, with strongly held views on social and political issues.

1773. With this starting point, it seems fair to consider this question on the fact that different trade unions may build their activities on quite different basic principles as regards social and political issues. Thus, it is of importance for the individual employee to be able to choose the trade union which – as far as possible – is in accordance with his or her basic views. A consequence of this view is that an employee should not be forced to contribute to the general activities of a trade union, whose basic views the employee does not share (cf. *Evaldsson v. Sweden* (2007, monitoring fees) paragraph 62, where the ECtHR pointed out that the employees 'had to pay the fees against their will to an organization[10] with a political agenda which they did not support', as well as *Sörensen and Rasmussen v. Denmark* (2006) paragraph 63 in regard to 'non-political membership'; the ECtHR held that 'there is no guarantee that "non-political membership" will not give rise to some form of indirect support for the political parties to which the specific trade union contributes financially'). Further, *Sigurjnsson v. Iceland* (1993) paragraph 37 should also be mentioned, where the ECtHR pointed out that he disagreed with the policy of the association and, therefore, the ECtHR held that Article II can, in the circumstances, be considered in the light of Articles 9 and 10, the protection of personal opinion being also one of the purposes of the freedom of association – a statement which the ECtHR repeated in *Sörensen and Rasmussen v. Denmark* (2006) paragraph 54.

1774. Thus the right to choose which trade union the employee wishes to join is closely related to political freedom, and restrictions on the freedoms of this kind will therefore have to be well founded; as stated by the ECtHR 'there must be a reasonable relationship of proportionality between the means employed and the aim sought to be realized' (cf. *Evaldsson v. Sweden* (2007) paragraph 55); observed should also be the most critical remarks of the ECtHR in *Sigurjönsson v. Iceland* (1993) paragraph 41, stating that the court was not convinced that compulsory membership... was required in order to perform certain functions, and expressed further the view that 'membership was by no means the only conceivable way of compelling the licence-holders to carry out such duties and responsibilities as might be necessary for the relevant function', concluding that there had been a violation of Article 11.

10. The trade union in the building and construction industry *Byggettan*.

1775. In considering the proportionality between the means employed and the aim sought to be realized, it seems fair to begin with the purpose of the tax reduction for members of trade unions, fulfilling the provisions stipulated in the Taxation Act. This purpose may – as mentioned above – be summarized as a contribution to smoothen the process of collective bargaining, negotiations, mediation etc., and to achieve that the development as regards wages, other working conditions etc. be kept within economic frames acceptable for the national economy, by promoting the position of the confederations of trade unions through tax reductions for members of the trade unions which are associated with the confederations.

1776. In a human rights context, the right to collective bargaining is expressed and recognized (cf. *inter alia* ILO Convention No. 154 (1981), especially Article 5, and ESC (1996) Article 6, stipulating that it is an obligation for the state to promote the required machinery for this purpose). The state will enjoy a wide margin of appreciation as to how the required machinery should be designed, and may to quite an extent distinguish between the different trade unions (cf. *inter alia*, *National Union of Belgian Police v. Belgium* (1975)). Thus, it can hardly be doubted that the purpose of the tax reduction system must be considered legitimate in this regard.

1777. However, while the purpose of the tax reduction system is to influence the position and activities of the trade unions in regard to collective bargaining etc., that system is designed in such a way that it aims at and will have direct effects on the individual employees and their choice between different trade unions. In other words, the effects for the individual employees will be direct, while the effects for the trade unions will be indirect.

1778. Thus, as pointed out by the ECtHR in *Sörensen and Rasmussen v. Denmark* (2006) paragraph 58, arrangements (in that case acceptance of the closed shop system) 'which run counter to the freedom of choice of the individual inherent in Article 11, the margin of appreciation must be considered reduced', underlining that 'although individual interests must on occasion be subordinated to those of a group, this does not simply mean that the views of a majority must always prevail'. Consequently, also such a tax reduction arrangement which is dealt with here, and the considerations of the legislator in that regard, must similarly be kept within the limits following from the freedom of the employee to choose which trade union she or he wishes to be a member of. In other words, the margin of appreciation is much more limited in this regard, as it has to be kept within the limits following of the principle of proportionality (cf. *Evaldsson v. Sweden* (2007) paragraph 55).

1779. In the context of organizational structure there is, of course, a difference between the negative right to organize (the right not to be organized) on the one hand, and on the other hand the right to choose which organization – which trade union – an employee wishes to be a member of.

1780. As regards the right not to be organized, an individual and unorganized employee does not, as such, represent any immediate threat for the organizational structure, established as an organized community, as long as this community acts in an organized manner, especially as a trade union. The individual and unorganized employee does however, represent at free rider-problem (cf. paragraph 1452 above), as he or she does not participate in, or contribute to the challenges and burdens of the employee community. Should this attitude develop into a larger trend – there may be a large number of unorganized employees at the enterprise or in the industry in question – a large number of unorganized employees may in the long run represent a danger for the organized community, as the unorganized employees may contribute to undermine the organized community; their behaviour as 'outsiders' may have as result that the solidarity between the employees disintegrates, and thereby so do the basic values on which the right to organize is built.

1781. Should, however, the individual and unorganized employees coordinate their attitudes, their views and their behaviour – and begin to act in an organized manner – a basic change takes place compared to the situation indicated above. This will especially be the case, if these employees act in an organized manner as regards questions related to wages, working conditions, etc.; in which case they have established a trade union. Such a trade union may represent a direct challenge to the previously established organizational structure. Then, there is no longer a 'free rider-problem' and there may no longer be a question of disintegrating the basic values of solidarity. Rather, it might be that a revitalization of the organizational democracy takes place, because different views and ideas may be brought to the surface more explicitly than before; anyway, the employees may now choose which trade union they prefer to be a member of. A consequence of such a development is, that there will be a competition between the trade unions, in order to have the employees as members.

1782. It seems necessary to keep in mind these basic realities and differences between the negative right to organize, and the right to choose between trade unions, when the question is to be considered, whether conclusions may be drawn from the negative right to organize to the right to choose organization. Otherwise, a conclusion might be drawn too hastily.

1783. Thus, it seems necessary to start with the positive right to organize – the right to form and to join a trade union – which is today undoubtedly a right for every employee. Once a trade union is established, the trade union is entitled to carry out its activities, and is also entitled to a certain degree of protection against interference from the state. The basic point is, however, that it is the right of the individual employee which is primarily protected, and the protection of the activities of a trade union follows as a diverted consequence of the right of the individual. This basic point is further illustrated through the development of the legal acceptance of the negative right to organize; there is no longer any doubt about it; a closed shop clause is not in accordance with the right to organize (cf. above paragraphs 1608–1609). Seen from the trade unions' point of view, in an organizational structure context, it might be argued that the validity of closed shop clauses would strengthen the position of the trade unions. That view is, however, not accepted; it is the right of the individual employee not to organize that is protected. Thus, the bottom line – that it is the right of the individual employee that is protected – should also apply as regards the right to choose between different trade unions, as the organizational structure, including the relationship between different trade unions, is necessarily of a subsidiary nature, also in this regard. Consequently, the right of the employees to choose between different trade unions may cause a competition between the trade unions, which again may counteract trends that might develop towards monopoly, conformity, etc.

These considerations may be summarized so, that the right of an employee to choose which trade union he or she wishes to be a member of, constitutes a part of the right to organize, irrespective of the organizational structure of the trade unions.

1784. Therefore, it is an important question whether the system with tax reduction for union dues – limited to the members of trade unions which are associated to one of the confederations of trade unions, or otherwise excepted – is appropriate for the purpose of making the process of collective bargaining etc. smoother, and thereby making the development acceptable for the national economy as regards wages and working conditions.

1785. It seems, that the question may not be answered in the affirmative, because it seems doubtful that this system will have the intended effect, especially because this system does not prevent the trade unions, whose members do not enjoy tax reduction benefits, from demanding negotiations with their counterpart on the employer side, or from presenting their claims in that regard, and thereafter possibly making use of strikes or other forms of industrial action; and vice versa as regards lock-out or other forms of industrial action from the employers' side. Whether or not such industrial action will lead to the solution desired by such a trade union – or its counterpart – will of course depend on several different circumstances, including the number of members, the economic backbone of the trade union, etc., but the problems arising from a collective bargaining situation where competing trade unions are involved, are not resolved by the tax reduction system.

1786. Of course, the questions related to industrial conflicts involving competing trade unions or confederations of trade unions are in many respects most complex. Thus, an industrial conflict involving competing trade unions may potentially be quite harsh indeed, and the underlying issues may deepen the conflict, as the involved trade unions may have quite different views on principal ideological and political values. Moreover, collective bargaining involving competing trade unions may, undoubtedly, be quite a challenge for all parties involved; the climate for negotiations and mediation may indeed be rather harsh, and should a solution not be arrived at, an industrial conflict may similarly be very harsh and hard to bring to an end.

1787. Such conflicts may arise, however, not just when one or more of the involved trade unions are not associated with a confederation of trade unions, while others are, but may also arise between confederations of trade unions, or trade unions associated with one or more of these. A complicated conflict on wages and working conditions for employees in the North Sea oil- and gas-production may e.g., be rather difficult to resolve, even when the trade unions involved are associated with different confederations of trade unions

1788. It may further be mentioned that the different views on competing trade unions may relate to questions as to how an increase or decrease within an economic frames should be divided between the employees involved in a collective bargaining process – e.g., as to whether a 3.5% increase or decrease of wages should be divided at a flat percentage for all employees, or as a specified amount for different groups of the employees – or perhaps should the 3.5% economic frame be used by shorter or longer working hours, and so on. In such conflicts, the economic situation for the nation will not be effected, irrespective of what solution the parties may end at – and, in principle at least – one solution may be chosen for one of the involved trade unions and the members of that trade union, while another solution may be chosen for the other involved parties and their members.

1789. Considering the complexity of industrial conflicts involving competing trade unions or confederations of trade unions indicated above, in regard to the tax reduction system for trade union dues, it is obvious that the aim of this system is to influence the activities of the trade unions. The indirect effects of the system chosen will, however, apply irrespective of whether a trade union should behave in a responsible or an irresponsible way as regards the national economy – a question which, by the way, is basically a political and not an economic one – which leaves the impression that the system is not properly adapted to the aims of the system. The system appears to be too simplified, as it does not distinguish between trade unions following the basic intention that national economic stability should be maintained, and trade unions presenting claims beyond the frames required in that regard.

1790. Furthermore, it follows of the whole collective bargaining system that the confederations of trade unions do have a considerable influence on the frames for the general collective negotiations, especially through their representation in the Coordinating Committee (cf. paragraph 1676 above). Consequently, it seems difficult in practice for any trade union to obtain terms that are significantly different from those frames.

1791. Moreover, according to the Taxation Act, members of a trade union are entitled to tax benefits only when the trade union has concluded a collective agreement. That provision should be seen in connection with the whole system on collective bargaining, but should also be considered on a more fundamental basis; that requirement is not based on the view that trade union activities should be encouraged, but on the *results* obtained by the trade union. Based on a democratic approach – as the activities of trade unions are often based on ideological views with social and political issues – encouraging trade union activities may encourage a broader and more nuanced approach to the complex questions that may arise in connection with collective bargaining. Thus, in this regard, it is a not only a weakness with the tax benefits system that a collective agreement must have been concluded by the trade union, but that provision may in practice also have a significant influence on the choice of the individual employee as to which trade union he or she would prefer to be a member of; he or she would undoubtedly feel that the choice would be more free, if it had been sufficient that the activities of a trade union were to promote the interests of the members, *inter alia* through negotiations and collective bargaining aiming at the possible conclusion of a collective agreement.

1792. Still further, it is a possibility that the tax reduction benefit system may also have as consequence that the number of unorganized employees will increase – contrary to the wish of the legislator – because the employees in question, who do not share the basic values etc. of the trade union, in which they may be members and enjoy the tax reduction benefit, may prefer to remain or become unorganized rather than to support such a trade union by their membership and union dues.

1793. Based on these considerations, it seems fair to conclude that the limitations of the Taxation Act section 6-20 on the income deductions for paid union dues seem to go beyond what is 'necessary in a democratic society' (cf. ECHR Article 11(2). Consequently, the Taxation Act, as well as the assessment of income tax for the employees in question, should be amended accordingly (cf. also the HRA section 3). As mentioned in paragraph 1588 above Oslo City Court (case No. TOSLO-2011-34224 decision of 9 January 2012) came to the conclusion that this provision of the Taxation Act was not at variance with the international conventions. The case was appealed to Borgarting Court of Appeal, but dismissed (case No. LB-2012-79354 of 1 November 2013). Further, a claim for compensation of costs connected to the case, raised by the trade union *(Fellesforbundet For Sjöfolk)* against the state was rejected by the CA (case No. 14-195663ASD-BORG/03 of 26. Oct. 2015), preliminary stating *inter alia* that the provisions of the Taxation Act were not at variance with the international conventions and the freedom to organize.

Selected Bibliography

Literature on Norwegian Labour Law in English

Aune & Fredriksen *Norwegian Employment Law – An Overview*. N.W. Damm & Søn AS, 2008.
Schwarz & Enkegaard (ed.). *Scandinavian Employment Law – A General Overview on Danish, Norwegian and Swedish Employment Law.* 2nd ed. Thompson Reuters Professional A/S, Copenhagen, 2009.

Literature in Norwegian

Aagaard, Erik C. (ed*.): Arbeidstvistloven. Kommentarer og praksis* (2014) [The Labour Dispute Act, Comments and Practice].
Allstrin, Tor et al. (2012): *Endring og opphør av arbeidsforhold* [Amendments and Termination of Employment Contracts].
Andersen, Kristen (1956): *Arbeidsretten og organisasjonene* [Labour Law and Trade Unions].
Andersen, Kristen (1967): *Fra arbeidslivets rett* [Labour Law].
Aune, Helga (2013): *Deltidsarbeid. Vern mot diskriminering på strukturelt og individuelt grunnlag* [Part-Time Work. Protection against Discrimination on the Structural and Individual Basis].
Aune, Fauchald, Lilleholt and Michalsen (ed.) (2009): *Arbeid og rett, festskrift til Henning Jakhellns 70-årsdag* [Labour and the Law, Liber Amicorum on Henning Jakhelln's 70-Year Anniversary].
Berg, Paal (1930): *Arbeidsretten* [Labour Law].
Björkholm, Mikaela (2007): *Fri rörighet i Europa ur ett sjöarbetsrättslig perspektiv (PhD)* [Free Movement in Europe, from a Maritime Labour Law Perspective].
Bjørnaraa, Gard and Selmer (2000): *Norsk tjenestemannsrett, kommentarer til tjenestemannsloven* [The Civil Servants Act with Comments and Remarks].
Dalheim, Urdal Sand and Østre (2008): *Sjømannsrett* [Norwegian Legislation regarding Seamen].
Dege, Jan Tormod (2009): *Arbeidsrett* individuell del (Del I – II) [Labour Law, the Individual Part (Volumes I–II)].
Eidsvaag, Tine (2009): *Handlaus gjæte. Vern mot utstøting og diskriminering av arbeidstakere med helseproblemer eller funksjonsnedsettelser* (PhD) [Protection against Ejection and Discrimination of Employees due to Health Problems or Disabilities].
Engelsrud, Gerd (2006): *Styring og vern – arbeidsrett for kommuner og fylkeskommuner* [Labour Law in relation to the Municipal and County Sectors].
Evju, Stein (1989) (ed.): *Aktuell arbeidsrett* [Current Labour Law].

Evju, Stein (1982): *Organisasjonsfrihet, tariffavtaler og streik* [Freedom of Association, Collective Agreements and Strikes].
Evju and Jakhelln, Henning (1979): *Arbeidsrettslige emner* [Labour Law Subjects].
Evju, Stein (ed.) (1977–78, 1979 and 1980 [LARD]): *Dommer og kjennelser av lokale arbeidsretter* [Local Labour Courts, Law Reports].
Fanebust, Arne (1997, with later editions): *Innføring i arbeidsrett. Den individuelle del* [Introduction to Labour Law. The Individual Part].
Fanebust, Arne (1985, and later editions): *Oppsigelse i arbeidsforhold* [Termination of Employment].
Fanebust, Arne (2001, 4th ed.): *Oppsigelsei arbeidsforhold* [Termination of Employment].
Fougner, Holo (2006): *Arbeidsmiljøloven* [Commentaries on the Working Environment Act].
Fougner, Jan and others (2007): *Endring i arbeidsforhold* [Changes in Working Conditions].
Fougner, Jan and others (2004): *Kollektiv arbeidsrett* [Collective Labour Law].
Fougner, Jan and others (2003): *Omstilling og nedbemanning* [Restructuring and Staff Cutbacks].
Fougner, Jan (1999): *Arbeidsavtalen – utvalgte emner* [Labour Law – Selected Subjects].
Hellum and Ketscher (ed.) (2008): *Diskriminerings-og likestillingsrett* [Antidiscrimination and Equality Law].
Jakhelln, Henning (4th ed., 2007): *Oversikt over arbeidsretten* [An Overview of Norwegian Labour Law].
Jakhelln, Henning (ed.) (2001): *Artikkelsamling i arbeidsrett* [Collection of Articles in Labour Law].
Jakhelln, Henning (vols. I–IV, 2000): *Arbeidsrettslige studier/ Rettslige studier* [Studies on Labour Law/Legal Studies].
Jakhelln, Henning, Aune, Helga, Kroken, Nina and Lenth, Claude (ed.) and 30 contributing authors (3rd ed. 2011): *Arbeidsrett.no, kommentarer til arbeidsmiljøloven* [The Working Environment Act with Comments and Remarks], Book and webpage: www.arbeidsrett.no.
Jakhelln, Henning, Aune, Helga, Gisle, Jon (ed.) (2012): *Arbeidsrett.no, kommentarer til arbeidstvistloven* [The Labour Dispute Act with Comments and Remarks], Book and webpage: www.arbeidsrett.no.
Jakhelln and Vidnes (1981–85, 1986, 1987, and 1988): *Norsk Arbeidsrettslig Domssamling [NAD]* [Norwegian labour law reports].
Lødrup, Kaasen and Tjomsland (last edited 2008): *Norsk lovkommentar* [General Comments on Norwegian Legislation].
Mork, Per Helge (2nd ed., 2007): *Hovedavtalen LO-NHO 2006–2009, kommentarer og veiledning* [The Main Collective Agreement between LO-NHO, with Comments and Remarks].
Pettersen, Terje Hernes et al. (2014): *Skipsarbeidsloven* [The Seamens Act].
Skarning, Nicolay (2005): *Nedbemanning og sluttpakker* [Workforce Reductions and Severance Payments].
Skarning, Nicolay (2009): *Permittering og nedbemanning* [Temporary Lay-Offs and Workforce Reductions].

Selected Bibliography

Skjønberg, Alexander Naess and Hognestad, Eirik: Indiduell arbeidsrett (2014) [Individual Labour Law].
Uggerud, Ken (1997): *Arbeidstvistlov og menneskerettigheter* [Labour Disputes Act and Human Rights].
Ulseth, Terese Smith (2006): *Daglig leders stillingsvern* [The Protection against Dismissals regarding General Managers].
Vigerust, Elisabeth (1998): *Arbeid, barn og likestilling* [Labour, Children and Equality].

Some Articles Written in English about Different Labour-Law Related Subjects

Evju, Stein (2010): *Arbeidsrett – Utvalgte artikler 2001 – 2010* (Labour Law – Selection of Articles 2001–2010):

- 'Principles of Public Law in Labour Law'
- 'Labour Courts and Collective Agreements'
- 'The Nordic Model'
- 'The Actors of Collective Bargaining'
- 'The Right to Strike in Norwegian Labour Law: An Insider-Outsider Perspective'
- 'A European Social Model? Experience from the Scandinavian Countries'
- 'Market Freedoms, Labour Market Regulation and Trade Union Rights – Worlds Apart in EU Law?'
- 'Labour-Only Contracting – The Norwegian Way'.

Jakhelln, Henning, *Copyright Protection for Collective Agreements, and Some Supplementary Remarks regarding the Copyright Protection of Standard Form Contracts*. UFITA 2001; Volume 2001 (III) pp. 683–756.

List of Useful Web Pages

www.arbeidsrett.no.: A web-based forum with over thirty lawyers and legal experts that has written comments on the Norwegian Working Environment Act, and topics within the international labour law, pension, lay-offs, the Holidays Act and Competition Clauses, etc. Professor Henning Jakhelln and post.doc. Helga Aune are the main editors of arbeidsrett.no)

www.arbeidsretten.no.: The Norwegian Labour Court

www.arbeidstilsynet.no.: The Norwegian Labour Inspectorate

www.barneombudet.no.: The Ombudsman for Children

www.domstol.no/hoyesterett.: The Supreme Court of Norway; Presentation of the Norwegian judicial system and summary of recent Supreme Court decisions

www.efta.int.: The European Free Trade Association

europa.euwww.europa.eu.: Gateway to the European Union

www.forbrukerombudet.no.: The Consumer Ombudsman and the Market Council

www.helsetilsynet.no.: The Norwegian Board of Health Supervision

www.konkurransetilsynet.no.: The Norwegian Competition Authority

www.ldo.no.: The Ombudsman for Equality and Antidiscrimination

www.lovdata.no.: A web-based forum which contains an overview of Norwegian legislation in force, regulations (both central and local), Supreme Court decisions, Appellate Court decisions, District Court decisions, decisions from the European Court of Human Rights, opinions by the Civil Ombudsman and special boards and councils, legal articles published in the main legal journals, and bibliographic references to legal literature, etc.

www.nato.int/cps/en/natolive/index.htm.: The North Atlantic Treaty Organization

www.nav.no.: The Norwegian Labour and Welfare Administration

http://www.ombudsmann.no/node/57.: The Parliamentary Commissioner for the Armed Forces

www.regjeringen.no.: The Norwegian Government

www.sivilombudsmannen.no.: The Civil/Parliamentary Ombudsman

www.ssb.no.: Statistics Norway

www.toll.no/.: Norwegian Customs Authority

List of Useful Web Pages

www.ub.uio.no/ujur/ulov/.: Translated Norwegian legislation, collected by the Faculty of Law Library, University of Oslo. The collection on the present site consists mostly of translations initiated by Governmental Agencies, Royal Ministries and private institutions. The translations are unofficial and only updated at the time of the translation.

www.ingramcontent.com/pod-product-compliance
Lightning Source LLC
Chambersburg PA
CBHW071412230926
51846CB00001B/67